The
Apocalypse

AND THE SHAPE OF THINGS TO COME

The Apocalypse

AND THE SHAPE OF THINGS TO COME

Edited by Frances Carey

Published for The Trustees of

The British Museum by

BRITISH MUSEUM 🏛 PRESS

*The publication of this book has been funded by
The Michael Marks Charitable Trust
in memory of the late Lord Marks*

Published to accompany an exhibition at the British Museum
December 1999 – April 2000

Published by British Museum Press
A division of The British Museum Company Ltd
46 Bloomsbury Street, London WC1B 3QQ

A catalogue record for this book is available from
the British Library

ISBN 0–7141–2623–3 (cased)
ISBN 0–7141–2620–9 (paper)

Designed and typeset in Apollo by Andrew Shoolbred
Project manager Elisabeth Ingles

Printed and bound in Spain by Imago

Frontispiece
Lucifer, Prince of Hell, fol.98r of *Le livre de la vigne nostre Seigneur*
(early 1460s), south-eastern France. Manuscript on parchment.
Oxford, Bodleian Library MS Douce 134 (see Ch. 3, cat. 22)

Contents

Preface

The approach of what is generally accepted as the end of the second millennium is a good pretext for re-examining the legacy of the work which has been the source of 'that vague millennialism and that hazy typological yearning which form part of the uncritical inheritance of the European imagination',[1] the Revelation of St John the Divine, otherwise known as the Apocalypse. The most controversial of all the books in the Christian canon, it underpinned the Western concept of linear, teleological time, defining the meaning of history in terms of its relationship to eternity and, by analogy, the purpose of all individual human lives whose meaning likewise lay in their end: 'In my beginning is my end'.[2] In the liturgical calendar, the readings for the Sundays immediately preceding Advent focus on death and the Last Judgement, while the Second Coming is the theme for the first Sunday of Advent. Past, present and future formed an integral whole susceptible to 'decoding' in the light of the unveiled prophecies of the apocalyptician, of whom the author of Revelation was the most famous and influential example.

The content of Revelation has been profoundly disturbing from the date of its composition at the end of the first century AD, when it was addressed to the seven churches of Asia Minor to bind together these early Christian communities against persecution from the Roman Empire without and guard against sectaries from within. Its rhetorical purpose was responsible for a text which 'radically suspends logic and opens up vertiginous possibilities of referential aberration',[3] working through metaphors which both invite and confound interpretation. The potential dangers of 'referential aberration' never ceased to alarm ecclesiastical authorities, from the early Church Fathers to the medieval Papacy, Martin Luther, the Anglican Church under Edward VI which included a condemnation of millenarianism among the forty-two Articles of 1552, Charles Wesley, and contemporary clerics of all denominations who have recently issued cautionary statements in anticipation of 'millennial fever'. St Augustine of Hippo's injunction to 'relax your fingers, and give them a rest' in the *City of God*[4] was directed against millenarians intent upon the precise calculation of something which he regarded as beyond the sphere of human understanding. Nonetheless, his warning against the naive application of apocalyptic numbers and symbols to contemporary events has gone unheeded throughout much of the intervening 1,570 years. The nineteenth-century historian Jules Michelet promulgated the romantic view of 1000 as a year of widespread calamity, perhaps reflecting the insecurities of his own epoch as much as anything, but the evidence of Anglo-Saxon homilectic literature, for example, does give some credence to the notion of the period *circa* 1000 as displaying a marked interest in millenarianism. Henri Focillon, writing his study *L'An Mil* during a time of worldwide anxiety prior to his death in 1943, referred to the different layers of belief, starting with the most primitive at the bottom: 'Perhaps history is only a series of exchanges and accommodations between these diverse stratifications, with periodic upheavals which expose the secrets of the depths. It is thus that I interpret the year 1000.'[5]

Within the modern period alone, the tragic consequences of too close an identification with the literal interpretation of Revelation have been the stuff of fact and fiction, from the Fifth Monarchy men (p.215) who were finally routed in 1661 in the environs of Caen Wood (now Kenwood in north London), to the Battle of Wounded Knee in 1890 or the recent instances of the Branch Davidians in Waco, Texas, and the Heaven's Gate sect in California, whose mass suicide was triggered by the appearance of the Hale-Bopp comet in 1996. 'Lou, the prophet', a simple Danish immigrant farmer in the American Mid-West who is the subject of Willa Cather's eponymous short story of 1892,[6] is but one example 'of the many people whose minds have been unhinged by misdirected study of the Book of Revelations'.[7] Their number has included prominent public figures, such as the Dutch diplomat and Burgomaster of Amsterdam, Conrad van Beuningen (1622–93), who in retirement in the late 1680s became obsessed with the end of the world; a mid-eighteenth century native of York, Adam Toppin, the ostensible subject of the quotation above and author of a number of lively illustrated woodcut sheets described elsewhere in this volume (see pp.214–15 and Ch.5, cat.9); and Aleister Crowley (1875–1947), the son of Plymouth Brethren and self-proclaimed Great Beast who wore the number 666, promulgating his occult beliefs from the unlikely setting of Richmond on Thames.

A more benign example would be that described by the French author Jean Giono (1895–1970) in a piece entitled *Le Grand Théâtre*, which he contributed to a lavishly illustrated volume of the Apocalypse executed as a unique work between 1958 and 1961, and announced somewhat melodramatically as 'perhaps the final witness of human art before the great leap into emotions as yet unknown of interplanetary space'.[8] The subject is his father, a radical cobbler of Italian origin in Provence, for whom the Apocalypse was a living reality to be conjured up nightly while surveying the sky from the rooftops. The subjunctive tense, because it expresses that which exists simply as an idea, and the imperfect tense, because it expresses continuity, were the preferred mode of dreaming for Giono's father, who believed the Apocalypse could happen anywhere at any time. After seeing a demonstration flight by an aeroplane, he read to his son from

Revelation about soaring angels; later, when Giono was struggling to convey the horrors of the First World War, his father admonished: 'Remember the Apocalypse – "In those days shall men seek death and shall not find it, and shall desire to die and death shall flee from them"' (Revelation 9: 6).[9]

Giono's narrative conveys what is in fact the main focus of this publication, the esemplastic or form-giving power of Revelation; the very concrete nature of the visualization of its signs and symbols which has engendered a pictorial tradition stretching from the earliest known representations of apocalyptic subjects in the fifth century (see p.44) to the present day. The essays by Sir Frank Kermode and Norman Cohn set the stage for understanding the psychological and biblical context of apocalypticism, while the art-historical contributions present, in chronological progression, some of the salient aspects of this vast subject from a western European perspective, concentrating on its transmission through graphic means and concluding with the cinema which in the twentieth century has further extended the pictorial vocabulary. Ekphrasis or 'the skill to create set descriptions, intended to bring visual reality to the mind's eye by means of words'[10] was central to the success of Revelation as a continuing source of inspiration. St Augustine emphasized the importance of devout seeing 'in the mind's eye' as part of a threefold process of visionary contemplation and Luther wrote that he found it impossible not to make visual images of theological truths;[11] this intuitive grasp of the vividness of biblical imagery was one of the factors in his change of heart about the status of Revelation between 1522 and 1530 and his ultimate refusal to align himself with the iconophobes (pp.102–4, 111–12).

Although the Book of Revelation and its related biblical texts may appear to encourage every kind of wild imagining, until comparatively recent times the development of its iconography was governed by theological sanction. Critics of Michelangelo's *Last Judgement* argued for the subjugation of the creative imagination to the dictates of religious truth (see Ch.4, cats 96–8), but there can be little doubt that artistic licence emerged as the winner for posterity. Prior to the advent of printing, the main public impact of any visual art form had to be achieved within a monumental setting, yet its diffusion was dependent on the agency of manuscripts. Illustrations of apocalyptic subjects appeared in a variety of liturgical and moralizing texts, but the most elaborate expression of that imagery was in the extended Apocalypse cycles, of which the earliest surviving manuscripts date from the Carolingian period of the ninth to tenth centuries. The principal written commentaries on the Apocalypse favoured by the monastic communities engendered their own distinctive iconographic traditions, of which the most famous was the group of manuscripts from Spain of the late tenth to twelfth centuries associated with the commentary of Beatus of Liébana (c.782–6). The vivid Mozarabic style of examples such as the Silos Apocalypse in the British Library (Ch.3, cat.4) and its companions in the Bibliothèque Nationale in Paris, the Pierpont Morgan Library in New York and elsewhere has captured the imagination of twentieth-century artists, including the Surrealists and Fernand Léger, as well as writers such as the notable critic and semiotician Umberto Eco. In *The Name of the Rose* (1980), which is full of apocalyptic references, he made an illuminated Beatus manuscript material to the conclusion of William of Baskerville's detective work. By the mid-thirteenth century Apocalypse manuscripts had become a luxury item, associated with the courtly status of certain secular patrons including women in Anglo-Norman society. It was probably a woman who commissioned the volume of exceptional magnificence known as the Trinity Apocalypse after the Cambridge college where it has been since 1660 (Ch.3, cat.10).

After the great manuscript cycles, and the early block-books which were the first attempt to translate the imagery into printed form, the defining moment in the development of the pictorial tradition was Dürer's publication of his set of fifteen woodcuts in 1498. 'Like Leonardo's *Last Supper*, Dürer's Apocalypse belongs among what may be called the inescapable works of art. Summarizing, yet surpassing an age-old tradition, these works command an authority which no later artist could ignore, except perhaps by way of a deliberate opposition which in itself is another form of dependence.'[12] Their resonance has been felt at all levels of subsequent portrayal, as has that of the next cycle of major significance, that by Lucas Cranach the Elder to accompany Luther's September Testament of 1522, which was the first to incorporate the theological presumptions of the Reformation. The influence of

these series was immediate and widespread thanks to the invention of printing, which by the mid-sixteenth century had conveyed their imagery as far afield as the monasteries on Mount Athos. In the twentieth century the Dürer woodcuts have provided the central motifs, among many possible examples, for the 1921 film *The Four Horsemen of the Apocalypse*, starring Rudolph Valentino (see pp.325–7), for Thomas Mann's novel *Dr Faustus* (1947; see pp.293–4), and for the work of a contemporary Polish artist, Andrzej Dudek-Dürer (b.1953), who sees himself as the reincarnation of his illustrious predecessor.[13]

Apocalyptic imagery was quickly exploited as a vehicle for propaganda and satire during the Reformation and the ensuing wars of religion across northern Europe, where it provided a standard repertoire of motifs largely among the Protestant community for the many pamphlets and broadsheets issued by the opposing sides. The same was true for the Civil War period and Commonwealth in Britain, in many respects the high-water mark of apocalyptic speculation there. Although eminent authorities such as Sir Isaac Newton continued to make efforts to reconcile millennialist calculation with the exercise of rational religion, apocalypticism thereafter lost its intellectual credibility, re-emerging as a weapon of secular satire at the hands of artists like James Gillray and Thomas Rowlandson in the latter part of the eighteenth century. Gillray's contemporary William Blake evolved, through his illuminated prophetic books of 1790–1820 and a series of watercolours c.1805–10, a concept of Apocalypse and Judgement that was part of a personal mythology responding to the millenarian currents and revolutionary upheavals of the period in question. One of the most remarkable of all Blake's overtly apocalyptic subjects, *The Great Red Dragon and the Woman Clothed with the Sun* (Ch.6, cat.29), like the Beatus manuscripts, has surfaced in contemporary fiction. Central to the plot of Thomas Harris's *Red Dragon* (1981) is the psychopathic interest displayed in Blake's watercolour by the principal character, who eventually makes a journey to see the original which he then eats, in a bizarre variation on Dürer's image of St John consuming the book.

The events of the twentieth century have conspired to ensure the survival of apocalyptic metaphor in all media as a vehicle for visions of destruction and regeneration, of nihilistic despair and futuristic fantasy; the real meaning of Apocalypse as 'unveiling' has been virtually extinguished by its contemporary usage as a synonym for catastrophe. In a largely secular society, perhaps it is by listening to music that we can recapture some of the original purpose of the revelations ascribed to St John, which were intended to provide solace to the believer as well as to inspire terror. Many twentieth-century composers have written pieces inspired by this theme, including John Tavener's *Apocalypse* of 1994, but especially affective among earlier examples are the Bach cantatas, written to adumbrate the liturgical cycle of the Lutheran Church in Leipzig. Cantatas such as 'O Ewigkeit, du Donnerwort' (O Eternity, thou voice of thunder, no.60; 1723), based on Revelation 14: 13, represent a dialogue between hope and fear, a meditation on death and judgement whose performance is succeeded on the following Sunday, the last before Advent, by 'Wachet auf, ruft uns die Stimme' (Awake, the voice is calling us, no.140), a joyful anticipation of the entry of the soul into heaven and eternity. In a post-Holocaust environment, the words of Isaiah quoted by St Augustine may not carry conviction: 'There will be a new heaven, and a new earth; and men will not remember the past, and it will not come to their minds', but the more oblique intimations of apocalypse and hope at work in the poetry of Paul Celan (1920–70), for example, may nonetheless be accessible: 'there are still songs to be sung on the other side of mankind' (from 'Thread Suns' in *Atemwende* (Breath-turn), 1967). Images of all kinds whether static or filmic retain their power to mediate experience, none more so than apocalyptic ones:

> For one road to reality is by way of pictures.... Pictures are nets: what appears in them is the holdable catch.... However, it's important that these pictures exist outside a person too; inside a human being, even they are subject to change. There has to be a place where he can find them intact, not he alone, a place where everyone who feels uncertain can find them. Whenever a man feels the precariousness of his experience, he turns to a picture. Here experience holds still, he can look into its face.... The pictures need *his* experience in order to awake.... There are several pictures that a man needs for his own life, and if he finds them early, then not too much of him is lost.[14]

Frances Carey

NOTES

1 Frank Kermode, *The Uses of Error,* London 1991, p.16.
2 T.S. Eliot, 'East Coker' from *The Four Quartets* in *The Complete Poems of T. S. Eliot*, London 1970, p.177.
3 Paul de Man quoted by Christopher Burdon in *The Apocalypse in England: Revelation Unravelling, 1700–1834*, London 1997, p.24.
4 *City of God*, London 1984, *Book XVIII*, p.838.
5 *L'An Mil*, Paris 1952, p.64.
6 Published in *Paul's Case and Other Stories*, New York 1996.
7 Campbell Dodgson in a letter to Dyson Perrins, dated 20 January 1905 (Huntington Library, California). I would like to thank my colleague Sheila O'Connell for drawing this to my attention.
8 Ed. Joseph Foret, *L'Apocalypse*, Paris 1962, p.vii exh. cat. Musée Jacquemart-André.
9 See also Giono's novel, *Le grand troupeau*, 1931, and Jay Winter's account of this work in *Sites of Memory, Sites of Mourning*, Cambridge 1995, pp.197–9.
10 Jean Hagstrum, *The Sister Arts. The tradition of literary pictorialism and English poetry from Dryden to Gray*, Chicago 1958, p.29. The quotation is excerpted from a passage discussing ekphrasis as a device of Classical rhetoric. See Murray and Jean Krieger, *Ekphrasis. The illusion of the sign*, Baltimore and London 1992; James Heffernan, *Museum of Words. The poetics of ekphrasis from Homer to Ashbery*, Chicago and London 1993; Ellen J. Esrock, *The Reader's Eye. Visual imaging as reader response*, Baltimore and London 1994.
11 See Bob Scribner, 'Ways of seeing in the age of Dürer' in *Dürer and his Culture*, ed. Dagmar Eichberger and Charles Zika, Cambridge 1998, pp.93–117.
12 Erwin Panofsky, *The Life and Art of Albrecht Dürer*, Princeton 1955, p.59.
13 This information has been kindly supplied by Joanna Tomicka, Curator of Prints at the National Museum in Warsaw.
14 Elias Canetti, *The Torch in My Ear*, London 1990, pp.113–14.

Acknowledgements

The number of those to whom acknowledgement should be made is almost as vast as the subject of the Apocalypse itself, but I must begin with the distinguished team of authors with whom I have had the privilege of collaborating on this publication. The Michael Marks Charitable Trust has generously provided the financial support which has made it possible. I would like to thank particularly Marina the Lady Marks, for her endorsement of the project; Christopher White, one of the trustees, for his efforts on my behalf, and my colleague Martin Royalton-Kisch, who first recommended the subject to their attention. The making of the book has devolved upon many other people, principal among whom are Elisabeth Ingles, the project manager, and Andrew Shoolbred, the designer; both of them have achieved wonders within a very compressed schedule, assisted by Teresa Francis of British Museum Press.

This project has only come to pass because so many people responsible for other collections, both public and private, have been willing to share their material, often their greatest treasures. I am grateful to all parties concerned, the private owners, governing bodies, museum directors, curators, librarians, conservators, exhibitions officers and photographic services who are acknowledged explicitly or by implication in the credits given elsewhere in this volume. The British Library has been the largest single outside contributor, offering every assistance throughout a period when its entire collections were moved from Bloomsbury to St Pancras. I would like to record my particular gratitude to staff there both past and present, especially Michelle Brown, Pam Porter and Jacqui Hunt in Manuscripts, and Janet Backhouse who helped me to embark upon the initial selection; John Goldfinch, Graham Jefcoate, Philippa Marks and Graham Nattrass in Early Printed Collections; Anne Rose of Exhibitions, Peter Barber of the Map Library and Malcolm Marjoram in Photographic Services. Alice Prochaska, Director of Special Collections, and Jane Carr, formerly Director of Public Affairs, were equally supportive. Elsewhere in London I have had every courtesy shown to me by Sam Fogg of Sam Fogg Rare Books and Manuscripts, Robert Harding and Bryan Maggs of Maggs Bros., Alastair Laing at the National Trust, Nick Savage of the Royal Academy, Robin Hamlyn and Christopher Webster of the Tate Gallery and Richard Aspin of the Wellcome Institute for the History of Medicine Library. Outside London I am indebted to Patricia Allderidge of the Bethlem Royal Hospital Museum; Michael Campbell in Kent; David McKitterick and Alison Sproston of Trinity College Library, Cambridge; Patrick Zutschi at Cambridge University Library; David Scrase and Jane Munro at the Fitzwilliam Museum, Cambridge; Kate Harris, Librarian and Archivist to the Marquess of Bath at Longleat; Peter McNiven of the John Rylands University Library, Manchester; Mary Clapinson and Martin Kauffmann of the Bodleian Library, Oxford; Marjory Szurko, Librarian of Keble College, Oxford, and Sir Paul Getty K.B.E., Wormsley, Oxfordshire.

I have been similarly dependent on the goodwill of collections and curators abroad, principal among whom are Ger Luijten and Peter Schatborn of the Rijksprentenkabinet, Rijksmuseum, in Amsterdam; Peter Märker and Irmgard Bröning of the Hessisches Landesmuseum and Landesbibliothek respectively in Darmstadt; Martin Schøyen in Norway; Bob Essick in California; Elizabeth Fairman of the British Art Center at Yale; Colta Ives at the Metropolitan Museum; Elizabeth Easton of the Brooklyn Museum in New York; Derick Dreher of the Rosenbach Museum and Library in Philadelphia; Andrew Robison and Ruth Fine of the National Gallery of Art in Washington D.C.

In addition to those who have assisted with loans to the exhibition linked to this publication, many others have helped me to find images for reproduction. For help in this connection I wish to thank particularly James Austin; Christopher de Hamel and Laura Nuvoloni of Sotheby's; Philippa Grimstone of Eton College Library; Alyson Rogers of the National Monuments Record; Mandy Rowson of the British Film Institute Stills Library; Simon Theobald of Christie's; Nick Wise of the V&A's Picture Library; Reiner Nolden of the Stadtbibliothek in Trier, Sarah Wentworth of the Walters Art Gallery in Baltimore, Kurtis Barstow and Jacklyn Burns of the J. Paul Getty Museum in Los Angeles.

Friends and colleagues all around the world have offered suggestions and assistance, and I apologize for lack of sufficient space to acknowledge them all. I must single out Nicholas Mann of the Warburg Institute for his support in connection with the joint Warburg/British Museum colloquium to be held on the Apocalypse in 2000 and the series of lectures sponsored by the British Academy, for which I also thank the Academy and the National Gallery where they will be held. Foremost among those who have given constant moral support are Linda Karshan and Celina Fox.

I have benefited from the advice and practical support of colleagues across the British Museum, in particular Terence Mitchell, former Keeper of Western Asiatic Antiquities, the staff of Western Pictorial Art under Heather Norville-Day, and photographers Bill Lewis and Lisa Baylis. The greatest debt, however, is to my own department, Prints and Drawings, to the excellent Special Assistants successively engaged to work on the exhibition and publication, principally Rhoda Eitel-Porter and Suzanne Meurer, who were briefly preceded by Lucy Pelz; and Janice Reading, Maureen Welby and Charlie Collinson who have been responsible for the loans administration and the practical arrangements. David Paisey has presented important work to the collection for the exhibition and made his wealth of knowledge of German material readily available, while Daniel Parker, formerly one of our Museum Assistants, kindly lent me a number of essential reference books. Everyone in Prints and Drawings, employees past and present, dedicated volunteers and visiting scholars alike, has made a significant contribution through their expertise, general interest, willingness to assume extra duties and abundant good humour; I am proud to be associated with them.   F.C.

1 Millennium and Apocalypse

Frank Kermode

The idea of a millennium would be much more manageable if it were a mere chronological convenience, meaning nothing more than a thousand-year lapse of time. In fact, because of other ideas that have long been associated with it, whether religious or merely superstitious or something in between, its connotations are much wider and much more difficult to define.

The calendrical sense of the term, though not entirely simple, is not particularly mysterious. A year is recognizably a natural cycle, and when dealing with multiples of it communities accustomed to the use of decimal systems for counting find it easy and convenient to talk in terms of decades, centuries and millennia. Of course that explanation leaves almost everything to be explained; it does not go into the history of this practice, and say what impulses have for so long prompted the wish or need to divide history in this way. What benefit, it may be asked, can be derived from investing time and emotion in red-letter dates of one kind or another, and why is it that a millennium, far from being no more than a computational convenience, seems to be an even redder-letter date than a year or a decade or a century? And why do all these units of historical time, but especially millennia, have the effect of encouraging suitably impressionable subjects to entertain conjectures and visions, whether dystopian or utopian, or both in that order, of things to come?

The year AD 2000 belongs, like all other dates, to an artificial chronology, but the conventional prefix AD, *anno domini*, indicates that this chronology serves purposes beyond the obvious one of counting, for it is not only a way of measuring history but also of celebrating especially memorable past events, and, further, can be thought of as a conceptual instrument for predicting the future. The point of origin of the system we use happens to be the date of the foundation of a religion, and although we do not normally have this in mind when we are making everyday use of the chronology, or worrying whether our computers will manage the transition to 2000, the system has not yet quite divested itself of its religious associations. The modern Jewish practice, now winning more or less general acceptance in the United States, of replacing AD with CE, meaning Common Era, and prefixing BCE (Before the Common Era) to dates traditionally designated BC, Before Christ, has the effect of neutralizing the Christian implications of the dates. The purpose of this change is not, of course, to replace the Christian calendar with a Jewish religious calendar, which is another matter entirely, but simply to exclude what are, in the ordinary course of life, taken to be irrelevant associations. There may conceivably be less practical considerations at work, such as a protest against what could be seen as a takeover by a majority, or even imperialist, religion, of the calendar, a property essentially to be held in common; but the main aim is to secularize a scheme that is in almost universal use. Having to concede, therefore, to this degree, one keeps to the dominant calendar, but strips it of its religious affiliations – reducing it to the point when it becomes, as it were, exactly and only as useful as the convention, long employed without much demur by practically everybody, that zero longitude passes through Greenwich.

The use of Christian dates in an entirely secular way may be necessary to the conduct of modern life and business, but we are occasionally reminded that the reduction of this usage is not yet complete, that its religious origins are still remembered. During the construction of the Greenwich Dome protests were heard from believers who suspected that the enterprise was ignoring the Christian implications of the date AD 2000, and insisting that it should make significant reference to the birth of Christ, the zero point of the current measurement system, and therefore the event that, in the view of the protesters, gives the date AD 2000 its prime significance. Every system of chronology of course requires a zero point, but the one we have selected and continue to use can have, for some, this additional importance as an inaugural event. For them it retains that value as well as serving a chronological function; indeed it gives that chronology a meaning much more important than it could have as a mere tally of time.

The inaugural moment, whatever it may be, is honoured as marking the moment when a series of new times began, when a new historical dispensation was established. This is especially true of the originating date of the Christian chronology, for since the Incarnation is the means by which the Fall was remedied, it divides the whole of time and also marks the direct intervention of God into human history, after which nothing can be as it was. So the desire for a new start arises not just from the need to nominate a moment from which to start counting; it is evidently much more portentous than that. And although the Christian arrangement is exemplary, this desire for a new start is not induced solely by a particular religious creed. Even the irreligious quite like the idea, which is why the beginning of each annual cycle, and *a fortiori* the end and the beginning of a millennium, is so generally regarded as an occasion for stocktaking, anxiety and celebration.

Such habits and assumptions may reflect an entirely private hunger in the individual to renovate his or her life, but they seem to be entailed on us in the

Fig. 1. Max Beckmann (1884–1950), 'And God shall wipe away all tears from their eyes', page 71 of *Apokalypse* (1943). Lithograph with hand-colouring. Washington DC, National Gallery of Art, Bequest of Mrs Mathilde Q. Beckmann (see Ch. 6, cat. 12).

first place by inherited cultural constraint. In my part of the world, the Isle of Man, New Year's Eve was the day when the house must be made free of dirt and ashes, and the first stranger to enter after midnight, bearing traditional gifts, was honoured as the first-foot. (Some cheating went on to ensure that the first-foot should be male and of dark colouring, though why this was thought desirable among a largely fair-headed community is a matter for conjecture; perhaps it was to ensure that the stranger should be genuinely strange, as the new year might be if we used it as an opportunity to be better behaved, to be strangely different from what we have been.) In the German Pietist tradition fathers on New Year's Eve heard the confessions of their children so that they might begin another year with clean consciences. No doubt a quasi-religious feast would follow. One supposes that behind these manifestations, or at any rate the more public gestures, there are pagan midwinter festivals, which seem to show that the desire for an end and a new start is ancient, and derives from human attempts to adapt to the undoubted inconvenience of living under the rule of time and the natural cycle.

Even when the occasion is celebrated impiously there is a general sense that it is good to be starting again from scratch: ''Tis well the old age is out', says Janus, the god of facing-both-ways, lord of the turn of time, in Dryden's *Secular Masque* (1700); 'And time to begin a new', adds Chronos, Time itself, urging the world onward to possibly better things.

The idea, then, is both very ancient and very general, and, since we tend to be awed by big numbers, it is likely to take firmer hold at the ends of centuries, and even more so the ends of millennia, than it can at the end of a year. It is within this context that celebration of the great turn of time may assume, for the devout, a theological or spiritual sense demanding a more mysterious formulation: there, at what for Christians is the pivotal moment of history, one which they annually, centurially and millennially commemorate, the timeless intersects with time. It hardly needs repeating that to those who hold such a belief the inaugural moment itself is of much more than mere chronological significance, and festivals commemorating it therefore acquire a certain solemnity, a shadow of which is likely to fall even on agnostic revels. We not only measure history from that primal moment but know it for its triumphant transcending of history. It admits the believer to an order beyond time. And, as we shall see, there is an assumption, not necessarily given expression and not always justified by specific religious belief, that we can participate in that different order of time as well as in the one in which we live from day to day; and this prompts our interest in some cardinal dates at the expense of all the others.

The custom of attending to origins, if not universal, is far from peculiar to cultures using our calendar. The Romans counted from an original point – *ab urbe condita*, from the foundation of the city. This arrangement presumably seemed satisfactory because it connected the present moment of the individual with the mythical origin of the state. It gave Romans what many societies seem to need, the sense of a duration by means of which its citizens could situate their lives in relation to the larger context of past and future, to an end that would not be entirely private and insignificant because, like the individual beginning, it acquires a larger sense from the history of a society bound together not only by the ordinary acts of social necessity but by an unbroken series of generations, whose lives and achievements can be celebrated by festivals which recur annually, like the seasons. From these sources each life might acquire a meaning beyond itself in the interval between its beginning and its end. It was not just a simple progress towards one's own death, not just one damned thing after another. Instead of remaining at the mercy of the passage of ordinary time a life could be felt as making sense in terms of a far more universal system of counting; and a lifespan is thus given significance by solidarity not only with those who shared membership of one's particular epoch but also with ancestors and descendants. Moreover, as one's beginning may be marked by a ritual which transforms it from a merely natural occurrence, and allows the child to have access to that other order of time, so death has rites that are not merely temporal. One way of making it generally as well as personally significant is to relate it to the end of history, which, for each of us, it so emphatically prefigures. As we shall see, millennia are prefigurations of the end, which is one reason why they continue to interest us; they also mark beginnings, and are thus, in one sense, celebrations of both death and survival.

To confer upon beginnings and endings the power of enriching the significance of the life in between is, as I have suggested, to assume that one lives in two related orders of time. This was an idea familiar to medieval scholars and jurists. It was at the root of a celebrated doctrine, made famous by Ernst Kantorowicz,[1] of the King's Two Bodies, one a mortal body subject to time, the other a Dignity that persisted in an intemporal order of duration that mediated between ordinary time and eternity. In the Middle Ages the point was made with an impressive allegory, for an effigy of the monarch, an image of the royal Dignity, of the body that does not die, travelled in the funeral procession with his coffin. The continuum, neither temporal nor eternal, in which the Dignity endured was called the *aevum*, originally, in scholastic thought, the 'time of the angels', whose duties as messengers required them to operate in normal time without being native to it, and who therefore inhabited this medium between time and eternity.

These theological fictions may strike us as bizarre relics of a superseded philosophy, but behind them there is a perfectly commonsense principle which we continue, without giving the matter much thought, to uphold. A third term between time and eternity, participating in both the temporal and the eternal, is needed not only by angels and the undying monarchy but also by legal corporations. An invention which began life in a context of refined angelology proved adaptable for political and commercial purposes. A corporation or company persists in a different kind of time from its members; they die in the course of ordinary time but it survives them, enjoying a sort of quasi-immortality while yet subsisting in that same temporal order. The idea may also have some personal use, enabling us to reconcile our conflicting senses of time: simple successiveness, an ever-rolling stream, an uncontrollable force bearing us on to our individually insignificant deaths; but also a continuum marked by moments of special grace or attentiveness, or simply by a sense of the intemporal relations that connect one moment with other great moments similarly distinguished, and foster our awareness of a vital relation to past and future time.

This capacity to distinguish, by varying our forms of attention, between significant and insignificant moments in time is sometimes expressed as the distinction between two Greek words, *chronos*, passing time, and *kairos*, waiting time or season. (Not all scholars agree that the words are so sharply opposed in New Testament Greek, but they are certainly not synonymous, and the distinction is one we can feel on our own pulses. We *know* this difference, living most of the time in *chronos* but recognizing our *kairos* moments and valuing them even when their occasion may seem trivial.)

The more one considers this temporal dualism the more obvious it becomes that it remains an inescapable part of our lives. One reason why we do not lead our lives as if they existed solely in an order of simple chronicity is that we cannot cease to be conscious of the existence of our parents and our children, which simply requires us to attend to a time that is not merely our time. As Aristotle remarked, the cycle of generation is a kind of second-best eternity ('eternal in the manner that is open to it'). Our lives, and the lives of creatures that are presumably not aware of the fact as we are, take their place in an order that is, if not eternal, then very remote from the merely successive. So, as the poet Spenser knew, it was necessary to think of nature as both eternal and mutable, a condition we can imagine in human terms by understanding that there is a kind of genetic perpetuity; though perishable as individuals we are, in Spenser's words, 'by succession made perpetuall,/Transformed oft, and chaunged diverslie', a notion not discouraged by modern genetics. This is the sense in which we 'raigne over change', or at least feel that, up to a point, we are doing so, for example by supposing that a person is the same person at twenty and seventy, that there is a substance in us that prevails despite the difficulties put in the way of this assumption by David Hume, for example.

Indeed the prospect of being merely an item in change, of having no continuous relationship to the past or the future, no trace of perpetuity, seems hard to bear. We mark the passing of the individual either with religious services which stress both the mortality of the body and the perpetuity of the spirit, or with agnostic celebrations that dwell on the past of the individual and his or her legacy to a future. We know that we must have ends that are more important than mere temporal cessations. And the millennium is an image of such important ends.

All of us are uneasily aware of the certainty of death, which is therefore immanent throughout our conscious lives. If given some relation to a common beginning, and to the patterned tract of time separating end from origin, we can perhaps worry less as to whether our lives, destined to annihilation, make any sense at all. In this way a chosen chronology that offers impressive images of end-times, and relates them to a great inaugural event, serves the same purpose as genealogical memory in preliterate societies, when the passage of historical time could be sanctified by the recitation of the names of generations of ancestors, a practice that not only marked out a different system of temporal progression but affirmed identification with the great names and so claimed a part in their achievements.

In short, the calendar has to provide us, as the complex temporal arrangements of some tribes provided others, with the means of measuring two sorts of time, and as it supplies a beginning it must also provide an end. It supplies images of that end, at the great centurial and millennial dates.

In our system the date of the transition from one to the next millennium was accessible only after much calendrical research. The accurate measurement of years, on which the definition of greater epochs clearly depended, took time, calling for progressive understandings of the natural cycle as measured by the sun and the moon, and solutions to the problems of reconciling the data. Our calendar is a version, much refined over centuries, of the Roman. Attempts have been made to depart from it, but it has proved too strong to be supplanted; the French Revolutionary Calendar, beginning in 1792, lasted only twelve years. Nevertheless, many non-Christian systems continue to operate; for example, each year Hanukkah and Ramadan fall on differing dates in the Christian calendar, and even within Christendom there are disputes about dates and epochs. In the Armenian Church, for instance, Christmas is celebrated on 6 January. The calendar of the Orthodox Church is thirteen days behind the Western because it has not yet adopted the calendrical reforms instituted by Pope Gregory XIII, who omitted ten days from the calendar in 1582; by the time the Gregorian calendar was adopted in England (1752) the number of lost days had risen to eleven. These adjustments were a cause of much concern and even some rioting, in England and elsewhere, for many citizens imagined that their lives were being arbitrarily shortened by the authorities.[2] But for all practical purposes there is now a chronological lingua franca, and it is, inevitably, ours. Yet it must be remembered that our millennial dates are quite without significance to communities who prefer another style and have their own red-letter-day arrangements.

The Christian practice of dating events from the Incarnation was instituted by the monk Dionysius Exiguus in the sixth century. He started his count from the Annunciation, and since he was working before the invention of zero he perforce dated this event in March AD 1. The removal of New Year's Day from 25 March to 1 January, and the aforementioned discrepancy between Julian (English) and Gregorian (European) systems, are the reasons why historians sometimes need to give three dates for events of the sixteenth and seventeenth centuries: thus an English contemporary would have given the date of the execution of Charles I as 30 January 1648 but to a foreign contemporary this would be 9 February 1649. By our calculation it was 30 January 1649. (I borrow this neat formulation of the confusion from Godfrey Davies.[3])

Dionysius' arrangement was adopted in England at the Synod of Whitby in 664, which achieved a settlement of the pressing problem of the date of Easter. The Synod decided in favour of the Roman as against the Irish calculations, and so, in a manner, we first joined Europe. The difficulty over this cardinal date had its origin in the Jewish way of calculating Passover, and the fact that we have traditionally accorded special significance to millennial dates is at least in part due to the influence of Jewish customs and calendrical speculations.

The whole span of history from the Creation was thought by the Jews to be six thousand years, a thousand for each day of the work of Creation, with a paradisal sabbath to follow. The equation one day = 1,000 years was supported by Psalm 90: 4 ('A thousand ages in thy sight are but as yesterday when it is past, and as a watch in the night') and the formula was taken up by Christianity on the testimony of II Peter 3: 8: 'one day is with the Lord a thousand years, and a thousand years as one day'.

The pre-Christian Jewish apocalypses had imagined a future Messianic earthly kingdom, on the analogy of the sabbath following the six days of divine work. Consequently the end of a span of a thousand years, a sixth of all the time there was or ever would be, was a matter of unusual interest, the end of each millennium being a consummation premonitory of the final end. Elements of this belief persisted into times when the age of the world was recognized as being a good deal longer than 6,000 years, and they still persist; our present interest in millennia may be said to have been, at least in part, a survival of Judaic thought that has been sustained in Christian circles, at any rate until recently, by a habitual and general reverence for the Bible, not least for the Book of Revelation, a Christian Apocalypse on strongly Jewish lines.

The time scheme of six millennia was taken up in his *Chronographia* by the third-century scholar Julius Africanus, who was somewhat exceptional among apocalyptic students in not fixing the date of the End during his own lifetime. He believed that 5,500 of the 6,000 years that would comprise the whole of history had already passed before the Nativity, so the end, though not exactly at hand, was reasonably nigh. The church historian Eusebius, who presided over the inaugural session of the Council of Nicaea, called by Constantine in 325 to sort out the doctrinal problems of the church he had now adopted, established a world dating-system which, with modifications, was still the pattern for Isaac Newton's chronological schemes; and the remains of these and many other apocalyptic fantasies are still with us. Evidently we have still not quite reached the stage where we can have the chronology without the apocalyptic trimmings, and without some reverence, at least vestigial, for the inaugural event; this was of course not accepted by Judaism, where there were alternative views of the Messiah, but like other elements of Christian teaching it was made to be consonant with much in the Jewish tradition.

The Jews, however, were not the first to divide time in this way. Norman Cohn[4] has made the case for the priority of Zoroastrianism, which was the official religion of the Iranian empire in the sixth century BC, long before the Jewish apocalypses. The length of time envisaged by Zoroaster seems to have been either 12,000 or 6,000 years, in 3,000-year sections, each in turn subdivided into 1,000-year epochs. Zoroaster, like most millenarian prophets, expected the great transformation of the end-time to occur in or soon after his own lifetime; it would be preceded, as it usually is in apocalyptic speculation, by a period of decadence, almost invariably the one in which the prophet happened himself to be living. In Zoroastrianism time was to reach its end and be succeeded by a last judgement awarding the saved an eternity of bliss. Cohn says the words denoting this transformation literally mean something like 'the making wonderful'. Zoroastrians celebrate its prefiguration at the New Year, which for them occurred in spring.

The comparative shortness of time allowed in our tradition between origins and ends – a brevity imposed on research until relatively recently by the time-indications of an inerrant Bible – has enabled us to continue the practice of celebrating or fearing these rather tightly organized millennial dates without giving much consideration to the fact of their gross irrelevance to the history of the universe as it is now calculated. We ought by now to be capable in principle of taking a Godlike view: two thousand years, after all, in relation to the history of the universe are in our sight like an evening gone. It is the power of tradition, of systems built in ignorance of modern knowledge though still active, that allows us to behave as if this were not so. As the Zoroastrians indicate, societies and religions not constrained by the Judaeo-Christian Bible use much larger numbers, and this presumably has some influence on the way they feel about dates. At the present time Hindus believe themselves to be living in the fourth *yuga* or division of time, and although the fourth is much shorter than the other three it still runs to 430,000 years, only about 6,000 of which have passed; so the transformation, the making wonderful, is still a long way off. It is interesting that the present *yuga* is thought to be a time of degeneration or decadence which will be corrected only with the birth of a new age. We have that much in common, but the time scale is such that the imminence of an end, which adds so much to the excitements of Western millennialism, must be absent when the cycles of world time are conceived so much more extensively.

The Jewish figures, unlike the Persian and the Indian, are part of our intellectual heritage, and their relative smallness makes specific eschatological prophecy easier to manage as well as more thrilling. It is, however, worth remembering that despite the vastness of the Indian numbers, which presumably deny the devotee the immediate frisson imparted by the threats and promises of our tradition, the idea of disorder and decay as the prelude to the end is still present.

Indeed it is nearly always easy to believe that times are so bad that the end must be nigh. A seventh-century inscription found at Poitiers reads 'Alpha and Omega, The beginning and the end. All things become every day worse and worse, for the end is drawing near.'[5] Thirteen centuries later the poet Yeats echoes this sentiment in his poem 'The Second Coming':

> Things fall apart, the centre cannot hold;
> Mere anarchy is loosed upon the world...
> Surely some revelation is at hand...

and the poem ends, not with the usual Second Coming, but with the vision of a rough beast slouching towards Bethlehem to be born.

The novelist D.H. Lawrence saw the Great War as the biblical time of Tribulation, when 'we give ourselves up to the flux of death'. He even found specific apocalyptic significance in Zeppelins; the Great War was to him equivalent to the disorders that signify the approach of the end. *Lady Chatterley's Lover*, with its ruined landscapes, its portraits of a decadent society and its bouts of apocalyptic sex, is probably the most elaborately designed apocalyptic novel in the language, an extension of his earlier meditations, first prompted by apocalyptic hymns in his chapel childhood; and his last book was a study of the subject (*Apocalypse*, 1931).

These are not the specific prophecies of naive or fundamentalist apocalyptists, though Lawrence treats the topic more literally than most serious writers. Great artists know too much about the relationship of their fictions and images to historical reality to be seduced by figures or promises of Armageddon, Rapture and Judgement; but apprehensions of terror, epochal change and possible renewal are still strong, and it is not difficult to see the history of the twentieth century as providing more than adequate confirmation of the horrible events imagined as preceding the end. Artists, by drawing on the visual and literary traditions, can give particular expression to the apprehensions of others, whether these are vague or given the appearance of precision by appeals to a Bible supposed to be literally inspired. Picasso's *Guernica* is said to owe something to the imagery of medieval apocalypses, and few can now look at illustrations in the medieval Beatus tradition, described elsewhere in this volume, or at the Renaissance frescoes of Signorelli in the cathedral at Orvieto, and not recognize, in their Last Judgements, the imagery of death camps and torturers, images provided in their time for the terrified edification of all. Modern artists, in giving precise expression to a vaguer, more general, less acute anxiety that all may share, find themselves repeating the old figurations of Apocalypse. Even when the old thought is modernized the old imagery recurs, and is potent because Apocalypse still has a date in the calendar.

Among fundamentalists the idea is widespread that millennial or even centurial dates, and certain other dates worked out arithmologically from numbers in Daniel and Revelation, will occur at times when human society is in a bad way, as it is regularly seen to be. The pattern is of decadence, as concisely and vividly described in the 'little apocalypses' of Mark 13 and Matthew 24: a time of disaster, false preachers, persecutions and abominations, 'affliction such as was not from the beginning of the creation', followed by renovation, the

Second Coming. The evangelists do not specify when this would happen; indeed the founding texts warn against attempts to do so: 'But of that day and that hour knoweth no man, no, not the angels which are in heaven, neither the Son, but the Father' (Mark 13: 32, Matthew 24: 36), though one is warned always to be looking out for it and ready to act when it arrives. What would happen next is also left unclear; perhaps, as in the Judaic tradition, the sequel would be the institution of an earthly kingdom of God, when the Messiah would reign for a thousand years, or perhaps earthly time would be no more, the end of the world being already upon us. The just would be taken up at once into a heavenly kingdom. And just as the Zoroastrians were disappointed, and are still waiting for the end, so in the Christian ecclesiastical tradition the notion that the Second Coming was at hand, and likely to occur in the lifetime of the current generation, had to be given up, and the eschatological prophecies given a more relaxed interpretation. This, of course, has not prevented dissident sects over the ages from working out and preparing for their own versions of the end time, as they still do.

It is safe to say that the millennial sentiments and celebrations of all who have abandoned the apocalyptic Grand Narrative and do not belong to any such sect — who remain unconvinced that upon them the ends of the ages have come — will lack the prophetic thrills and expectations of the true apocalyptist. In this way they will differ — and the difference is admittedly rather large — from the fundamentalist interpreters already alluded to, who expect a very detailed confirmation of the numbers and allegories of Revelation. It is they, with their embarrassing literalism, who stand most directly in the long tradition of apocalyptic and millennial thinking. For the rest of us the importance of 2000 must be, in comparison, very dilute, but even so the fainter excitement felt at the imminence of a new millennium derives some of its character from chronologies, numerologies and allegories long since consciously discarded.

Since modern scepticism closes off direct access to the grand tradition we may well wonder why the desire to observe and celebrate the end of the second millennium in a manner descended, however enfeebled, from that tradition is apparently so general. Of course to many it is simply an occasion for a New Year's Eve party on a scale grander than usual, though even that may be read as the exploitation of an exceptionally good opportunity to elude the constraints of diurnal consciousness. Others, without acceding to naive millenarianism, may take this great New Year rather more seriously and perhaps more ethically, imagining a future in which they will give up bad habits, be better people, renounce personal decadence and pursue personal renovation. For such resolutions are made annually and, given our habits of calculation, may well be felt more keenly at the ends of centuries, and, *a fortiori*, at this greater turn of time.

But there may be more serious reasons for an interest not directly related to biblical prophecy or mere calendrical obsessiveness. One such is precisely our attachment to a past which, despite the historiographical nihilism of the post-modernists, we can still think of as ours, and as relevant to us. And it is a past of which the historical record is crammed with apocalyptic interpretations, some of which have had a positive effect on the constructions and the mentalities of times quite close to our own, if not on our own. For another good reason we may look beyond the historical record and ask whether human beings have not generally had, what in some form they still retain, a need to make more sense of the world than is available without some grasp of the idea of an end in relation to an origin.

As to the first of these reasons, there is no shortage of information concerning the historical importance of the millennial idea. It is part of a myth that is also the myth of Apocalypse, since that revelation is always timed according to the numerological opportunities offered by the biblical apocalypses, Daniel's in the Old Testament, and in the New, Matthew and Mark, Revelation, and a passage or two in the Epistles, notably I Thessalonians 4: 16–17, the source of much cultic modern interest in what is called the Rapture, when, at the end of time, the born-again will be snatched up to meet the Lord in the air. The identification of persons (Napoleon, Hitler) as characters from the biblical Apocalypse, and the detailed application of prophecies to a modern Armageddon, seem to be as common now as they have ever been, and Hal Lindsey's guide to these persons and events, *The Late Great Planet Earth* (1st edn 1970), is a famous best-seller in the United States, though it has many competitors.

At what may be a slightly loftier level of interest, apocalyptic eschatology has at various times had powerful political influence. John Foxe, whose *Acts and Monuments* is one of the supreme examples of Tudor propaganda, uses apocalyptic numbers to establish Elizabeth's Settlement as a *renovatio*. She herself was an incarnation of Virgil's Astraea in the Fourth Eclogue, a prophecy of the Golden Age to come. Spenser's *Faerie Queene* also enlists Apocalypse in the justification of the Elizabethan Settlement. At the time of the English revolution the Fifth-Monarchy men took their cue from Daniel's four monarchies (of Babylon, Persia, Greece and Rome) and daily expected the advent of the fifth; this was a variant way of estimating the date of the millennium. Milton's political fervour included exalted evocations of the new age about to be born, and was sure that the millennial empire would have its capital in England; for, as he announced in *Areopagitica*, 'all concurrence of signs' shows that God is about to inaugurate 'some new and great period in his church' – 'what does he then but reveal himself to his servants, and, as his manner is, first to his Englishmen?'

The Book of Revelation, which despite its originality is in the tradition of other, apocryphal, Jewish apocalypses of the intertestamentary period, had some difficulty getting into the canon, and even Luther doubted whether he should include it in his translation of the Bible. It is interesting to speculate on what difference it would have made to the world had it been left out from the beginning, like other apocalypses. Here one thinks again of the popular eschatologies that treat the events of Revelation as a direct prophecy of the times of the interpreter; but a more serious matter is the historical scheme of Joachim of Fiore, a Calabrian abbot who died in 1202, of whom it has been not implausibly said that he has had an influence on European history comparable with that of Marx.

Joachim divided history into three phases, one for each Person of the Trinity, with a period of transition between them: the last transition would begin in 1260, the date arrived at by multiplying forty-two, the number of generations between Abraham and Christ, by thirty, the estimate of a generation. There would be an Antichrist, and his victorious opponent, the Emperor of the Last Days; and there would be an Angelic Pope. A new gospel, the *evangelium aeternum*, would become manifest, transcending the New Testament as that did the Old, and appropriate to the Third Age, that of the Holy Spirit. Joachim's writings were sometimes taken to be this gospel, and various contemporary figures were identified as the emperor and the pope.

What makes Joachim extraordinary, as Norman Cohn, Marjorie Reeves and others have demonstrated, is the persistence with which, over the centuries, he was read, interpreted and distorted by commentators hungry for apocalyptic prophecy. Yeats and Lawrence, already mentioned as apocalyptists, studied Joachim and used him in their writings; in doing so they were carrying on a tradition of a nineteenth-century Joachimite revival involving names as serious as those of Hegel, Comte and Renan, and carried on by Spengler and Ernst Bloch in the twentieth. In earlier times Savonarola was a Joachimite, as George Eliot knew when she wrote *Romola* (1862–3), and so was William Blake, influenced perhaps by the lingering memory of the doctrines promulgated by dissenters in the mid-seventeenth century; and so, perhaps, was Hitler, or at any rate his propagandists, for the expression 'Third Reich' seems to have been related to the Third Dispensation or *status* of Joachim.

As Marjorie Reeves and Warwick Gould are careful to remind us, in their *Joachim of Fiore and the Myth of the Eternal Evangel in the Nineteenth Century* (1987), not every tripartite historical theory need derive directly from Joachim; but when there was a distinct tendency to 'think in threes', vague, second-hand notions of the abbot's theory may have been complicit. There were those, like Ernest Renan, who, having had preliminary instruction from George Sand, eventually sought out the original texts, although Joachim's genuine works were not republished after the sixteenth century. Joachim's scheme was of course much varied, even in the thirteenth century, when rival groups put partisan interpretations on it, and the modern versions tend not to reproduce his views with any accuracy, particularly since his programme for the third peaceful *status* was, as might be expected from an abbot, monastic in character. But the least one can say is that this apocalyptic variant, though it is not bound to the idea of thousand-year partitions of history, reflects a similar desire to read the providential pattern of universal history in numerical terms derived from the Bible, here strongly affected by Trinitarian considerations. Joachim's was for seven centuries an influential attempt to find a plausible basis for the vague but still strong desire that there should be such a pattern, even if the authority of the biblical model had been reduced.

In earlier times the work of Joachim most cited was his commentary on Revelation, which was used by Foxe and others in their anti-papal interpretations. The proclamation of the Three Ages suited the thought of extreme dissenters, such as the Ranters and Muggletonians, who might treat the Eternal Evangel not as a book, or a gospel for the new age, but as a figure for the Second Coming, and the Third Age, a time when the other testaments were no longer needed, since the Holy Spirit would henceforth speak directly to every heart. In this new age all were exempt from the old Law. It was a good doctrine for the innocently licentious.

The revival of varieties of Joachimism in the nineteenth century was clearly a consequence of a general feeling that the age was one of transition. It had respectable scholarly support, and coexisted with the more vulgar manifestations of millenarianism. If we now turn to a consideration of the more general human interest in temporal epochs and endings, we may discover that this sense of transition, embodied in Joachim's theory but common to all who saw history in thousand-year periods, or even hundred-year periods, as part of a divine arrangement, is a clue to the nature of that interest.

It is not easy, in the world as it is, to imagine what it would be like to have no sense that one was living in a time of transition, though there may recently have dawned a new sense that the transition itself is endless, that it has in fact turned into an epoch or age, with nothing on the temporal horizon but more of the same, more transition. In the last century the sense that one was living in a terminable age of transition was a common, indeed almost unavoidable notion, and the literature of the time is full of it. Perhaps the sense of transition grew less vague, and more apprehensive, at the beginning of the twentieth century, when the excitement of the idea was accompanied by certain terrors that were soon to be justified. 1900 was the date Freud placed on the title-page of *The Interpretation of Dreams* (the book was published in 1899 but he wanted the centurial date); Max Planck, whether because of the interest of the date or merely by chance I do not know, published his quantum hypothesis in December 1900, so modern physics, which made possible, among other things, the atomic bomb, began at the exact end of the century, provided one happens to accept the argument that the new century began on 1 January 1901 (and the millennium, by the same token, on 1 January 2001, though in respect of the present millennium we appear to have agreed on the earlier date). For political historians 1900 is, as George Lichtheim has argued, a watershed in European power struggles because, under the influence of A.T. Mahan's *The Influence of Sea Power upon History* (1890), the great powers began to build enormous battle fleets, the Germans taking the decision to do so in 1900.[6]

This development underlies the change – transition was now to be seen as in large part a transition to an age of technology. With our eyes on other kinds of change, and our anxious awareness of military technologies far more destructive, we are inclined to forget the invention of the Dreadnought; as Buckminster Fuller used to say, when it became possible to fire a shell weighing a ton from a gun fixed on a rolling, pitching platform moving forward at 30 knots, with good hope of hitting a target moving at the same speed on a different course and sixteen miles away, the technology of the moonshot was born, and the moonshot surely belongs to our own age of transition.

These are not the kinds of thing we think of first when contemplating the phenomena that are often described as *fin de siècle*. That description of the mood of the time has always, since it came in, been used to connote decadence, the mingling of hope and anxiety, with a particular date, and it is strongly associated with the mood of the last years of the nineteenth century. The *O.E.D.* records its first English use in 1890, though that was in a newspaper, and since the expression had already acquired an extended sense ('The finance of the year has been special – *fin de siècle*') we can assume it had been in use for some time before that. The *Westminster Gazette*, in 1898, described it as a pessimistic expression, indicating 'a weariness and weakening of purpose', and later uses are normally meant to bring to mind the age of the *Yellow Book* and Oscar Wilde (who spoke of the *fin du monde*) and of the artistic cult of decadence, which found its most extravagant spokesman in Joris-Karl Huysmans and its canonical expression in his *A Rebours* ('Against Nature', 1884; pp.275–6). Arthur Symons is said to have called his influential book *The Decadent Movement in Literature* until, in the aftermath of the Wilde trials, he changed it to *The Symbolist Movement in Literature* (1899). Yeats, a friend of Symons and incidentally a convinced Joachimite, eventually wrote his *A Vision*, in which he continued to see his time as a time of transition – 'This foul world in its decline and fall', as he puts it in a late poem – a time soon to end in a supreme crisis, with new terrors, and a new annunciation.

The true end of the century, it has often been argued, may have been 1914, when all over Europe young men, having felt that they had been born into a decadent time, welcomed the war as a means to be rid of the old, dying culture, a means of regeneration: 'Now God be thanked/Who has matched us with this hour', cried Rupert Brooke; and Ortega y Gasset heralded the end of one world and the birth of another. This exalted mood was often nationalistic, though not confined to a single nation;[7] of course it changed completely when the enthusiasts encountered the conditions under which the fighting was to be done, but the notion of war as a terror that ended a decadence and made possible a renovation was strong. In prospect the conflict had some of the properties of the biblical Tribulation, for which all too soon it was to provide an updated imagery of horror. And probably only the static anxieties of the Cold War, and the self-evident absurdity of supposing atomic war to be in any sense liberating or ennobling, put such attitudes out of court. The Tribulation now became a dull fear, incapable of exaltation and apparently without end. When it came, the end of the Cold War was attended with scenes that might have been thought benignly apocalyptic, the destruction of the Berlin Wall a peaceful Armageddon, though we find, as so many have discovered before us, that the habits of modern tribulation persist, few swords have been beaten into ploughshares, and persons as apt as Nero or Hitler for the role of Antichrist continue to plague the world.

This meditation on millennia has tried to say why we make so much of arbitrary calendrical divisions, and to say something about the relatively occult concerns that induce us to do so. They may now be less urgent than they were at other times, when the figures found in the Bible had to be taken literally, but they persist. Everybody knows of the many superstitions about numbers, degenerate descendants of the extraordinary arithmological obsessions of our ancestors in times when mathematics, which was to be the ground of the new science, also contributed to forms of magic not yet clearly differentiated from science.

So numbers, including those enshrined in our calendar, belonged to an order of reality independent of the mundane world though reflected in it, like the numbers of Pythagoras or the Forms of Plato, and had themselves the power to excite. The importance of the number 10 was understood by the Pythagoreans as arising from its being the total of 1, 2, 3 and 4, and 100 is 10 squared and 1,000 is 10 cubed, with correspondingly increasing weight and importance. When to this basis of numerical superstition one adds the idea that millennia represent ends and beginnings, and that the end of a particular millennium will mean the end of time, the portentousness of the millennium is increased. And when, through long ages of interpretation, a body of apocalyptic writing can be adduced to support the idea that the End, of which the end of every millennium is a prefiguration, will be preceded by terrors and followed by judgement, there is grave cause for the sort of anxiety, however manifested, that seems to attend the great turns of time. The position is presumably most serious for believers in a providential design of history from the Creation to the End, divided by millennia, which endows with supreme relevance the date at which the modern calendar began.

Here it is necessary to recall the duality of our consciousness of temporal matters. What we remember of our lives as we narrate them to ourselves are the *kairoi*, and the relations between disparate *kairoi*. We remember history in the same way. No history, not even the barest annals, can be entirely concerned with mere successiveness, and so it is when we are trying to understand what our lives mean. The incidents thus remembered may be, on a general view, commonplace enough: falling in love, bereavement, the births of children. Somehow we can make these matters hang together. I take it that our interests in millennium and Apocalypse are projections of these existential musings. We like lives, and the world itself, to have a plot; a plot helps us to make sense of our lives and of the world. Plots have endings, perhaps not the tying up of loose ends that we find in older fiction, for scepticism has entered also into plot-making; but even if the end is dubious, ambivalent, it must still be more than a mere cessation of narrative. That the end of the world plot should be extremely spectacular, with justice and punishment meted out to all, as it is in the apocalypses and in some old novels, is a view now confined to the admittedly very large number of modern fundamentalists. What everybody else, more critical of this Grand Narrative, experiences may not be much more than a mild interest, rather like an interest in the number 13, or systems for winning the lottery or breaking the bank at roulette.

Still, it is there, and when the number is large, as in the year 2000, faint atavistic memories of the once significant chronologies and the once alarming imagery may stir in the mind of the sceptic and stimulate an interest not only in the history of these manifestations but a determination to enjoy the complex pleasures of the millennial moment, even though the moment is a fiction and our responses to it as human and as fallible as all the other stories we tell ourselves of our own lives.

NOTES

1 *The King's Two Bodies*, Princeton: Princeton University Press, 1957.

2 For an interesting account of reactions to these lost days see David Ewing Duncan, *The Calendar*, London: Fourth Estate, 1998, pp. 288–320.

3 *The Early Stuarts, 1603–1660* (Oxford History of England), Oxford: The Clarendon Press, 1937 (ed. of 1952), p. xvii.

4 'How time acquired a consummation', in Malcolm Bull (ed.), *Apocalyptic Theory and the Ends of the World*, Oxford 1995, pp. 21–37.

5 Bernard McGinn, 'The end of the world and the beginning of Christendom', in Bull, op. cit., pp. 58–89.

6 George Lichtheim, *Europe in the Twentieth Century*, London: Weidenfeld & Nicolson, 1972, pp. 7–8.

7 See Robert Wohl, *The Generation of 1914*, London: Weidenfeld & Nicolson, 1980.

2 Biblical Origins of the Apocalyptic Tradition

Norman Cohn

In contemporary usage 'The Apocalypse' has two meanings. It can indicate the last book of the New Testament, and thus of the Christian Bible: the work known as the Revelation of St John the Divine or, more usually, simply as Revelation. Or it can indicate the prodigious events which, in Christian tradition, are expected to usher in the end of the present world and its replacement by the world to come. As a common noun, 'apocalypse' is also used to indicate a whole category of literary productions, of which Revelation is the most celebrated example. The Greek word *apokálypsis* means 'unveiling', 'uncovering'; sometimes the secret knowledge that is unveiled in the Apocalypse concerns the heavenly world, but chiefly it is about the destiny of this our world. Eschatology, which is at the very heart of Revelation, bulks large in many other apocalypses.

The earliest of these writings are of Jewish origin; they were produced in Judaea in the third and second centuries BC.[1] Whether they were produced for the benefit of particular sects is uncertain, but the notions they express about the end of this world and the coming of another had no place in the official Judaism of the time. This is true of the one and only Apocalypse that has been accepted into the Hebrew Bible, and so into the Christian Old Testament: the Book of Daniel.[2]

In its present form the Book of Daniel is a product of the Antiochan persecution of Judaean Jews in the 160s BC. Almost two centuries had elapsed since Alexander's campaigns had inaugurated the Hellenistic period in the eastern Mediterranean world. After Alexander's death the vast empire he had founded was divided amongst dynasties of Macedonian descent. In the second century BC Judaea was under the rule of one such dynasty, the Seleucids, which was based in Syria.

Governments in the Greek-speaking world did not generally interfere with ancestral religions, but in the 160s the Seleucid monarch Antiochus IV Epiphanes interfered drastically with Judaism. He proceeded with singular brutality. In 169 he entered the Temple in Jerusalem, stole cultic ornaments and stripped the building of its gold decoration. Two years later he turned on the city itself. It was pillaged and burned, many of its inhabitants were killed, women and children were taken as slaves. All the observances and customs of the Jewish religion were prohibited, the sacred scrolls were to be destroyed and infringement of any of these prescriptions was punishable by death. In the Temple the cult of Yahweh was replaced by that of a Syrian god, Baal Shamen; a new altar was superimposed on the old, where sacrifices of those taboo animals, pigs, were carried out. In the provinces, too, altars to pagan gods were set up, and everywhere offerings had to be made in honour of the king. Throughout the land everyone was required to take part in the foreign cult and the royal officials had to ensure that this was done. The guaranteed right that the Jewish community had always enjoyed, to live according to its own religious laws, was thereby abolished. Many Jews were prepared to fight, if need be to die, rather than commit the sacrilege demanded of them. The result is known to history as the Maccabaean rising. It was a successful rising: in 164 the Temple was liberated and the rightful cult restored; a couple of years later the Jewish community was again granted its traditional rights.

Such is the background of the Book of Daniel as we know it. Ostensibly the work is concerned with the actions of a Jew called Daniel – a legendary figure of wisdom and righteousness – at the Babylonian court in the sixth century. But although some of the stories it contains may have originated at that time, all the apocalyptic passages were written between 169 and 165 BC, and probably by more than one author.

Chapters 2 and 7 contain famous apocalypses. Chapter 2 tells how King Nebuchadnezzar dreamed of a huge and fearsome image, with head of gold, breast and arms of silver, belly and thighs of bronze, legs of iron, and feet part iron and part terracotta. While he watched, a stone hewn from a mountain – but 'not by human hands' – struck the feet of the image and shattered them, whereupon the other parts of the image disintegrated and vanished, leaving no trace behind. But the stone grew into a great mountain, filling the whole earth. What none of the wise men of Babylon could do, God enabled Daniel to do: in a vision the sage was shown not only what the king had dreamed but also what the dream meant.

The golden head, according to Daniel, was the king himself, while the silver and bronze parts of the image stood for future kingdoms, inferior to the Babylonian. Daniel's main interest was reserved for the fourth kingdom, represented by the iron legs and the feet of iron and terracotta. As iron shatters and destroys all things, so, he foretold, that kingdom would break and shatter the whole earth: he was of course foreseeing the history of Alexander's empire and its successor states. Nevertheless, that kingdom would suffer from internal weaknesses: attempts to bind its several parts together by means of dynastic marriages would fail, for those parts would be as incompatible as iron and terracotta – clearly a reference to the troubled relationship between the Syrian Seleucids and the Egyptian Ptolemies. Finally God himself would intervene:

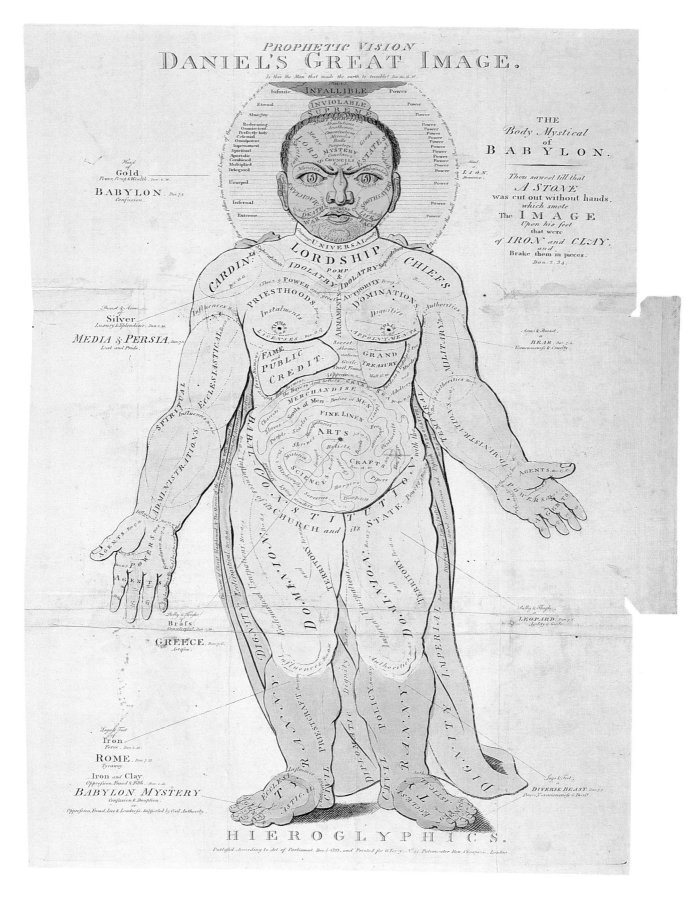

> In the period of those kings the God of Heaven will establish a kingdom which shall never be destroyed; that kingdom shall never pass to another people; it shall shatter and make an end of all these kingdoms, while it shall itself endure for ever. This is the meaning ... of the stone being hewn from a mountain, not by human hands, and then shattering the iron, the bronze, the clay, the silver, and the gold.[3]

The stone in fact represents a kingdom which God is to establish 'at the end of this age'. That kingdom will be universal and everlasting. Moreover, it will be terrestrial – why else the assurance that it can never pass to 'another people'? But indeed, what else could be meant by a stone that fills 'the whole earth'?

The scheme of four successive world empires, or 'kingdoms', was well known to the Ancient Near East, but in the hands of the author(s) of Daniel, working at the height of the Antiochan persecution and the Maccabaean rising, it took on a new significance. This is still more apparent in Chapter 7. For Chapter 7 foretells much the same future as Chapter 2, only it presents the story in quite a different symbolic guise, of far greater imaginative power; and it carries it further on in time. It also explains things far more precisely. Here Daniel figures not as an interpreter of dreams but as the dreamer, while the task of interpretation is taken over by an angel.

In his dream, or nocturnal vision, Daniel sees four beasts come up out of the tumultuous sea, one after another, each beast different, and each bizarre. A lion with eagle's wings, a bear-like creature, a four-headed winged leopard are followed by a more fearsome beast. Again it is the fourth item that claims Daniel's attention:

> I saw a fourth beast, dreadful and grisly, exceedingly strong, with great iron teeth and bronze claws. It crunched and devoured, and trampled underfoot all that was left. It differed from all the beasts which preceded it in having ten horns. While I was considering the horns I saw another horn, a little one, springing up among them. ... And in that horn were eyes like the eyes of a man, and a mouth that spoke proud words.[4]

The emergence of the little horn is the signal for the consummation of history. God himself appears, as 'the Ancient of Days' or 'Ancient of Years'. White-robed, white-haired, God is seated on a throne of fire, attended by myriads of beings making up the heavenly host. The court sits and – as in a contemporaneous court of law – the books are opened. At the command of the divine judge the fourth beast is destroyed and its carcass given to the flames. Then 'one like a son of man' appears 'with the clouds of heaven'. He is presented to the Ancient of Days, who bestows on him a sovereignty which will never pass away, a kingly power such that all peoples and nations in the world serve him.

Though it is commonly assumed that all this takes place in Heaven, there are abundant indications that the author imagined it as taking place on earth. The beasts emerge from the sea – and the sea was a traditional symbol of chaos, hostile to God and eternally threatening the ordered world. The land on to

Fig. 1. Garnet Terry (active 1770–1800), *An Hieroglyphical Print of Daniel's Great Image, or Mystical Man* (1793). Engraving. Altadena, California, Collection Robert N. Essick (see Ch. 5, cat. 16).

which they emerge is the same as the land which the fourth beast tramples – and that surely can only be Judaea. And when the thrones are set in place and the Ancient of Days, attended by myriads of angels, takes his seat, that must surely take place in Judaea as well. There are other such theophanies in the Hebrew Bible: in Psalm 96, for instance, and in Zechariah and Joel.[5] What the symbol of the four beasts is meant to convey is explained in the same Chapter 7: like the four parts of the image in Chapter 5 they stand for the imperial powers that have ruled over the Jews. The fourth beast, so much more terrible than its predecessors, is identified as Alexander's empire and its successor states: the ten horns are various monarchs, with Antiochus represented both by the tenth horn and by the 'little horn'.

The Book of Daniel was not a Maccabaean manifesto. Its aim was not to recruit troops but to encourage the civilian population – or rather an elite within that civilian population – to stand firm under persecution. For the deliverance was to be God's work: the Maccabaean forces were but instruments in his hand; their victory, when it came, would really be his victory. In the great vision of 'the Ancient of Days' it is God himself who judges the Seleucid kingdom symbolized by the fourth beast and sentences it to destruction. And it is God himself who bestows everlasting sovereignty over the whole world on 'the one like a son of man'.

This 'one like a son of man' who appears 'with the clouds of heaven' is a mysterious figure.[6] In itself the phrase meant no more than 'one like a human being', 'one in human likeness', but the figure in Daniel's dream clearly has a special significance. What it signifies has been much debated, yet it seems clear enough. Of the man-like figure it is said that 'his sovereignty was to be an everlasting sovereignty which should not pass away, and his kingly power should never be impaired'. Of the 'saints of the Most High' it is said that 'their kingly power is an everlasting power and all sovereignties shall serve and obey them'.[7] Surely, then, the 'one like a son of man' must be either a symbol of 'the saints of the Most High' or their representative. In either case he embodies the sense of election, the certainty of future vindication and exaltation of the Jews – or rather, of the Jews for whom the author(s) of Daniel wrote.

The 'saints (or holy ones) of the Most High' are in turn surely to be identified with those Jews. All that ever belonged to the great pagan empires will pass to them. All and more: for whereas each of those empires exercised a dominion only until it was replaced by another empire, no such fate is in store for the dominion exercised by Daniel's Jews: 'their kingdom shall never pass to another people, it shall shatter and make an end of all these kingdoms, while it shall itself endure for ever and ever'.[8] All this, too, will happen on this earth. The future empire, which will also be the kingdom of God, will be as purely terrestrial as the pagan empires of the past – indeed, its beginning will be marked by the reconsecration of the Jerusalem Temple, desecrated by Antiochus. Yet the future empire will be utterly different from any previous empire, in fact it will stand in total opposition to everything that has happened in history.

Fig. 2. John Martin (1789–1854), *Belshazzar's Feast* (1832). Mezzotint. London, British Museum (see Ch. 5, cat. 38).

Hitherto righteousness has been largely absent from the earth – only in Heaven has it obtained fully; with the realization of the kingdom of God righteousness will obtain on earth also, the divinely appointed order will have become all-embracing. The Jews who preside over the kingdom will likewise be different from the Jews of the past. The very phrase 'people of the saints of the Most High' hints at a people wholly without sin and wholly reconciled with God; and so does the association with the awe-inspiring figure of 'one like a son of man'.

There are indications in Daniel that these people are, in particular, the Jews who have followed the teachings of 'the wise' – of the visionaries such as the author of Daniel. From them they will have learned the technique of non-violent resistance; by standing firm under persecution they will have undergone an inner refinement and purification so that they will have become 'shining white'.[9] They will also have learned the technique of eschatological interpretation – how to relate both the text of the Bible and visionary experiences to the 'end-time'. Inwardly changed and endowed with esoteric wisdom, they will constitute an elite raised far above the normal condition of mankind. Furthermore as a community of 'holy ones' on earth, they will correspond to the angelic 'holy ones' in Heaven. And whereas the kingdoms symbolized by the beasts were in their day so many embodiments of purely human, political power, so these denizens of the coming kingdom will be vehicles of divine power.

The establishment of the empire of the saints, or holy ones, as the final and everlasting empire will be preceded by a divine judgement – and this will determine the fate not only of the Seleucid empire but of every individual Jew. After the overthrow and death of Antiochus all the faithful Jews – 'everyone who is written in the book' – will be saved from further suffering. And there will be an even more marvellous benefaction. Chapter 12 – the last in the book – closes with the remarkable prophecy: '… many of those who sleep in the dust of the earth will wake, some to everlasting life and some to the reproach of eternal abhorrence'. This passage has no parallel in the Hebrew Bible: it marks a decisive break with the traditional Israelite notion of death. The prospect of Sheol, 'the pit', 'the land of oblivion', that lay before the righteous and unrighteous alike, is replaced by a very different prospect: at the great consummation the dead are to be resurrected, judged and either rewarded or punished.[10]

Who were those dead? This again is a matter on which scholars have expressed widely differing opinions. On the whole it seems likely that the apocalyptist was thinking not of the mass of mankind, nor even of Jews as such, but of two categories of Jews. On the one hand there were the martyrs who, under the Antiochan persecution, had perished rather than betray their god. On the other there were those who had capitulated and who were now secure in the tyrant's favour. For why should the pious perish, not so much despite as because of their piety, and why should apostasy be rewarded with life and often with a prosperous life at that? The prophecy in Daniel 12 affirms that a state of affairs which offended monstrously against Jewish standards of justice would not last. Daniel 12 was written while the persecution was still raging – what more natural than for it to offer a solution to a problem that was all too real to its readers?

The state of the apostates and the martyrs after their resurrection is indicated clearly enough. The bodies of the apostates are exposed to vilification. As for the martyrs, if they were to live forever in the body, would that body not have to be incorruptible and unageing? The revelation that was supposed to have been granted to the sage Daniel, four centuries in advance, would seem to imply all this. The fate that awaited the 'wise leaders' was more wonderful still. It is indicated in Chapter 12: 'The wise leaders shall shine like the bright vault of heaven, and those who have guided the people in the true path shall be like stars for ever and ever.' Some scholars have interpreted these images as mere metaphors, signifying no more than that the glory of these men's achievements will remain for evermore. Yet there is abundant evidence, from the next three centuries, in Jewish and Christian sources, that exceptionally holy individuals expected, at the End, to receive garments of glory that would make them resplendent and fiery. The apocalyptist is surely foretelling that he and his fellows will exist for ever as superhuman beings, angelic, star-like.

Expectation of an imminent transformation of the world is as unmistakable in parts of the New Testament as it is in the Book of Daniel; but the transformation is imagined in a new way. Jesus and his disciples were convinced that the coming of the kingdom of God was imminent, but that it was obstructed by a supernatural being of terrifying power, which they called Belial or Satan. It seems they regarded their preaching and exorcisms as part of a struggle which they were waging, on God's behalf and with God's help, against Satan.[11]

It was a desperate struggle, for they knew only too well that Satan would not easily give up his hold over the world; there would be no gradual giving way to the coming kingdom. Jewish apocalyptic writings had long foretold a period of terrible tribulation which would precede the final salvation; the war waged by the fourth beast against the people of God, in Daniel, is an example. The so-called 'Marcan apocalypse' tells how wars and rumours of wars, earthquakes and famines, persecutions and flights, darkening of sun and moon, disturbances of the stars will usher in the great consummation[12] – and even if this particular prophecy was constructed by the early Church, the dread it reflects may well have been shared by Jesus. The wording of the Lord's Prayer suggests as much, for originally 'lead us not into temptation' or 'do not put us to the test' referred to the tribulation planned by Satan as a last, desperate stratagem to subvert the faithful and to retain his power on earth.[13] That is why, in the version from St Matthew, the appeal is reinforced by another: 'Save us from the evil one', i.e. Satan. The Book of Revelation was to have much to say about all this.

The kingdom of God did not come, and Jesus was executed. But meanwhile certain Jewish groups had been elaborating a concept of a transcendent, supernatural being, manlike in appearance, but in effect a second divine figure, who would carry out the great transformation at the end of time.[14] In some sayings attributed to Jesus, too, we meet such a figure. We are told that 'the Son of Man' will be sent down from Heaven, accompanied by angels, to judge mankind. Not every scholar accepts those sayings as authentic, and even among those who do accept them, some believe that Jesus was referring not to his own destiny but to a divine being who was yet to come. The early Church none the less set much store by those sayings, thereby ensuring that later generations would do so too.[15]

In one passage of the New Testament after another – in the synoptic Gospels, in Acts, in the Pauline epistles – Jesus appears as judge of the world, alongside God or even in God's place. Above all he was expected to act as God's plenipotentiary at the Last Judgement. In the words of Acts, God 'has fixed the day on which he will have the world judged, and justly judged, by a man of his choosing; of this he has given assurance to all by raising him from the dead',[16] and again and again Jesus is referred to as the one who is to judge the living and the dead. Nor was all this imagined as lying in some remote, unpredictable future. The early Christians were certain that Jesus would return very soon indeed: ' The time we live in will not last long'; 'It is far on in the night; day is near'; 'The end of all things is upon us'.[17] The same certainty is reflected in the promise which Jesus is supposed to have made to his disciples, whether he really made it or not: 'I tell you this: there are some of those standing here who will not taste death before they have seen the kingdom of God already come in power.'[18]

What the Last Judgement will mean in practice is made perfectly clear: Christ will allot eternal joy to some, while to others he will allot eternal torment – and the test will be whether they have accepted or rejected him and his teaching. Already John the Baptist is supposed to have prophesied this: 'His shovel is ready in his hand and he will winnow his threshing-floor; the wheat he will gather into his granary, but he will burn the chaff on a fire that can never go out.'[19] Jesus himself is supposed to have expected the same. Sayings ascribed to him by Matthew make this abundantly plain. 'Whoever then will acknowledge me before men, I will acknowledge him before my Father in heaven; and whoever disowns me before men, I will disown him before my Father in heaven.'[20] And again:

> When the Son of Man comes in his glory and all the angels with him, he will sit in state on his throne, with all the nations gathered before him. He will separate men into two groups, as a shepherd separates the sheep from the goats, and he will place the sheep on his right hand and the goats on his left. Then the king will say to those on his right hand, 'You have my Father's blessing; come, enter and possess the kingdom that has been ready for you since the world was made.'

These are the people who gave food, drink, shelter and succour of every kind to those whom Jesus calls his 'brothers'.

The fate of those who refused to support Jesus's followers, and who now stand at his left hand, is terrible. To them Jesus says, 'The curse is upon you; go from my sight to the eternal fire that is ready.'[21] And again: '… at the end of time the Son of Man will send out his angels, who will gather out of his kingdom everything that causes offence, and all whose deeds are evil, and these will be thrown into the blazing furnace, the place of wailing and grinding of teeth. And then the righteous will shine as brightly as the sun in the kingdom of their Father.'[22]

Whatever doubts there may be about the authenticity of such passages, there can be no doubt that they faithfully mirror the expectations of the first generations of Christians. The same expectations permeate the only full-length Christian Apocalypse to have been admitted into the canon, the Book of Revelation.[23] Revelation forms as it were a Christian counterpart to the Book of Daniel, on which indeed it draws heavily. The work was probably composed towards the end of the reign of Domitian, around AD 95–6. The author was clearly a Christian of Jewish and Palestinian origin; moreover, his strange and ungrammatical Greek suggests that he normally thought in Hebrew or Aramaic. He calls himself John, and traditionally he has been identified with the apostle John, son of Zebedee. This attribution, which was accepted by various first- and second-century Fathers of the Church, was partly responsible for the inclusion of Revelation in the New Testament canon, and even today it is defended by some scholars. Yet apostolic authorship is not even hinted at in the work itself; moreover, it would presuppose that the apostle composed this intensely emotional work when he was eighty-five or more. It is more likely that the John in question was an itinerant prophet circulating among the churches of the Roman province of Asia, which comprised, approximately, the western coast of what is today Turkey.

The book was written for Christians who still felt themselves to be Jews — indeed, the only true Jews, the rest being 'the synagogue of Satan'. The Jewishness of the work is everywhere apparent. Not only is it influenced by the Jewish apocalypses; many passages are simply translated from the Hebrew Bible, and in addition there are more than 300 references to the passages in the Bible, including of course the Book of Daniel.

The seer's acute sense of the continuity of Israel and the Christian branch of Judaism (it was not yet called 'Christianity') explains much that would otherwise be quite mysterious. The 144,000 'servants of God' who have seals set upon their foreheads, to protect them from the catastrophes visited upon the rest of mankind, are certainly Christians, yet they are described as belonging to the twelve tribes of Israel. To indicate the Christian Church, persecuted by the heathen yet secure in God's protection, the seer uses the image of the earthly Jerusalem or Mount Zion. And when, after the Last Judgement, the New Jerusalem comes down from Heaven, the names of the twelve tribes are found to be inscribed over its twelve gates, just as the names of the twelve apostles are inscribed on the twelve foundation stones of the city wall.

Revelation is nevertheless a profoundly Christian work throughout. Whatever is taken over from the Hebrew Bible is reinterpreted in a Christian sense and integrated into a Christian world-view. Jewish prophecies and oracles are invoked precisely in order to show that the history of the Church is faithfully following the course foretold in Scripture, and, conversely, that what Scripture foretold is now coming to pass. The prophets and the Book of Daniel are made to testify to the imminent victory of the Christian Church; Revelation itself takes on the appearance of a Christian conclusion to the prophetic tradition of Israel.

The work opens with a statement of its nature and purpose. God has revealed to Jesus what must shortly happen, at 'the hour of fulfilment'. Jesus in turn has conveyed the revelation of 'his servant John', who now comes forward as a prophet, charged with the task of passing on the message to the Church, represented by seven churches in the neighbourhood of Ephesus. The whole work has the form of a letter, and there are signs that it was intended for liturgical reading.

John received the message on the island of Patmos, in a series of visions of overwhelming power. Already the first vision presents the risen Jesus as a transcendent being of inconceivable majesty, lord of the seven churches and of the Church as a whole. But it is the last part of the work, chapters 10 to 23, that has done most to inspire the Western pictorial tradition. In the form of a great red dragon with seven heads and ten horns Satan appears in Heaven and sets about reducing the ordered world to chaos.[24] With its tail the Dragon attacks the stars, those supreme symbols and guardians of the divinely appointed order, and flings a third of them down from their proper places on to the earth. Then he confronts the 'woman clothed with the sun' as she is about to give birth – and when her son is born, he tries to devour him. But God snatches up the child to himself and to his throne, and for the woman he prepares a place of refuge in the wilderness, where she can hide for the critical period (inherited from the Book of Daniel) of three and a half years. The providential rescue of the child is the signal for war in Heaven. The Archangel Michael – the same who in Daniel and other apocalypses figures as the patron angel of Israel – emerges as champion of the Christian Church. With a host of angels he fights Satan, who likewise commands a host of angels. Michael is victorious, and Satan and his host are thrown down from Heaven to earth.

As usual in Near Eastern belief, what happens in Heaven determines what happens on earth. Almost certainly, the 'woman clothed with the sun' represents Israel and the child symbolizes the Christian community – heavenly counterparts of the real Israel and its Christian offspring on earth. Now the persecution and rescue of the Church must be played out in the world of human beings, where the dragon-Satan, expelled from Heaven, is frantically active. It is the fated, final tribulation foretold in the Jewish apocalypses and indeed by Jesus: 'But woe to you, earth and sea, for the Devil has come down to you in great fury, knowing that his time is short!'

In his pursuit of 'those who keep God's commandments and maintain their testimony to Jesus',[25] Satan has allies. He is aided by two beasts, one coming from the sea, the other from the depths of the earth. On the first beast Satan confers 'power and rule' and 'authority over every tribe and people, language and nation'.[26] As for the second beast, it is wholly devoted to strengthening the power of the first beast: it makes men erect an image in its honour, it causes all who will not honour the image to be put to death. There is no doubt about the sources of these images or about what they symbolize in Revelation. The first beast is modelled on the four beasts in Daniel, amalgamated, and its role too is akin to that of the blasphemous world-tyrant in Daniel – only, the symbol that once stood for the Seleucid monarchy stands here for the Roman empire. The second beast, otherwise called 'the false prophet', owes much to the prophecy in II Thessalonians of 'the wicked man whose coming will be attended by all the powerful signs and miracles of the Lie'.[27] Later, that prophecy was to generate the notion of Antichrist, but here the false prophet and the second beast stand for the priesthood of the official Roman religion.

That Revelation was written in the reign of Domitian is widely agreed, but there is less agreement about the situation of Christians in that reign. Did Domitian really regard himself as a living god? Did he really demand that sacrifices be offered to him in his lifetime? Did he really persecute Christians who refused to practise such idolatry, and have some of them executed? Scholars are anything but unanimous on these matters. What is certain is that John, the author of Revelation, had a notion of cosmic order which was in total contrast with the notions sanctioned by the Hellenistic world, in general, and by the Roman empire, in particular. So far from reflecting divine government, the rule of kings and emperors was an expression of Satan's power; and John awaited, eagerly, the day when God would put an end to both.[28]

That would be the day of the Second Coming. And what a Coming! In a vision the seer sees Jesus as a fierce warrior on a white horse, at the head of a host of angels: 'His eyes flamed with fire, and on his head were many diadems … From his mouth there went a sharp sword with which to smite the nations: for he it is who shall rule them with an iron rod, and tread the winepress of the wrath and retribution of God the sovereign Lord.'[29]

The first beast and the kings of the earth muster to do battle with Jesus. This battle of Armageddon ends in total defeat for the demonic powers and their human allies. The beast is captured and thrown alive into a lake of fire. As for the kings and their armies, they are killed by the sword issuing from Jesus's mouth. The glory of Rome is at an end; and while her fall will be greeted with lamentation by the merchants of the earth, the followers of Jesus will rejoice: 'But let Heaven exult over her; exult, apostles and people of God; for in the judgement against her he has vindicated your cause.'[30]

The fate of the Devil himself is less final. An angel comes down from Heaven, chains him, throws him into an abyss and shuts and seals it over him – not, however, for all eternity but for a thousand years, after which 'he must be let loose for a short while'.[31] During that thousand years – the original 'Millennium' – the Christian martyrs, those who have preferred to be executed rather than worship the beast, receive their special rewards: they are resurrected and reign with Christ on earth. Nor are they the earth's only inhabitants: it is made clear that in this intermediate period the nations of the world are required to submit to the authority of Christ and the resurrected martyrs, who rule them with a rod of iron.

After his thousand-year imprisonment, Satan reappears on earth and summons his legions. It is likely that the seer imagined these legions as consisting not of human beings but of demons, rising from the depths of the earth in a last effort to destroy the Church.[32] When these last, supernatural enemies are destroyed by fire from Heaven, the way lies open for the Last Judgement. All the dead are resurrected, and judged according to their records. While those whose names do not appear in 'the roll of the living' are cast into the lake of fire, there to suffer torment for ever and ever, all the righteous – and not simply the martyrs – pass into a realm of bliss, where they dwell for ever with God, as his children, free from death and from suffering and grief of every kind: 'All this is the victor's heritage'.[33] Time has reached its consummation.

The realm of bliss is something wholly new, a fresh creation that will replace the old:

> Then I saw a new heaven and a new earth, for the first heaven and the first earth had vanished, and there was no longer any sea. I saw the holy city, new Jerusalem, coming down out of heaven from God, made ready like a bride adorned for her husband. I heard a loud voice proclaiming from the throne: 'Now at last God has his dwelling among men!'[34]

By the descent of the heavenly Jerusalem earth and Heaven are made indissolubly one, a realm where human beings will share the bliss of the angels. The New Jerusalem is portrayed in imagery of great concreteness. The city is built as a square, with each side 12,000 furlongs in length, its walls of jasper 144 cubits in height. The city itself is of pure gold, 'bright as clear glass', and the foundations of its walls are adorned with jewels of every kind. The kings and the nations bring their wealth and splendour to it. It becomes a source of salvation for the whole earth. The work ends as it began, with an assurance that the stupendous drama which is its theme is about to open: '… the hour of fulfilment is near'. Jesus himself confirms it: 'Yes, I am coming soon, and bringing my recompense with me, to requite everyone according to his deeds! … Yes. I am coming soon!' And the seer replies: 'Amen. Come, Lord Jesus'.[35]

In the New Testament book known as the Second Letter of Peter (or simply as II Peter) one finds the same tense expectation of the Second Coming and the Last Judgement. Although the traditional view is that II Peter is a late work, composed some time between AD 125 and 150, it has been persuasively argued that it dates from around AD 90 – which would make it contemporaneous with the Book of Revelation.[36] Whatever the date of the text's composition, the author is passionately concerned to prevent his readers from forfeiting their entry into Christ's eternal kingdom. Many are likely to do so, for they are openly scoffing at the notion of Christ's return to judge mankind; as a result they feel free to live lives of greed, intemperance and licentiousness.

The parallel with the story of the Flood, as recounted in Genesis, is obvious, and the author exploits it to the full:

> … there were heavens and earth long ago, created by God's word out of water and with water; and by water that first world was destroyed, the water for the deluge. And the present heavens and earth, again by God's word, have been kept in store for burning; they are being reserved until the day of judgement when the godless will be destroyed….
>
> But the Day of the Lord will come; it will come, unexpected as a thief. On that day the heavens will disappear with a great rushing sound, the elements will disintegrate in flames, and the earth with all that is in it will be laid bare.
>
> Since the whole universe is to break up in this way, think what sort of people you ought to be, what devout and dedicated lives you should live! Look eagerly for the coming of the Day of God and work to hasten it on; that day will set the heavens ablaze until they fall apart, and will melt

the elements in flames. But we have his promise, and look forward to new heavens and a new earth, the home of justice.[37]

There is no obvious source for this notion in the Old Testament, but the Stoics believed the world would be periodically destroyed and purified by fire, Zoroastrians expected a last judgement when the metal in the mountains would melt and stream over the earth, destroying all evil beings while preserving all good ones, and a second-century Christian could easily have had contact with Stoics or Zoroastrians or both. However that may be, II Peter's version of the coming judgement was to become a stock feature of Christian eschatology. Late in the seventeenth century an eminent English cleric, Thomas Burnet, could still write a whole book – the celebrated *Theory of the Earth* (1681) – in which the primeval deluge and the final conflagration are brought into intimate relation with one another.[38]

But indeed, all the prophecies outlined in this account have proved extraordinarily adaptable and long-lived. Reinterpreted again and again to fit everchanging circumstances, they have continued to affect the perceptions of millions of both Christians and non-Christians right down to the present day.

NOTES
The version of the Bible quoted in the text is The New English Bible.

A fuller bibliography of modern works, notably articles, is given in the Notes to Chapters 9 and 11 of N. Cohn, *Cosmos, Chaos and the World to Come*, London, 1993.

1 Works on Jewish apocalyptic, or Jewish and early Christian apocalyptic in general, in order of publication: J. Bloch, *On the Apocalyptic in Judaism*, Philadelphia 1952; H.H. Rowley, *The Relevance of Apocalyptic*, 3rd rev. edn, London 1964; D.S. Russell, *The Method and Message of Jewish Apocalyptic, 200 BC–100 AD*, London 1964; J.D. Schreiner, *Alttestamentliche-jüdische Apokalyptik: Eine Einführung*, Munich 1969; W. Schmithals, T*he Apocalyptic Movement: Introduction and Interpretation*, Nashville 1975 (trans. from the German, 1973); M.E. Stone, *Scriptures, Sects and Visions*, Philadelphia 1980; G.W.E. Nickelsburg, *Jewish Literature between the Bible and the Mishnah*, London 1981; C. Rowland, *The Open Heaven. A Study of Apocalyptic in Judaism and Early Christianity*, London 1982; J.J. Collins, *The Apocalyptic Imagination: An Introduction to the Jewish Matrix of Christianity*, New York 1984.

2 Relatively recent studies of and commentaries on Daniel are those of E.W. Heaton, London 1956; N.W. Porteous, London 1965; M. Delcor, Paris 1971; A. Lacocque, Atlanta 1979; R. Hammer, Cambridge 1976, in the series *The Cambridge Bible Commentary*; L.F. Hartman and A.A. Di Lella, Garden City, New York, 1978, as a volume in the Anchor Bible. On the eschatology of Daniel in particular: J.J. Collins, *The Apocalyptic Vision of the Book of Daniel*, Missoula 1977.

3 Daniel 2: 44–45 and 2: 28.

4 Daniel 7: 7–8.

5 Psalm 96: 12–13; Zechariah 14: 5; Joel 3: 12.

6 On the Son of Man in Daniel: A. Caquot, in *Semitica* 17, Paris 1967, and M. Casey, *The Son of Man*, London 1979 (at pp. 30ff.), provide surveys of the various interpretations offered up to those dates.

7 Daniel 7: 14, 27.

8 Daniel 2: 44.

9 Daniel 12: 10.

10 On the significance of this prophecy see G.W.E. Nickelsburg, *Resurrection, Immortality, and Eternal Life in Intertestamental Judaism*, Cambridge, Mass., and London 1977, pp. 18–27.

11 cf. B. Noack, *Satanas und Soteria: Untersuchungen zur neutestamentlichen Dämonologie*, Copenhagen 1948; J.M. Robinson, *The Problem of History in Mark*, London 1957, pp. 43–51; R.H. Hiers, *The Historical Jesus and the Kingdom of God in the Synoptic Tradition*, Gainesville 1973, pp. 59–64; J.B. Russell, *The Devil, Perceptions of Evil from Antiquity to Primitive Christianity*, Ithaca and London 1977, pp. 227–39.

12 cf. Mark 13: 7–10 and 24–25.

13 cf. Hiers, pp. 25–6.

14 cf. J. Thiesohn, *Der auserwählte Richter*, Göttingen 1975.

15 cf. B. Lindars, *Jesus Son of Man*, London, 1983 esp. p. 14.

16 Acts 17: 31.

17 I Corinthians 7: 29; Romans 13: 12; I Peter 4: 7.

18 Mark 9: 1.

19 Matthew 3: 12.

20 Matthew 10: 32-33.

21 Matthew 25: 31–34 and 41.

22 Matthew 13: 41–43.

23 Valuable works on Revelation include: R.H. Charles, *A Critical and Exegetical Commentary on the Revelation of St John*, London and New York 1920; T.F. Glasson, *The Revelation of St John*, Cambridge 1965; G.B. Caird, *A Commentary on the Revelation of St John the Divine*, London and New York 1966; W. Harrington, *Understanding the Apocalypse*, Washington 1969; P.S. Minear, *I Saw a New Earth*, Washington D.C. 1968; J.M. Court, *Myth and History in the Book of Revelation*, London 1979; A. Yarbro Collins, *Crisis and Catharsis. The Power of the Apocalypse*, Philadelphia 1984; L.L. Thompson, T*he Book of Revelation: Apocalypse and Empire*, New York and Oxford 1990; R. Bauckham, *The Theology of the Book of Revelation*, Cambridge 1993.

24 That this part of Revelation owes much to the Near Eastern combat myth was argued already in H. Gunkel, *Schöpfung und Chaos in Urzeit und Endzeit*, Göttingen 1885. For a more up-to-date presentation of the argument see R. Halver, *Der Mythos im letzten Buch der Bibel*, Hamburg-Bergstadt 1964.

25 Revelation 12: 12 and 17. Unless otherwise stated, the following references are to the Book of Revelation.

26 13: 7.

27 II Thessalonians 2: 9.

28 cf. Thompson, op. cit., esp. pp. 16, 55, 104, 132, 171–81.

29 19: 12, 16.

30 18: 20.

31 20: 3.

32 cf. A. Wikenhauser, *Die Offenbarung des Johannes*, 3rd edn, Regensburg 1959 (*Regensburger Neues Testament* 9); W.W. Reader, *Die Stadt Gottes in der Johannesapokalypse*, Göttingen 1971, pp. 240–1.

33 21: 7.

34 21: 1–3.

35 22: 12 and 20.

36 cf. *The Anchor Bible: The Epistles of James, Peter and Jude*, trans. and notes by Bo Reicke, Garden City, New York, 1964, p.144.

37 II Peter 3: 5–7 and 10–13.

38 Thomas Burnet, *The Sacred Theory of the Earth*, was first published in Latin in 1681, then in English in 1684. The second part, *On the Conflagration of the World and the Future State of Things*, appeared in 1689/90. On *The Theory of the Earth* see N. Cohn, *Noah's Flood: The Genesis Story in Western Thought*, New Haven and London 1996, ch. 5.

3 The Last Things: Representing the Unrepresentable

The Medieval Tradition

Jonathan Alexander

The earliest Christians believed that the end of the world was imminent, and indeed likely to come in their own lifetime. They have left no artistic record of how they might have visualized the cataclysm, and it was not until Christians had grown in numbers and spread over all areas of the Mediterranean, three whole centuries later, that a visual iconography of the 'Last Things' began to develop. Images of the judging Christ, of the resurrection of the dead, of Heaven and hell, were created from the fourth to the ninth centuries which were to remain powerfully vivid to the end of the Middle Ages and indeed right up to the present. The continuity of Christian visual imagery is one of its most striking features. From the beginning the imagery had an ideological function, aiming to teach the events of a holy history in which God's purpose had been fulfilled in the past and so would be in the future. Christian art thus reinforced Christian dogma. The familiarity of images was part of their power, and their repetition in easily recognizable forms was therefore essential. The pictorial content and to a notable degree the formal aspects of Christian imagery were in this way controlled and restricted.[1]

Christian dogma was founded on written texts, which were held to enshrine truth. This canon of texts collected into a single whole, the Bible, was known to Western medieval Christians above all in the 'Vulgate' Latin Bible as translated by St Jerome from the Hebrew and Greek originals at the end of the fourth century. Extracts from the Vulgate Bible were read aloud during the Church year in religious services. Numerous commentaries both in Latin and in the vernacular European languages were written during the Middle Ages to aid understanding, and preachers also drew on the Scriptures in their sermons. Though Latin remained the Church's primary language, there was an increasing tendency for the vernaculars to be used in both oral discourse and in written texts. This was necessary, of course, because of the widely varying levels of Latinity and of literacy in medieval society.[2]

The most relevant among the biblical texts to our enquiry is the Book of Revelation or, to give it its Greek title, since that was the language in which the text was originally written, the Apocalypse. In the Old Testament canon similar visionary experiences are recorded of the prophets Ezekiel (ch. 1) and Daniel (ch. 7), and there was a rich tradition of Jewish apocalypticism in the two centuries before and after the birth of Christ. The Apocalypse of St John the Divine was therefore only one, though clearly an outstandingly creative example, of a genre of prophetic writings foretelling a violent end to the world.[3] In the West during the Middle Ages it was universally believed that the Apocalypse had been written on the island of Patmos c.AD 70 by St John, author of the fourth Gospel. This belief goes far back and finds its explanation in the controversies surrounding the adoption of a canon of Scripture in the earliest centuries of Christianity. It was no doubt originally intended to give the text a special authority as written by the disciple 'whom Jesus loved' and to whose care he entrusted his mother at the Crucifixion. A number of medieval illustrated Apocalypse manuscripts underline the authorship by including a prefatory cycle of illustrations of St John's life and miracles (cats 10, 11, 18, 20; in the case of the Trinity Apocalypse, the cycle both precedes and concludes the main sequence of illustrations to the Apocalypse).[4] Almost all Apocalypses begin with a depiction of him experiencing his vision on the island of Patmos, usually accompanied by his symbol as evangelist, the eagle. This vision is also illustrated in many other contexts in both monumental art and manuscript illumination (cat. 23).

For these reasons of textual dependence and because their images had to be easily recognizable, as well as for other reasons linked to the artistic practice of their craft, for example their use of model books, Christian artists tended to base their images on a previous visual tradition. This tradition altered over time in both style and content, but for the most part the process was gradual.

Some of the early images based on the Apocalypse had been created for buildings which not only survived down the centuries, but which had great general importance for the Christian faith. A prime example was St Peter's in Rome, that is, 'Old St Peter's', which was built in the fourth century and pulled down only in the fifteenth. The tomb of St Peter and the many other saints' shrines in Rome were an object of Christian pilgrimage throughout the Middle Ages. A mosaic of the Adoration of the Lamb by the twenty-four elders, based on Revelation 4–5, was placed on the façade of Old St Peter's and thus could be said to be one of the most central images of Western Christianity. As it was destroyed in the later rebuilding, we know it only

Fig. 1. *Funeral of Gregory the Great with Façade of Old St Peter's showing Adoration of the Lamb by the Twenty-Four Elders.* John the Deacon, *Life of Pope Gregory the Great*, fol.122 (early twelfth century), Windsor, Eton College Library.

from a series of drawings including that in an early twelfth-century manuscript in the library at Eton College (fig. 1).[5] It was a public and continually visible image to the countless visitors of widely varying status and rank who came to Rome from every part of Europe on diplomatic, economic, political and religious business of all kinds.

Others of the Roman basilicas, built at the same date and which were also pilgrimage churches, still exist. San Paolo fuori le Mura (St Paul's outside the Walls), though destroyed by fire in the nineteenth century, was rebuilt, while Sta Maria Maggiore survives to the present, though not without damage and restoration to its mosaic cycles. At San Paolo the twenty-four elders and the four living creatures were shown in mosaic on the triumphal arch, while at Sta Maria Maggiore the throne, the book with the seven seals and the four living creatures were shown, again in mosaic, on the triumphal arch above the entry to the sanctuary.[6]

Churches were also erected in the Holy Land by the emperor Constantine (c.274–337) after his vision and conversion at the battle of the Milvian Bridge in 312. These too were the sites of continuous pilgrimage and devotion over the centuries, but either have not survived or have been drastically altered, so that their influence on Christian representation has in large part to be reconstructed archaeologically.[7]

The Eastern, Byzantine church, centred on the refounded city of Constantinople, consecrated by the emperor in 330, both preserved and developed the early Christian pictorial tradition. After a period of estrangement during the iconoclastic controversy in the eighth and ninth centuries, when images were banned altogether, contact with the West was renewed from the tenth century onwards. Enhanced by the Crusades and the establishment of the Latin Kingdom of Jerusalem after the capture of Jerusalem from the Muslims in 1099, this led to an enrichment of pictorial imagery throughout Western Christendom from Eastern sources in the eleventh and twelfth centuries (cat. 3).

The Apocalypse was not accepted into the canon of the Eastern Church until the early fourteenth century (see Ch. 4, cat. 117). Nevertheless, in both the East and the West, God as the all-powerful judge at the final end of the world, a figure so vividly described in Revelation, took a similar pictorial form in the early centuries. The artists' task had been to represent a series of unrepresentables. God was defined in the texts as eternal and timeless, omnipotent and all-knowing. Even to attempt such a task had been prohibited by Jewish law, according to the second of the commandments handed down by God on Mount Sinai to Moses as recorded in Exodus 20: 4: 'Thou shalt not make to thyself a graven image, nor the likeness of anything that is in heaven above, or in the earth beneath, nor of those things that are in the waters under the earth.'[8]

Meyer Schapiro in his book on the semiotics of Christian art pointed to the distinction between the frontal and the profile image, describing the former as the 'theme of state' and the latter as the 'theme of action'.[9] This is suggestive, since both the Greek 'Pantocrator' (all-powerful) image of God and the Latin

Fig. 2. *Christ in Majesty with two Angels and St Vitalis and Bishop Ecclesius* (c.547). Mosaic in the apse of San Vitale, Ravenna.

image known as the 'Majestas' (God in Majesty) are frontal figures. In both types God, whether Father or Son, is shown frontally seated on the globe or on a rainbow or on a throne. He typically holds a book or scroll in his left hand and blesses with his right. A famous example is the apse mosaic of the church of San Vitale in Ravenna of *c.*547 (fig. 2). The contemporary popular topos today of God as a white-bearded figure, thus an old man, which is also how he is described in the Book of Daniel and in Revelation, is not how the early Christian artists envisioned him. At Ravenna the Christ is a beardless young man who holds the scroll with the seven seals of Revelation. If he is shown bearded, and this is by no means the rule, the beard is almost always black, implying the power of maturity, not the feebleness of age. The monumental apse mosaics of the twelfth century in the Sicilian churches, the Cappella Palatina in Palermo and the cathedrals at Cefalù and Monreale, are among the most imposing of such Byzantinizing images, though they are frontal half-length figures.

It is not possible to say when or where, still less by whom, this powerful and majestic image was created. But other religions had earlier shown their god or gods enthroned in symmetrical frontal poses. Egyptian, Assyrian, Greek and Roman examples are familiar. Earthly rulers also were often similarly shown and in the light of Schapiro's observations this is unsurprising. We do not have to think of one modelled on the other, but rather recognize a shared semiotic function.[11] The Christian image has two other features, the first, the nimbus or halo, being invariable, the second, the mandorla, being more common in the early Middle Ages than in the later centuries. The first is a zone of light signifying sanctity, and in its circular form perfection. The second also signifies timelessness and is one of Jung's archetypal symbols, being found in Asian as well as European art.

Though the frontal 'Majesty' type could be used by itself in non-narrative contexts, it also appeared in the scene of the Ascension as narrated in Acts 1.[12] This type continued in use by Byzantine artists (cat. 3), whereas in the West a profile type existed in which the Christ was depicted as actively stepping up the mountainside of the Mount of Olives to be received by the hand of God. The angels told the apostles gathered below that (1: 11): 'This Jesus who is taken up from you into Heaven, shall so come, as you have seen him going into Heaven.' The iconography of the Ascension was thus necessarily linked with that of the Second Coming and Last Judgement.

The earliest surviving illustrated manuscripts of the Apocalypse were made on the Continent during the Carolingian period of the ninth to tenth centuries.[13] It is thought that their lengthy cycles of pictures are not original creations, but that they are copied from early Christian manuscript models of the fifth to sixth centuries, one stemma being connected with Rome, another with North Africa and Spain. These cycles transpose the various visions described by the text into a series of framed images in which John as narrator/viewer is generally present. The Apocalypse in Trier made in the early ninth century in northern France contains seventy-five miniatures in which the artist has retained many aspects of the classical style of his model (fig. 3). Whether or not the manuscript cycles came first and the monumental scenes at Old St Peter's and elsewhere were excerpted from them is unknown.

Other early images in monumental contexts, however, had tended to represent the Last Judgement symbolically. Thus the parable of the Wise and Foolish Virgins from Matthew 25: 1–13 and that of the division of the sheep and goats from Matthew 25: 31–3 are shown in the Catacombs, and the latter occurs among the Gospel scenes in mosaic in the nave of the sixth-century church of Sant'Apollinare Nuovo in Ravenna. The empty throne prepared for the reign of Christ (known in Greek as the *Hetoimasia*) is seen in mosaic in several of the churches at Ravenna and on the triumphal arch at Sta Maria Maggiore, Rome.[15]

Such indirect and largely symbolic references to the Last Judgement tended to drop out of use in the West, however. This observation qualifies what was said earlier about the continuity of Christian imagery, for there were indeed changes, newly adopted scenes and updated ways of showing even canonical subjects.

Fig. 3. *Majestas Domini with Twenty-Four Elders*. Trier Apocalypse, fol.16v (ninth century), northern France. Trier, Stadtbibliothek.

The symbolic references were replaced with the narrative image of the Last Judgement which is probably most familiar in Michelangelo's version in the Sistine Chapel in the Vatican, painted 1535–41 (see Ch. 4, cat. 96). This narrative image, which also incorporates motifs from Christ's teaching in Matthew 25, developed only gradually by putting together a variety of motifs from various sources to produce what was to become its standard form.[16] An ivory now in the Victoria and Albert Museum, London (inv. 253–1867; fig. 4), is often quoted as the earliest example of the Last Judgement iconography. Earlier opinion dated it *c.*800 and ascribed it to Anglo-Saxon England, but more recently it has been considered continental of the later ninth century. Whatever its origin, there was certainly an interest in the Apocalypse in Ireland and England in the early period of conversion to Christianity in the seventh to ninth centuries. Bede recounts that Benedict Biscop brought back from his fourth visit to Rome, on which he set out in 676, 'scenes of the visions of the Apocalypse of St John' to decorate the north wall of the church of St Peter, Wearmouth. An image in an Irish Gospel book of the second half of the eighth century, now preserved at St Gall, also shows Christ as Judge with apocalyptic trumpeting angels and the twelve apostles below.[19] Later Anglo-Saxon art of the tenth and eleventh centuries shows a similar interest in apocalyptic subject-matter, which mirrors a considerable contemporary theological interest in the Apocalypse.[20]

Fig. 4. Leaf of ivory showing the *Last Judgement* (ninth century?). Probably continental. London, Victoria and Albert Museum.

Early monumental versions of the Last Judgement on the Continent occur in the wall-paintings at Müstair in Switzerland of the late ninth century and at Reichenau Oberzell on Lake Constance in the eleventh century. Around 1070 the scene was painted on the west wall of Sant'Angelo in Formis in southern Italy, a dependent church of the great Benedictine abbey of Monte Cassino. Other famous versions in Italy include the twelfth-century mosaics in the cathedral at Torcello in the Venetian lagoon, and those of the thirteenth century in the Baptistery at Florence. Giotto's fresco in the Scrovegni Chapel at Padua was painted *c.*1305 and Signorelli's version in the Cappella S. Brizio at Orvieto Cathedral, 1500–3. Throughout this period the idea of a final judgement in which all wrongs are to be set right, the righteous rewarded and the wicked definitively punished, must have had powerful resonances for contemporaries dependent on the often corrupt courts of contemporary rulers. The twelve men of the medieval English jury are the same in number as the apostles who number the tribes of Israel and who in representations flank the throne of God as Just Judge. The presence of the Virgin Mother and St John as merciful intercessors must have been equally moving for a medieval audience, who recognized the role of their own medieval queens as intercessors, for example Philippa of Hainault obtaining mercy for the burghers of Calais from her husband, Edward III of England, after the siege of Calais in 1346.

The Last Judgement was most often painted on the inside of the west wall of the church, it being believed that when the Last Trump sounded God would appear from the west. The mosaic at St Peter's was also on the outside of the west façade. It is on the outside west wall of the church, too, that the famous stone-carved representations of the Romanesque and Gothic periods usually occur, for example at St-Lazare at Autun in Burgundy, or at the Gothic cathedrals of Paris, Amiens and Rheims. At the Romanesque Benedictine abbeys of Moissac[21] and of Conques in southern France and at Gothic Chartres it is on the south side, but in all cases these are main entrances for the laity, reminding them that entrance to the gate of Heaven is achieved via the Church on earth.[22]

At Autun, though the figure of the judging God is greatly enlarged and placed frontally enthroned in the centre of the tympanum in a mandorla, the composition achieves its effect by contrasting this static, timeless figure with a multiplicity of details (figs 5, 6).[23] Among the many unforgettable subsidiary vignettes is that of the resurrected man to the right on the lintel whose head is about to be grasped by a gigantic pair of hands (fig. 7). The surreal quality is the more horrific in contrast to the poignancy of the soul embraced by an equally enlarged but gentler archangel on the way to Paradise on the other side of the lintel. Paradise is on the right hand of God, where the blessed congregate to pass through the gates of the heavenly city of Jerusalem. Hell and its tortures are on God's left, in Latin the 'sinister' side. The devouring jaws of the mouth of hell already appear in the ivory in the Victoria and Albert Museum mentioned above (fig. 4; cf. cats 1, 6).

All the evidence suggests that these sculpted portals were painted and in fact at Conques, the largest of all the Last Judgement tympana, a great deal of colour is still clearly visible. So the tympana must have been even more striking and vivid to their original audiences. Both Conques and Autun also bear carved inscriptions. On the mandorla of the Christ at Autun is carved a Latin inscription: 'I alone dispose of all things and crown the Just. Those who follow crime I judge and punish'. Below on the lintel the inscriptions read: 'Thus shall rise again everyone who does not lead an impious life. And endless light of day shall shine on him'. 'Here let fear strike those whom earthly error binds, for their fate is shown by the horror of these figures'. The warning is clear and similar to that in one of the earlier of the surviving Spanish copies of the commentary of Beatus on the Apocalypse, that of the late tenth century in the Morgan Library. Its colophon states: 'I have depicted the wonderful words of the story in sequence, so that those who know of them will be terrified by the events of the future judgement'.[24] Two centuries later the Life of St Hugh of Lincoln (*d*. 1200) tells how he admonished King John by pointing to a carved Last Judgement portal on which kings were shown being consigned to damnation[25] (cf. cat. 6).

Above Fig. 5. *Last Judgement* (c.1130). Tympanum of west door of S. Lazare, Autun.

Far left Fig. 6. *Angel Embracing a Soul*, detail of *Last Judgement* (c.1130). Tympanum of west door of S. Lazare, Autun.

Left Fig. 7. *Pilgrim Grasped by Giant Hands*, detail of *Last Judgement* (c.1130). Tympanum of west door of S. Lazare, Autun.

The tympanum at Autun was carved *c*.1130, well over a hundred years after the completion of the first millennium. Historians consider the year 1000 an important turning-point which saw the beginnings of many significant changes. Increased population, improvements in technology, the development of a profit economy based on coinage rather than barter, the spread of literacy beyond the monks and clergy to the laity with the creation of a written as opposed to an oral vernacular literature: these are some of the most important. There was reform in the Christian Church, new experiments in monastic practice, new educational developments in cathedral schools and somewhat later the start of the universities, which in turn led to the formation of larger libraries and the establishment of a professional book trade catering to individuals as well as institutions. By all these measures it was a time of self-confident optimism and hope, rather than of fear and despair at the approaching end of the world. The capture of Jerusalem in 1099 signalled a triumph of Christ over the heretics and disbelievers, not the triumph of Antichrist.

However, there is historical evidence that some Christians at least thought the world might come to an apocalyptic end in the year 1000 or perhaps in 1033. Abbo, abbot of Fleury, tells of a preacher in Paris *c*.970 who foretold the advent of Antichrist in 1000. It is impossible to tell how widely such prophecies were circulated or how strongly they were believed, and historians disagree on this.[26] The distinguished French art historian Henri Focillon, in a posthumously published book (see p.6), argued for millenarianism as a factor in the creative upsurge of Romanesque art, referring in particular to a well-known text, the *History* of Radulphus Glaber (*c*.985–1047), who ended his career as a monk of Cluny. Radulphus writes in the early eleventh century that the world on the threshold of the thousandth year 'had cast off her old age and clothed herself in a white garment of churches'.[27]

The Apocalypse could always be invoked as a threat of retribution whether eventual or immediate. That meant it was always a message of hope for millenarian Christians, who based their belief that their present suffering was about to end on the key, though highly abstruse, passage in Revelation 20: 1–10, especially verses 4–5: 'And I saw seats; and they sat upon them; and the judgement was given unto them; and the souls of them that were beheaded for the testimony of Jesus, and for the word of God, and who had not adored the beast nor his image, nor received his character on their foreheads, or in their hands: and they lived and reigned with Christ a thousand years.' If this was interpreted as a literal prophecy then the way was opened to calculations of when exactly the millennium might be expected.

The monumental sculpted and painted Last Judgements, however, did not necessarily reflect a belief on the part of the churchmen who commissioned them in the immediate or proximate end of the world. The official church line was to follow St Augustine in the *City of God* (Book 20: 9) in interpreting the Apocalypse text as having mystical, not literal significance. Augustine warned in particular of the dangers of arithmetical calculation to produce a firm date for the end of the world. The most influential later commentaries, especially that of Berengaudus (cats 2, 10–13, 18, 20), took a similar line in interpreting the text spiritually as a symbolic conflict of good and evil.[28]

The great Romanesque tympana thus stood as general rather than specific warnings and the event they portrayed, though it was believed inevitable, was not for that reason necessarily thought imminent, except in the sense that all die and the hour of death is unpredictable. The monumental images, painted or carved, remained in place throughout the Middle Ages, and there was no idea of dismantling them as irrelevant when the deadlines prophesied by a variety of writers came and went. Nor were such writers discouraged either by Augustine or by previous failures from making their complicated numerical calculations, especially those relating to the famous number of the beast, six hundred and sixty-six (Revelation 13: 18). It was only in 1766 that the door at Autun was plastered over. It was no doubt considered crude and unseemly on aesthetic grounds, and its graphic and literal-minded depiction of damnation may also have offended Enlightenment sensibilities. The head of the Majesty figure was broken off at the same time and was retrieved and replaced only in 1948.

At Autun some of the saved are shown carrying the wallet and staff of the pilgrim. Here there is a clear sense of division. Some virtuous Christians will be saved eternally, others will be damned eternally. This signals a difference from the early Christian community who saw themselves as the elect and therefore certain of salvation as opposed to the pagans around them.[29] In the twelfth century Virtues and Vices are shown symbolically battling it out on some of the Romanesque portals, for example at Aulnay in western France. Interestingly, they are shown as female knights, since Latin, the language of the Church and of culture, is gendered, and all the Virtues – Fides, Spes, Caritas, Fortitudo (Faith, Hope, Charity, Courage, etc.) – are female nouns, as for that matter are the Vices too. The text lying behind such images is a fifth-century poem by a Spanish Christian author, Prudentius, illustrated probably in his lifetime and then copied in numerous manuscripts surviving from the tenth and eleventh centuries.[30] The Wise and Foolish Virgins also appear on Romanesque and Gothic portal sculpture, and they are the protagonists of the earliest eschatological play, the *Sponsus*, from the end of the eleventh century.[31]

In thirteenth-century sculpture on the Gothic cathedrals, at Notre-Dame in Paris, for example, the Virtues are peacefully enthroned females each holding her symbol, the Chalice for Faith, the Lion of Courage, etc. Virtue in this context is a matter of personal responsibility and of inward disposition. Individuals were beginning to see their salvation in more personal terms rather than as a matter of their religious or social status. Earlier it was believed that salvation was reserved not for individuals so much as for categories among the faithful and just, those who fought the just fight, that is, for monks, clergy, pilgrims or crusaders, as we see them at Autun and Conques. In the late eleventh century St Anselm, archbishop of Canterbury, wrote that only monks could be assured of entering Heaven, and not even all of them.[32]

In the later Middle Ages, however, individual conscience and a person's own conduct in life were increasingly examined. Confession at least once a year was enforced as a duty for every Christian by the edicts of the Fourth Lateran Council under Pope Innocent III in 1215. Personal faith in the redemptive power of Christ and his saints and personal choice between good and evil in the actions of life were believed to be the keys to salvation. For these reasons the wealthy and powerful increasingly built commemorative tombs and chantries (chapels endowed with land or property) yielding an income that was paid to priests to pray for their individual souls and those of individually named members of their families. The implication was that death does not inevitably decide things, and that there can still be an opportunity for the account to be levelled out before the Last Trump. That event was thus by implication pushed further into the future.

The belief in Purgatory as an intermediate state where souls were to be purified, like metal ore in the furnace, brought with it what has been called an economy of salvation in the shape of papal indulgences and chantry masses.[33] Purgatory is also represented, though relatively rarely, as a physical space. Merchants made wealthy by lending money, a practice officially condemned by the Church as 'usury', could direct some of their gains to buy pardons from the pope ('indulgences'), and masses to be said for their own souls or those of family members. A famous example is the chapel in Padua founded by Enrico Scrovegni, whose father had been depicted by Dante as a usurer in hell. Giotto depicts Enrico offering the chapel to the Virgin at the Last Judgement painted on the interior of the west wall.[34]

Death remained the crucial moment of transition, which had to be constantly kept in mind and carefully prepared for, and the way in which a person died was, therefore, of the utmost importance. At Autun the angels are shown battling the devils, who vainly try to weigh down the scales so that a soul, who has just risen from the tomb, may be condemned. In the later Middle Ages a similar struggle is shown in individualized death-bed scenes, an early example being in the thirteenth-century Burckhardt-Wildt Apocalypse (cat. 13). In Books of Hours, the main prayer book of the laity, an individual in following the Office of the Dead could see portrayed his own death-bed as it were, surrounded by his family and friends as well as the priest giving Extreme Unction (fig. 8).[35] The same Books of Hours often included prayers to be said to avoid sudden death. Their owners were motivated as much by fear of being deprived of the opportunity to prepare for the next world through confession, shriving and the Last Sacrament as by their terror of assassination. A text on the art of

Fig. 8. *Struggle over the Dying Man's Soul*. Book of Hours, Office of the Dead, fol.117 (fifteenth century), France. Baltimore, Walters Art Gallery.

dying, the *Ars Moriendi*, was composed by an anonymous, probably Dominican, author at the time of the Council of Constance in 1415. Sequences of illustrations to the *Ars Moriendi* are found in a set of engravings by the Master E.S. and in a contemporary block-book of the mid-fifteenth century. There are also manuscript copies (cat. 20) and numerous later editions with woodcuts.[36]

With an increasing preoccupation with personal subjectivity, the people of the late Middle Ages came to entrust themselves to their own personal guardian angel, one of that legion of light who hovered round the Throne of God (cat. 19), and of whom images were placed high in the roofs of numerous churches, carved in stone at Rheims and Lincoln cathedrals, for example, and in wood in many English parish churches, for example March in Cambridgeshire or Wymondham and Cawston in Norfolk.[37]

Spiritual life is already described by St Paul as a battle in Romans 13: 12: 'Let us therefore cast off the works of darkness, and put on the armour of light'. In the twelfth and thirteenth centuries the Christian knight, especially in his role as crusader, could be pictured as virtue personified (cat. 8). The famous series of English thirteenth-century Apocalypse manuscripts (cats 10–12, 15–16) contain scenes of combat and slaughter, in which malevolent armed riders hew down the innocent who are shown as unresisting, powerless and passive. St Michael and his angels fight on God's side to destroy the devil. Such scenes (cats 4, 16, 26) contrast with the images of a static, hieratically ordered and compartmentalized Heaven (cat. 19).

Much study has gone into determining the origins of the pictorial cycles in these manuscripts, and their relationships to each other and also to the separate traditions seen in the twelfth-century texts, the *Liber Floridus* of Lambert of St Omer and the *Hortus Deliciarum* of Abbess Herrad of Hohenburg,[38] as well as in the French *Bibles moralisées* made in Paris from *c.*1220 on (cat. 7). The thirteenth-century Apocalypses produced both in England and on the Continent are highly individual in their varying combinations of texts and commentaries in Latin and the French vernacular. They are also original in the experimental ways they find of relating text and image in varying page layout (cats 10–12, 14). It has been argued that their miniatures, in which the figure of John acts as role model to the reader who likewise is able to witness the events narrated in the text, respond to speculations current in the thirteenth-century universities, where figures such as Roger Bacon wrote on optics and made use of works on natural science by Aristotle and Arabic commentators, newly available in Latin translation.[39]

These richly illustrated Apocalypse manuscripts, which must have been very expensive for their patrons to acquire, were in demand from a variety of owners, including high churchmen and magnates, and also, increasingly, ladies of the nobility (cats 10, 11).[40] These patrons shared an ideological acceptance of ordained roles, and of Christianity as a favoured religion which guaranteed salvation for its adherents. Those outside the pale, the 'Others', especially the infidels, the Jews and the Mohammedans, and the heretics inside the boundaries of

Christendom, were assured of defeat and final damnation.[41] But the very popularity of such imagery may have concealed anxiety at a time when the Holy Land had to be abandoned and Islam once again increasingly threatened the West in the Mediterranean and in Eastern Europe. Matthew Paris (d. 1259), the monk of St Albans (see cat. 9), both chronicler and artist, included c.1250 a marginal note in his *Chronica Majora* on the coming of the Antichrist, and linked the Mongol invaders in the East with Gog and Magog.[42] The emperor Frederick II (d. 1250) was labelled as the Antichrist by his papal opponents, though such polemics were soon to become routine propaganda (cats 9, 14).

The Apocalypse evidently struck a chord, or rather many chords, for it was illustrated in such a wide variety of contexts and in so many different media over so long a period that its images reached a multiplicity of viewers. Illuminated manuscript copies continued to be made even after the invention of printing (Ch. 4, cats 1, 117). Among the relatively complete surviving monumental cycles made in England are the early fifteenth-century wall-paintings in

Fig. 9. John Thornton of Coventry, *The Chaining of the Beast before the Millennium*, detail of the Great East Window (1408) in York Minster.

the chapter house of Westminster Abbey,[43] and the east window of York Minster documented as by John Thornton of Coventry and bearing the date 1408. The latter has a particularly elaborate iconographical programme, dominated by the image of God the Father at the apex of the window holding a book originally inscribed 'I am Alpha and Omega', thereby emphasizing the first and last books of the Bible from which the subjects are taken and making the typological links between the Old Testament and the Apocalypse; for the Apocalypse itself there are seventy-eight narrative panels each 86 cm wide (fig. 9).[44]

Some of the Italian representations of the Last Judgement have already been mentioned, and narrative Apocalypse cycles are found there too, though perhaps not as frequently as in the North.[45] From the lands of the old Holy Roman Empire there is the Apocalypse altarpiece by Master Bertram of Hamburg, now in the Victoria and Albert Museum, London (see cat. 14),[46] of about the same date as the window in York Minster. The Chapel of the Holy Cross (1357–67), containing the crown jewels and most important relics at the summit of the castle built outside Prague for the emperor Charles IV, was decorated with gilded glass, semi-precious stones and painted scenes of Revelation, including the Adoration of the Lamb and the apocalyptic God, in a simulacrum of the heavenly Jerusalem. In the adjoining chapel of the Virgin was another cycle of Apocalypse scenes of similar date though by a different hand, which likewise served to emphasize the emperor's personal and dynastic role within the fulfilment of Christian eschatology.[47] From the Netherlands there is the famous monumental altarpiece of the Adoration of the Mystic Lamb painted by Hubert and Jan van Eyck and completed for St Bavon in Ghent in 1435;[48] also by Netherlandish artists are the Last Judgement paintings by Rogier van der Weyden in the Hospice at Beaune in Burgundy, c.1443–52, and by Hans Memlinc in Danzig (Gdansk), 1473.[49]

Perhaps the most extraordinary set of illustrations of the Apocalypse is found on the series of tapestries made for Louis I, duke of Anjou (1339–84), now housed in the castle at Angers.[50] The ducal accounts record payments from 1377 to 1379 to Jean Bondol, responsible for the cartoons, and to Nicholas Bataille, responsible for the weaving. The duke borrowed an English Apocalypse, which still survives, from the library of his brother, King Charles V, to serve as a model for Bondol.[51] This illustrates the interconnections of the pictorial arts at this period. Three tapestries were delivered on Christmas Day 1379. The set as commissioned originally included six tapestries, each with a seated figure and fourteen narrative scenes. Today sixty-seven of the narrative panels, each measuring about 180 × 280 cm, survive. Even in its present incomplete state it is one of the most awe-inspiring works of art of the later Middle Ages.

Such cycles, whether monumental or more private in manuscripts, were ordered and paid for by the powerful and wealthy. There seems little room for millenarians in the sense of those who formed a counter-culture of dissent, hoping for a different and better future.[52] The message is rather that the poor of God are part of the divine plan and must accept their fate, and even welcome it as ensuring their salvation. In the Campo Santo at Pisa a famous image shows the beggars to whom death, which they desire, will only come to release them from their suffering in God's own good time, as in Revelation 9: 6: 'In those days men shall seek death and shall not find it: and they shall desire to die, and death shall fly from them'. In the orthodox view the millennium cannot be brought forward as the result of human volition and even calculations as to its likely timing, as we have seen, were suspect. They might well lead, as they did with the writings of Joachim of Fiore (c.1132–1202), to condemnation for heresy.[53]

Nevertheless the responses to wealth, power and poverty within Christianity in the Middle Ages were always conflicting, even contradictory, and the message to the rich and powerful was not always comforting; witness the representations of popes, emperors and kings among the damned in Gothic Last Judgements and the story of Hugh of Lincoln. St Francis (1182–1226), the *frate poverello*, canonized two years after his death, had a special interest in the Apocalypse. In the church at Assisi in which he was buried, scenes from Revelation were painted by Cimabue in the 1280s in the crossing so that they were visible to the brothers as they said their office. The church had been built and sumptuously decorated by his followers, that wing of the order which triumphed in the bitter debate of the conventuals and the spirituals on apostolic poverty and the order's possession of worldly goods (cat. 9).[54]

The Book of Revelation was a continuing source of inspiration for mystics throughout the Middle Ages. Highly novel visionary imagery was created in emulation of St John's visions and in an important way was authorized by them and thus protected from the taint of heresy. One such mystic is Hildegard of Bingen (1098–1179), who arranged for her visions to be written down at her dictation. They were then illustrated with fully painted and gilded miniatures which, though absolutely original in content, are also unthinkable without knowledge of the Apocalypse text and its illustrations.[55] Another outstanding example of original mystical imagery is in the so-called Rothschild Canticles, made somewhere in the region of Thérouanne in French Flanders at the turn of the fourteenth century for an unidentified but almost certainly female owner, who may also have been a member of a religious order.[56]

As to the reality of the next world, it could be described in visions that were based on the Apocalypse itself. The most famous is that of Dante in the *Divine Comedy*, a text frequently illustrated in the fourteenth and fifteenth centuries in Italy (cat. 21).[57] There were other tales, many circulating orally and invoked by preachers in their sermons, for example the Miracle of Diocrès, a canon of Notre-Dame, Paris. It was related how during the vigil in church after his death he sat up in his coffin to testify to the torments he had witnessed in hell. He told his horrified listeners that he would shortly return there, together with any who doubted his testimony. The scene is painted in the *Très Riches Heures* of Jean de Berry.[58] There was also the account of the Visions of Tundal, of which a manuscript copy was made for Margaret of York, married to Charles the Bold, duke of Burgundy, and illustrated by Simon Marmion of Valenciennes in

Fig. 10. Attributed to Simon Marmion, *The Beast Acheron* (1475), from the *Visions of Tundal*, fol.17. Los Angeles, J. Paul Getty Museum.

the 1470s (fig. 10).[59] This has vivid representations of the tortures of the damned in hell-fire.

These were warnings to expect and prepare for death, which in the Middle Ages, with its continued violence, its plagues and famines, was always a present and vivid threat. Other powerful images of this kind are the Dance of Death and the legend of the Three Living and the Three Dead. The latter, which first appeared in a French poem of the late thirteenth century, is very frequently illustrated in a variety of contexts.[60] It is the story of three noble youths who are out hunting when they are confronted by three skeletons who issue the famous warning: 'As you are, so once were we, as we are so shall you be'.[61] It is seen in the already mentioned frescoes in the burial ground adjacent to Pisa Cathedral, the Campo Santo, whose date, whether just before or just after the Black Death of 1348, has been so much debated (fig. 11).[62] The former, the Dance of Death, was illustrated on the walls of the main burial ground of medieval Paris, the Cemetery of the Innocents, where the skulls and bones of the dead were piled up around the walls as their corpses were exhumed to make room for their successors.[63] There are also manuscripts of the *Danse macabre* with illustrations of Death dancing with a sequence of either men or women of different status.[64] The dance was evidently such a familiar subject that it could be shown in abbreviated form in the margin of a Netherlandish Book of Hours (cat. 24). Like the *Ars Moriendi* and the Three Living and the Three Dead, it remained a frequent subject in woodcut illustrations.[65]

Images like these are again common to both manuscripts and monumental contexts, the one relatively restricted to private perusal by the wealthy, the other visible to all sections of society. The Dance of Death is structured as a dance of status, from the pope and emperor downwards to the peasant labourer. Death is shown as a leveller in a society in which consciousness of status was everywhere apparent. It is possible that some of those who hoped for a millennium in which a juster society might prevail and God's saints be rewarded, may have been reassured by such imagery. But more likely it served only to strengthen the sense of the inevitability of social distinctions, as did the iconography of tomb sculptures, which similarly emphasized rank and hierarchy.[66]

The dissident sects, for example the followers of Wycliffe (*c.*1330–84) in England and of Jan Hus (*c.*1372–1415) in Bohemia, on the whole returned to the Old Testament prohibitions on images observed by the Jews and the earliest Christians. The patronage of art was too much associated with the *status quo* and with those very social and religious abuses they wished to reform.

If we can speak of a popular culture in the later Middle Ages, we have to speak mainly, I believe, in terms of audience, not patrons. In visual terms this would apply to the medieval liturgical and pageant plays as well as to the works of visual art accessible to mass audiences, above all the wall-paintings and stained glass in the parish churches.[67] Works such as the late fifteenth-century Doom painting on the chancel arch of the parish church of St Thomas Becket, Salisbury, or the early fifteenth-century stained-glass window with imagery of the Last Signs based on a Middle English poem, the *Pricke of Conscience*, in All Saints, North Street, York, were certainly created *for* the people, that is for the congregation seated below in the nave, whoever they might be.[68] Some of the extra-apocalyptic imagery, such as that from Matthew 24 of the Last Signs (cat. 22), may have come via texts such as the *Legenda aurea* (Golden Legend), which acted as preachers' manuals and so must have been widely familiar.

Moreover, since the majority of the artisans who produced such works were also of comparatively humble social status, the images were popular in the sense that they were made for the most part by the people. But they were paid for by richer citizens in the case of York, or richer parishioners, perhaps local landowners or wealthier peasant farmers, or perhaps the stipendiary clergy, as in the case of St Thomas's, Salisbury.

Fig. 11. Attributed to Bonamico Buffalmacco, *The Three Living and the Three Dead*, detail of *The Triumph of Death* (c.1340). Fresco. Pisa, Campo Santo.

Fig. 12. Giovanni di Paolo, *God Wipes Away the Tears of the Faithful* (1442). Illuminated initial 'A' in an antiphonal from Lecceto. Siena, Biblioteca comunale degli Intronati.

Bernard Guinée, the distinguished French historian, has written that 'Paradise was the Christian's country in the Middle Ages'. That comment emphasizes for us how the Christian doctrine of an eternal reward, whether in hell or in Heaven, was a socially unifying belief as strong as any incipient sense of national identity in medieval European society. Visual references to that belief, which were repeated constantly in so many varying contexts, performed, therefore, a necessary function as ideological cement in a society filled with conflict. A last image shows how the Apocalypse text provided for the faithful hope, rather than the despair on which modernist thought, which is less firmly attached to the concept of the afterlife, often tends to focus. In an antiphonal illuminated in 1442 by the Sienese artist Giovanni di Paolo for the church of the Augustinian hermits of Lecceto near Siena, an initial 'A' (fig. 12) introduces the beautiful, consolatory words of Revelation 21: 4: 'And God shall wipe away all tears from their eyes and death shall be no more, nor mourning, nor crying, nor sorrow shall be any more, for the former things are passed away.' The Lord is shown wiping the eyes of the faithful kneeling before him, thus confounding the huge, threatening, scaly dragon with fierce biting jaws which makes up the shape of the letter 'A'.[69] The believer is here shown not as one of a group of the elect confidently proclaiming the Eternal Ruler (fig. 1), nor as a helpless victim of the malevolent power of devils (fig. 5), but rather as a humble yet trusting servant of a gentle and above all merciful Lord.

NOTES

1 Jonathan J.G. Alexander, 'Iconography and ideology: uncovering social meanings in Western medieval Christian art', *Studies in Iconography*, XV (1993), pp.1–44.

2 There has been great interest more recently in the question of levels of medieval literacy due to the influence of 'Reception theory' on literary studies generally. See, for example, Brian Stock, *Listening for the Text*, Baltimore 1990, and Michael Camille, 'Seeing and Reading: some visual implications of medieval literacy and illiteracy', *Art History* 8 1985, pp.26–49.

3 For an account of that tradition see Bernard McGinn, 'Introduction: John's Apocalypse and the apocalyptic mentality' in Richard K. Emmerson and Bernard McGinn (eds), *The Apocalypse in the Middle Ages*, Ithaca and London 1992 (henceforth cited as *Apocalypse*), pp.3–19.

4 For the English medieval illustrated Apocalypses of the thirteenth and fourteenth centuries see most conveniently Nigel Morgan, *Early Gothic Manuscripts (1) 1190–1250, (2) 1250–1285* (J.J.G. Alexander (ed.), *A Survey of Manuscripts Illuminated in the British Isles*, vol. 4), London 1982, 1988, and Lucy F. Sandler, *Gothic Manuscripts 1285–1385* (J.J.G. Alexander (ed.), *A Survey of Manuscripts Illuminated in the British Isles*, vol.5), London 1986. For a wider discussion see Suzanne Lewis, *Reading Images. Narrative Discourse and Reception in the Thirteenth-Century Illuminated Apocalypse*, Cambridge 1995, with a full bibliography.

5 Eton College, MS124, f.122. The text is John the Deacon's Life of St Gregory the Great, and the miniature represents the pope's funeral. The manuscript belonged to and was probably written at the Cluniac abbey of Farfa in the early twelfth century. It was first discovered by Montague R. James. See his book *The Apocalypse in Art*, London 1931, p.32. The original mosaic was put in place between 440 and 461. It was altered probably between 692 and 701, and it is thought that a Lamb was substituted then for a figure of Christ in Majesty. It was again remade in 1227–41 and finally destroyed between 1608 and 1618. For this and the other earliest monumental images drawn from the Apocalypse see Dale Kinney, 'The Apocalypse in early Christian monumental decoration', *Apocalypse*, pp.200–16.

6 See Kinney (op. cit. n.5), for other churches in Rome and elsewhere with Apocalyptic motifs.

7 Richard Krautheimer, *Early Christian and Byzantine Architecture* (Pelican History of Art), Baltimore 1965. These monuments were known in the West again via pilgrims, some of whom brought back visual mementoes, such as the small silver flasks for holy oil of the sixth century preserved at Monza and Bobbio. André Grabar, *Ampoules de Terre Sainte*, Paris 1958.

8 All biblical quotations are in the Douay–Rheims version, first published in 1582, New Testament, and 1609, Old Testament.

9 Meyer Schapiro, *Words and Pictures. On the Literal and the Symbolic in the Illustration of a Text*, Hague 1973, reprinted in *Words, Script and Pictures: Semiotics of Visual Language*, New York 1996.

10 Christa Ihm, *Die Programme der christlichen Apsismalerei vom vierten Jahrhundert bis zur Mitte des achten Jahrhunderts*, Wiesbaden 1960. Gertrud Schiller, *Ikonographie der christlichen Kunst*, vol. 3: *Die Auferstehung und Erhöhung Christi*, Gütersloh 1971. Frederik van der Meer, *Maiestas Domini: visions from the Book of Revelation in western art*, London, New York 1978. J.-M. Spieser, 'The Representation of Christ in the Apses of Early Christian Churches', *Gesta* 37/1 1998, pp.63–73.

11 Thomas F. Mathews, *The Clash of Gods. A reinterpretation of Early Christian Art*, Princeton 1993, critiques an earlier derivation of much of Christian iconography from imperial imagery. Compare for example the earlier account of André Grabar, *Christian Iconography. A study of its origins*, Princeton 1968.

12 See Schiller (op. cit. n.10), figs 460ff.

13 These are the manuscripts kept in the libraries of Valenciennes, Trier and Cambrai and at the Bibliothèque Nationale de France, Paris. For an authoritative account with supporting bibliography of medieval Apocalypse illustration in all media see Peter K. Klein, 'The Apocalypse in medieval art', *Apocalypse*, pp.159–99. An earlier, shorter but still useful account, mainly of the illustrated manuscripts, is that by M. R. James (op. cit. n.5).

14 Beat Brenk, *Tradition und Neuerung in der christlichen Kunst des ersten Jahrtausend. Studien zur Geschichte des Weltgerichtsbildes* (H. Hunger (ed.), Wiener Byzantinische Studien), Vienna 1966, pp.36ff., figs 1–2. Pamela Sheingorn, '"For God is such a Doomsman": Origins and development of the theme of Judgment', in *Homo, Memento Finis: the iconography of Just Judgment in medieval art and drama* (Early Drama, Art and Music Monograph Series 6), Kalamazoo, Mich., 1985, pp.19–22, fig. 1.

15 Gertrud Schiller, *Ikonographie der christlichen Kunst*, vol. V. 1 and 2, *Die Apokalypse des Johannes*, Gütersloh, 1991–2; also Kinney (op. cit. n.5).

16 Beat Brenk (op. cit. n.14) describes this process.

17 London, Victoria and Albert Museum, 253–1867. Brenk op. cit. n.14), pp.118–20, 164, 223, pl.35. John Beckwith, *Ivory Carvings in Early Medieval England*, London 1972, pp.23–4, 118 (cat. 4), figs 1, 16, as Anglo-Saxon, c.800. Sheingorn (op. cit. n.14), pp.25–8, fig. 3. On the back was carved, probably in a Late Carolingian workshop, a scene of the Ascension, though this, too, was considered Anglo-Saxon by Beckwith, who dated it late tenth century, cat. 22. See also Leslie Webster, in L. Webster and Janet Backhouse (eds), *The Making of England. Anglo-Saxon Art and Culture AD 600-900*, British Museum, London 1991, cat. 140 (Victoria and Albert Museum, 254.1867, ivory recarved with companion scene to that on the back of 253.1867, of the Transfiguration).

18 'Imagines visionum apocalypsis beati Iohannis.' Paul Meyvaert, 'Bede and the church paintings at Wearmouth Jarrow', *Anglo-Saxon England*, 8 1979, pp.63–77.

19 St Gall, Stiftsbibliothek, Cod. 61. Brenk (op. cit. n.14), pp.68–9, pl.17. Jonathan J.G. Alexander, *Insular Manuscripts 6th to the 9th century* (Survey of Manuscripts illuminated in the British Isles, vol. 1), London 1978, pp.66–7 (cat. 44), ill. 206. A second Irish Gospels, now in Turin, datable to the first half of the ninth century, shows another early stage in the evolution of the iconography, ibid., cat. 61, ill. 280. George Henderson, *From Durrow to Kells. The Insular Gospel-Books 650–800*, London 1987, has emphasized apocalyptic elements in Insular iconography, pp.80ff., etc.

20 For example an ivory in Cambridge of the early eleventh century shows the Last Judgement. Beckwith (op. cit. n.17), pp.38, 121 (cat. 18), ill. 41. The Old English literary sources include poems in the Exeter book, and homilies by Aelfric and others. I thank Leslie Webster for bringing this material to my attention.

21 Historiated capitals in the cloister at Moissac also include an Apocalypse cycle. Meyer Schapiro, *The Romanesque Sculpture of Moissac*, New York 1985.

22 For the Romanesque churches see Yves Christe, *Les grands portails romans. Etudes sur l'iconologie des théophanies romanes*, Geneva 1969, and id., 'The Apocalypse in the Monumental Art of the Eleventh through Thirteenth Centuries', *Apocalypse*, pp.234–58. The same author's *L'Apocalypse de Jean*, Paris 1996, is unavailable to me. Also Millard F. Hearn, *Romanesque Sculpture. The Revival of Monumental Stone Sculpture in the Eleventh and Twelfth Centuries*, Oxford 1981. For the Gothic cathedrals see Willibald Sauerländer, trans. J. Sondheimer, *Gothic Sculpture in France 1140–1270*, London 1970, and Paul Williamson, *Gothic Sculpture 1140–1300* (Pelican History of Art), New Haven and London 1995.

23 Denis Grivot and George Zarnecki, *Gislebertus, Sculptor of Autun*, London 1961.

24 New York, Pierpont Morgan Library, M. 644. *A Spanish Apocalypse. The Morgan Beatus Manuscript*, Introduction and commentaries by John Williams, Codicological analysis by Barbara Shailor, New York 1991, p.17. See also John Williams, *The Illustrated Beatus: a Corpus of Illustrations of the Commentary on the Apocalypse*, vols1–3 so far published, London 1994–8.

25 Sheingorn (op. cit. n.14), p.38. The passage from the *Magna Vita Sancti Hugonis* (Rolls Series, London 1864, p.289) is given at greater length by A. Caiger-Smith, *English Medieval Mural Paintings*, Oxford 1963, pp.40–1.

26 For a recent full discussion of millenarianism at this historical juncture see Richard Landes, *Relics, Apocalypse and the Deceits of History. Ademar of Chabannes, 989–1034*, Cambridge, Mass., 1995, especially pp.285ff. He considers that millenarian anxiety was widespread and in some areas intense. But see the somewhat more sceptical comments of Henry Mayr-Harting, *Ottonian Book Illumination. An Historical Study. Part 2. Books*, London 1991, pp.45–8, in relation particularly to the making of the early eleventh-century Bamberg Apocalypse, and of Derk Visser, *Apocalypse as Utopian Expectation (800–1500). The Apocalyptic Commentary of Berengaudus of Ferrières and the relationship between exegesis, liturgy and iconography*, Leiden 1996, pp.126–8. For a general account of millenarianism and beliefs on the coming of Antichrist in the Middle Ages see Richard K. Emmerson, *Antichrist in the Middle Ages. A study of medieval apocalypticism, art and literature*, Manchester 1981. The visual tradition of representing Antichrist is discussed by Rosemary M. Wright, *Art and Antichrist in Medieval Europe*, Manchester 1995.

27 H. Focillon, *L'An Mil*, Paris 1952, published after his death in 1943. The text is translated in Cecilia Davis-Weyer, *Early Medieval Art 300–1150* (Sources and Documents in the History of Art Series, ed. H.W. Janson), Englewood Cliffs 1971, p.124. For Radulphus's linking of heresy in the late tenth century to the coming of the millennium see Landes (op. cit. n.26), p.292.

28 For the commentaries see the essays in *Apocalypse*, especially those by E. Ann Matter, 'The Apocalypse in early medieval exegesis', *Apocalypse*, pp.38–50; by John Williams, 'Purpose and imagery in the Apocalypse commentary of Beatus of Liébana', ibid., pp.217–33; and by Suzanne Lewis, 'Exegesis and illustration in thirteenth-century English Apocalypses', ibid., pp.259–75. Also Barbara Nolan, *The Gothic Visionary Perpéctive*, Princeton 1977. For Berengaudus see Visser (op. cit. n.26), who argues for identifying him with the ninth-century monk of Ferrières.

29 This important point is rightly emphasized by Sheingorn (op. cit. n.14).

30 Adolf Katzenellenbogen, *Allegories of the Virtues and Vices in Medieval Art to the Thirteenth Century*, Warburg Institute, London 1939, repr. Nedeln 1977.

31 Sheingorn (op. cit. n.14), pp.31–6, with further literature on the play.

32 Richard W. Southern, *Saint Anselm and his Biographer*, Cambridge 1963, p.109.

33 For the medieval 'economy of salvation' see Jacques le Goff, trans. R. Ranum, *Your Money or your Life*, New York 1988. Also Eamon Duffy, *The Stripping of the Altars. Traditional Religion in England c.1400–c.1580*, New Haven and London 1992, ch. 10, 'The pains of Purgatory'. For its artistic consequences see Paul Binski, *Medieval Death. Ritual and Representation*, London 1996, especially pp.187–8.

34 See James H. Stubblebine, *Giotto: the Arena Chapel Frescoes*, New York and London 1969, especially Ursula Schlegel, 'On the picture program of the Arena Chapel', pp.182–202.

35 Roger Wieck, *Time Sanctified. The Book of Hours in Medieval Art and Life*, exh. cat., Walters Art Gallery, Baltimore, and New York 1988, p.124, pl.37 (W.457, f.117).

36 Thomas S. R. Boase, *Death in the Middle Ages. Mortality, Judgment and Remembrance*, London 1972, ch. 5. Binski (op. cit. n.33), pp.39ff. For the block-book and its relation to the engravings by Master E.S. see Arthur M. Hind, *An Introduction to the History of the Woodcut*, reprinted Dover Publications, New York 1, 1963, pp.224ff. Also Wilhelm L. Schreiber and H. Zimmermann, 'Ars moriendi', in Otto Schmitt (ed.), *Reallexicon zur deutschen Kunstgeschichte* 1, Stuttgart 1937, pp.1121–7.

37 Arthur Gardner, *English Medieval Sculpture*, Cambridge 1951, p.265, figs 514, 519.

38 These are conveniently surveyed by Wright (op. cit. n.26), ch. 2.

39 Michael Camille, 'Visionary Perception and Images of the Apocalypse in the Later Middle Ages', *Apocalypse*, pp.276–89. Lewis (op. cit. n.4), pp.6–10. Michael Camille, *Gothic Art. Glorious Visions*, New York 1996, pp.16–25.

40 An example is the Apocalypse, Lambeth Palace Library, MS 209, made c.1274 for Lady Elizabeth de Quincy. Nigel Morgan, *The Lambeth Apocalypse: Manuscript 209 in Lambeth Palace Library*, London 1990 (commentary to facsimile).

41 Robert I. Moore, *The Formation of a Persecuting Society. Power and Deviance in Western Europe 950–1250*, Oxford 1987.

42 Suzanne Lewis, *The Art of Matthew Paris in the 'Chronica Majora'*, University of California Press 1987, pp.102–3.

43 Paul Binski, *Westminster Abbey and the Plantagenets. Kingship and the Representation of Power 1200–1400*, New Haven and London 1995, pp.185–95.

44 Thomas French, *York Minster. The Great East Window*, British Academy, London 1995.

45 See Klein (op. cit. n.14), pp.180–1, 194–6.

46 C.M. Kauffmann, *An Altar Piece of the Apocalypse from Master Bertram's Workshop in Hamburg*, Victoria and Albert Museum Monographs, London 1968.

47 Vlasta Dvořáková *et al.*, *Gothic Mural Painting in Bohemia and Moravia 1300–78*, London 1964, pp.92–100, pls.140–61.

48 Visser (op. cit. n.26), ch. 6.

49 Otto Pächt, *Early Netherlandish Painting from Rogier van der Weyden to Gerard David*, London 1997, pp.40–51, 228–9, figs 33, 172–4, pls 28–9, folding plate.

50 Francis Muel *et al.*, *La tenture de l'Apocalypse d'Angers* (Cahiers de l'Inventaire 4), Paris n.d. [1995].

51 Paris, Bibliothèque Nationale de France, fr.403. It was not the main model used, however. See George Henderson, 'The

manuscript model of the Angers Apocalypse', *Burlington Magazine*, 127 1985, pp.209–18.

52 Norman Cohn, *The Pursuit of the Millennium: Revolutionary Millenarians and Mystical Anarchists of the Middle Ages*, rev. edn, Oxford and New York 1972.

53 E. Randolph Daniel, 'Joachim of Fiore: Patterns of History in the Apocalypse', *Apocalypse*, pp.72–88, with earlier literature, especially Marjorie Reeves, *The Figurae of Joachim of Fiore*, Oxford 1972. A useful anthology is *Apocalyptic Spirituality. Treatises and Letters of Lactantius …*, trans. and intro. Bernard McGinn, London 1979.

54 Umberto Eco writes of this conflict and the mobilization of the Apocalypse text in his novel *The Name of the Rose*, trans. W. Weaver, San Diego 1983.

55 Maura Böckeler, *Hildegard of Bingen, Wisse die Weg, Scivias*, Berlin 1928, repr. Salzburg 1954; Madeline Caviness, 'Artist: to see, hear, and know all at once', in Barbara Newman (ed.), *Voice of the Living Light. Hildegard of Bingen and her world*, Berkeley 1998, pp.110–24.

56 Jeffrey Hamburger, *The Rothschild Canticles. Art and Mysticism in Flanders and the Rhineland c. 1300*, New Haven and London 1990.

57 Peter Brieger, Millard Meiss and Charles S. Singleton, *Illuminated Manuscripts of the Divine Comedy*, 2 vols, Princeton 1969.

58 Chantilly, Musée Condé, f.86v, one of the miniatures finished by Jean Colombe c.1485. Millard Meiss, Jean Longnon and Raymond Cazelles, *The "Très Riches Heures" of Jean, Duke of Berry*, London and New York 1969.

59 Malibu, J. Paul Getty Museum, MS30. Thomas Kren and Roger S. Wieck, *The Visions of Tundal from the Library of Margaret of York*, J. Paul Getty Museum, Malibu 1990. *Margaret of York, Simon Marmion, and the Visions of Tundal*, ed. Thomas Kren, Malibu 1992.

60 Karl Künstle, *Die Legende der drei Lebenden und der drei Toten und der Totentanz*, Freiburg i. B. 1908.

61 Binski (op. cit. n.33), pp.134–8.

62 Millard Meiss, *Painting in Florence and Siena after the Black Death*, Princeton 1951. Luciano Bellosi, *Buffalmacco e il Trionfo della Morte*, Turin 1974. Henk van Os, 'The Black Death and Sienese painting: a problem of interpretation', *Art History*, 4 1981, pp.237–49.

63 See Michael Camille, *Master of Death. The lifeless art of Pierre Remiet*, New Haven and London 1996, pp.195-6. Also Duffy (op. cit. n.33), ch. 9, 'Last Things'.

64 Binski (op. cit. n.33), pp.153–9. Camille (op. cit. n.63), pp.158–9 etc. Helmut Rosenfeld, *Die mittelalterliche Totentanz. Entstehung, Entwicklung, Bedeutung*, 2nd edn, Cologne and Graz 1968. A.T. Harrison (ed.), *The Danse Macabre of Women. Ms. fr. 995 of the Bibliothèque nationale*, with a chapter written by S.L. Hindman, Kent, Ohio, and London 1994.

65 See for example William J. Ivins, *The Dance of Death printed at Paris in 1490. A reproduction made from the copy in the Lessing J. Rosenwald collection, Library of Congress*, Washington DC 1945. It was the subject, too, of musical composition, for example the round dance *Ad mortem festinamus* from the *Llibre Vermell* (Red Book), a manuscript copied at the turn of the fourteenth and fifteenth centuries.

66 For this reading see Jean Batany, 'Les "Danse Macabre": une image en negatif du fonctionalisme social', in Jane H.M. Taylor (ed.), *Dies Illa. Death in the Middle Ages* (Proceedings of the 1983 Manchester Colloquium), Manchester 1994, pp.15–27.

67 For the plays see the collection of papers in *Homo, Memento Finis: the iconography of Just Judgment in Medieval Art and Drama* (Early Drama, Art and Music Monograph Series 6), Kalamazoo, Mich., 1985, with further references. For a general overview of stained glass in England see Richard Marks, *Stained Glass in England during the Middle Ages*, London 1993. In the absence of a fuller, more up-to-date account of the wall-painting see the overview by Caiger-Smith (op. cit. n.25).

68 For St Thomas's, Salisbury, see Margaret Rickert, *Painting in Britain. The Middle Ages* (Pelican History of Art), 2nd edn, Harmondsworth 1965, pp.188–9, pl.193. For All Saints, North Street, York, see E.A. Gee, 'The painted glass of All Saints' Church, North Street, York', *Archaeologia*, 102 1969, pp.151–202.

69 'Absterget Deus omnem lacrimam'. Grazia Vailati Schoenburg Waldenburg, 'Testo e immagine: Giovanni di Paolo e la Leccetana "Comunella dei Santi"', in Melania Ceccanti and M. C. Castelli (eds), *Il codice miniato. Rapporti tra codice, testo e figurazione* (Atti del III Congresso di Storia della Miniatura), Florence 1992, p.303, fig. 8. Keith Christiansen, Laurence B. Kanter and Carl B. Strehlke, *Painting in Renaissance Siena 1420–1500*, Metropolitan Museum, New York 1988, cat. 30,col. pl.

The catalogue entries for this section have been prepared by Giulia Bartrum, Rhoda Eitel-Porter and Frances Carey

1 The Tiberius Psalter

Gallican Psalter with Old English gloss

Winchester, *c*.1050

Manuscript on parchment, 248 × 146 mm; 129 leaves

Fol. 13v: *The Three Maries at the Tomb*

Fol. 14r: *The Harrowing of Hell*

Lit: E. Temple, *Anglo-Saxon Manuscripts 900–1066. A Survey of Manuscripts illuminated in the British Isles*, 2, London 1976, no.98; *The Golden Age of Anglo-Saxon Art 966–1066*, exhib. cat., Janet Backhouse, D.H. Turner and Leslie Webster (eds), British Museum, London 1984, no. 66; *English Romanesque Art 1066–1200*, exhib. cat., G. Zarnecki, T. Holland and Janet Holt (eds), Hayward Gallery, London 1984, no.1.

London, British Library Cotton MS Tiberius C VI

Despite the damage it received in the fire at the Cottonian Library at Ashburnham House in 1731, this is one of the most important monuments of late Anglo-Saxon culture to have survived. It contains illustrated tables for calculating astrological and astronomical correspondences during the year (ff.2–7v), seventeen full-page prefatory miniatures (ff. 8–16), a treatise on musical instruments (ff.16v–18), Prefaces for the Psalms (ff.19–23), an order for Confession (ff.23–7), two homilies in Anglo-Saxon (28v–30) and St Jerome's edition of the Latin Psalter with collects and Anglo-Saxon gloss.

The scribe of the psalter has been identified with that of at least five manuscripts from Winchester. These include the Old Minster, Winchester Cantatorium (Oxford, Bodleian Library MS Bodley 775) (a manuscript used by the chief cantor at Winchester), as well as another Gallican psalter from New Minster (Winchester), London, British Library Stowe MS 2, which displays the same order of collects. The five full-page miniatures of the life of King David and eleven of the life of Christ form the earliest prefatory cycle of this type from any psalter. Many such cycles have survived from the twelfth century; they became popular all over Europe by the thirteenth. The highly personal nature of the compilation of both texts and images has suggested to some scholars that the very idea of a prefatory cycle of images for a psalter, one of the key artistic vehicles for images in the Middle Ages, may have originated in England in either this or a slightly earlier manuscript of the same type. There is every likelihood that a calendar prefaced the miniatures and text and, as the manuscript is incomplete, it can be suggested that it may have had a litany and prayers. The emphasis placed on the old three-part division of the psalter text through the placing of further full-page miniatures at Psalms 1 (f.30v), 51 (f.71v) and 101 (f.114v) is of also of interest. The eight-part liturgical division of the psalter is marked by large

1, Fol. 13v

decorative initials with Psalm 109 (f.126v) given a half-page miniature. The combination of these two systems provides an antecedent for the later English practice of maintaining a ten-part liturgical division for the reading of the psalter, by retaining the divisions at Psalms 51 and 101, when the rest of Europe was content with eight.

The two miniatures displayed depict the Three Maries confronted by the angel at the empty tomb of Christ, inscribed *Angelus tribus Mulieribus Loquitur* (The angel speaking to the three women), and the Harrowing of Hell, inscribed *Christus infernu[m] despoliat* (Christ robs hell). The looming giant figure of Christ above the mouth of hell is balanced by that of the huge angel confronting the women at the tomb. The tinted drawing effect, with agitated hemlines and voluminous draperies, has its roots in 'Winchester school' illumination of the later part of the tenth century. But

1, Fol. 14r

the quality of line, varying in speed of execution from thick repeated inking to quick thin strokes, is characteristic of the eleventh century.

The Harrowing (literally 'robbing' – the Latin *despolio*) of Hell is the equivalent in Western Christianity to the Anastasis of Byzantine art (see cat. 3), and both iconographies have their textual origins in the Apocryphal Gospel of Nicodemus, also known as the Acts of Pilate. The Apostles' Creed (widely used in the West from earliest times) had developed by *c*.1000 to include the phrase attributed to St Thomas: *Descendit ad inferna, tertia die resurrexit* (He descended into hell and rose again on the third day). It is probably this more general statement that is reflected in the iconography here rather than the more textually accurate Anastasis iconography of Byzantine art.
M.M.

2 Longleat Apocalypse

Apocalypse in Latin with commentary of Berengaudus

Canterbury? *c*.1100

Manuscript on parchment, 213 × 119mm; 128 leaves

Fol.1: The Holy Trinity in a mandorla surrounded by the evangelist symbols (above) and St John seated at a lectern being instructed to write by the Angel of the Apocalypse (below).

Lit: M.A. Michael, 'An Illustrated "Apocalypse" manuscript at Longleat House', *Burlington Magazine*, cxxvi 1984, pp.340–3; Suzanne Lewis, *Reading Images. Narrative, Discourse and Reception in the Thirteenth-Century Illuminated Apocalypse*, Cambridge 1995, pp.42–3; P. Klein, 'The Apocalypse in Medieval Art', in *The Apocalypse in the Middle Ages*, R.K. Emmerson and Bernard McGinn (eds), Ithaca and London 1992, pp.159–99; D.Visser, 'Apocalypse as Utopian Expectation (800–1500). The Apocalypse Commentary of Berengaudus of Ferrières and the relationship between exegesis, liturgy and iconography', *Studies in the History of Christian Thought*, lxxiii, Leiden 1996, p. 17.

Longleat (Wiltshire), Marquess of Bath, Longleat House MS 2

The choice of the Berengaudus commentary as early as *c*.1100 for this small portable book suggests there was a general acceptance of the reading of the glossed Apocalypse as a separate text in monastic communities, long before the first fully illustrated English Apocalypses emerge. There are a number of other early commentators on the Apocalypse, but it is the commentary of Berengaudus, which survives in copies from the eleventh century onwards, that was most widely read in northern Europe, while the commentary of Beatus was read in Spain and southern France (see cat. 4). Almost nothing is known about Berengaudus, although his work was used by German writers from the eleventh century onwards. Visser has recently suggested that he may have come from the archdiocese of Sens and lived *c*.840–92, but admits that his research found 'little that suggests who Berengaudus was or when he lived'. The text is arranged into seven 'visions' and, like many commentators on the Apocalypse from Jerome onwards, he is interested in the prefiguration of events in the New Testament and how this sheds light on God's 'revelation'. Nigel Morgan suggests Berengaudus's popularity was based on the way in which he addresses the central question of 'what shall come to pass at the end of time', while Suzanne Lewis believes he was preferred to other commentaries, such as that in the *Glossa Ordinaria* (the preferred text of the university scholar), because his interpretations were imbued with the values of Benedictine monasticism. Visser has recently suggested that it was Berengaudus's positive and utopian vision of the future that was so attractive to later readers.

The opening rubric of the Longleat text introduces the manuscript as an Apocalypse and Berengaudus is only later mentioned on f.3, which suggests that the book was regarded as an Apocalypse *per se* and not merely a commentary. The carefully structured text may have proved attractive to the thirteenth-century compilers of fully illustrated

2

of the evangelists which surround this Trinity are commonly found in twelfth-century sculptural depictions of the Last Judgement. Their use here serves as a reminder that the source of this iconography is linked to the visual cross-reference between the beasts described by Ezekiel (Ezk. 1: 10) and those in the Apocalypse (Rev. 4: 6–8). St John and the angel below, although only presented as an author portrait in this miniature, bear a remarkable likeness to compositions found in a number of the tinted-drawing Apocalypses of the thirteenth century.

M.M.

3 The Four Gospels in Greek

Eastern Mediterranean, late eleventh or early twelfth century

Manuscript on parchment, 230 × 165mm; 1+ 269 leaves

Fol.206v: *The Anastasis* (Resurrection) from the Gospel of St Luke; image size 110 × 120mm

Lit: A.W. Carr, *Byzantine Illumination 1150–1250*, Chicago 1987, pp.55–69; D. Buckton (ed.), *Byzantium. Treasures of Byzantine Art and Culture from British Collections*, London 1994, no.194.

London, British Library Harley MS 1810

The Anastasis is one of the twelve feasts (*dodecaorton*) of the Byzantine Church. Known as the Harrowing of Hell in Western European art, it provides the focus for the Easter celebrations in the Orthodox Church and thus came to symbolize the Resurrection itself, whereas it remained part of the Passion cycle in the West (cat. 1).

The rubric above the miniature acts as a label (it states: 'The Resurrection') below, the text refers to Christ's own words that he would rise on the third day. Christ breaks down the doors of hell and rescues those who had died under the Old Law (of the Old Testament), but who, nevertheless, believed in his coming. This Descent into Hell is recounted in the Apocryphal Gospel of Nicodemus, also known as the Acts of Pilate, which has survived in both Greek and Latin recensions. The breaking down of the doors is graphically described:

> …Hades heard the voice a second time, he answered as if he knew it not, and said: Who is this King of glory? The angels of the Lord said: The Lord strong and mighty, the lord mighty in battle. And straightway at the word the gates of brass were broken in pieces and the bars of iron were ground to powder, and all the dead that were bound were loosed from their chains, and we with them, and the King of glory entered in fashion of a man, and all the dark places in hell were lightened [Book VIII].

The narrative goes on to describe St John the Baptist preaching in hell, and identifies Adam and his son Seth, who recount the story of Adam's death and his long wait (for five thousand and five hundred years) for the oil from the tree of

Apocalypses, as they could easily take interpretative extracts where needed to append to the biblical text.

There is no indication that the Longleat Apocalypse miniature was ever part of a larger cycle, but it certainly fills a gap in our knowledge of the development of Apocalypse decoration in England during the Middle Ages. Its two-tier format is found in the picture-book Apocalypses of the Morgan group, which included text in scrolls inside the miniatures (see Rylands cat. 19). A scroll is used in the Longleat miniature on which the lamb and dove rest in front of God the Father, who is seated in a mandorla. The symbols

+ ἡ ἀνάστασις·

3

but whose main images were illuminated by the artist Basilius in a Byzantine style, probably in the Holy Land in the early twelfth century. Such manuscripts show a fusion of Western European and Byzantine styles which antedates by over a hundred years the stylistic experimentation typical of the thirteenth and early fourteenth centuries in both Eastern and Western European art. Stylistic analysis of this manuscript is further complicated by the fact that the characteristic paint-flaking of Byzantine illumination has led to extensive reworking of some of the surfaces, and the images found in its margins may post-date the initial campaign to illuminate the book.

M.M.

4 The Silos Apocalypse

Beatus of Liébana's Commentary on the Apocalypse in Latin

San Sebastián (later Domingo) de Silos, Spain, written by 18 April 1091 (f.265v) and illuminated by 1 July 1109 (f.275v)

Manuscript on parchment, 380 × 250mm; 280 leaves

Fols 147v–148r: *The Woman Clothed with the Sun and The Dragon* (Rev.12: 1–18); image size 311–446mm

Lit: *Los Beatos*, Chapelle de Nassau, Bibliothèque Royale Albert 1er, Brussels 1985, no. 10; P. Klein, *Beatus a Liebana in Apocalypsin comentarius: Manchester, The John Rylands University Library, Latin MS 8* (Codices Illuminatio Medii Aevi 16), Munich 1990; J. Williams, *The Illustrated Beatus*, IV, no.16, forthcoming

London, British Library Additional MS 11695

The commentary on the Apocalypse compiled by Beatus of Liébana in Visigothic Spain c.782–6 was illustrated in a unique way. It represents a strain of Apocalypse decoration that ties later Spanish painting directly into the culture of the first Christian churches in North Africa. As much as it reminds us of the Islamic influences present in Mozarabic culture, the forms and ideas found in these manuscripts represent an unbroken link with North African Christianity in the first few centuries of the millennium after Christ's birth.

A number of recensions of the text have been identified and a canonical set of 108 images established (there are ninety in this volume, two of which may belong to another manuscript). This copy carries the final (third) edition of the AD 786 text. Although Carolingian copies of the Apocalypse with up to seventy-four framed illuminations have survived, suggesting that a late Roman tradition of Apocalypse illustration existed, these are not thought to have inspired the decoration of the Beatus Commentary. The main reason for this view is that the texts from the Apocalypse in the Beatus manuscripts rely on an old Latin pre-Vulgate exemplar, probably known to Beatus only through an earlier commentary on the Apocalypse written in North Africa by Tyconius, from which he quotes freely.

life. King David and Isaiah also rebuke Satan and Hades with reminders of their prophecies. Finally Christ delivers the righteous from the jaws of hell:

> The Saviour blessed Adam upon his forehead with the sign of the cross, and so did he also unto all the patriarchs and prophets and martyrs and forefathers. And he took them and leaped up out of hell.

Byzantine images of the Anastasis, like this one in the Harley Gospels, follow this text quite closely by showing Adam and Eve (who signify the salvation of mankind in general), followed closely by King David, his son Solomon and St John the Baptist as the *Prodromos* and last prophet. As in most versions of this scene from the mid-Byzantine period, the legend that Christ's sceptre split the hill of Golgotha at the moment of his return is visualized by the two hills either side of him. Ultimately the image may derive from ancient Roman depictions, often found on coins, of the victorious emperor pulling up supplicant figures of the vanquished at his feet; the earliest surviving paintings are from early ninth-century Rome.

This Greek Gospel has stylistic characteristics which suggest that it should be grouped with manuscripts such as the Melisende Psalter (London, British Library, Egerton MS 1139), written in Latin for Queen Melisende of Jerusalem,

4

Beatus comments on the Apocalypse text and the images provided through a series of Incipits he calls 'Explanatio supra cripta storiae' (explanation of the hidden meaning of the 'imagery' – here meaning verbal as well as pictorial images suggested by the text, f.148v). These are based on various sources such as Isidore of Seville, Jerome and Tyconius. The Vision of the Woman as the *Amicta Sole* became a central theme in Franciscan theology in the later Middle Ages and Renaissance, eventually providing the images of the Immaculate Conception made famous by Spanish artists such as Murillo. But these interpretations of the *Amicta Sole* appear to have been unrecognized by Beatus, who identifies her solely with Ecclesia (the Church) attacked by the devil. A continuous narrative is provided of the *Amicta Sole* on the left, the bad angels who lose their wings as they fall to hell in the bottom right, the dragon attacking

the Woman who seeks refuge, centre and left, and the Child who represents the Saviour, presented to God in the top right-hand corner.

Despite the clear colophons and dates inserted into the manuscript there is still confusion as to who illuminated the manuscript and when. A certain Dominicus and his fellow monk Munnio appear to have executed the manuscript ('exigui libri huius') under Abbot Fortunio (f.277v), but a Prior Petrus claims to have completed the book and illuminated it ('ab integro illuminabit', f.275v). It would seem best to assume that it was written and then illuminated between 1091 and 1109, but it is possible that Prior Petrus may only have had the illumination finished and not necessarily have illuminated it himself.

M.M.

5 Beatus of Liébana's Commentary on the Apocalypse

Spain, Burgos? *c.*1175?

Manuscript on parchment, 455 × 325mm; 248 leaves

Fols181v–182r: *The Destruction of Babylon with Onlookers*

Lit: John P. O'Neill (ed.), *The Art of Medieval Spain, A.D. 500–1200*, Metropolitan Museum of Art, New York 1993, no.145; P. Klein, *Beatus a Liebana in Apocalypsin comentarius: Manchester The John Rylands University Library Latin MS 8* (Codices Illuminatio Medii Aevi 16), Munich 1990; J. Williams, *The Illustrated Beatus*, V, no. 20, forthcoming

Manchester, John Rylands University Library MS Latin 8

Williams has suggested that the Rylands Apocalypse should be associated with the monastery of San Pedro de Cardeña, as the Cardeña Beatus (now split between four collections: New York, Girona and two in Madrid) copies an otherwise anomalous arcade from the Rylands frontispiece. Like the Silos Apocalypse, the Rylands illustrations may ultimately rely on a much earlier copy of the text, such as the late tenth-century Tábara Beatus of Magius, the oldest surviving fully illustrated copy (Madrid, Archivo Histórico Nacional Cod. 1097B). Stylistically, it is far less interested in the neo-Mozarabic effects of the Silos Apocalypse. The clear drawing and complex fold structures of the figures suggest an awareness of wall-painting of the later twelfth century. Indeed, there is a hint of the Byzantinizing effects achieved by English artists at Sigena in Cataluña that gives this Apocalypse an international flavour.

That the careful organization of the figures and even the somewhat subdued colour scheme should recall northern European art as much as they do Spain, should not be so surprising at this date. A manuscript such as the Rylands Beatus may ultimately have been a model when the Trinity Apocalypse (cat. 10), one of the earliest of the English Apocalypses, was created in the thirteenth century around the commentary of the northern European Berengaudus, rather than the Spanish Beatus.
M.M.

5

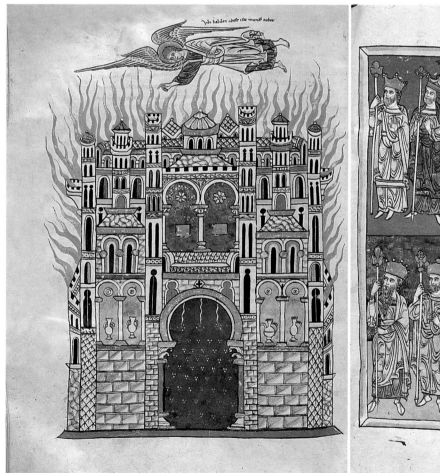

6 The Winchester Psalter

Winchester?, mid-twelfth century

Manuscript on parchment, 320 × 230mm; 142 leaves

Fol. 39r: *Hell Mouth*, image size 275 × 178mm

Lit: G.F. Warner, *Illuminated Manuscripts in the British Museum*, London 1903, pl. 12; E. Gulden, 'Das Monster-Portal am Palazzo Zuccari in Rom. Wandlungen eines Motivs vom Mittelalter zum Manierismus', *Zeitschrift für Kunstgeschichte* 1969, pp.229–61, esp. p.258; C.M. Kauffmann, *A Survey of Manuscripts Illuminated in the British Isles, Romanesque Manuscripts 1066–1190*, London 1975, no.78; F. Wormald, *The Winchester Psalter*, London 1973; K.E. Haney, *The Winchester Psalter. An Iconographic Study*, Leicester 1986

London, British Library Cotton MS Nero C IV

This manuscript contains a parallel text of the psalter in Latin and French and has contemporary French inscriptions describing each of thirty-eight prefatory miniatures, but is missing important miniatures of a Tree of Good and Evil for which the rubric survives on f.142v. The miniatures have been damaged by the heat of the fire in the Cotton Library in 1731 and subsequent attempts at repair have spoilt many of the backgrounds. Warner first signalled the importance of the manuscript and suggested the connection with Winchester and its most important twelfth-century patron, Henry of Blois (1120–71). But Henry's involvement with the manuscript has recently been questioned. There is no firm evidence to suggest he should be connected with it other than a conjectural interpretation of the saints in the calendar, two of whom, being Cluniac, may reflect Henry's early training in that order. The calendar and prayers are certainly based on St Swithun's usage, but there is also a clear Benedictine bias from Hyde Abbey. It is certain that the book went to Shaftesbury Abbey, probably in the thirteenth century. Additions to the calendar, which include feasts of St Edward King and Martyr and the dedication of the abbey at Shaftesbury by St Anselm, are typical of this use. The inclusion of the obit of Stephen Bauceyn (d. 1257), probably a relation of the abbess Juliana Bauceyn (d. 1279), suggests that these additions were made in the thirteenth century, but the pen-flourish work added over the twelfth-century initials is of the fourteenth century.

The angel locking the door of hell is one of the most striking paintings to have survived from medieval England. Clearly labelled 'Ici est enfers e li angels ki enferme les portes' (Here be hell and the angel who closes the doors), the composition depicts a gaping hell mouth, its door locked by an angel who stands outside the miniature confidently turning the key, with kings, queens, clerics and men and

6

women tormented by devils inside. It is closely linked iconographically with Anglo-Saxon images of the early eleventh century such as the hell mouth in the Tiberius Psalter (cat. 1) and in particular the scene of Judgement in the New Minster, Winchester, *Liber Vitae* (London, British Library Stowe MS 944). The image of the Gates of Hell is compared visually in the latter with the Gates of Heaven above. The same idea of locking the door is also found in the Caedmon Genesis (Oxford, Bodleian Library MS Junius II) with its Anglo-Saxon verse poem *Christ and Satan*. The vertical composition in the Winchester Psalter is rare, but can be found in the thirteenth-century Blankenburg Psalter (Wolfenbüttel, Herzog-August-Bibliothek, Cod. Blank. 147), which suggests a wider dissemination of this idea across Europe.

M.M.

7 *Bible moralisée*

Paris, *c*.1230–40

Fols 116v–117r: opening of *The Apocalypse*

Manuscript on parchment, 395 × 275 mm; 153 leaves

Lit: Alexandre de Laborde, *La Bible moralisée conservée à Oxford, Paris et Londres; reproduction intégrale du manuscrit du XIIIe siècle accompagnée d'une notice*, 5 vols, 1911–27, pls 475–624 (description vol. 5, pp. 34–51); Robert Branner, *Manuscript Painting in Paris during the Reign of St Louis*, Berkeley 1977, pp. 49–57, 207; Peter Klein, 'The Apocalypse in Medieval Art', *The Apocalypse in the Middle Ages*, Richard K. Emmerson and Bernard McGinn (eds), Ithaca and London 1992, pp. 179–83, 192; Gerald B. Guest, *Bible moralisée. Codex Vindobonensis 2554. Vienna Österreichische Nationalbibliothek*, London 1995; R.M. Wright, *Art and Antichrist in Medieval Europe*, Manchester 1995, ch. 3, figs 20–4; H.-W. Stork, *The Bible of St Louis. Commentary to complete facsimile edition of Ms. 240 from the Pierpont Morgan Library, New York*, Graz 1996, pp. 12, 28, 40–1; Patricia Stirnemann, 'Note sur la Bible moralisée, en trois volumes, conservée à Oxford, Paris et Londres, et sur ses copies', *Scriptorium*, 53/2 (1998), forthcoming.

London, British Library Harley MS 1527

The *Bible moralisée* combines on the same page an excerpted biblical text, moralizing interpretations of that text, and images, which illustrate both the text and the interpretations. Paired openings of versos and rectos match, each with their other sides left blank. In the present copy eight roundels on each page contain the images, and the text is arranged next to the relevant roundel on its left, the biblical text coming first, and below it its interpretation.

Two earlier *Bibles moralisées* are both now in Vienna, one of which is in French and incomplete (O.N.B. Cod. 2554), and the other in Latin (O.N.B. Cod. 1179). These have been variously dated at some time between *c*.1215 and *c*.1230. There are also two other copies of the thirteenth century, both complete. One, datable *c*.1220s–30s and now in Toledo, is in three volumes, with eight leaves detached from the end now in the Pierpont Morgan Library, New York. The second is also in three volumes, one each in the Bodleian Library, Oxford, the Bibliothèque Nationale de France, and the British Library. The third volume is now bound in two parts, Harley 1526 and the present manuscript, Harley 1527.

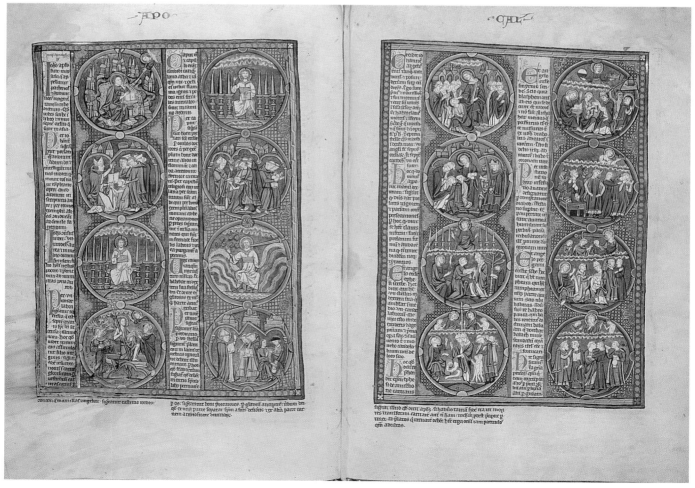

It is likely that these huge undertakings were under royal patronage, and two of them (Vienna, Cod. 1179 and Toledo/New York) contain royal portraits. As the dates of the bibles cannot be determined with exactitude, it is not possible to identify the kings shown with certainty: they could be Philip II (r. 1180–1223), his son Louis VIII (r. 1223–6) or his son Louis IX (St Louis, b. 1215, r. 1226–70). There is no evidence as to the original ownership of the other copies, but the present copy seems to have been in England perhaps as early as the thirteenth century, and the Harley volume contains the name of John Thwayte entered in the second half of the sixteenth century. Patrica Stirnemann has recently made the suggestion that the present copy might have been owned by Henry III, king of England.

The Apocalypse cycles have been said by Peter Klein to be based on the French Romanesque Family III cycles. It is however questionable whether any similarities are not as easily explicable in terms of their reliance on a common text. The illustrations of the moralizations after all can have no models, so must have been invented by the Parisian artists who worked in groups and used standard and repetitive conventions for figures, architecture, etc.

Folio 116v shows St John on Patmos and the visions of God with the Seven Candlesticks, the Sword and the Seven Stars (Rev. 1: 9–16). At the top left the interpretation tells us that 'By John are signified the prelates who hear the word of God.' At the bottom right we are told that by the sword is signified the word of the Lord which on the one hand separates the spirit from its desires, and on the other the flesh from the desire for wealth.

On f. 117r the texts are Revelation 1: 17–20 and 2: 1, 5, 8–10, 12–14. In the roundels John is seen falling at the feet of the Lord and then follows the writing of the letters to the Churches. There is a strong anti-Jewish aspect to the imagery in the bibles, exemplified in the second roundel on the right, which shows the Jews with their money bags. They are accused of avarice in the moralization. At the bottom right are three other kinds of sinners, including those corrupted by sexual sins and by greed.

J.J.G.A.

8 William Peraldus, *Summa de Vitiis*

London? after 1236, *c*.1250?

Manuscript on parchment, 278 × 172mm; leaves 27–71v

Fols 27v and 28r: *The Christian Knight*; image size 199 × 145mm

Lit: Morgan, 1, no. 80; Michael Evans, 'An Illustrated Fragment of Peraldus's Summa on Vice: Harleian MS 3244', *Journal of the Warburg and Courtauld Institutes*, xlv 1982, pp.14–68

London, British Library Harley MS 3244

This book appears to have been made for an unknown Dominican friar (depicted on f.27r) who had bound together various texts useful for preaching, including an illustrated bestiary. This diagrammatic double-page spread of the Christian Knight riding forth to combat the seven vices provides a visualization of ideas that came together from a number of disparate sources within medieval society. The somewhat gloomy title 'Militia est vita hominis super terram' (Armed struggle is the lot of man on earth) covers a whole range of concepts from secular and religious sources. Through a transference of ideas stemming from popular chivalric romances, Christ is identified as the bridegroom (the lover) of the Church (the lady), who battles to save her from the devil. For the Dominican preacher the Christian Knight emulates Christ. His armour takes on an emblematic significance which can be interpreted in a moralizing way, just as the commentaries on the Apocalypse did so with elements in the visualization of the text of St John. The explanations given through a reading of each part of the image act as signs leading to a greater signification as progressive images (or labels) are unravelled and related to each other.

Thus each of seven vices – *Superbia* (Pride), *Invidia* (Envy), *Ira* (Anger), *Accidia* (Sloth), *Avaricia* (Covetousness), *Gula* (Gluttony) and *Luxuria* (Self-indulgence) – is subdivided (giving a total of 69), and countered by virtues – *Pauperitas* (Poverty), *Mansuetudo* (Gentleness), *Luctus pro peccatis* (Struggle with Sin), *Esuries Iusticie* (Desire for Justice), *Misericordia* (Mercy), *Mundicia cordis* (Pureness of Heart) and *Pax* (Peace). Each part of the knight's armour and horse-trappings is also labelled with a virtue:

Helm: *spes futuri* (optimism)
Shield: *fides* (faith)
Lance: *perseverantia* (perseverance)
Reins: *discretio* (discrimination)
Saddle-cloth: *humilitas* (humility)
Spurs: *disciplina* (penance)
Horse-shoes: *delectatio* (delight), *consensus* (concord), *bonum opus* (good work), *consuetudo* (duty)
Hauberk: *caritas* (charity)
Sword: *verbum dei* (the word of God)
Pennant: *regni celestis desideriam* (desire for the Kingdom of Heaven)
Saddle *christiana religio* (Christianity)
Horse: *bona voluntas* (willingness)
Stirrups: *propositum boni operis* (good intentions)

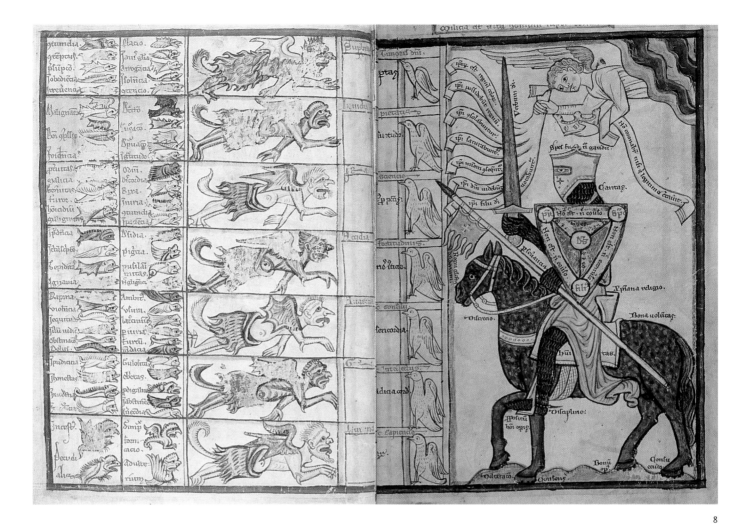

8

This is one of the earliest images of its type and others emerge only slightly later from independent sources. They would seem to have been influenced by ideas which derive from the endorsement of the crusades by writers such as St Bernard of Clairvaux and such books as Ramon Lull's *Libre qui és de l'orde de cavalleria* (c.1275), which lists twenty pieces of armour in a similar arrangement and was widely read in French. The necessity to engage in physical combat to preserve and maintain Christianity was particularly pertinent to many preachers during this period, as the Mongol hordes had reached Poland and defeated the

Teutonic Knights at Liegnitz in 1241. Evans has suggested that the design of this image may have originated with Matthew Paris, the great chronicler and artist who was a monk at St Albans (d. 1259; cat. 9), but the style of the miniatures and the patronage behind the book suggest London as the centre in which it was produced. Similar ideas of chivalry lie behind the image of a knight crowned by an angel added to the Westminster Psalter (London, British Library MS Royal 2.A XXII), almost certainly made in London in the middle of the thirteenth century.
M.M.

9 *Liber Additamentorum* (Book of Additions) of Matthew Paris of St Albans

St Albans, 1250–9

Manuscript on parchment, 350 × 235mm; 202 leaves

Fol.156: *The Apocalyptic Christ* by Brother William (Rev. 1)

Lit: H. Luard, *Matthew Paris. Chronica Maiora*, 6 vols, Rolls Series, London 1882, 6, p.515; A.G. Little, 'Brother William of England, Companion of St Francis, and some Franciscan drawings in Matthew Paris manuscripts', *Collectanea Franciscana*, A.G. Little, M.R. James and H.M. Bannister (eds), Aberdeen 1914, pp.1–8; A.G. Little, *Franciscan History and Legend in English Medieval Art*, Manchester 1937, p.38, Ch. IV pl.1; Morgan vol. 1, no. 87b; S. Lewis, *The Art of Matthew Paris in the Chronica Majora*, Cambridge 1987, pp.64–5 and 467.

London, British Library Cotton MS Nero D.I.

The Book of Additions (*Liber Additamentorum*) made by Matthew Paris, the Benedictine monk of St Albans, to his Chronicles is one of the most remarkable illuminated manuscripts to have survived from the Middle Ages. It is important for its marginal miniatures by Matthew himself, its armorial (the earliest illuminated roll of arms to have survived) and its exceptional miniatures. These include a cycle of the lives of the Offas (kings of England), which was finished by a court artist in the fourteenth century, his painting of Henry III's elephant, a gift from St Louis (IX) of France, and the added full-page miniature of the Apocalyptic Christ.

Matthew's origins are obscure, but he counted kings, princes, dukes and duchesses as his friends. He was held in high regard internationally, and was invited to Norway by King Haakon to help with the reform of the Benedictine order. But Matthew did not execute the miniature of the Apocalyptic Christ. He tells us in an inscription at the top right-hand corner of the miniature:

> *Hoc opus fecit frater Willelmus de ordine minorum socius beati francisci* [sic], *secundus in ordine ipso, conversacione sanctus, natione anglicus* [This is the work of Brother William of the order of Minors, companion of St Francis, second in that order, holy in conversation, English by birth].

This indicates that this exceptional miniature was illuminated by the brother William whom Matthew had depicted twice in his *Chronica Majora* (Cambridge, Corpus Christi College MS 16 ff.26 and 67) in his Franciscan habit – taking care to show his bare feet and knotted tunic.

The miniature displayed is of particular importance because of the associations of the Apocalypse with the establishment of the mendicant orders. As Freyhan has pointed out, the writings of Joachim of Fiore were widely read during this period and predicted the coming of the Antichrist perhaps in 1260. Matthew saw Frederick II of

9

Hohenstaufen as 'the devil's herald, the vicar of Satan, the forerunner of Antichrist… drunken with the blood of the saints'. For many at this time the Franciscans were the witnesses of the Apocalypse themselves; at Assisi scenes from the Apocalypse were chosen when the west end of St Francis's church was decorated, while the Franciscan brother Alexander of Bremen started writing his illustrated commentary on the Apocalypse as early as *c.*1240 (cat. 14). The image of the Apocalyptic Man is based on the opening texts of the Apocalypse where John states:

> …And being turned I saw seven golden candlesticks. And in the midst of the seven candlesticks one like unto the Son of Man, clothed with a garment down to the foot and girt about the paps with a golden girdle… and out of his mouth went a sharp two-edged sword…[Rev. 1: 12–16]

The visionary nature of this image and its direct contact with St Francis through his *socius* (companion) William is further underlined by the unique inscription on the back of the thin, almost translucent page. At the top of the page a prayer of St Edmund of Abingdon, archbishop of Canterbury (d. 1240, canonized in 1246), to St John the Evangelist shows through and disturbs the design of the miniature. In red, on the right-hand side of Christ's leg, we are instructed as much as informed:

> Nichil Amplius scribatur in hac pagina ne deterioretur ymago, quia percamenum diaphonum est, et melius videri potest si opponatur luci [Nothing more is to be written on this page lest the image be injured, since the parchment is transparent, and it can be seen better if held up to the light].

This appears to have been written after the rest of the page had been cleaned with a pumice stone. A number of faded notes can be seen under ultra-violet light and there is evidence to suggest that the seated man at the foot of the page may have related to some lost text. Moreover, examination of the Apocalyptic Christ under ultra-violet light reveals the diminutive figure of a supplicant at his feet, who is indeed visible if the page is held up to the light. Executed in the distinctive style of Matthew Paris himself, it is now hidden by an inscription in red ink. Little (1937) first recognized that 'the outline of a small kneeling figure, no doubt St John' could be detected, but the inscription (not recorded by Luard or Lewis) refers to a woman:

> Hec [autem] mulier antea Marcella vocabatur, que omnibus relictis sicut apostoli, christi in terra predicantis vestigia sequebatur iugiter ['iugiter' is marked for insertion before 'sequebatur' in the manuscript] [(Now) this woman was formerly called Marcella, having left all things behind like the apostles, constantly followed the footsteps of Christ's teaching on earth].

It is unclear if the erased figure is that of a woman or the more normal iconography of St John. Long hair can be detected in ultra-violet light, but he is often shown in this way, although the hands, just visible to the naked eye, suggest quite a delicate form. No other image of a supplicant woman before an apocalyptic image of Christ has survived from the Middle Ages, and it seems extraordinary that her image should be erased to make way for an inscription telling us of her presence. The praying figure may well be St John, as Little (who first read the inscription) suggested. It may be that the instruction to hold the page up to the light was made in the knowledge that the figure would be clearer if this were done. The three red lines marked before the start of the inscription suggest that the artist had copied it from elsewhere, and it is also clear that the sheet is an addition which he had to cut down to fit into the *Liber Additamentorum*. Marcella's identity remains a mystery. Little (1914) noted that she is referred to again on the reverse of the miniature in a longer inscription, and assumed that she was the Martella who is referred to in the *Golden Legend* as a servant of St Martha and who wrote her life.
M.M.

10 Trinity College Apocalypse

Abbreviated Apocalypse with extracts from the commentary of Berengaudus in Anglo-Norman French

London? *c*.1255–60

Manuscript on parchment, 430 × 304mm; 1+32 leaves

Fol. 2r: *St John Banished to Patmos; the Sea Journey to Patmos*

Fol. 24v: *The Last Judgement* (Rev. 20: 11–15)

Fol. 25v: *Heavenly Jerusalem* (Rev. 21: 10–27)

Lit: P.H. Brieger, *The Trinity College Apocalypse*, London 1967 (facsimile); G. Henderson, 'Studies in English Manuscript Illumination I, II and III', *Journal of the Warburg and Courtauld Institutes*, XXX 1967, pp.1–104, 104–37; XXXI 1968, pp.103–47; Morgan 2, no.110; S. Lewis, *Reading Images. Narrative Discourse and Reception in the Thirteenth-Century Illuminated Apocalypse*, Cambridge 1995, p.340, no.2 and *passim*

Cambridge Trinity College MS R 16 2

This is one of the most lavish of all thirteenth-century illuminated Apocalypses, with three pages of prefatory and eight pages of concluding scenes from the life of St John the Evangelist (the author of the Apocalypse) and seventy-one fully painted miniatures illustrating the text. These are placed in the text (not at the top of each page; cat. 11) and

10, Fol. 2r

10, Fol. 24v

vary in size – an almost unique format in the thirteenth century; it is, however, commonly found in fourteenth-century French prose texts such as BL Add. MS 38842 (cat. 16), and was generally used for the later copies of the Beatus Commentary such as the Rylands Manuscript (cat. 5). Because of its unusual format, disparate iconographical sources and early date, the Trinity Apocalypse has been seen by some authors as the model from which nearly all other thirteenth-century English Apocalypses derive their formats. Morgan has convincingly argued that this is probably not the case.

It has been suggested, for several reasons, that it was made for Eleanor of Provence, wife of Henry III. A female patron depicted in a number of the miniatures could certainly be the queen, and a number of the miniatures appear to be uniquely related to the tradition of the Spanish Beatus Commentary on the Apocalypse, a copy of which she could have brought to England. This is a plausible hypothesis, but it is no stronger than van der Meer's suggestion that the branches of the tree on the New Jerusalem page suggest the monogram 'E' of the queen's name. Such monograms were used in the period of Richard II at the end of the fourteenth century, but are not appropriate to the interpretation of a thirteenth-century manuscript. What is more certain is that a female patron owned the manuscript and that she was of high social rank. Indeed, there is nothing known of the early history of the book until it was given by Anne Sadleir, daughter of Chief Justice Edward Coke and wife of Ralf Sadleir of Standon (Herts), to

Ralph Brownrig, bishop of Exeter (1592–1659), on 20 August 1649. She instructed him to pass it on to Trinity College, Cambridge, where it arrived in 1660.

In common with both M.R. James's so-called 'first' and 'second family' of Apocalypse recensions (based on their iconography), the Trinity Apocalypse displays an elaborate series of illustrations placed at the beginning and end of the text telling the story of St John's preaching mission (see cats 12, 13 and 18). The scene displayed shows the emperor Domitian exiling St John to the Aegean island of Patmos (f.2). It is on this island that John has his vision, called the *Apocálypsis* (revelation or discovery) in the original Greek. The idea that John's vision was in fact a dream and that dreams could reveal hidden meanings is a common one in Late Antique and medieval culture.

The four artists of the Apocalypse have been studied in detail by Henderson and Morgan and appear to be working c.1255 in courtly circles, but their work also resembles that in books associated with southern England such as the Evesham Psalter (London, British Library Add. MS 44874) and the Amesbury Psalter (Oxford, All Souls MS 6). The New Jerusalem page is the sole example painted by the third artist who, like the fourth, shows a full awareness of the new French style of angular flat folds which has become known as the broad-fold style. His use of the bird's-eye-view format for the city, combined with the inclusion of the names of tribes of Israel and those of the apostles written over the gates and on the stones of the city, is common in the Beatus tradition, but is not used in other English Apocalypses despite the fact that it follows the text of the Apocalypse quite closely:

> …a wall great and high, and had twelve gates, and at the gates twelve angels, and names written thereon, which are the names of the twelve tribes of the children of Israel…
> And the wall of the city had twelve foundations, and in them the names of the twelve apostles of the lamb [Rev. 21: 12–14].

The magnificent Last Judgement page, which precedes this, is also of particular interest as it shows a composition familiar from English wall-paintings, which have not survived in anywhere near as good a condition as this miniature. The text illustrated is not that which was chosen for the commentary (Rev. 20: 7–10), but the one immediately after:

> And I saw the dead, small and great, stand before God; and the books were opened: and another book was opened, which is the book of life: and the dead were judged out of those things which were written in the books, according to their works [Rev. 20: 12].

The iconography of the Last Judgement in medieval art is based on this last text. It also serves as a reminder that books of life were commonly kept in Benedictine monasteries. Christ sits on his throne in the centre flanked by angels on the left carrying the instruments of the Passion. On the right

cumegez. eas honuridei. eas formaturs. e as uein
maurs. eas idolatres. e as truz menturs. lur partie
serra en le estaunk ardaunt de fu e de sufre. la que
le est la secunde more.

e plꝰ dutent le curs des houmes. ke de deu. eil purrunt aider a ceus plus apse. e deliurer de pil. e en treisaunt sofrent
ceus innocens cheir en gꝛt damage. e akeuns donet tortenus iugemens pur pour des houmes. e pur paer les. ceste
pour est male. Mescraius ne mie gius e paens solement. mes cristiens kine creient pas a la dreiture de deu. Ples escu
meges poum entendre. ceus ki sunt si sens hunte. ke il ne put point de hunte fere escumeges choses deuaunt gent.
Homicides il apelet ceus ki tuꝰvent houmes. e ceus ki portent haine en lur quoꝛl. Autres maneres sut de forniscatiuns.
En tutes les maneres ke houme fer le desir de lur char sauns sa femme espuse. ceo est apele fornicatiun. Cil i a forni
catiũ de pensee. Venimaurs sut ceus ki tuꝰuent la gent pueni. e ceus ki semient descord entre freres. Idolatres sunt cei
ki aurent ydles. e les autres ausi. Mensunges sut akeuns ki sunt nuũbres entre legers pecches. Nul menturs suuent p
qꝺaunte. e paruesure. ene en mi p malice. il ne dist pas de ceus mensunges. Autres mensunges sut ki sut mortaus. si tu
mesunge. de desleaute. e de blasfemie. eki uenent de haine. e de enuie. e de auarice. e deuente glorie. E sachez ke se
tur iohan dist. deus est uerite. enule rꝛe ne est si cuntraie a uerite cũ mensunge. Dunt la paie des menturs serra en les
taunk de fu e de sufre. Dunt la misericoꝛde de deu nus garde p sa pite. ki uit en regne en secle de secles amen.

Il i ad bone pour. de ki li saumistre dist. Li seurt pour
de nostre seignur pmeint en seele de seele. E males pour
sunt. De ceste male pour dirrai. Akeuns sut as queus
deu a done science des leis temporeles. ki sut nul iuge
ment ki ueient akeuns estre trauaile a toꝛt de puisauns.

the naked souls of the dead given up out of the sea and those delivered from purgatory in hell come forward. The book of life can be clearly seen in the hands of the naked souls on the upper right. Below a gaping hell mouth consumes the damned, while at 'God's right hand' five figures are introduced by St Peter. This is of particular interest as they clearly represent the laity (a youth), the Benedictine order (a monk and a nun) and the mendicant orders (a Franciscan and a Dominican friar), in that order. This suggests a favouritism for the preaching orders which was almost certainly deliberate, as they were commonly held to be the heralds of the second coming of Christ and the Last Judgement during the thirteenth century.

M.M.

II Apocalypse in Latin with extracts from the commentary of Berengaudus

London, c.1260

Manuscript on parchment, 109 × 161mm; 38 leaves

Fols 7v–8r: *The Second Seal. The Red Horse* (Rev. 6: 3–4) and *The Third Seal. The Black Horse* (Rev. 6: 5–6)

Lit: P. Brieger and P. Verdier (eds), *Art and the Courts. France and England 1259–1328*, 2 vols, Ottawa 1972, no. 20; Morgan, vol 2, pp.385–6, no. 67S; P. Klein, *Apokalypse Ms Douce 180 der Bodleian Library, Oxford. Codices Selecti. Phototypice impressi. Facsimile vol. LXXII. Commentarium vol. LXXII,*Graz 1983, pp.65–70; Lewis, *Reading Images*, p.341, no.4, and *passim*

London, British Library Additional MS 35166

A sister manuscript to the Dyson Perrins Apocalypse (now Los Angeles, J. Paul Getty Museum, MS Ludwig III.I.83.MC.72), it follows the iconographical cycle found in the so-called 'Westminster group' of Apocalypses studied by Klein, some of which were made for royal patrons such as the Douce Apocalypse (Oxford, Bodleian Library Douce MS 180). The design of these books, with illustrations taking up the upper part of each page (both recto and verso), and text and commentary beneath, exemplifies the demand for picture books with explanatory texts from courtly patrons.

The tinted drawing effect of the seventy-six miniatures (which include scenes from the life of St John the Evangelist), set against unpainted parchment at the top of each page, may have suggested antiquity and thus authority to English patrons, as such effects were common in Anglo-Saxon manuscript illumination. This technique also allowed artists to complete large numbers of illustrations without the painstaking layering of colours necessary for fully painted images. The drapery and figure style employed by this artist may be compared with courtly manuscripts such as the *Histoire de Saint Aedward le Rei* (Cambridge University Library MS Ee 3. 59) and the *Flores Historiarum* Manuscript of Matthew Paris (formerly Manchester, Chetham's Library MS 6712, now British Library Loan MS), which was finished probably by Westminster artists c.1265.

St John stands both inside and outside the main scenes of the Apocalypse observing and being guided through the 'revelations' by various intermediaries, in a sequence that is uncannily like that of Dante being guided through the underworld. Revelation 6 relates the story of the opening of the seven seals. Each seal is opened by the Lamb, but it is the

four beasts, who were earlier referred to in Revelation 4: 6–8, who call to St John, 'Come and see.' These beasts gained a symbolic meaning so that each had the signification of an evangelist: the Lion (St Mark), the Calf (St Luke), the Winged Man/Angel (St Matthew) and the Eagle (St John), a reading based on the typological interpretation of the vision of Ezekiel (Ezk. 1: 10), who also describes the same beasts. The second seal releases the Rider on the Red Horse:

> And when he had opened the second seal, I heard the second beast say, Come and see. And there went out another horse that was red and power was given to him that sat thereon to take peace from the earth, and that they should kill one another: and there was given unto him a great sword.

The third seal releases the rider on the White Horse:

> And when he had opened the third seal, I heard the third beast say, Come and see. And I beheld, and lo a Black horse; and he that sat on him had a pair of balances in his hand [Rev. 6: 3–6].

M.M.

12 The Abingdon Apocalypse

Apocalypse in Latin with extracts from the commentary of Berengaudus in French.

London? before 1262 and c.1270–80

Manuscript on parchment, 330 × 215mm; 85 leaves

Fols 17v–18r: *The Angels holding the Winds* (Rev. 7: 1); image size 116 × 144mm

Lit: Morgan vol. 2, no. 127; S. Lewis, 'Giles de Bridport and the Abingdon Apocalypse', *England in the Thirteenth Century. Proceedings of the 1984 Harlaxton Symposium*, ed. W.M. Ormrod, Nottingham 1984, pp.107–19; S. Lewis, 'Tractatus adversos Judaeos in the Gulbenkian Apocalypse', *Art Bulletin*, lxviii 1986, pp.543–66; *The Lambeth Apocalypse MS 209 in Lambeth Palace Library*. A Critical Study by Nigel Morgan with a contribution on the Palaeography by Michelle Brown, London 1990, esp. pp.25–37 and 39–43; S. Lewis, *Reading Images*, p.341 no. 5 and *passim*

London, British Library Additional MS 42555

Despite its unfinished state, the Abingdon Apocalypse holds a key position in the history of English art. Like its sister manuscripts the Gulbenkian Apocalypse (Lisbon, Museu

Calouste Gulbenkian MS L.A.139) and the Lambeth Apocalypse (Lambeth Palace Library MS 209), it belongs iconographically to the so-called 'Metz group' (a mid-thirteenth-century English Apocalypse formerly at Metz, Bibliothèque Municipale Salis 38 [olim 1184], destroyed by bombing in 1944). The complex images visualize extracts from a French translation of the Berengaudus commentary on the Apocalypse (see cat. 2) which reflect the contemporary interest in moralizations on a biblical text, as exemplified by the French royal *Bible moralisée* (see cat. 7). In the two images displayed, the angels holding the four winds at the four corners of the earth are compared with the unity of the holy Church and the four ancient kingdoms of Assyria, Persia, Macedonia and Rome. Each kingdom is visualized as a walled city with a bishop, signifying spiritual authority, at an altar and a king seated in his palace exercising temporal power. Rome takes pride of place on the right (the pope as bishop of Rome is signified by his triangular mitre). By the four angels the commentary directs the reader to understand that Rome alone could appropriate the power of the four kingdoms.

The technique of painting is of huge importance for establishing the background for the precocious experiments in plastic form in English painting on the famous Westminster Retable (Westminster Abbey, *c*.1270?). Indeed, so advanced is the system of grading tones using white paint mixed with deep colours that, before the emergence of the Abingdon Apocalypse from obscurity, scholars were convinced that the Gulbenkian Apocalypse was retouched in Italy in the fourteenth century.

A fourteenth-century inscription suggests that it was bequeathed to Abingdon Abbey by Giles de Bridport, bishop of Salisbury (d. 1262), and that it was then lent to Joan, queen of Scotland, in the year of her death, 1362, no doubt because its commentary is in Anglo-Norman French and it could be easily read by her. Morgan has convincingly argued that it should not antedate the Gulbenkian Apocalypse, despite the iconographical arguments put forward by Lewis. A more convincing analysis of the evidence might be that it was written for Giles de Bridport before 1262, but left with only its pen-flourishing largely complete at his death. It was then partly completed in the 1270s by the artists of the Gulbenkian/Lambeth group. This is supported by the fact that the pen-flourishing appears to have been completed before the illumination throughout the book.

M.M.

13 The Burckhardt-Wildt Apocalypse

Single leaves cut from an Apocalypse with extracts from the commentary of Berengaudus in Latin and French

Lorraine, *c*.1280–90

Manuscript on parchment, full-page miniatures *c*.200 × 140mm; cuttings from the Apocalypse *c*.105 × 145mm (five large and twelve small cuttings)

Lot 31: Three allegorical miniatures of the *Bride of Christ*; Lot 32: *The Tree of Virtues and the Tree of Vices*; Lot 33r: *St John on Patmos woken by the Angel* (Rev. 1: 1–3); Lot 34r: *The Vision of Christ and the Candlesticks*; Lot 35v: *St John weeping* (Rev. 5: 1–5); Lot 40r: *The Angels holding the Winds* (Rev. 7: 1–8); Lot 42r: *The Incense cast on the Earth and the First Trumpet* (Rev. 8: 5–7); Lot 57v: *The Second Angel and the Fall of Babylon* (Rev. 14: 8)

Lit: Sotheby's sale catalogue, London, 25 April 1983, lots 31–5, 40, 42, 57 and 68; N.J. Morgan, The Burckhardt-Wildt Apocalypse, *Art At Auction*, 1982–3, p.168; P.M. de Winter, 'Visions of the Apocalypse in Medieval England and France', *Bulletin of the Cleveland Museum of Art*, lxx 1983, pp.396–417; G. Henderson, 'The manuscript model of the Angers Apocalypse tapestries', *Burlington Magazine*, cxxvii 1985, pp.209–18; R. Emmerson and S. Lewis, 'Census and bibliography of manuscripts containing Apocalypse illustrations *c*.800–1500, II, Anglo-French Apocalypses', *Traditio*, 41 1985, pp.370–409, no.38; M. Camille, '"Him whom you have already desired you may see." Christian Exegesis and the Prefatory Pictures in a French Apocalypse', in *Studies in Cistercian Art and Architecture*, ed. M.P. Lillich,

13, Lot 31a

13, Lot 31b

13, Lot 31c

13, Lot 32a

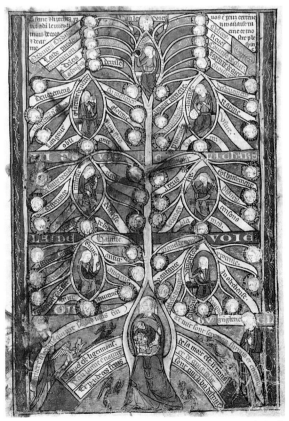

13, Lot 32b

13, Lot 33r

13, Lot 34r

13, Lot 35v

13, Lot 40r

Kalamazoo, Mich., 1987, pp.137–60; Jeffrey F. Hamburger, *The Rothschild Canticles. Art and Mysticism in Flanders and the Rhineland c.1300*, New Haven and London 1990, pp.49–50; R.S. Wieck, '"Folia Fugitiva", The pursuit of the illuminated manuscript leaf', *Journal of the Walters Art Gallery*, LIV 1996, p.237; *The Beck Collection of Illuminated Manuscripts*, Sotheby's sale, 16 June 1997, Lot 15; New York, Pierpont Morgan Library, 28 January–2 May, *The Wormsley Library, a Personal Selection by Sir Paul Getty, KBE*, ed. H. George Fletcher, London 1999, no. 7

Wormsley (Oxfordshire), Collection of Sir Paul Getty, KBE

The dismembered manuscript to which these cuttings once belonged appears to have entered the collection of Peter Birmann, a Swiss art dealer, after the French Revolution. He seems to have cut off the text and sold it as an album to Daniel Burckhardt-Wildt of Basel in 1796. It remained in that family until it was sold in part lots by Sotheby's in 1983. Many of the great museums and libraries of the world now possess cuttings from this manuscript, but none is as

important to the study of the use and purpose of the Apocalypses as those in the Wormsley Library.

Iconographically these miniatures belong to the so-called 'Metz group' (see above, cat. 12), also known more loosely as the 'second family'. Although originally sold as English, both Morgan and de Winter have re-attributed the cuttings on stylistic grounds to the Lorraine, and have pointed out a close iconographical and textual relationship with two other thirteenth-century Apocalypses (London, British Library Add. MS 22493 and Florence, Biblioteca Laurentiana MS Ashburnham 415). Henderson has convincingly demonstrated that they provide a possible model for the Angers Apocalypse tapestries ordered by Duke Louis I of Anjou *c.*1376–81.

The full-page miniatures appear to have formed a prefatory cycle which provided the reader with an allegorical introduction to the Apocalypse based on St

Bernard's commentary on the Song of Songs, where the Sponsa (bride) symbolizes an ungendered 'soul' and the Sponsus (bridegroom) Christ the Redeemer. In the first miniature, framed by passages from the Book of Lamentations, the sinful Sponsa lies in a bed of pestilence tormented by devils who take relish in writing on a scroll behind her the reasons for her torment : 'thou art unmindful and have forgotten God that formed thee'. Christ appears at the doorway standing, like St John in the Apocalypse, outside her locked chamber with the host in his hand, quoting a chorus from the Song of Songs as his breath falls on her exposed chest. Quotes from the Psalms frame and run across the second miniature as the Sponsa, now garlanded for her wedding, is pulled through the open doors of her chamber by Christ in a gesture derived from the Harrowing of Hell iconography (see cat. 1). She is seen in the next scene seated on a mound of earth, smiling in ecstasy as Christ appears to her, birds sing and an angel makes music.

The two trees that follow, one of Virtue and one of Vice, originate in the visualization of a parable in Matthew 7: 16–20; they are commonly found in twelfth-century theological works, but became a popular means of decorating psalters and books of hours for lay use by the early fourteenth century. The message is simple but clear: virtue is rooted in Humility and, in this case, vice in Pride (symbolized by the disc of a man falling from his horse which she holds). The woman seated on the ground (*Humus*) in ecstasy is based on the image of Humility (*Humilitas*) in the Tree of Virtues page. She should be compared with later representations of the Virgin of Humility which exploit this motif in devotional imagery, particularly in books of hours from the region of the Lorraine and diocese of Metz in the fourteenth century. The inclusion of miniatures using redemptory themes in this way can be paralleled with the thirteenth-century Lambeth Apocalypse (London, Lambeth Palace MS 209), but they are in some ways closer in spirit to the elaborate eschatological illustrated tracts included in the

Wellcome Apocalypse of the fifteenth century (cat. 20). It suggests a culture of lay devotional practice based on a much more conceptual level than just a simple relationship between words and images might imply.
M.M.

14 Friar Alexander, Commentary on the Apocalypse

Saxony, second half of the thirteenth century

Manuscript on parchment, 248 x174mm; 205 leaves

Fol. 74v: *The Seventh Trumpet* (Rev. 11: 15–17). Preachers preaching the story of Dives and Lazarus to the people of England

Lit: J.P. Gilson, 'Friar Alexander and his historical interpretation of the Apocalypse', *Collectanea Franciscana*, ii, 1922, ed. C.L. Kingsford *et al.*, p.20; M. Huggler, 'Der Bilderkreis in den Handschriften der Alexander Apokalypse', *Antonianum*, ix, Rome 1934, pp.85–150 and 269-308; *Monumenta Germaniae historica. Die deutschen Geschichtsquellen des Mittelalters, 500–1500. Quellen zur Geistesgeschichte des Mittelalters*, vol. 1, Alexander Minorita Expositio in Apocalypsim, ed. Alois Wachtel, Weimar 1955, p.258; C.M.Kauffmann, *An Altar-Piece of the Apocalypse from Meister Bertram's Workshop in Hamburg*, London 1968, pp.14–26

Cambridge University Library MS Mm.V.31

Extraordinarily rich in imagery, this manuscript is one of three thirteenth-century illustrated copies of a Commentary on the Apocalypse written by Frater Alexander, a German Franciscan probably from the area of Bremen in Saxony (the other two are in Dresden, Staatliches Bibliothek MS A.117, and Wroclaw, University Library MS I.Q.19). He is depicted taking communion and writing in his habit in two prefatory miniatures in this manuscript (f. 1v). The Wroclaw manuscript states that he died in 1271, and he appears to

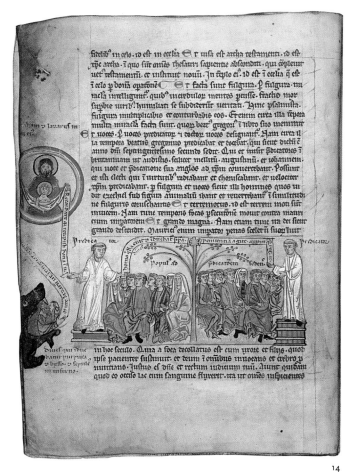

14

and is eclectic in his use of previous commentators and histories as source material of equal value. Pictorially, elements of the Beatus tradition can be found in the illustrations, notably the standing image of the Woman Clothed with the Sun and the Moon under her Feet (Rev. 12: 3–5; see cats 4, 16), but most of the imagery is unique to his commentary and reflects its idiosyncratic approach. The page illustrated demonstrates this. A long preamble about Pope Gregory the Great and his mission to the people of England through his representatives Sts Augustine and Mellitus, in the early seventh century, moves swiftly to a discussion of the struggles between the early Byzantine emperors Phocas and Maurice. The illustration is a fascinating piece of reportage depicting two preachers (labelled 'predicator', preacher), possibly to the English, apparently standing on plinths holding scrolls with the parts of a sermon based on the parable of Dives (literally 'rich man') and Lazarus inscribed on them ('indeed the man was Dives who wore purple silk'). A crowd of men and women seated below a central tree for shade are labelled 'Populus ad predicatorem sedens' (the people seated before the preachers). On the left the parable of Dives and Lazarus is depicted (Luke 16: 19–31): Lazarus the pauper is sent away from Dives the rich man's table; when he dies, Lazarus is taken up to Heaven by angels to rest in the lap of Abraham, but Dives is tormented in hell. His scroll forms part of a dialogue with Abraham. Dives asks for Lazarus to be sent to him with a little water, but the reply is sent back that he should remember the good things he received in his lifetime whereas Lazarus received only evil things when he was alive. This parable has all the elements one could hope for in preaching preparedness for the end of the world, and underlines the didactic nature of the Apocalypse text for the Franciscans.

Alexander's text also had considerable impact in Franciscan circles and was referred to widely by Nicholas of Lyra in his commentaries; several fourteenth-century copies have survived, illustrated outside Saxony. The often peculiar iconography of this Apocalypse is also reflected in panel painting from the area of Hamburg, as has been demonstrated by C.M. Kauffmann in his publication of the altarpiece of the Apocalypse from the workshop of Master Bertram in the Victoria and Albert Museum. This cycle, in turn, appears to have affected the planning of the wall-paintings of the Apocalypse in the chapter house at Westminster Abbey of the late fourteenth century.
M.M.

have compiled his work over a long period of time starting in the 1240s.

Frater Alexander almost certainly joined the Franciscans because he believed in the Joachimite prophecy that the world would come to an end in 1260 and that the friars, led by St Francis of Assisi (who had died in 1226 and was canonized in 1228), were the witnesses necessary to a process that would lead to the Second Coming. He follows the same lines of reasoning as Matthew Paris (see cat. 9) when he demonizes Frederick II (d. 1250) as Antichrist and identifies with the Moslem world many of the evils spoken of in the Apocalypse.

Unlike Berengaudus, Frater Alexander uses direct references to chronicles of world history to illustrate his text

15 'The Queen Mary Apocalypse'

Apocalypse with commentary in French prose

London, c.1310–25

Manuscript on parchment, 304 × 208mm; 45 leaves

Fols 13v–14r: *The Opening of the Seventh Seal* (Rev. 8: 1–7), image size: left 131 × 131mm, right 92 × 131mm

Lit: L. Delisle and P. Meyer, *L'Apocalypse en français au xiiie siècle (Bibliothèque Nationale MS fr 403)*, Paris 1901, pp.cccxi ff.; M.R. James, *The Apocalypse in Art, Schweich Lectures of the British Academy, 1927*, London 1931, no. 25, p.7; R. Freyhan, *Joachimism*, JWCI 1955, p.211; Sandler, no. 61 p.69; L. Dennison, 'The Apocalypse Royal MS 19.B.XV: a reassessment of its artistic context in early fourteenth-century English manuscript illumination', *British Library Journal*, 20, 1994, pp.35–54

London, British Library Additional MS Royal 19 B XV

This manuscript takes its name from an anonymous artist who worked on one of the most beautiful of all English early fourteenth-century illuminated manuscripts, the Queen Mary Psalter (London, British Library MS Royal 2 B VII, given to Queen Mary Tudor after being seized by a customs official in 1553). He collaborated with two other artists on this manuscript, at least one of whom worked on a book of hours made for a lady of the De Lisle family (New York, Pierpont Morgan Library MS G.50, c.1316–31). His flowing broadfold style underlines the close contacts between English and French art at this time, and an artist working in this style has been identified in a book probably illuminated in Paris (an Aristotle collection, Paris, Bibliothèque Nationale MS 17155).

The Apocalypse is written in a cursive book hand known as *Anglicana Formata*, in common with its slightly later sister manuscript, the Lincoln College Apocalypse (Oxford, Lincoln College MS 16). This type of hand had developed as a form of current handwriting for documents and records and became favoured for use with books that circulated in both scholarly and courtly circles, where a smaller script was required. It is easier to write than the formal gothic book hands and gives what must have seemed a more accessible page design, together with its use of French, the courtly vernacular at the time.

The images are partly in a continuous narrative illustrating the silence that comes over the earth at the opening of the seventh seal and the appearance of the angel who comes with a golden censer to the altar. The silence is likened in the text to the coming to rest of the souls of the martyred saints at the death of Antichrist. The angel signifies the incarnation of Christ (i.e. in his human form) and the golden censer (carefully gilded by the artist) the holy Church.

The next commentary is tinged with an avowed anti-semitism, which reminds us that the Jews were officially expelled from England by Edward I in 1290, not to return officially until the more enlightened days of the Commonwealth, when they were readmitted by Cromwell in accordance with the requirement that the Jews must be converted to fulfil the prophecy of Revelation. The hail and fire mingled with blood of the second image are likened to the evil words and great anger of the Jews who shed the blood of Christ and the saints.

M.M.

15

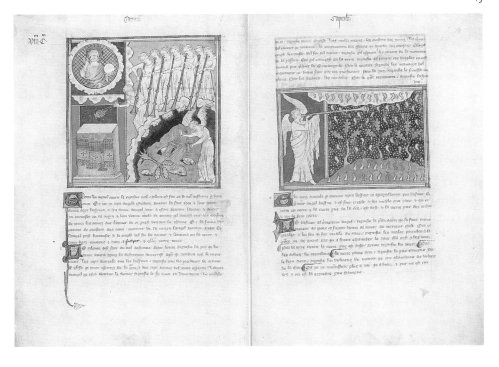

16

16 Apocalypse with Commentary in the French prose version

London? c.1325–30

Manuscript on parchment, 290 × 198mm; 8 leaves

Fols 3v–4r: *The Woman with the Child* (Rev. 12:3); *The Battle of the Angels* (Rev. 12:7) and *The Woman given the Wings of the Eagle* (Rev.12:14); image size c.134mm wide and between 55 and 65 mm high

Lit: M.R. James, *The Apocalypse in Art, Schweich Lectures of the British Academy, 1927*, London 1931, no. 72

London, British Library Additional MS 38842

The images displayed here describe a short narrative about the vision of the Woman Clothed with the Sun and the Moon under her Feet who gives birth to a child who is to rule all nations. A great red dragon with seven heads appears ready to devour him, but he is 'caught up unto God' and St Michael and the angels come to her aid. Each element of the scene is given a signification. The beast with seven heads is identified as the devil and the child is 'Christ born of the holy church which governs the people by firm Justice'. Thus the woman can be interpreted as an allegory of the Virgin as Ecclesia protecting and nurturing Christ. In the last scene she grows the wings of an eagle to escape the beast. These are given a signification encapsulating the typological purpose that

often lies behind this type of visualization, for they are 'the two testaments by which the holy Church teaches us'.

This fragment of an Apocalypse was illuminated by an important court artist who worked on the *Treatise on Good Government* given by Walter of Milemete to Edward III on his accession to the throne in 1327 (Oxford, Christ Church MS 92). His work can be found in a number of other luxury manuscripts which were probably made for patrons in London and East Anglia such as the All Souls Psalter (Oxford, All Souls MS 7) and the Bible in Dublin (Trinity College MS 35 [A.I.2]).

The French prose text of this Apocalypse is close to that of the 'Queen Mary Apocalypse' (cat. 15). Unlike the latter manuscript all the images were fully painted, often with gold backgrounds, making it a much more expensive book in terms of materials than its current appearance would indicate. The two-column format, with images varying in size depending on their position in the text, follows the tradition set by the much more lavish Trinity Apocalypse (cat. 10). This alternative type of design appears to have been thought particularly suited to French texts of the Apocalypse with Commentary. Such Apocalypse manuscripts were regarded in the same light as illuminated Romance manuscripts, whose design in two-column texts is often similar; such books were almost a necessary possession for any courtly lady.

M.M.

17 Apocalypse in Latin and French prose

Northern France, early fourteenth century

Manuscript on parchment, 326 × 224mm; 2+47+2 leaves

Fols 8v and 10r (f.9 miniature cut out, lower half of page visible only): *The Angels Holding the Four Winds* (Rev. 7: 1–8); *The Incense Cast on the Earth* (Rev. 8: 5); miniatures, c.146 × 180mm

Lit: F. Deuchler, J. M. Hoffeld and Helmut Nickel, *The Cloisters Apocalypse. An early fourteenth-century manuscript in facsimile*, Greenwich,Conn. 1971; P. Klein, *Apokalypse, Ms Douce 180 der Bodleian Library, Oxford. Codices Selecti phototypice impressi. Facsimile vol. LXXII. Commentarium vol. LXXII*, Graz 1983, p.67

London, British Library Additional MS 17333

This is one of a small group of exceptionally fine Apocalypse manuscripts produced in the first quarter of the fourteenth century, probably in north-western France, that ultimately derive their iconographical programmes from the lost English Apocalypse once in Metz (see cat. 12). The other three (Paris, Bibliothèque Nationale MS lat. 14410; New York, Metropolitan Museum of Art, Cloisters Treasury MS; Namur, Grand Séminaire MS 77) contain only the Latin text of the Apocalypse without the French translation provided in the London manuscript. Few British or American scholars had any idea where these manuscripts could have been made, and they were often called merely 'continental'. François Avril first suggested a connection between the closely related Paris, London and New York manuscripts with a Pontifical made for Guillaume Thiéville, bishop of Coutances in Normandy (Paris, Bibliothèque Nationale MS lat. 973).

Despite the dependence on an English Apocalypse cycle of the thirteenth century, the conception of the figures and scenes is completely different in this group of manuscripts. The heaviness and corporeality of the figures adds a tangibility to the fantastic nature of the scenes. In the London manuscript, the Angels with the Four Winds stand elegantly in a scene of calm and disinterested serenity. The angel with the incense, on the other hand, leans over in an atmospheric scene which gives the impression of a momentous and quite believable storm. The extremely careful execution and the elegant realism of the protagonists is made more beautiful by the delicate colours and extraordinarily fine harmony of unexpected tones.

The man and woman who commissioned the New York manuscript appear in a unique final miniature praying to the Virgin and Child and the man's patron. In the London manuscript two repeating armorials are placed in the initials at ff.11v, 12, 13, 14, 15, 16 and 16v. This also suggests that a husband and wife owned the London manuscript, as the shields are shown dimidiating each other (split in half within one shield) on three of these folios, indicating that a marriage had taken place. The heraldic devices have not led to any clear identification of the owners of these manuscripts, but they almost certainly came from the area of Normandy and showed considerable discernment in their choice of artist. M.M.

17, Fol. 8v

17, Fol. 10r

18

18 Picture-book Apocalypse with explanatory inscriptions from the commentary of Berengaudus

Northern France or Flanders, after c.1350

Manuscript on parchment, 265 × 200mm; 24 leaves

Fol. 6v: *The Incense cast on the Earth* (Rev. 8: 5); *The First Trumpet: the Rain of Fire on the Earth* (Rev. 8: 6–7); *The Second Trumpet: the Fire cast on the Sea* (Rev. 8: 8–9); *The Third Trumpet: the Burning Star falls from Heaven* (Rev. 8: 10–11)

Fol 7r: *The Fourth Trumpet: the Darkening of the Sun and the Moon; the Angel cries Woe* (Rev. 8: 12); *The Fifth Trumpet: the Locusts come up from the Pit* (Rev. 9: 3–4)

Lit: M. Delisle, *L'Apocalypse en français au XIIIe siècle*, Société des anciens textes français, 1901, p.lxxvii; M.R. James, *A Descriptive Catalogue of the Latin Manuscripts in the John Rylands Library at Manchester*, Manchester 1921, pp.57–8; M.R. James, *The Apocalypse in Art*, London 1931; J.J.G. Alexander, *Medieval Illuminators and their Methods of Work*, New Haven and London 1992, p.135

Manchester, John Rylands University Library MS Latin 19

Almost identical in format to the two surviving thirteenth-century English picture-book Apocalypses (New York, Pierpont Morgan Library MS M. 524 and Oxford, Bodleian Library Auct. MS D.IV.17), the ninety-six scenes which survive in this manuscript supply the iconography for the four missing in the latter and are very close to another copy of this cycle produced in Flanders in the fourteenth century (London, British Library Add. MS 38121). All of these manuscripts are, in turn, thought to derive their iconography, with characteristically elaborate extra-biblical Antichrist scenes and life of St John the Evangelist, from a lost English model that may date from before c.1250. M.R. James (following Leopold Delisle) christened this the 'first family' of English Apocalypses in his 'The Apocalypse in Art' lectures for the British Academy published in 1931. The thirteenth-century English Apocalypse owned by King Charles V of France (d. 1380), now in Paris (Bibliothèque Nationale MS fr. 403), derives its iconography from a picture-book Apocalypse in this group. This example serves to emphasize how important it is to remember that books from the thirteenth century could be admired because of their antiquity and association with a bygone age and used as models for inspiration in later centuries. Louis I of Anjou, brother of Charles V of France, directed the court artist Jean Bondol to use a thirteenth-century manuscript (see p.56) when he ordered him to design a set of Apocalypse tapestries which still survive at Angers Cathedral.

The artists of this manuscript have been described as

both French and Flemish, but no one has suggested any particular source for the confident and assured drawing style of the St John scenes (especially the Trial and Banishment of St John, fol.1v). These bear comparison with the work of the Parement de Narbonne Master, who worked for Charles V in the 1370s, about twenty years after this manuscript was illuminated. Nevertheless, in the emphasis on the eyes and in the accurate depiction of fashionable clothes there is, perhaps, an indication of a common origin for both of these artists, probably outside France.

The pages displayed here are executed by the second artist and depict a continuous narrative of scenes ranging from *The Incense Cast on the Earth* (Rev. 8: 5) to the sounding of the first five of the seven trumpets of the Apocalypse (Rev. 8: 6 to 9: 4) and their consequences. The labels form an integral part of the design of these miniatures, and the texts are carefully planned to act as a foil to the figures. Each angel is given a label with its signification ('Tertius Angelus prophetas significat', the third angel refers to the prophets; 'Quartus Angelus Christum et Apostolos significat', the fourth to Christ and the Apostles). These labels form a résumé of the fuller explanation of the scene from Berengaudus's commentary included on scrolls or in text blocks within the miniatures in red (the text of the Apocalypse is always in black). Thus, a mnemonic system of signs associated with images and texts can be postulated for these images. Their constant use must have eventually rendered the text unimportant so far as the interpretation of the scenes was concerned.

M.M.

19 Matfré Ermengaud, *Breviari d'Amour*

Catalonia (Gerona?), *c*.1400

Manuscript on parchment, 360 × 240 mm; 1 + 259 leaves

Fol. 40v: *The Nine Choirs of Angels adoring God*

Lit: P. Meyer, 'Matfré Ermengau of Béziers', *Histoire Littéraire de la France*, 32, 1898, pp.16–56; M.R. James, 'Catalan prose version of the Breviari d'Amour', *A Descriptive Catalogue of fourteen illuminated manuscripts in the library of Henry Yates Thompson*, vol. 4, Cambridge 1912, pp.1–22; H.Y. Thompson, *Illustrations from One Hundred Mss. in the Library of Henry Yates Thompson*, vol.7, London 1918, pp.11–12, pls 45–7; K. Laske-Fix, *Der Bildzyklus des Breviari d'Amor* (Münchner Kunsthistorische Abhandlungen, Bd. V), Munich 1973, p. 132

London, British Library Yates Thompson MS 31

Most of the little we know of Matfré Ermengaud is derived from his own works, principally the present poem. He was probably born about 1250 and is mentioned as still alive in the diocese of Béziers in 1322. He describes himself as a Franciscan in another poem which he presented to his sister.

19

The *Breviari* is a compendium of theology and natural science structured around a favourite medieval teaching diagram, the tree. The poem was written in Provençal between 1288 and 1292, and later translated into other vernaculars including Catalan, the language of the present prose version. Ermengaud seeks to demonstrate that God's love is the moving principle of the universe. Human virtues, especially love of one's neighbour, derive from this love. Its denial leads to the works of the devil and there are vivid representations of the vices and their consequences as well as of the Last Judgement. Matfré explains that he wrote at the request of troubadour poets desirous to know the origins of true love.

The illustrations, which are copied in most of the numerous surviving manuscripts of the text, were undoubtedly created under the close supervision of the author (see Laske-Fix). Rubrics in the text and inscriptions in the illustrations help to explain to the reader the often complex and unusual iconography. The image of the Nine Orders of Angels depends not on the well-known Pseudo-Denis text, but on Gregory the Great's Homilies on the Gospels (Bk II, ch. 34). It shows God at the centre above, flanked by Christ and the Virgin. The Nine Orders consist in the first hierarchy of Cherubim, Seraphim and Thrones (six angels in each division); in the second hierarchy of Dominions, Principalities and Powers (three angels in each division); and in the third hierarchy of Virtues, Archangels and Angels (three angels in each division). The texts which surround the images are *Sanctus, Sanctus, Sanctus* (Rev. 4: 8), *Gloria in excelsis* (Luke 19: 38), and *Salus Deo nostro qui sedet super thronum et agno*, 'And they [the great multitude] cried with a loud voice: salvation to our God who sitteth upon the throne, and to the Lamb. And all the angels stood round about the throne …' (Rev. 7: 10–11).
J.J.G.A.

20 Apocalypse with extracts from the commentary of Berengaudus and the *Glossa Ordinaria*, *Ars Moriendi*, Medical Tracts and Tables of Virtue and Vice

Germany, *c.*1420

Manuscript on parchment, 400 × 30mm; 69 leaves

Fols 12v–13r: Antichrist scenes

Lit: F. Saxl, 'A Spiritual Encyclopedia of the Later Middle Ages', *Journal of the Warburg and Courtauld Institutes*, v 1942, pp.82–134; G. Bing, 'The Apocalypse Block-Books and their Manuscript Models', *Journal of the Warburg and Courtauld Institutes*, v 1942, pp.143–58; S.A.J. Moorat, *Catalogue of the Western Manuscripts on Medicine and Science in the Wellcome Historical, Medical Library*, 1, London 1962, pp.32–7; R.K. Emmerson, *Antichrist in the Middle Ages. A study of medieval apocalypticism, art and literature*, Manchester 1981; A. Seebohm, *Apokalypse, Ars Moriendi, Medizinische Traktate, Tugend- und Lasterlehen. Die erbaulich-didaktische Sammelhandschrift London, Wellcome Institute for the History of Medicine, MS 49, Codices illuminati medii aevi*, 39, Munich 1995 (in English)

London, Wellcome Institute for the History of Medicine Library MS 49

This extraordinary manuscript was first studied together with its slightly later sister manuscript, Rome Casanatense Library MS Basil. A.V.23, by Friz Saxl in a seminal article published in 1942, supplemented by an article in the same journal on the Apocalypse itself by Gertrude Bing. The encyclopaedic nature of the compilation, combined with its juxtaposition of Apocalypse iconography with detailed gynaecological and medical illustrations and works on virtue and vice, makes it one of the most important sources for interpreting the ideology behind late medieval society. The fine condition of the text and images, as well as the contemporary white deerskin stamped binding, suggests that it was never intended to be used as a work-book, but was a luxury presentation piece to be handled with care. Its size indicates that it was intended to be read on a lectern and the text has passages which encourage the monastic life, suggesting that it was intended for a monastic library. It makes links between mortality, the functions of the body, childbirth, sinful behaviour and the Last Judgement both explicitly and implicitly by including advice on death, menstruation, drunkenness, the nature of prophecy, the ages of man and the physiology of men and women. All of this indicates that it was compiled as a book of almost 'secret' information that could be consulted by a privileged few. St John's Revelation (the Greek *Apokálypsis*) and its commentaries themselves represent eschatological 'secrets' which can be revealed to those who know how to interpret the text. The macrocosmic idea of creation leading to the end of the world at the Last Judgement is placed next to the

25 Book of Hours. Use of Rome

Ghent or Bruges, c.1500

Manuscript on parchment, 237 × 152 mm; ii + 237+ ii leaves

Fol.134v: *The Last Judgement with the Blessed above and the Damned below*

Lit: *Catalogue of Additions to the Manuscripts in the British Museum in the years 1894–99*, British Museum, London 1901, pp.253–4; G.F. Warner, *Reproductions from Illuminated Manuscripts. Series II*, London 1907, pl.36; F. Winkler, *Die flämische Buchmalerei des XV. und XVI. Jahrhunderts. Künstler und Werke von den Brüdern Van Eyck bis zu Simon Bening*, Leipzig 1925, reprinted Amsterdam 1978, pp.120, 127, 178, pl.75; O. Pächt, *The Master of Mary of Burgundy*, London 1948, p.59, n.39; G. Dogaer, *Flemish Miniature Painting in the 15th and 16th Centuries*, Amsterdam 1987, pp.164, 166, 177; *Renaissance Painting in Manuscripts. Treasures from the British Library*, ed. T. Kren, New York 1983, cat. 8

London, British Library Additional MS 35313

25

This richly illuminated Book of Hours (commonly referred to as the Rothschild Hours) was attributed by Friedrich Winkler to the Master of James IV of Scotland, now convincingly identified with Gerard Horenbout of Ghent (cf. cat. 23), and the Master of the Hortulus Animae, named after a manuscript in Vienna now believed to be illuminated by Simon Bening of Bruges. The miniatures by the second illuminator are mainly half-length figures of saints. Thomas Kren, however, considers them inferior to Bening's accepted work.

The scene of the Last Judgement, which introduces the Seven Penitential Psalms, shows the Lord as judge seated on a rainbow and surrounded by angels and the blessed in Paradise in a great circle in the sky. Below, the damned fall into the pit of hell. On the recto opposite, King David as author of the Psalms is shown kneeling in prayer.

Otto Pächt noted that among the miniatures by Horenbout, a number are close copies of compositions by the Master of Mary of Burgundy, the leading Netherlandish illuminator of the previous generation. Thus the miniature for the Office of the Dead (f.158v) shows a woman on horseback confronted by three skeletons, a variation on the theme of the Three Living and the Three Dead seen in the Berlin Hours of Mary of Burgundy. The Last Judgement too is based on a miniature by the Master to be found in the Hours of Engelbert of Nassau, where it similarly introduces the Seven Penitential Psalms (Oxford, Bodleian Library MS Douce 220, f.181v; J.J.G. Alexander, *The Master of Mary of Burgundy. A Book of Hours*, New York 1970). The Master of Mary of Burgundy used aerial perspective to suggest the numberless crowd of the blessed extending into the distance, in dramatic contrast with the vivid expressions of horror and pain and the contorted poses of the damned shown as if closer to us. This play-off between near and far, all represented in the tiny space of a miniature, is typical of the Master. The effect is somewhat weakened in the version by Horenbout, who, as Pächt observed, also lessens the spatial impact by flattening the rainbow and placing Christ frontally in the centre of the page.
J.J.G.A.

26 Prayer-book

Germany (perhaps Nuremberg?), early sixteenth century

Manuscript on parchment, 247 × 178mm; ii + 59 + ii leaves

Fols 48v–49r: *Kneeling female donor; St Michael fighting the Dragon*

Lit: Malcolm B. Parkes, *The Medieval Manuscripts of Keble College Oxford*, London 1979, pp.129–38

Oxford, Keble College MS 35

St Michael makes his first biblical appearance in the Old Testament, where he is a prince of the heavenly host and the special guardian and protector of Israel (Daniel 12: 1). In the Book of Revelation (12: 7–9) he is once again the principal fighter of the heavenly battle against the forces of evil: 'And there was a great battle in heaven, Michael and his angels fought with the dragon, and the dragon fought and his angels: And they prevailed not, neither was their place found any more in heaven. And that great dragon was cast out, that old serpent, who is called the devil and Satan, who seduceth the whole world; and he was cast unto the earth, and his angels were thrown down with him.'

Thus Michael was regarded from the time of the early Church as the helper of Christian armies against their heathen opponents, and as the protector of individual Christians against the devil, especially at the hour of death, when he conducts souls to God – a belief echoed in the traditional text of the Roman Mass for the Dead. Following apparitions of the archangel, pilgrims flocked to the shrines at Monte Gargano in southern Italy and at Mont Saint-Michel in Normandy. The medieval iconography of St

Michael consisted of two main scenes, with the saint shown either weighing souls or slaying the dragon.

The Keble College manuscript must post-date the publication in 1498 of Dürer's woodcut series for the *Apocalypse*, since the illuminator has clearly been inspired by elements of Dürer's treatment of the same subject (Ch. 4, cat. 16); St Michael and the angel with the bow and arrow have been copied in reverse, while the landscape below also reflects the artist's knowledge of Dürer's design.

On the opposite page is a prayer to St Michael in German, underneath which, in a foliate scroll, is an unidentified woman, presumably the patron of the book. She is shown kneeling, facing the image of the archangel, praying with the aid of her rosary. The German prayers in this manuscript (in an East Franconian dialect) and the pictures related to them are arranged on opposite sides of each opening, a surprisingly rare example of one method of linking together devotional texts and images. The female patron also appears (with an unidentified coat of arms) at the beginning of the book, meditating upon a miniature of the Trinity. The main series of prayers and pictures is based on incidents in the life of Christ. The wonderfully varied figures who inhabit the foliate scrolls beneath each text look at or gesture towards the images, and are often identifiable as biblical or traditional characters having some connection with the events shown. The prayers to St Michael come immediately after the christological sequence, which ends with the Last Judgement; they are followed by suffrages to St Margaret (who herself overcomes a dragon) and St Barbara.
M.R.K.

26

ulating on astrology as well as other natural and preternatural evidence. Making a new claim to authority in this enterprise required many Protestants to reconsider the nature of miraculous signs and the means for their verification. Were celestial events and preternatural phenomena to be treated alike? How were the insidious operations of the devil to be distinguished from those of legitimate origin? In a world of often unenforceable regulations governing publication, and in the absence of systematic means of scientific explanation, what should finally constitute sufficient testimony for confirming a miracle or separating a random act of nature from a consequential sign? In questioning these matters Protestant apocalypticism had some bearing on the development of the empirical method and what we now term the scientific revolution.[16]

The compulsion to prophesy on the basis of natural phenomena gradually ran counter to the emergence of Baconian science and new analytical approaches to historical evidence, developments fostered more often among Protestant intellectuals than among Catholics. Rational scepticism in the interpretation of nature and human events was as prevalent in the late sixteenth and the seventeenth centuries as was rampant eschatological speculation. It is tempting to see these coeval tendencies as a form of ideological schizophrenia dividing progressive modes of natural philosophy from reformed theology and outmoded superstition. But the situation was certainly more complex than that, especially in learned circles. The dictates of reason and manifest evidence of the irrational were in a constant state of tension.

Sixteenth-century religious polemic

The violent contest for souls provoked by the Reformation movement and the Catholic response led to the appropriation of imagery from Revelation for explicitly sectarian propaganda. On the Reformation side the earliest programmatic instance of this is the *Passional Christi und Antichristi*, a pamphlet fashioned by Cranach and his workshop and printed under Lutheran auspices in 1521 in both Latin (cat. 26) and German editions. Here thirteen pairings of woodcuts illustrate often ingenious parallels from the life of Christ and the legend of the Antichrist. For example, the 'Crowning of Thorns' appears paired with the 'Antichrist Crowned with the Papal Tiara', 'Christ Washing the Feet of the Apostles' with the 'Kings of the World Kissing the Feet of the Antichrist', the 'Tribute Money' with the 'Antichrist Issuing Indulgences', 'Christ's Entry to Jerusalem' with the 'Antichrist in Triumph', and finally the 'Ascension' with the 'Descent of the Antichrist into Hell'.

Although explicit references to the Antichrist in Scripture occur only in the first and second Epistle of St John, the legend had a lengthy history evolved in Jewish and Christian texts and mystery plays as well as in block-book and manuscript illustration (cats 1, 3; Ch. 3, cat. 20). The Antichrist legend appears to have had a distinctly popular appeal by the later Middle Ages. Accordingly,

Septima etas mūdi

Fig. 6. *Fall of Antichrist*, woodcut from the *Nuremberg Chronicle* (Nuremberg: Anton Koberger 1493), f. cclix (verso). London, British Museum.

the *Nuremberg Chronicle* of 1493 culminates its account of the sixth age of the world with a full-page woodcut of the *Fall of the Antichrist* alongside a brief summary of his story (fig. 6). This woodcut served as a direct source for the same episode in Cranach's *Passional* with the addition that here and throughout the *Passional* the figure of the Antichrist is portrayed in the garb of the pope, an association not made in the *Nuremberg Chronicle* but one that became common in the Reformation period. Somewhat later Luther composed his own tract on the Antichrist, a spectre that achieved so much currency in Catholic and Protestant diatribe that it gave some reformers cause for concern. Calvin was among them, and in his commentary on Genesis even Luther expressed the view that there was altogether too much talk of the Antichrist and too little of the true Saviour.[17]

To be sure anti-clerical satire was not a new phenomenon that came with the Reformation; lampooning the clergy had long been familiar terrain. If not exactly sanctioned by the Church in an official sense, it seems to have been regarded as benign or at the very least constructively directed to the reform of clerical abuses. Many a tonsured soul can be found roasting in hell in fifteenth-century panels of the Last Judgement. Now, however, as the venom of Protestant rhetoric began to escalate, the stakes were a great deal higher. The impulse behind Reformation satire of the clergy had become revolutionary rather than reform-minded, no longer the agitation of a loyal opposition but something that constituted a clear and present danger to Church authority. By pairing the pure life of Christ with the Antichrist, Cranach's *Passional* constructed a kind of profaned typology illustrating the corruption of sacred and secular power and prophesying the imminent fall of the Church of Rome. Accordingly the format of the *Passional* purposely mimics medieval typological cycles such as the *Biblia Pauperum* which juxtapose Old Testament types with the New Testament events they were deemed to foretell. The *Passional* is thus not only a blatant satire but a subtle parody of Church teachings and the Catholic tradition of biblical exegesis. In the *Passional* the complementary relationship between type and antetype represented in orthodox picture books is converted to a set of antitheses, a blunt dialectical contrast of good versus evil. The vernacular texts beneath the woodcuts are taken from the Bible and from papal decretals. They are brief and to the point. This simple perversion of a familiar format for explaining the prophetic nature of Scripture reveals a didactic ingenuity of unusual force and clarity.[18] Typical of later Protestant and Catholic broadsheets, the *Passional* makes its case in a 'show and tell' fashion that perhaps served as a point of reference for popular preachers and other religious agitators.

As is characteristic of polemic in general, the structure and the message of the *Passional* are declarative. Polemic typically contains no real argument and thus admits of no counter-argument. Declarations of this sort, whether they be framed in texts or in pictures, are neither interrogative nor likely to be persuasive about conditions of belief. Certainly they are bound to be even less persuasive about intricate theological matters. Although printing is widely credited with the rapid spread of Reformation ideas, and no doubt rightly so, the question remains whether polemical pamphlets and broadsheets were really instrumental in changing people's thinking. Since by its very nature polemic caricatures ideas and plays to the prior conviction of its audience rather than an inclination to be convinced, it serves mainly to articulate and reinforce existing discontents.[19] Suffice it to say that apocalyptic imagery proved ideal for preaching to the converted. Paradoxically Revelation, the most elusive and obscure text of Scripture, helped provide the foundation for a new mode of popular expression that required dogmatic clarity in order to be effective.

Luther's initial scepticism about Revelation involved not just its canonicity but its susceptibility to interpretation altogether. However, his view on these questions changed between 1522 and 1530 in the wake of the cataclysmic events of the Peasants' War in 1525 and the Sack of Rome in 1527. The peasants' uprising suddenly confronted Luther with the radical social implications inferred from his preachings. Two years later a large number of German mercenaries enlisted in the army of Charles V participated in the looting of Rome. They had seen the astonishing wealth of 'Babylon', consumed and destroyed it.[20] These experiences seemed to confirm the worst of Luther's fears and compelled him to rethink the application of Revelation to history. He recast his preface to acknowledge the topical relevance of the text and its usefulness for instructing the community of believers about the internal corruption of the Church and the external threats posed to it in the past and the present.

Luther's revised position on the authority of Revelation deemed the value of the text to be twofold. First, it gave comfort by assuring us of impending purification under the sword and the eventual triumph of true belief. Secondly, it gave warning of the assaults against the faith and those trials already endured to defend it. In his revised preface Luther assigns Revelation to the category of inspired dreams and visions visited upon holy people in earlier times, and he applies specific passages to the history of the Church and events to come.[21] Consistent with well-established tradition, Luther identifies particular historical references in the prophecies of the text. According to his interpretation, embedded in it are predictions of the Saracens, the subjugation of the empire to Mammon, the illegitimate adoption of temporal powers by the papacy, and finally the coming of false prophets in his own time. Many believed that the vision of St John even predicted Luther's role as the leading prophet of the new age. We cannot say whether Luther shifted his position on Revelation for purely

opportunistic reasons or because he decided in the interim that the urgency of John's prophecies had somehow become manifest and their historical accuracy thus confirmed. In either case he reopened the way for his followers to exploit it for immediate political and evangelical ends.

The paralleling of true and false beliefs that constitutes the polemical structure of the *Passional Christi und Antichristi* set the pattern for Matthias Gerung's images of the Antichrist (cats 62–3) and an additional series of allegorical woodcuts he made between 1544 and 1558 (cats 59–61).[22] Gerung's allegorical cycle illustrates a commentary on Revelation composed by Sebastian Meyer, a Protestant cleric active in Bern, and was carried out under the patronage of Ottheinrich of Neuburg who had formally embraced the Reformation in 1541. Although the meaning of Gerung's inventive woodcuts is often obscure, the cycle seems closely aligned with Luther's anti-Catholic views. Gerung's own religious allegiance is difficult to determine on the basis of these woodcuts, his other work, or what else we know of his life. Even for those such as Gerung who elsewhere engaged in outright religious and political diatribe it is often the case that an artist's particular confession of faith may not be reflected in his imagery or in the conviction of his patrons. Lucas Cranach himself continued to execute important commissions for Catholics during the period in which he was effectively Luther's 'in-house' artist.

This protean ability of an artist to move from one camp to another is all the more surprising given how entwined religious conviction and artistic patronage had become by the middle of the sixteenth century. It is useful to be reminded that artists were neither politicians nor theologians, but typically hired professionals who worked to contract in a proto-capitalist setting. Printing was as much a business as it was a means of propagating ideas and expressing deeply felt personal convictions. As we shall see, there are indeed cases in which artists betray a close personal identification with an apocalyptic theme. However, one must be cautious about drawing romantic conclusions regarding the private implications of an artist's religious work, even where it is sharply sectarian in content.

The increasingly virulent contest between Catholics and Protestants encouraged pictorial inventions that were often vulgar and grotesque but also humorous. This applies especially to *ad hominem* attacks, for example Hans Brosamer's 1529 anti-Protestant caricature of *Luther with Seven Heads* (cat. 99), and its later counterpart, the anonymous *Seven-Headed Calvinist Phantom* of 1619 (cat. 108). Among the most potent and disturbing pictorial satires to arise in this climate of hatred and fear is the *Allegory of Iconoclasm*, an etching attributed to Marcus Gheeraerts the Elder and known only in one example (fig. 7). Gheeraerts appears to have been a follower of the Calvinists who began preaching in the Netherlands during the 1560s. He fled his native Bruges for England two years after the iconoclastic outbreak there in 1566 and may have executed his bilious attack on Catholic abuses either in England or even prior to leaving the Continent.[23] The etching depicts the rotting head of a monk – identifiable by

Fig. 7. Marcus Gheeraerts the Elder, *Allegory of Iconoclasm*, etching. London, British Museum.

his habit and tonsure – emerging from a rocky landscape outcropping, infested with little figures who swarm over it like ants scavenging the flesh of a corpse. A diabolical mass is being conducted inside the gaping mouth, and on the pate sits a figure of the pope enthroned beneath a canopy with a wealth of indulgences pinned up on the staves. In the foreground Protestant iconoclasts are busy sweeping up bits of altarpieces, religious sculptures, sundry vanities and other church paraphernalia.

Presuming the attribution to Gheeraerts is correct, it would seem that here we do have a case in which personal conviction played a role in generating an image of exceptional potency. In retrospect the autobiographical implications of Gheeraerts's etching are striking. Outright hostility to religious images on the part of many reformers, especially Calvinists, had dire professional consequences for an artist. After all, much of the art made in this period was religious, and its systematic destruction not only obliterated a tradition but eroded commissions altogether. We can only speculate on how Gheeraerts might have responded to this aspect of the Calvinist campaign, although the print seems to portray dutiful iconoclasts sweeping up a field of Catholic abominations. Religious deviance could provoke severe legal responses under the Spanish regime governing much of the Netherlands, and the publication of Protestant propaganda was a serious offence. Gheeraerts seems not only to have promoted the decline of his own profession but placed himself at risk in doing so. None the less there are other documented cases of artists who subscribed to iconoclastic acts or were persecuted by the authorities merely for practising their beliefs.[24] With its charge of horror and ritual cleansing Gheeraerts's strange anthropomorphic landscape evokes the hyperbole of apocalyptic foreboding. The iconoclastic campaign that swept over the southern Netherlands in 1566 caused this to be termed 'het wonderjaar', an *annus mirabilis* of unprecedented violence and repression. No doubt for victims on both sides of the confessional divide the uprising portended a final reckoning with the Antichrist.

The personal crisis of Revelation

A striking departure from the evolving German tradition of printed Apocalypse illustration emerged in the publication of Jean Duvet's bizarre and extravagant cycle of engravings made between 1544 and 1555 (cats 64–81).[25] Duvet was by profession a goldsmith and a tapestry designer but was also adept at laying out fortifications, a range of expertise that led to his employment by the Catholic French court. On its publication in 1561 his *L'Apocalypse figurée* carried an imperial privilege, a sure sign that it was not considered by official censors to conceal any recognizable Protestant infections. Furthermore, the French version of the text of Revelation accompanying Duvet's engravings has never been identified as either Catholic or Protestant in origin. Finally, the sundry pictorial sources on which Duvet drew for his eclectic illustrations include both orthodox and Reformation models, extending from Dürer to Lutheran bibles and incorporating Italian engraving styles as well.[26] Despite the vigilant religious climate in which it was produced, with the authorities constantly alert to heretical deviation of any kind, scholarly attempts to align Duvet's cycle with one camp or another have proved unsuccessful.

Duvet provides a means of eluding this dilemma in a kind of signature image for the cycle, a darkly allegorical self-portrait of the artist in the role of St John (cat. 64). Before him on a table is a tablet arched at the top so as to mimic the engraved plates for the Apocalypse cycle itself. A burin is neatly laid out alongside it, thus aligning Duvet's act of conceiving his own engraved phantasms with the divinely inspired visions of the prophet. This erudite 'double author portrait' is replete with arcane reflections on the artist's condition of melancholy and the burdens of saturnine genius.

Here Duvet offers a response to Revelation of a sort not clearly evident in the work of those several predecessors he acknowledged by imitation: the undertaking of a programme of Apocalypse illustration for profoundly personal reasons. Rather than being motivated by sectarian interests, Duvet's *Apocalypse* may best be understood as confessional, a declaration of spiritual and existential miasma undertaken by a seventy-year-old man confronting the nearness and ultimate consequence of his own death.[27] Not that Duvet intended his audience to understand this publication as having largely autobiographical significance; such a motive would be altogether inconsistent with the production of works of art in this period, especially in the design of print cycles for an open market. Rather, his pictorial evocation of Revelation responds to the text with an immediacy and subjectivity that earlier illustrators typically avoided in their desire to clarify the text's often incoherent clashes of descriptive and figurative language. With the exception of Dürer's images, Duvet's swarming compositions and the turbulent contours of his draughtsmanship suggest an unprecedented sense of being 'in the spirit' of John's experience. Because the spread of Apocalypse illustration in sixteenth-century Europe was so often driven by propagandistic and evangelical motives, we are inclined to overlook the fact that for most people Revelation must have held very potent private implications.

One should be less surprised to find the portrayal of Revelation as a testimonial of personal crisis in an independent cabinet painting or a series of prints. It is far more remarkable to discover such a private expression in an authorized Catholic setting of the highest order. And yet Michelangelo seems to have left such a confession in his fresco of the *Last Judgement* in the Sistine Chapel, where he included the famously grotesque self-portrait painted onto the flayed skin of St Bartholomew. Although the Sistine *Last Judgement* was completed in 1541, shortly before Duvet began work on his *Apocalypse*, there is no indication that Duvet knew Michelangelo's fresco, though he might well have seen an engraving of it (cat. 96).[28] Michelangelo's *Last Judgement* was widely known and much imitated, and given its location at the centre of Western Christendom it necessarily bore the stamp of pure orthodoxy. In its epic scale the Sistine fresco is a magisterial statement that reflects the religious and historical perils confronting the papacy, not only the challenge posed by Protestant heresies to the north but also the terrifying events of the Sack of Rome. Yet despite the institutional prominence of the Sistine *Last Judgement*, Michelangelo was apparently permitted the liberty of declaring his own deeply personal identification with the subject.[29] This autobiographical revelation can be partly accounted for by the influence of Dante's *Divine Comedy*, an epic poem that permeated Italian popular culture in the fifteenth century to the extent that it is said to have been often quoted in the streets of Florence. Although Michelangelo drew upon it lavishly in his conception of hell, he must have been as much affected by the spiritual odyssey that structures Dante's poem, making of it an allegorical self-portrait of unprecedented scale, as he was by the intensely evocative imagery of damnation.

Over the course of the next century in both northern and southern Europe the Sistine Chapel *Last Judgement* broadly influenced representations of the subject. Whereas Duvet's eccentric formulations proved inimitable, Michelangelo's fresco provided an example of multi-figure composition of previously unrealized complexity and dynamism as well as a model for heroic realizations of the nude figure, a lesson not lost on Rubens. Rubens and other northern artists who took up the subject were compelled more by the consuming grandeur and awesomeness of Michelangelo's apocalyptic vision than by any allegorical subtext. It was the overwhelming spectacle that had greatest effect, a quality that perfectly invoked the sensation of personal jeopardy that determined the meaning of the Apocalypse for so many subsequent generations.

By the second half of the sixteenth century programmatic cycles illustrating the Book of Revelation such as the picture bibles of Virgil Solis, Jost Amman and Tobias Stimmer (cats 82, 95) had become less innovative in content. Bibles of this type are extensively illustrated with woodcuts, often set off in elegant strapwork frames, many of these frames individually designed for each subject. The texts are brief, in effect aphoristic, in the vein of an emblem book. For example, Stimmer's woodcuts are headed with a citation to the appropriate passage from Scripture and complemented with a few banal rhyming couplets describing each episode. Bibles of this type were printed in great numbers, presumably for collectors of finely crafted books or for use as *alba amicorum*.[30]

Independent cycles of Apocalypse illustration are rare in the later sixteenth century. Gerard van Groeningen's set of twelve plates made between 1565 and 1571 reflects the Italianate style adopted in the Netherlands around mid-century (cats 83–94) and is accordingly expansive and histrionic in its pictorial realization of the text. Since these prints are accompanied by German, Latin and French translations of the relevant passages from Revelation, it is clear that they must have been distributed to a wide geographical audience and certainly to a literate one. Like Stimmer's picture Bible they may have been meant to be collected in portfolios and albums of biblical subjects although, as Giulia Bartrum points out, the series is fitted out with frames that make it suitable for display as a frieze (cat. 83). Virtuoso engravings such as Hieronymus Wierix's *St Michael Triumphing over the Devil* (cat. 103) or Jan Sadeler's *Vision of the Holy Lamb* (cat. 104) better exemplify the dramatic potential of apocalyptic themes for single compositions. In northern Europe by the later sixteenth century the illustration of the Apocalypse had also become a more purely aesthetic enterprise.

The Apocalypse and the new empiricism

In the Dutch struggle for independence from the Spanish Netherlands, and later in the throes of the Thirty Years War, political and religious rhetoric grew further entangled. It was a context in which apocalyptic imagery expressed an unbridgeable divide that left no room for ambiguity or reasonable doubt. The once reassuring sense that human fallibility in matters of faith was something that could be absolved through the mercy of the Church was now replaced by an ultimatum. For Protestants this meant a stark choice between salvation and eternal damnation: one was either bound by divine providence to a state of grace or hopelessly abandoned to the jaws of Satan. Although the true condition of one's soul was finally unknowable, a commitment of faith had to be made. This brutal set of alternatives was surely at odds with the unsettled disposition of many believers for whom recondite theological arguments must have remained largely inaccessible. In an ambiguous and unstable world political and evangelical speech grew all the more uncompromising. It was a milieu in which apocalyptic allegory found renewed purpose in the lucid expression of irreconcilable polarities.

A firm separation of knowledge from belief lies at the root of Lutheran and Calvinist theology. This separation is best expressed in the Protestant doctrine that justification (i.e. being made righteous) depends not on certain knowledge nor on the exercise of good works but on faith alone. At base this is a problem of epistemology, and it affected many other dimensions of European thought, including academic propositions about the writing of secular history and the pursuit of the new science. How sharply divided were the truths of religion, history and nature, and how might the prophecies of Revelation be confirmed according to revised empirical measures? To what extent should secular history and biblical prophecy be interpreted alike? Under the pall of apocalyptic expectation these were all the more pressing philosophical issues, and much of the debate about them sprang from deep within Protestant intellectual culture.

The evolution of new critical methods for historical writing during the late Renaissance has been traced back to the Protestant approach to biblical exegesis, in particular Luther's insistence on the absolute authority and inherent transparency of Scripture. It was precisely this conviction that led him to discard centuries of biblical interpretation in favour of a return to early patristic sources, and of course to the Bible itself. Luther's scepticism regarding the canonical status of Revelation is a case in point, reflecting the shift towards an empirical method of text criticism that takes care to discriminate between valid and invalid sources. From Luther to the late sixteenth-century French writer Jean Bodin and eventually Isaac Newton, historians influenced by Protestant hermeneutics returned time and again to Revelation as a touchstone for mapping divine prophecy on to the chronicle of human events. In the opening lines of his seminal text on history writing Bodin adopts a conventional division among categories of historical enquiry. 'Of history, that is, the true narration of things, there are three kinds: human, natural and divine.'[31] But in ordering his approach to each of these Bodin took issue with his forerunners. He made clear that although the interpretation of divine history had primacy over the investigation of nature and human events, it should properly come under consideration last so that it might rest on a solid foundation of what could be known through observation of sensible things.

> So it shall come about that from thinking first about ourselves, then about our family, then about our society we are led to examine nature and finally to the true history of Immortal God. . . . Those who start with divine history, without thinking about human affairs and natural science, and explain to boys or unlearned men difficult problems about divine matters, not only are mistaken in their expectations but also discourage many by the very magnitude of these problems. In the same way that we urge those who come from a thick blackish mist into the light to observe attentively the splendour of the sun first on earth, then in the clouds, then on the moon, in order that, having strengthened their vision, they may be able some time to gaze upon the sun itself, we must act for the benefit of the unlettered also.[32]

In an elegantly deployed Platonic metaphor Bodin lays out the peril of proceeding from an assumed understanding of extra-sensible things to the interpretation of the mundane. Underlying his concern were the prevailing claims among zealots that they had sure knowledge of the divine will moving through history. Most disturbing to Bodin was the tendency of false prophets to inflict their ungrounded authority on the young and unlettered. Bodin's sceptical reasoning gains added moral force against the backdrop of apocalyptic rhetoric and polemical image-making at the time. In Bodin's view the history of human affairs had to be subjected to the analysis of reason, that capacity which is quintessentially and exclusively ours.

For Bodin Revelation stood apart from most other writings of sacred history because it presumes to predict events of the distant future and because its language is inherently figurative and obscure. The elusiveness of Revelation had always concerned commentators on the Apocalypse: which among its prophecies had already occurred, which might be unfolding at the very moment, and which were yet to be fulfilled? Specific readings that bore on the historical moment were then always susceptible to being disconfirmed, and disconfirmed they inevitably were. Thus the interpretation of Revelation was constantly subject to revision, not in the usual sense of biblical exegesis but because disconfirmation came about in the inexorable course of lived time. Hence the problem this text posed was not only acute but unique for theorists of history as much as for theologians. As Scripture Revelation had special status, and if specific readings were regularly disconfirmed, the text itself could by definition never be discredited.[33] Bodin recognized that centuries of falsified readings of biblical prophecy were clear testimony to the relative and errant perspectives adopted in the past. And as a matter of general principle he cautioned against interpreting textual sources that were self-evidently cryptic. 'I thoroughly approve of the reply of Calvin, not less polished than sagacious, when he was asked his opinion about the book of the Apocalypse. He candidly answered that he was totally at a loss regarding the meaning of this obscure writer.'[34] In academic discourse the Apocalypse was destined to become the decisive location for measuring the limits of religious and historical understanding.

And yet despite the care and scepticism being exercised in learned commentaries on Revelation, it continued to be exploited with great vigour as a repertoire of familiar imagery for political and religious diatribe. Whereas rational scepticism became ever more important in academic circles, political and religious rhetoric took a course of its own. Polemicists bent on characterizing the present in apocalyptic terms were likely to regard learned debates about the reading of prophecy as little more than a scholarly diversion. For publishers of broadsheets the Apocalypse was taken as a source of allegory, the visual stridency of Revelation being perfectly suited to ennobling local heroes and slandering enemies.

In Germany and the Netherlands polemical broadsheets and pamphlets were produced more or less continuously from the early years of the Reformation onward, and during the wars of the seventeenth century apocalypticism and the image of the Antichrist were once again deployed for political and religious propaganda.[35] By this stage apocalypticism had become largely a Protestant theme. A broadsheet of 1632 titled *The Town of Augsburg under Siege* (cat. 110) is characteristic, if more finely executed than the average sheet of its type. The etching gives a conventional bird's-eye view of the town with its principal buildings labelled. The two monsters looming over it are derived from Revelation, as the text beneath indicates. On the left is the crowned seven-headed beast, its sinister tail encircling the city, and on the right the horned beast in the form of a lamb wearing a Jesuit's cap. Both monsters vomit up Jesuit priests and monks over the town. The text recounts the events of a three-year period in which Augsburg was subjected to intense re-Catholicization. This broadsheet was provided with a pendant also dated 1632 declaring the liberation of the town from Catholic pollution (cat. 111). Here the two beasts of the Apocalypse

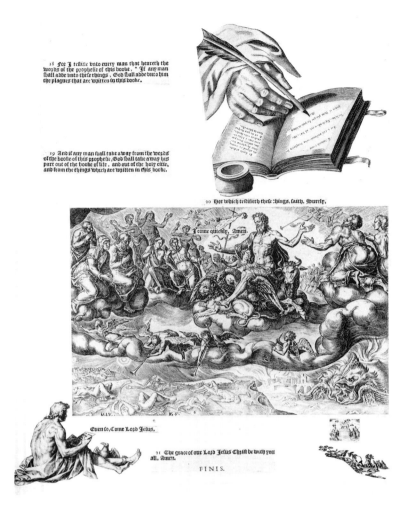

have been slain by the sword of the Swedish king Gustavus Adolphus, who wears the mantle of the true Christian Knight acting in defence of the faith. The corpse of the horned lamb has lost its cap, and lying before it is a clearly identified indulgence, for Protestants the ubiquitous sign of Catholic venality.[36] The Apocalypse offered a vocabulary for demonizing the Catholic opposition: Jesuits and monks regurgitated by the foul beasts of the Antichrist and the Protestant king granted the triumphant role of the Archangel Michael.

In its public and private appeal apocalyptic imagery in the seventeenth century reflects two general tendencies. As we have seen, the first of these is the migration from narrative to allegory in political broadsheets and pamphlets where the exegetical complexity of Revelation is reduced to a mode of caricature. This is the rhetoric of ideological combat addressed to partisans rather than a matter of personal conviction. Elsewhere apocalypticism yielded images of a very different sort. Although the requirements of Baroque naturalism necessarily rejected the unlikely phantasms attempted in earlier pictorial accounts of Revelation, the text offered possibilities of another sort perfectly attuned to the new style. The vision of fear, suffering and damnation in Lucas Vorsterman's engraving of *St Michael fighting the Rebel Angels* after Rubens (cat. 109) and Rubens's own spectacles of overly fleshed souls cast into hell-fire are noteworthy examples, as are Stefano Della Bella's gruesome images of death, a subject with a history extending as far back as the medieval *danse macabre*, now grotesquely reconceived as the very stuff of nightmares (cats 112–16). With much the same degrees of abstraction and palpability Milton would evoke the vaults of hell as something utterly strange and yet vividly experienced and undeniable. Milton, too, believed that the Antichrist reigned in the world.

For Catholics and Protestants alike the imagery of the Apocalypse conveyed the visceral horror of damnation and the ecstatic promise of final salvation. We find expressions of a tortured sense of inner turmoil and an almost blithe and confident acceptance of the inevitable. The latter sentiment appears uppermost in a remarkable group of volumes known as the *Little Gidding Concordances*, compiled by the Anglican community consisting largely of the family members of Nicholas Ferrar who were centred at Little Gidding Manor in Huntingdonshire from 1626 to 1646. Their *Concordances* or scriptural harmonies were part of an elaborate exercise in which the New Testament text was excerpted and illustrated on album pages with fragments most ingeniously cut from dozens of individual engravings and book illustrations, principally the work of Dutch and Flemish printmakers of the mid- to late sixteenth century. Among these is an album dated 1635 devoted to the Acts of the Apostles and the Book of Revelation which is thought to have been made for Charles I. The concluding page of Revelation shown here (fig. 8) is counterpointed by an opening page with twenty-four carefully clipped out oval and roundel scenes and an author portrait of St John. In four of the little scenes and elsewhere in the *Concordances* the figure of God the Father has been meticulously rubbed out and replaced in pen with the Tetragrammaton, the four consonants of the Hebrew word for God, elisions meant to avoid the hint of idolatry.[37] The Little Gidding treatment of Revelation is charming testimony to the private response to this text among a family whose Protestantism was High Church and contemplative rather than evangelical. It offers us a close view into a manner of devotional practice that is unabashed in its acceptance of divine providence, an intimate meditation on salvation emerging, as it were, from the family hearth. We know that at least the clipping of prints for these albums was done by two nieces in the household, and it might well be that the *Concordances* reflect a gendered perspective in quite particular ways. Among the pious middle class, perhaps especially among women, the confrontation with Last Things may often have been like this, a mixture of anxious anticipation and modest application to duty. The popular illustrated martyrologies of John Foxe and others detailing the sufferings of Protestants and Catholics for their faith served as similar reminders of personal devotion and the perils of temporal existence.

Early modern Europe was undergoing an epistemological crisis bound to affect both the public and private spheres. The contest between Catholics and Protestants, the trials of the Thirty Years War, and the English Revolution severely tested the soundness of claims to the sufficiency of empirical knowledge regarding the world of nature and the polity.[38] Popular books of astrology and collections of natural prodigies filled with dire prediction continued to be issued in great number, especially by Protestant authors.[39] Meanwhile, Francis Bacon set forth the dogma that the Book of Scripture and the Book of Nature necessarily had to be read differently, that one could never be understood by recourse to the other. And yet late in the seventeenth century none other than Isaac Newton turned his attention to Revelation and fundamentally contradicted Bacon's premise. He drafted a massive treatise investigating the meaning of its figures and their true application to history, and in doing so he followed much the same analytical procedure he employed for his scientific studies. Newton found Revelation not only accessible to human intelligence but its prophecies able to be determined with the sureness of a mathematical proof. 'A meer naturall man, how wicked soever, who will read it, may judg of it and perceive the strength of it with as much perspicuity and certainty as he can a demonstration in Euclide.'[40] Though Newton rejected the possibility of reading the Apocalypse as foretelling the immediate future, he subscribed to the view held by many contemporary divines that its applications to the historical past were sure and recoverable.[41]

Even for Newton the most vexing book of Scripture could not be abandoned as either divinely inscrutable or merely literary. He was, in Frank Kermode's words, 're-enacting the familiar dialogue between credulity and scepticism'.[42] For Kermode the compulsion to credulity is embedded deep in the human psyche and finally irresistible even to a materialist age. It betrays an insurmountable desire to confirm an absolute alpha and omega that will contain the uncertain fragment of time experienced in life, a final unwillingness to accept the notion of infinity. From such a perspective apocalypticism becomes a necessary consequence of acknowledging mortality, the most essential conclusion we draw from our capacity for inferential reasoning. The persistence of apocalyptic thought in the face of its perpetual disconfirmation seems none the less bewildering, a hapless resistance to an overwhelming chronicle of error. And yet in seventeenth-century Europe, where Saturn was everywhere devouring his children, it once again seemed the better alternative.

NOTES

1 For the medieval background to apocalypticism, Richard K. Emmerson and Bernard McGinn (eds), *The Apocalypse in the Middle Ages*, Ithaca 1992, esp. essays in part III. Robin Bruce Barnes, *Prophesy and Gnosis: Apocalypticism in the Wake of the Lutheran Reformation*, Stanford 1988, pp.20–9, for a general discussion of apocalypticism in the later period. On the prophetic implications of Columbus's voyage: Pauline Moffitt Watts, 'Prophecy and discovery: on the spiritual origins of Christopher Columbus's "Enterprise in the Indies"', *American Historical Review*, XC 1985, pp. 73–102.

2 The literature on Dürer's cycle is immense. The subtlest account of its place in his early career is given by Erwin Panofsky, *Albrecht Dürer*, Princeton 1948, vol. 1, pp. 47–59. For a recent, far more thorough reading of the woodcuts stressing their dramatic character and poetic dimension: Peter Krüger, *Dürers 'Apocalypse'. Zur poetischen Struktur einer Bilderzählung der Renaissance*, Wiesbaden 1996. For a convincing refutation of attempts to link Dürer's cycle to unorthodox theologies and revolutionary political sentiments, notably the interpretations offered by Max Dvořák, Alexander Perrig and Rudolf Chadraba: David Price, 'Albrecht Dürer's representations of faith: the Church, lay devotion and veneration in the *Apocalypse* (1498)', *Zeitschrift für Kunstgeschichte*, LVII 1994, pp. 688–96.

3 Arnd Müller, *Geschichte der Juden in Nürnberg 1146–1945*, Nuremberg 1968, pp. 81–5.

4 At a later stage, when Dürer had experienced the Reformation, he may have considered the print especially suited to religious expression because of its simplicity rather than its evocative power. See Donald Kuspit, 'Melanchthon and Dürer: the search for the simple style', *Journal of Medieval and Renaissance Studies*, III 1973, pp. 177–202.

5 The literature on Luther's complex and evolving attitude towards images is vast. See especially Sergiusz Michalski, *The Reformation and the Visual Arts: The Protestant Image Question in Western and Eastern Europe*, London and New York 1993. A probing and subtle analysis of his views is developed in Joseph Koerner, *The Moment of Self-Portraiture*, Chicago and London 1993, ch. 16. For a summation of reformers' opinions on images and earlier bibliography: Peter and Linda Parshall, *Art and the Reformation. An Annotated Bibliography*, Boston 1986, esp. the entries in part 2, and the intro. pp. xxiv–xxxii.

6 A detailed examination of the Lutheran tradition of Apocalypse illustration and its dependence on and deviation from Dürer's example is given in Peter Martin, *Martin Luther und die Bilder zur Apokalypse. Die Ikonographie der Illustrationen zur Offenbarung des Johannes in der Lutherbibel 1522 bis 1546*, Hamburg 1983. See also Philipp Schmidt, *Die Illustration der Lutherbibel, 1522–1700*, Basel 1977; Heimo Reinitzer, *Biblia deutsch. Luthers Bibelübersetzung und ihre Tradition*, exhib. cat. Wolfenbüttel, Herzog August Bibliothek, 1983, pp. 138–9; and Werner Hoffmann (ed.), *Luther und die Folgen für die Kunst*, exhib. cat. Hamburg, Kunsthalle, 1983.

7 Revelation had been a preferred text for illustration. For example, the second edition of the Low German *Cologne Bible* (Cologne: Heinrich Quentel, 1479) included fifteen woodcuts for the entire New Testament, nine of them from Revelation. Richard K. Emmerson, *Antichrist in the Middle Ages*, Seattle 1981, p.221.

8 Christoph Walther, *Von unterscheid der Deudschen Biblien und anderen Büchern des Ehrnwirdigen und seligen Herrn Doct. Martini Lutheri*, Wittenberg: Hans Lufft, 1563, fols Bii-Biii.

Und hat befohlen / das man auffs einfeltigst den inhalt des Texts solt abmalen und reissen / Und wolt nicht leiden / das man uberley und unnütz ding / das zum Text nicht dienet / solt dazu schmieren / Wie itzt die Nachdrücker in iren Biblien gethan haben / Die figuren in iren Biblien sind klein / und was den Text belanget / fast unkentlich / Umb die figuren aber herumb / haben sie viel Narrenwerck / Puppenwerck / und Teufels werck lassen malen / Denn sie haben etliche Leisten umb die Figuren lassen machen / weil die Figuren so klein sind / darauff stehet so nerrische fantasey / von Teuflischen angesichten / Uhu und andern unfletigen greslichen ange-sichten und monstris. Und haben solche Leisten umb die Figuren geschlossen und gesatzt / welche viel besser in Marcolfo / denn in der Biblia / neben Gottes wort / stehen solten.

The only publication of his translation that Luther is known to have overseen in detail is the last to be printed in his lifetime, the so-called 'Ausgabe letzter Hand' (Wittenberg 1545). Here he certainly must also have authorized the selection of illustrations.

9 All quotations are taken from the Douay-Rheims version of the Bible. On the woodcuts see Martin, op. cit. n.6, pp.28–32.

10 Richard Gassen, '"Kom, lieber jüngster Tag", Die Apokalypse in der Reformation', in Richard W. Gassen and Bernhard Holeczek (eds), *Apokalypse. Ein Prinzip Hoffnung?* exhib. cat., Ludwigshafen am Rhein, Wilhelm Hack Museum 1985, pp.75–7; Karl Arndt, 'Hans Burgkmair illustriert die Offenbarung des Johannes', in Stephan Füssel and Joachim Knape (eds), *Poesis et Pictura. Studien zum Verhältnis von Text und Bild in Handschriften und alten Drucken. Festschrift für Dieter Wuttke zum 60. Geburtstag*, Baden-Baden 1989, pp. 255–76, points out the correspondences and original departures of Burgkmair's 1523 cycle, itself very closely attentive to the text, in comparison with those of Dürer and the September Testament. Holbein's pictures are preceded by a title-page that introduces the woodcuts as 'comely pictures in which the most difficult of things can be easily understood', precisely Luther's objective. Attention to the text and prototypes of course varies. Beham's title woodcut of the *Vision of the Seven Candlesticks* (cat. 58) proudly sets the stage with eight tapers rather than seven, a startling lapse.

11 The episode of the well spouting up a plague of lion-headed locusts (Rev. 9: 3) is a case in point. These creatures are better left to the imagination than to the precise requirements of an image that strives for objectivity. In a different respect the rain of flaming stars (Rev. 6: 13), the harvesting of wheat and grapes (Rev. 14: 14–20) and the millstone being dropped into the sea (Rev. 18: 21) are likewise tamed by Cranach. Some of the later illustrators such as Burgkmair were less constrained.

12 Robert W. Scribner, *For the Sake of Simple Folk. Popular Propaganda for the German Reformation*, Cambridge 1981, pp.127–32.

13 *Zeichen am Himmel. Flugblätter des 16. Jahrhunderts*, exhib. cat., Germanisches Nationalmuseum, Nuremberg 1982, cat. 10, pp.24–5.

14 For the early history of news-sheets and their sensationalist character: Karl Schottenloher, *Flugblatt und Zeitung. Ein Wegweiser durch das gedruckte Tagesschrifttum*, rev. edn Johannes Binkowski, Munich 1985, vol.1. On the presumed eye-witness status of these reports see Peter Parshall, 'Imago contrafacta: images and facts in the northern Renaissance', *Art History*, XVI 1993, pp.554–79.

15 'Vorrhede Martini Luthers auff die weissagung des Johannis Lichtenbergers', *D. Martin Luthers Werke. Kritische Gesamtausgabe*, vol.23, Weimar 1901, pp.7–12. See also Barnes, op. cit. (n.1), pp. 47–8; 98–9. Luther differed from Melanchthon

and many later German Protestant sixteenth-century commentators on the viability of astrology and divination. On the currency of Lichtenberger's prophecies and Luther's stance see D. Kunze, 'Prophecy and History', *Journal of the Warburg and Courtauld Institutes*, XXI 1958, pp. 63–85.

16 Lorraine Daston, 'Baconian facts, academic civility, and the prehistory of objectivity', *Annals of Scholarship*, VIII 1991, pp. 337–63; Lorraine Daston, 'Marvelous facts and miraculous evidence in early modern Europe', *Critical Inquiry*, XVIII 1991, pp. 93–124. On the interpretation of private languages and authority in the context of Protestant exegesis: D.P. Walker, 'Esoteric symbolism', in *Poetry & Poetics from Ancient Greece to the Renaissance: Studies in Honor of James Hutton*, Ithaca 1975, pp. 218–32.

17 The concept of paralleling the figures of Christ and Antichrist can be traced back to the third century. For the history of the Antichrist legend through the Reformation see especially Bernard McGinn, *Antichrist*, New York 1994. For further discussion Emmerson, op. cit. (n.7); Oswald Erich, 'Antichrist', in *Reallexikon zur deutschen Kunstgeschichte*, Stuttgart 1937–, vol. 1, cols 720–30; Hanns Bächtold-Stäubli and Eduard Hofmann-Krayer (eds), *Handwörterbuch des deutschen Aberglaubens*, Berlin 1987, vol. 1, cols 479–502. Luca Signorelli painted a series of frescoes in Orvieto Cathedral between 1499 and 1504 pairing the 'Rule of the Antichrist' with the 'Last Judgement'. For apocalypticism and the representation of the Antichrist in Italy see Jonathan B. Riess, 'Luca Signorelli's "Rule of Antichrist" and the Christian encounter with the Infidel', in Claire Farago (ed.), *Reframing the Renaissance*, New Haven and London 1995, ch. 14. Christopher Hill, *Antichrist in Seventeenth-Century England*, Oxford 1971, pp.6–7, notes the demurrals of Luther and Calvin on the Antichrist obsession.

18 Christiane Andersson and Charles Talbot, *From a Mighty Fortress. Prints, Drawings and Books in the Age of Luther. 1483–1546*, exhib. cat., Detroit Institute of the Arts, 1983, cat. 202, pp.358–9. On the structural principles of Reformation propaganda and the advantages and limits of polemic see Konrad Hoffmann, 'Typologie, Exemplarik und Reformatorische Bildsatire', in Josef Nolte *et al.* (ed.), *Kontinuität und Umbruch. Theologie und Frömmigkeit in Flugschriften und Kleinliteratur an der Wende vom 15. zum 16. Jahrhundert*, Stuttgart 1978, pp. 189–210.

19 Much has been said on both sides of this question. See Frederick J. Stopp, 'Reformation satire in Germany: nature, conditions and form', *Oxford German Studies*, III 1968, pp. 53–68; and Parshall, op. cit. (n.5), intro. pp. xxxii–xxxvii. The recent, sustained case for the efficacy of pictorial propaganda in the Reformation can be found in the writings of Robert W. Scribner, especially op. cit. (n.12), and Christiane Andersson, 'Polemical prints in Reformation Nuremberg', in Jeffrey Chipps (ed.), *New Perspectives on the Art of Renaissance Nuremberg*, Smith, Austin, Texas 1985, pp.41–62.

20 André Chastel, *The Sack of Rome, 1527,* trans. Beth Archer, Princeton 1983, ch. 2, for the effect of this episode on recharged perceptions of the pope as Antichrist, the importance of prognostications and the vision of Roman corruption.

21 For the original texts of the two prefaces: *Luthers Werke*, vol. 7, pp.404; 407–21. Martin, op. cit. (n.6), pp. 100–23. A brief overview of the medieval approach to interpreting Revelation in relation to history, with particular reference to Nicholas de Lyra's commentary of 1329 and also the thirteenth-century prophet Joachim of Fiore: Philip D.W. Krey, *Nicholas of Lyra's Apocalypse Commentary*, Kalamazoo, Mich., 1997, pp.11–23.

22 On Gerung's Protestant iconography: Petra Roettig, *Reformation*

als Apokalypse: Die Holzschnitte von Matthias Gerung im Codex germanicus 6592 der Bayerischen Staatsbibliothek in München, Berne 1991; Scribner, op. cit. (n.12), pp.181–4, especially on his image of the Antichrist; Andersson and Talbot, op. cit. (n.18), cats 165–6, pp.298–300.

23 Gheeraerts was apparently in England by 1568. The engraving is labelled throughout with letters that indicate it once had a key attached, presumably explaining each detail or supplying each with a suitable passage from the Bible or some other appropriate text. Nevertheless, the sense of the satire is clear from the image alone. The fullest interpretation of it is given by Christine Göttler, 'Ikonoklasm als Kirchenreinigung: Zwei satirische Bildfiktionen zum niederländischen Bildersturm 1566', *Georges-Bloch-Jahrbuch des Kunstgeschichtlichen Seminars der Universität Zürich*, IV 1997, pp.61–87. See also Edward Hodnett, *Marcus Gheeraerts the Elder of Bruges*, Utrecht 1971, pp.26–7; David Freedberg, *Iconoclasm and Painting in the Revolt of the Netherlands 1566–1609*, New York and London 1988, pp.184–6; and Margaret Aston, *The King's Bedpost: Reformation Iconography in a Tudor Group Portrait*, Cambridge 1993, pp.168–71, which gives a vivid characterization of Gheeraerts's grotesque.

24 Peter Parshall, 'Kunst en reformatie in de Noordelijke Nederlanden – enkele gezichtspunten', *Bulletin van het Rijksmuseum*, XXXV 1987, pp.164–75.

25 Colin Eisler, *The Master of the Unicorn: The Life and Work of Jean Duvet*, New York 1979, gives a thorough examination of Duvet's career as an engraver and devotes the majority of his text to a detailed explication of the *Apocalypse* series. More recently on the previous tradition of Apocalypse illustration in France, but without reference to Duvet: Alicja Karlowska-Kamzowa, 'Die Rezeption von Dürers "Apokalypse" in der französischen Druckgraphik des frühen 16. Jahrhunderts', *Wiener Jahrbuch für Kunstgeschichte*, XXVI–XXVII 1993–4, pp.267–73; 437–40.

26 Eisler, op. cit. (n.25), accepts the view of most scholars that the Duvet employed by the French court is identical with a goldsmith simultaneously active in the Calvinist community of Geneva. This proposal has recently been brought into doubt. If indeed Duvet shuttled back and forth between these divided arenas we are left in doubt not only about his sectarian allegiance but also about how his *L'Apocalypse figurée* might have been received by Catholics and Protestants. However, Henri Zerner has questioned this identification, and if he is correct then there remains no basis for assuming the designer of *L'Apocalypse figurée* was anything but orthodox in his convictions. See *The French Renaissance in Prints from the Bibliothèque Nationale de France*, exhib. cat., Los Angeles, New York and Paris 1995, cat. 22, pp.216–18, 470.

27 Eisler, op. cit. (n.25), ch. 47, gives a detailed and convincing reading of the allegory, its sources and ambiguities. See also Zerner, op. cit. (n.26), cat. 22, pp.216–18. There are suggestive similarities between Duvet's allegorical self-portrait engraving and Giorgio Ghisi's *Allegory of Life* published in 1561. Suzanne Boorsch, Michal and R.E. Lewis, *The Engravings of Giorgio Ghisi*, exhib. cat., Metropolitan Museum of Art, New York 1985, cat. 28, pp.114–20.

28 Although the engravings after Michelangelo's *Last Judgement* were quite intricate, the discrepancy in scale would render a detail such as the self-portrait unrecognizable, and Vasari's report of it (which, in any case, does not mention the self-portrait) would probably not have reached Duvet by the time he completed his *Apocalypse* in 1555. On the Counter-Reformation and the later response to Michelangelo's fresco: Susanne Pfleger, 'Die Apokalypse in der Gegenreformation', in Gassen and Holeczek, op. cit. (n.10), pp.107–12.

29 It has often been suggested that Michelangelo harboured quasi-Protestant attitudes, specifically that he held Nicodomite sympathies, a leaning current among Italian literati such as his close friend Vittoria Colonna. On reflections of this disposition in Michelangelo's *Last Judgement* see most recently (with further bibliography) Mosche Arkin, '"One of the Marys...": An interdisciplinary analysis of Michelangelo's *Pietà*', *Art Bulletin*, LXXIX 1997, pp.506–7.

30 An example of a picture Bible used for an *album amicorum* is *Bibliorum utriusque Testamenti icones* (Frankfurt am Main: Hieronymus Feyerabend, 1571), with woodcuts by Sigismund Feyerabend and texts by Conrad Weiss now in the British Library (*Album Amicorum Henr. Wellingii*, Bibl. Edgerton 1,190). An *album amicorum* is a book in which colleagues and friends wrote dedications to the owner and sometimes drew pictures to go with them. These were especially popular in Protestant university faculties in the 16th and 17th centuries and were often constructed out of picture Bibles of this kind.

31 Jean Bodin, *Method for the Easy Comprehension of History*, trans. Beatrice Reynolds, New York 1945, p. 15.

32 ibid., p. 16.

33 Frank Kermode, *The Sense of an Ending: Studies in the Theory of Fiction*, Oxford 1967, p. 17.

34 Bodin, op. cit. (n.31), p.291.

35 David Kunzle, *The Early Comic Strip*, Berkeley 1973, part 1; Philip Benedict, 'Of Marmites and martyrs: images and polemics in the Wars of Religion', in *The French Renaissance in Prints* (op.cit. n.26), pp.109–37; William A. Coupe, *The German Illustrated Broadsheet in the Seventeenth Century: Historical and Iconographic Studies*, Baden-Baden 1966–7, 2 vols; and W.A. Coupe, *German Political Satires from the Reformation to the Second World War*, New York 1993, vol.1, pp.xi–xl, for an overview of the subject and further bibliography.

36 Coupe, op. cit. (n.35), vol.1, p.141.

37 On this practice: David Freedberg, 'The Hidden God: Image and interdiction in the Netherlands in the sixteenth century', *Art History*, V 1982, pp.140–1. For the Little Gidding Concordances see George Henderson, 'Bible illustration in the age of Laud', *Transactions of the Cambridge Bibliographical Society*, VIII 1986, pp.185–98. The one discussed here, containing Revelation, is in the British Library (C23.c.23) together with two others (C23.c.2 and C23.c.4).

38 Bernard Capp, 'The political dimension of Apocalyptic thought', in C.A. Patrides and Joseph Wittreich (eds), *The Apocalypse in English Renaissance Thought and Literature*, Ithaca, N.Y., 1984, pp.93–124.

39 Barnes, op. cit. (n.1), pp.146–81.

40 Frank E. Manuel, *The Religion of Isaac Newton: The Fremantle Lectures 1973*, Oxford 1974, appendix, p. 124. For an extended discussion of Newton's beliefs with particular reference to his interpretation of Revelation see ch. 4. On Newton's method and its correspondence with his scientific method: Maurizio Mamiani, 'The rhetoric of certainty: Newton's method in science and in the interpretation of the Apocalypse', in Marcello Pera and William R. Shea (eds), *Persuading Science: The Art of Scientific Rhetoric*, Canton, Mass., 1991, pp. 157–72. Newton's essential postulate was that simplicity be preferred in all explanations (p.165).

41 Manuel, op. cit. (n.40), p.99, notes that at a much younger age Newton believed the future might also be demonstrated through reading the Apocalypse, and he conjectured about the date of the Second Coming.

42 Kermode, op. cit (n.33), p.18.

The catalogue entries for this section have been prepared by Giulia Bartrum with Rhoda Eitel-Porter and Frances Carey

The Vision of the Apocalypse in the Fifteenth Century

I Apocalypse in Latin

German, *c*.1463–70

Manuscript on parchment, 290 × 212 mm; 32 leaves

Fols 8v–9r: *Antichrist Ordering the Deaths of Elias and Enoch; Unbelievers Killed, Antichrist Performs a Miracle; Antichrist Distributing Gold to his Followers, Execution of a King, a Bishop and Two Monks, Antichrist in Majesty; Devils Dragging Antichrist into Hell; His Supporters Lament*

Lit: L. Delisle and P. Meyer, *L'Apocalypse en français au XIII siècle*, Paris 1901, p.cvii; M.R. James, *The Apocalypse in Art*, London 1931, no.17; L. von Wilckens, 'Hinweise zu einigen frühen Einblattholzschnitten und zur Blockbuchapokalypse', *Anzeiger des Germanischen Nationalmuseums*, 1978, pp.13ff.; Sabine Mertens and Cornelia Schneider (eds), *Blockbücher des Mittelalters: Bilderfolgen als Lektüre*, exhib. cat., Gutenberg-Museum, Mainz 1991, pp.114ff.

London, British Library, Additional MS 19896

This manuscript is related to the type of picture-book Apocalypses first introduced in England in the thirteenth century (Ch. 3, cats 18, 20), but its style and iconography are so close to the block-book Apocalypses that it is probably one of the earliest manuscript copies of a printed original to have been produced (see cat. 2). Details of both image and text show that it was copied fairly precisely from the earliest edition of the block-book Apocalypse (Netherlandish, *c*.1440–50), with the exception of one page with the *Opening of the Seventh Seal* and the *Angel throwing the Censer of Fire to the Ground* (Rev. 8), which was copied from the fourth edition (German, *c*.1463–5). As in the earlier manuscripts and block-books, this Apocalypse cycle is preceded by four subjects from the life of St John, and followed by five further scenes ending with his death; a complete text of Revelation has been added at the end. The pages illustrated here show the four scenes from the Antichrist story (see cat. 3): Antichrist is interpreted as the Beast of the bottomless pit who kills the two witnesses (Rev. 11: 7), represented as the prophets Enoch and Elias (Elijah); the other scenes from his life are incorporated at this point in the chronology of Revelation.

Despite the uneven quality of this manuscript, the popularity of its subject is evident, and is displayed in the care taken with its preservation. The sixteenth-century binding of wooden boards covered in stamped leather has a half-length figure of the Virgin in Limoges enamel inserted into the upper cover.
G.B.

1

2 Apocalypse in Latin

German, *c.*1470

Unbound block-book, with three sets of folded sheets, containing 16 woodcuts in each.

Sigs. G and H: *The Third and Fourth Horsemen of the Apocalypse; Opening of the Fifth and Sixth Seals: Clothing of the Elect, and an Earthquake* (Rev. 6: 5–17)

Sigs. BB and CC: *Beast with Lamb's Horns and the Beast with Seven Heads; Worshippers bringing Gifts to the Beast with Lamb's Horns; the Appearance of the Lamb on Mt Sion* (Rev. 13–14)

Sigs. SS and TT: *Victory of Christ and the Heavenly Armies, and the Beast locked up for One Thousand Years; Judgement and First Resurrection of Believers; Final Battle with Satan's Knights attacking the City of Saints* (Rev. 19–20)

Woodcuts with hand-colouring and Latin text; each woodcut approx. 255 × 197mm

Watermark: bull's head with a crown and a petal (similar to Piccard XV, 360–1 and 381–2)

Lit: W.L. Schreiber, *Manuel de l'Amateur de la Gravure sur Bois et sur Métal au XVe siècle*, vol. 4, Leipzig 1902, p.167 (edition VI); Mainz 1991, pp.91, 371

London, British Library, IB 14

The great era of Apocalypse manuscripts of the thirteenth century had no immediate successor, but played an important role in a significant period of Apocalypse illustration during the fifteenth century, when the subject appeared in large numbers of block-books. These early printed books, in which text and image were cut from a single block on each page, were, in contrast to the exclusive nature of manuscript patronage, aimed at a wider market and printed in editions of several hundred. Their main purpose was to provide for preachers a visual interpretation of popular subjects, in which an abbreviated form of the text was incorporated within the design. Other block-book subjects include the *Biblia Pauperum* (Bible of the Poor), the *Ars Moriendi* (Art of Dying) and the *Speculum Humanae Salvationis* (Mirror of Human Salvation). The vast majority have not survived because they would have deteriorated rapidly with constant use. Of the few Apocalypse block-books that do remain, six different editions of Netherlandish or German origin produced between *c.*1440 and *c.*1470 have been recorded; only those that were well cared for have survived, like this hand-coloured edition which, according to Schreiber, formerly belonged to some Franciscan monks in Passau and then to the print scholar and book-dealer Theodor Oscar Weigel (1812–81). This example belongs to the sixth and last edition of *c.*1470, although it was probably printed later because the paper possesses a watermark similar to those appearing in publications of 1474–85.

The wide selection of subjects shown in the forty-eight scenes in the Apocalypse block-books stems directly from the illuminated manuscript tradition, particularly the incorporation of scenes from the life and death of St John, added before and after the Revelation, and the scenes from the story of Antichrist (see cats 1, 3). The three major thirteenth-century Apocalypse manuscripts which were

2, Sig. G

2, Sig. H

2, Sig. BB

2, Sig. CC

2, Sig. SS

2, Sig. TT

influential in this respect are Paris, Bibliothèque
Nationale Cod. fr. 403; New York, Pierpont Morgan
Library MS M. 524; and Oxford, Bodleian Library Auct.
D.IV.17, in which two scenes are represented on each
page with short pieces of text on scrolls or tablets in a
format similar to that of the block-books. The actual
prototypes for the block-books were probably later
copies of these manuscripts, such as Manchester, John
Rylands Library MS 19 (Netherlandish, *c*.1360–70; see
Ch. 3, cat. 18) and London, British Library Add. MS
38121 (Dutch, *c*.1400) which are based on Oxford Auct.
D.IV.17. The fifteenth-century manuscript from the
Wellcome Institute (MS 49; see Ch. 3, cat. 20), which is
derived from a different, earlier source, also contains
iconographic details used in the Apocalypse block-books.
G.B.

3 *The Book of Antichrist* [*Das puch von dem entkrist*]

German, *c*.1470–75

Fol. 22: *Antichrist Attacked by St Michael as he Attempts to Ascend to Heaven*

Woodcut with hand-colouring, four lines of German text above,
247 × 161mm

Lit: Schreiber, p.219 (edition I); Mainz 1991, p.375

Manchester, John Rylands University Library, inv. no.9403

The name Antichrist is not mentioned specifically in the
text of Revelation, although it is elsewhere in the New
Testament (I John 2: 18, 22; II John 7). Further references
in Mark to 'false Christs and false prophets' who it is
supposed will appear during the last days on earth (Mark 13:
22) and in Paul's Second Epistle to the Thessalonians to the
'man of sin' who exalts himself above God and 'whose
coming is after the working of Satan' (II Thessalonians 2:
3–12) helped formulate the character. The idea of a human
antithesis for Christ was developed by early commentators
on the text of Revelation, including Augustine and Bede.
Links were made with the various beasts of Revelation,
particularly the beast of the bottomless pit who makes war
on the two witnesses of Chapter 9, and also with the beast
from the sea of Chapter 13, the evil being who it was believed
would help Satan rule the world in the last days before
Christ's return. The notion of Antichrist was also stimulated
by the anthropomorphism of the beasts of the Apocalypse in
Carolingian manuscripts of the ninth century, such as the
Trier Apocalypse, in which Satan is represented as an
upright bestial figure, and the third beast as a tiny humanoid
form of the false prophet (see fig. 3, p. 47).

The first illustration of Antichrist as a man, identified by
an inscription, is in a manuscript commentary on the
Apocalypse by Beatus of Liébana of *c*.930–50, where he is

3

shown murdering the two witnesses, Enoch and Elias
(Madrid, Biblioteca Nacional MS Vitr.14–1 fol.105v.). The
most original and influential of all medieval commentators
was Joachim of Fiore (see pp.22–4, 63, n.53), who interpreted
Antichrist as a false teacher within the context of the
twelfth-century reformation of the Church. Antichrist was
considered to have performed outward 'wonders', in
contrast with Christ's revelation of the inner soul and
spiritual life through contemplation.

By the fifteenth century the figure of Antichrist was well
established, and the series of German block-books devoted
to Antichrist and the Fifteen Last Signs before Doomsday,
produced between *c*.1455 and 1480, gives the fullest visual
account of the subject (see B. McGinn, *Antichrist: Two
Thousand Years of the Human Fascination with Evil*, New
York 1994, pp.193ff. and cat. 1; Ch. 3, cat. 20). This block-
book contains forty-four scenes from his life, the majority of
which are printed two to a page, with five full-page scenes at
the end, including *Antichrist attacked by St Michael*. The
main source for the story of Antichrist was Book VII of the
Compendium of Theological Truth, a popular work written by
a Strasbourg Dominican, Hugh Ripelin, in *c*.1265 which was

first printed in 1473. The text above each scene here refers to the *Compendium* and to the Apocalypse; in this case, to Chapter 13, in which Antichrist is associated with the beast from the sea with seven heads and ten horns, to whom power was given, 'over all kindreds and tongues and nations' (Rev. 13: 7). References are also given elsewhere to the *Golden Legend* by Jacobus de Voragine, written 1255–66, which was first printed in 1470. The first scene of the conception of Antichrist has been torn out of this block-book, and the series begins with his birth by Caesarean section and the death of his mother. The story continues with his circumcision; his development of a group of associates; the prophets Elias and Enoch preaching against him and their subsequent deaths; his performance of various 'miracles' before admirers; his conversion of Jews and others, and his torture and murder of unbelievers. The subject of this woodcut, *Antichrist attacked by St Michael*, occurs at the end of his life. An angel resurrects the souls of Elias and Enoch and the associates of Antichrist refuse to preach any more, whereupon Antichrist simulates his own death. After three days he assembles all in the Garden of Gethsemane to witness his ascension, when he is attacked by St Michael and dragged into hell by devils.
G.B.

4 German Bible

A. Koberger, Nuremberg 1483

Fols 577 v–578r: *Four Angels Holding back the Winds and the Marking of the Elect* (Rev. 7: 1–8) (not illustrated), *The Lamb Breaking the Seventh Seal and the Seven Trumpeters* (Rev. 8: 1–12)

Woodcuts with hand-colouring, 119 × 190mm, 118 × 190mm

Lit: Mainz 1991, pp.119ff.

London, British Library, C.11 d.5

This Bible was published by Dürer's godfather, Anton Koberger, and provides the background for Dürer's

innovative series of Apocalypse prints in 1498. The book contains eight woodcut illustrations to Revelation, the blocks of which first appeared, with one other, in the so-called 'Cologne Bible', printed by Bartholomäus von Unkel or Heinrich Quentel in Dutch and Saxon editions in Cologne in *c*.1478. These illustrations were particularly influential, and were used directly or indirectly in all subsequent pre-Reformation printed bibles of the late fifteenth century, including the Grüninger Bible (Strasbourg 1485), to which Dürer also referred when producing his own series; the Czech Kuttenberg Bible of 1487; the Schönsperger bibles (Augsburg 1487 and 1490); the Italian bibles published by Malermi (Venice 1490) and Tridino (Venice 1493); and two bibles published after the appearance of Dürer's set by Johann and Silvan Otmar in Augsburg, 1507 and 1518.

Koberger was one of the leading German publishers of his day and may have belonged to a consortium which provided financial backing for the publication of the Cologne Bible. It is also possible that the designer of the blocks, who has not been identified, worked in Nuremberg; but in any case, Koberger acquired eight of the nine blocks used in the Cologne Bible for the purpose of illustrating his own High German translation five years later in Nuremberg. The designs are very loosely based on the block-book Apocalypses (cats 1–2) derived from the medieval manuscript tradition, of which the latest edition was probably still in print. Koberger's publication was a highly commercial enterprise in a sophisticated business dominated by efficiency of output; not surprisingly, the designs in his bible are therefore greatly simplified in technique and substantially reduced in number. With only a few exceptions, notably the *Four Horsemen*, each woodcut shows two or more scenes to represent a complete chapter of the Book of Revelation. In contrast also to Dürer's large, self-sufficient compositions, these images are always subservient to the text. They are cut in a naive style which ignores modulation of form, and hand-colouring was applied to enhance their appearance (see also p.104, fig. 2).
G.B.

4

Albrecht Dürer

5 Albrecht Dürer (1471–1528)

The Apocalypse [Apocalipsis Cu[m] Figuris], Nuremberg 1511

Title-page: *The Virgin Appearing to St John*

Woodcut, inscribed by a sixteenth-century owner *N. Foucquart*, 183 × 183mm (image)

Watermark: tower with crown and flower (Meder 259)

Lit: Adam von Bartsch, *Le Peintre-graveur*, 21 vols, Vienna 1803–21, no. 60; Campbell Dodgson, *Catalogue of Early German and Flemish Woodcuts Preserved in the Department of Prints and Drawings in the British Museum*, vol. I, London, 1903; vol. II, London 1911, I, p.262, 6; Joseph Meder, *Dürer-Katalog: ein Handbuch über Albrecht Dürers Stiche, Radierungen, Holzschnitte, deren Zustände, Ausgaben und Wasserzeichen*, Vienna 1932, no.163; Heimo Reinitzer, *Biblia deutsch. Luthers Bibelübersetzung und ihre Tradition*, exhib. cat., Herzog August Bibliothek, Wolfenbüttel 1983–4. no.75

London, British Museum 1895-1-22-580. Presented by William Mitchell

5

Dürer designed and published his series of fifteen full-page woodcuts of the Apocalypse in both German and Latin editions in Nuremberg in 1498, only three years after he had opened his workshop, where he intended from the outset that prints should provide his main source of income. It is remarkable for being the first book in Western art to be both designed and published by a major artist. Dürer's choice of the Apocalypse theme for the first of his series of religious prints must have been determined as much by the approaching half-millennium as by the traditional popularity of the subject. In many late fifteenth-century bibles, the superlative quality of the Apocalypse imagery of earlier manuscripts and block-books is merely acknowledged in so far as the Book of Revelation was the only section to be illustrated at all beyond the title-page. In aesthetic terms, Dürer's printed work stands out as the true successor to the medieval tradition, and the dramatic effect of its wide circulation cannot be underestimated. The appearance of full-page woodcuts of such superior technical quality and boldness of design that they could stand apart from the text made a sensational impact on the history of printmaking. As a subject, the cycle established an iconographic standard on which all future printed interpretations of the Apocalypse were based; and indeed, the designs were copied not just in woodcuts and engravings, but also in paintings, reliefs, tapestries and enamels, both within Germany and in France, Italy and Russia. Through intermediary copies, their influence extended as far as the monasteries of Mount Athos.

This series is the second edition of Dürer's Apocalypse, which he published with a Latin text in Nuremberg in 1511, and in which the woodcut on the title-page seen here appears for the first time. The series is bound with editions of Dürer's *Life of the Virgin* and *Large Passion* which he re-issued at the same time, and the signature of a very early owner on the title-pages of all three indicates that this set has remained united since the sixteenth century.

G.B.

6 Albrecht Dürer (1471–1528)

The Martyrdom of St John, 1498

Woodcut, borders trimmed slightly, 388 × 281mm

Watermark: imperial orb (Meder 53)

Lit: Bartsch, 61; Campbell Dodgson, I, p.272, 10; Meder, 164 (before text); Giulia Bartrum, *German Renaissance Prints 1490–1550*, exhib. cat., British Museum, London 1995, no.13

London, British Museum 1895-1-22-575. Presented by William Mitchell

The fifteen woodcuts of Dürer's Apocalypse described here do not come from a single series. This print, together with cats 9, 17, 19, 20, are on paper with the same watermark, and were all issued without text at an early stage of the printing. To judge from the numerous examples of impressions without text of the Apocalypse, and of Dürer's other large woodcut series in major print rooms today, Dürer clearly foresaw some demand for loose impressions of the series by issuing a sizeable number of them in this way. The remaining prints (cats 7, 8, 10–16, 18) come from a complete set of the first Latin edition (Nuremberg 1498) which was removed from its original binding before it entered the British Museum.

Dürer has represented the *Martyrdom of St John* as a prologue to the scenes of the Apocalypse, following a tradition established by Jacobus de Voragine in his *Golden Legend* that the author was tortured in a vat of boiling oil at the order of the Roman emperor Domitian for his refusal to worship pagan gods. After his miraculous escape from this ordeal, he was banished to Patmos, where he wrote down his Revelation. The subject was used in an illustration in the Cologne Bible (1478) in which the martyrdom, together with John on Patmos and the first vision of the Revelation, are shown in a small cut on the title-page (fig. 2). The block was reprinted in the bible published by Dürer's godfather Anton Koberger (cat. 4), from which Dürer borrowed the typeface and translation for the text of his series. Dürer's radical interpretation of the scene is typical of his determination to create woodcut compositions of a vastly superior quality. He placed the martyrdom in a sixteenth-century setting, thereby providing an earthly counterpoint to the visionary scenes that follow: the numerous bystanders are wearing contemporary dress, there is a view of a Venetian-style palace in the background and the Roman emperor is represented as a Turkish sultan, who would have been instantly recognized as the arch-enemy of Christianity and therefore the personification of Antichrist to contemporary viewers.

G.B.

6

7 Albrecht Dürer (1471–1528)

St John's Vision of the Seven Candlesticks, 1498 (Rev. 1: 10–16)

Woodcut, 397 × 288mm

Lit: Bartsch, 62; Campbell Dodgson, I, p.261, 2; Meder, 165 (Latin edition)

London, British Museum 1895-1-22-560. Presented by William Mitchell

Dürer has followed the treatment of this subject, in which John kneels before a vision of God seated on a rainbow, from the first illustration to Revelation in the Cologne and Koberger Bibles (see p.104, fig. 2). No further comparison can be made, however, because Dürer's sophisticated interpretation in terms of technique and design is overwhelming. The variety of decorative forms he introduced to the candlesticks also reveals his close connection with the goldsmiths' art, in which as a youth he received training from his father.
G.B.

Dürer's vision of Heaven, set above a peaceful landscape, is not only a clear contrast with the catastrophes to come later in Revelation, but also reveals his desire to interpret the text in terms of a contemporary, earthly setting. He probably designed the landscape on the basis of numerous landscape watercolours of the Alps and of scenes around Nuremberg which he produced during 1494–6; although the small hillside town and water-mill seen here may not show specific locations, they certainly represent buildings of the period.
G.B.

8 Albrecht Dürer (1471–1528)

St John Kneeling before Christ and the Twenty-Four Elders, 1498 (Rev. 4: 2–8)

Woodcut, 395 × 284mm

Lit: Bartsch, 63; Campbell Dodgson, I, p.261, 2; Meder, 166 (Latin edition)

London, British Museum 1895-1-22-561. Presented by William Mitchell

9 Albrecht Dürer (1471–1528)

The Four Horsemen of the Apocalypse, 1498 (Rev. 6: 1–8)

Woodcut, borders trimmed slightly, 392 × 282mm

Watermark: imperial orb (Meder 53)

Lit: Bartsch, 64; Campbell Dodgson, I, p.272, 11; Meder, 167 (before text b); *German Renaissance Prints*, 14

London, British Museum 1895-1-22-576. Presented by William Mitchell

7

8

The text in Revelation associated with Dürer's *Four Horsemen*, one of the most memorable images in the history of printmaking, relates to the Lamb with Seven Horns and Seven Eyes who takes a scroll from Christ and breaks its seven seals. Each opening is associated with events which are described at some length in the text, but unlike the early block-book woodcuts, which show these episodes individually, Dürer displayed the opening of the first four seals in one image. In this he follows the tradition of the Cologne and Koberger Bibles; but his powerfully designed and superbly cut composition fully maximizes the dramatic effect of the subject. The first rider on a white horse, with a bow and crown, is the Conqueror; the second, on a red horse and holding a sword, represents War; the third, on a black horse and brandishing a pair of scales, Famine; and the fourth, on a 'pale horse', is Death, followed closely by Hell. The figure of an emperor is the first to be swallowed by Hell, and the inevitability of the fate of all social classes is signified by the different figures trampled underfoot.
G.B.

10 Albrecht Dürer (1471–1528)

The Opening of the Fifth and Sixth Seals, 1498 (Rev. 6: 9–17)

Woodcut, 394 × 285mm

Lit: Bartsch, 65; Campbell Dodgson, I, p.261, 2; Meder, 168 (Latin edition)

London, British Museum 1895-1-22-563. Presented by William Mitchell

The upper section of this print represents the opening of the fifth seal, which was accompanied by a vision of the martyrs of Roman persecution 'under the altar' awaiting their vindication. They are presented with white robes and told to 'rest yet for a little season' for their fellow martyrs to be killed. In contrast to earlier and later interpretations of the event, where this is shown as a single scene, Dürer has combined it with the breaking of the sixth seal, which brought the day of wrath: 'there was a great earthquake; and the sun became black as sackcloth of hair, and the moon became as blood; and the stars of heaven fell unto the earth, … and the heaven departed as a scroll when it is rolled together; and every mountain and island were moved out of their places'.
G.B.

9

10

11

12

11 Albrecht Dürer (1471–1528)

Four Angels Holding back the Winds, and the Marking of the Elect,
1498 (Rev. 7: 1–8)

Woodcut, 396 × 286mm

Lit: Bartsch, 66; Campbell Dodgson, I, p.261, 2; Meder, 169 (Latin
edition)

London, British Museum 1895-1-22-564. Presented by William
Mitchell

Four angels armed with swords on the left restrain the four
winds of the earth, represented as heads in the upper section
of the print, so that an angel can mark the foreheads of
144,000 people who were to be protected from the
impending disasters. The four winds have been interpreted
as the great empires of antiquity. Dürer has represented a
motionless tree, laden with fruit, between the angels to
emphasize the atmosphere of calm they instilled.
G.B.

12 Albrecht Dürer (1471–1528)

The Opening of the Seventh Seal and the Eagle Crying 'Woe', 1498
(Rev. 8: 1–13)

Woodcut, 393 × 284mm

Lit: Bartsch, 68; Campbell Dodgson, I, p.261, 2; Meder, 170 (Latin
edition)

London, British Museum 1895-1-22-565. Presented by William
Mitchell

Dürer's prime interest in the composition of a striking series
of prints, rather than elucidation of a difficult text, always
governed his selection of subjects from the Book of
Revelation. Here he has displayed an extensive landscape to
show in one single drama the catastrophic events connected
with the opening of the seventh seal, which were usually
treated separately. The eagle crying 'Woe' to warn those on
earth of the sounding of the last trumpets appears in the
centre of the design. The various disasters include the
raining of hail and fire mingled with blood, the casting of a
burning mountain into the sea with destruction of creatures
and ships, the burning of one third of the earth, the
destruction of one third of the life in the sea and the
poisoning of one third of the rivers. The descent of the
burning star, Wormwood, seen here on the left, unleashed a

13

14

plague of monstrous locusts which Dürer has ignored. He evidently felt that his composition was complete without the locusts, which are often seen in earlier representations of the text and were also given considerable significance by the reformer Martin Luther in his translations of the Bible (see cats 35, 45, 56).

G.B.

13 Albrecht Dürer (1471–1528)

The Four Angels of Death, 1498 (Rev. 9: 13–19)

Woodcut, 392 × 282mm

Lit: Bartsch, 69; Campbell Dodgson, I, p.261, 2; Meder, 171 (Latin edition)

London, British Museum 1895-1-22-566. Presented by William Mitchell

The sixth trumpet released from the river Euphrates the four angels of death and their cavalry, whose horses had lions' heads and serpent-headed tails. They were responsible for slaying one third of all mankind, which Dürer has represented by showing a knight, a bishop, an emperor and a pope dead in the foreground.

G.B.

14 Albrecht Dürer (1471–1528)

St John Eating the Book, 1498 (Rev. 10: 1–11)

Woodcut, 394 × 287mm

Lit: Bartsch, 70; Campbell Dodgson, I, p.261, 2; Meder, 172 (Latin edition)

London, British Museum 1895-1-22-567. Presented by William Mitchell

This print is one of Dürer's most precise interpretations of the subjects of Revelation. The angel who appeared to John was holding a little book and was clothed with cloud, with a rainbow on his head and a face like the sun. He had feet like pillars of fire and stood on the earth and the sea, with one hand raised to Heaven. The notion of John literally eating the book, shown here for the first time, influenced all later representations of the subject: 'And I took the little book out of the angel's hand, and ate it up; and it was in my mouth sweet as honey: and as soon as I had eaten it, my belly was bitter'.

G.B.

I5 Albrecht Dürer (1471–1528)

The Woman of the Apocalypse and the Seven-Headed Dragon, 1498
(Rev. 12: 1–6)

Woodcut, 393 × 281mm

Lit: Bartsch, 71; Campbell Dodgson, I, p.261, 2; Meder, 173 (Latin edition)

London, British Museum 1895-1-22-568. Presented by William Mitchell

After the seventh trumpet sounded, an earthquake and storm were followed by the appearance of the vision in Heaven: 'a woman clothed with the sun, and the moon under her feet, and upon her head a crown of twelve stars'. A dragon with seven heads and ten horns stands nearby, waiting to devour the child she is about to bear; but the child is carried safely to Heaven, and the woman is provided with wings to escape from the dragon. The woman was identified by early commentators as a symbol of Israel or Jerusalem, but during the thirteenth century she came to be associated with the Virgin Mary. The newborn child symbolized Christ and the Church. During the Counter-Reformation in the seventeenth century veneration of the Virgin intensified considerably, and representations of the 'woman clothed with the sun' as a symbol of the Virgin, very much in the manner of Dürer's figure but without the wings, were commonly seen.

The dramatic power of Dürer's design here has much to do with his selection of memorable images from the text, without concern for chronological sequence. The battle between St Michael and the dragon, which is the subject of the following print of Dürer's series, takes place in Chapter 12 of Revelation after the dragon appears to threaten the woman and her newborn son, but before she is provided with wings to escape, and before the great torrent of water pours from the mouth of the dragon, 'that he might cause her to be carried away of the flood' from which she is saved by the earth, which 'opened, and swallowed up the flood' (Rev. 12: 14–16). Dürer has represented a particularly powerful apocalyptic monster here, due in no small part to the vigorous emanation of water from its mouth beneath the woman's feet.

G.B.

15

16 Albrecht Dürer (1471–1528)

St Michael fighting the Dragon, 1498 (Rev. 12: 7–9)

Woodcut, 394 × 284mm

Lit: Bartsch, 72; Campbell Dodgson, I, p.261, 2; Meder, 174 (Latin edition)

London, British Museum 1895-1-22-569. Presented by William Mitchell

The dramatic form of this composition, with its focus on the figure of St Michael and its striking contrast between the battle above and the peaceful landscape below, is entirely unrelated to earlier Apocalypse iconography and was not taken up by Lucas Cranach and his followers in illustrations to Luther's Bible. It became, however, a central image of the triumph of Christianity over evil and was commonly treated as a subject apart from the Apocalypse cycle, particularly in Counter-Reformation imagery (see cats 103, 109). The idea of setting the figures in the sky against a densely hatched background stems from engravings by Martin Schongauer, such as his *Temptation of St Anthony* (Bartsch 47).

The influence of Dürer's Apocalypse series is evident from an early date. His composition of *St Michael* was a source of inspiration to the anonymous illuminator of the early sixteenth-century German prayerbook at Keble College, Oxford (see Ch. 3, cat. 26).
G.B.

17 Albrecht Dürer (1471–1528)

The Beast with the Lamb's Horns and the Beast with Seven Heads; Christ holding the Sickle, 1498 (Rev. 13: 1–20; 14: 14–18)

Woodcut, borders trimmed slightly; repaired upper left; 387 × 282mm

Watermark: imperial orb (Meder 53)

Lit: Bartsch, 74; Campbell Dodgson, I, p.272, 13; Meder, 175 (before text)

London, British Museum E. 2–286. Bequeathed by Joseph Nollekens (1737–1823) subject to a life interest to Francis Douce, 1834

Dürer has here combined episodes from two chapters of Revelation. The beast with seven heads and ten horns emerging from the sea, with a mortal wound which healed (represented by the head which falls back as if dead) and bearing the number 666, has been interpreted at different stages as the emperor Nero and Antichrist (see cat. 3). The appearance of a second beast with lamb's horns, which made fire rain from Heaven, caused people to worship the first beast. The figure of Christ with a crown and a sickle enthroned above is related to the vision of the harvest of the world in the following chapter. Angels are sent out to gather grapes and cast them into 'the great winepress of the wrath of God': a symbol of the fate of the damned at the Last Judgement.
G.B.

16

17

18 Albrecht Dürer (1471–1528)

The Hymn in Adoration of the Lamb, 1498 (Rev.7: 9–14; 14: 1–5)

Woodcut, 393 × 282mm

Lit: Bartsch, 67; Campbell Dodgson, I, p.261, 2; Meder, 176 (Latin edition)

London, British Museum 1895-1-22-571. Presented by William Mitchell

Dürer's composition of the hymn in praise of the Lamb, which tells of God's forthcoming victory over Satan, also refers to different parts of the text. In terms of the iconography of his series, it was probably important to represent a positive subject between two woodcuts representing evil aspects of the Book of Revelation. The multitude of people clothed in white holding palms and the conversation between John and one of the Elders, seen here in the foreground, come from Chapter 7; but the subject also refers to the vision of the Lamb on Mount Sion at the beginning of Chapter 14.

G.B.

19 Albrecht Dürer (1471–1528)

The Whore of Babylon, the Destruction of Babylon and the Vision of the Knight Faithful and True, 1498 (Rev. 17, 18, 19)

Woodcut, borders trimmed slightly; 391 × 282mm

Watermark: imperial orb (Meder 53)

Lit: Bartsch, 73; Campbell Dodgson, I, p.272, 12; Meder, 177 (before text)

London, British Museum 1895-1-22-577. Presented by William Mitchell

Although this composition is dominated by the elegant figure of the Whore of Babylon from Chapter 17 (Rev. 17: 3–6), Dürer has created a dramatic background by adding episodes from the two following chapters, which were usually represented separately. The central figure represents a woman clothed in purple and scarlet, decked with jewellery and mounted on a scarlet beast that had seven heads and ten horns; she holds a gold cup full of 'abominations and filthiness of her fornication'. Dürer gives this colourful description a contemporary feel by copying the details of her costume and headdress from his drawing of a Venetian lady made in Italy in 1495 (Vienna, Albertina, inv. no. 3064 D37). Her admirers also wear contemporary dress. The Turkish sultan figure, seen here in the centre with his back to the viewer, appeared in the *Martyrdom of St John* (cat. 6), and a woman from Nuremberg and a German mercenary soldier, with tall feathers in his hat, stand behind the kneeling figure of a monk on the left. At a very early stage commentators associated the Whore of Babylon with Rome, because of the reference in the text to the seven hills represented by the beast's seven heads (Rev. 17: 9).

G.B.

18

19

20 Albrecht Dürer (1471–1528)

The Angel with the Key of the Bottomless Pit and the Vision of the New Jerusalem, 1498 (Rev. 20: 1–3; 21: 9–27)

Woodcut, 391 × 281mm

Watermark: imperial orb (Meder 53)

Lit: Bartsch, 75; Campbell Dodgson, I, p.272, 14; Meder, 178 (before text)

London, British Museum 1895-1-22-579. Presented by William Mitchell

The final print concludes the series on a triumphant note: an angel with the key of hell chains Satan, 'that serpent of old', and locks him in a pit for one thousand years. In the background, another angel shows John a vision of the New Jerusalem, which is represented as a medieval town with only the appearance of an angel at the gate to give a clue of its heavenly nature.

The countless copies and derivations of Dürer's Apocalypse series were due in part to its rapid circulation. It possibly even inspired the work of contemporary Italian Renaissance artists. A drawing after a lost original by Leonardo da Vinci of *c*.1508 in the Royal Collection at Windsor Castle records a monster which bears many of the attributes of Dürer's figure of Satan seen here (inv. no. 12371; see K. Clark and C. Pedretti, *The Drawings of Leonardo da Vinci at Windsor Castle*, London 1968). Leonardo may have

produced the drawing in connection with a projected series of illustrations to Dante's *Divine Comedy*, bearing in mind the well-known series of drawings of the same subject by Sandro Botticelli of *c*.1480–*c*.1503 (Berlin, Kupferstichkabinett, and Vatican City).

G.B.

21 Albrecht Dürer (1471–1528)

Recto: *Death riding a Horse*, 1505

Verso: *An Owl*

Charcoal, inscribed by the artist '*A memento of me* [*ME*/[*M*]*ENTO*/ *MEI*] 1505' with his monogram, 211 × 265mm

Watermark: imperial orb with a star (similar to Briquet 3058)

Lit: John Rowlands with the assistance of Giulia Bartrum, *Drawings by German Artists and Artists from German-speaking Regions of Europe in the Department of Prints and Drawings in the British Museum: The Fifteenth Century and the Sixteenth Century by Artists born before 1530*, 2 vols, London 1993, no.163

London, British Museum 1895-9-15-971

The large inscription indicates that Dürer possibly made this drawing for a friend. The image recalls the figure of Death in his woodcut of the *Four Horsemen of the Apocalypse* of seven years earlier (cat. 9). This crowned figure is more skeletal, however, and the attributes of a scythe and a bell emphasize the role of Death as the Grim Reaper. It has been thought that the drawing was prompted by the epidemic of plague that broke out in Nuremberg in 1505.

This drawing has been cited as one of the possible sources for a group of works (two drawings and a painting) of 1933–5 by Salvador Dalí, all of which have as their subject the horseman, Death (see R. Gassen and B. Holeczek (eds), *Apokalypse. Ein Prinzip Hoffnung?*, exh. cat., Ludwigshafen am Rhein, Wilhelm Hack Museum, 1985, p.258, no.128).

G.B.

20

21

St John writing the Book of Revelation on Patmos: the Landscape Tradition

22 Martin Schongauer (c.1450–91)

St John on Patmos, c.1480–5

Engraving, trimmed slightly, 160 × 113mm

Lit: Bartsch, 55; Max Lehrs, *Geschichte und kritischer Katalog des deutschen, niederländischen und französischen Kupferstichs im XV. Jahrhundert*, 9 vols, Vienna 1908–34, V, no.60

London, British Museum 1845-8-9-269

St John the Evangelist is shown, with his eagle nearby, seated on the island of Patmos. He is in the act of writing the Book of Revelation, which lies open on his left knee, when he is distracted by the subject of his vision, the Woman of the Apocalypse clothed with the Sun and crowned with twelve stars described in Chapter 12, who appears in the upper left corner. The subject of John on Patmos appeared frequently in manuscripts (see Ch. 3, cat. 23) and was also represented on the title-page woodcut to Revelation in the Cologne Bible of *c.*1478, which Schongauer probably would have known,

cut in a simplified form together with the *Martyrdom of St John* and the *Vision of Seven Candlesticks* (see p.104, fig. 2). The scene was represented in two engravings during the 1460s by Master E.S., in which the figure of the Woman of the Apocalypse also appeared (Lehrs vol. II, nos 150–1).

Martin Schongauer's print is notable, however, for its treatment of the landscape setting. Schongauer lived and worked around Colmar and was the first well-known painter to develop the medium of engraving. Many of his prints are figure compositions with only a slight indication of background, but the particular attention paid to the landscape here, seen in the central position of the tree, the different types of plants and the shoreline beyond, reflects the interest in contemporary Netherlandish painting in using this theme as a pretext to display elaborate landscapes. Paintings such as the right wing of the *Altarpiece of St John*, 1479, by Hans Memlinc (Bruges, Hospital of St John); *St John on Patmos*, c.1480/1510, by Hieronymus Bosch (c.1450–1516; Berlin, Gemäldegalerie), or *St John writing his Gospel in a Landscape*, c.1475/1500, by an artist who worked in the circle of Dirk Bouts (c.1415/20–75; Rotterdam, Boymans-van Beuningen Museum) are certainly related to Schongauer's design.

G.B.

22

23

23 Jan Wellens de Cock (c.1490–c.1527)

St John on Patmos, c.1520/5

Woodcut, trimmed along right edge, 269 × 375mm

Lit: J.D. Passavant, *Le Peintre-graveur*, 6 vols, Leipzig 1860–4, II, 287, 1; F.W.H. Hollstein, *Dutch and Flemish Etchings, Engravings and Woodcuts, c.1450–1700*, Amsterdam 1949 – no. 2

London, British Museum 1918-7-13-70

The idea of emphasizing the landscape in connection with the subject of John on Patmos is further developed in this Netherlandish woodcut of the second decade of the sixteenth century. The earliest predominantly landscape prints date from this period, such as Albrecht Dürer's *Landscape with a Cannon* of 1518 and Albrecht Altdorfer's landscape etchings of *c*.1520–1. Printmakers were unsure how the market would react to scenes of pure landscape, and there is a significant amount of other detail in this print to link it with the subject of John writing his Book of Revelation. The appearance of the devil stealing the inkpot and holder in an attempt to prevent the author from

completing his work stems from the painting of *St John on Patmos* by Hieronymus Bosch (see cat. 22), to whom this print was formerly attributed. In the painting, the devil is apparently prevented from stealing the inkpot by a stern glance from the eagle. A similar idea is expressed in the painting *St John writing his Gospel in a Landscape* (circle of Dirk Bouts, see cat. 22) in which the devil is shown pouring ink away. The woodcut also shows images of death in the left background which serve as a reminder of the catastrophes of the Apocalypse: the skeleton of a fish, the wheels on long posts to which victims of torture were strapped and the human skull underneath. The peaceful view of a town on the right, underneath the figure of the Woman of the Apocalypse, perhaps refers to the New Jerusalem.

Jan Wellens de Cock was a painter and draughtsman from Antwerp whose work is little known; he was the father of the landscape painter Matthijs Cock (*c*.1510–*c*.1548) and the successful printmaker and publisher Hieronymus Cock (*c*.1510–70).

G.B.

24

24 Monogrammist HWG

St John on Patmos, c.1545–55

Woodcut, trimmed along right edge, 193 × 370mm

Lit: G.K. Nagler, *Die Monogrammisten*, 5 vols, Munich 1858–79.
Facsimile reprint, Nieuwkoop 1977, III, no.1722, 2; Passavant, IV,
p.303, no.1; *Prints and Drawings of the Danube School*, exhib. cat.
ed. A. Shestack and C. Talbot, New Haven, Yale University Art
Gallery 1969, no.112

London, British Museum 1848-2-12-83

Nothing is known about the designer of this woodcut, which
is one of three prints of landscapes to have survived signed
with the initials HWG. It is possible that he worked in the
studio of Virgil Solis in Nuremberg (see cat. 82) but the clear
emphasis on the landscape with its panoramic view across
woodland, hills and water, and the treatment of pine trees
cut off at the edge of the design, is more reminiscent of work
of the Danube school artists, Albrecht Altdorfer
(*c.*1482/5–1538) and Wolf Huber (*c.*1480/5–1553). St John is
here relegated to the lower right corner, with the subject of
his Revelation, the Woman of the Apocalypse, only just
visible in a cloud on the upper edge. Unlike Jan Wellens de
Cock's interpretation of the subject (cat. 23) the few signs of
human activity in the landscape give no indication of the
disasters of the Apocalypse, but rather signify the pastoral
existence of John on Patmos in contrast to the violence of his
visions.
G.B.

The Book of Revelation in Sixteenth-Century Bibles and the influence of the Reformation

25 Giovanni Andrea Vavassore

(active 1510–72)

Apocalypse [*Apocalypsis Ihesv Christi flvctvabit sed non de
mergetvr*], A. Paganini, Venice 1516

Fig. II: *St John's Vision of the Seven Candlesticks* (Rev. 1: 10–16)

Woodcut, 265 × 190mm

Lit: Passavant, V, pp.86f., 63

London, British Museum 1883-11-10-260

The title-page to this Italian publication of the Apocalypse is
illustrated with a woodcut of Christ asleep on the boat in the
storm on Lake Galilee. The fifteen illustrations to Revelation
are, with one exception, much simplified copies cut in
reverse after Dürer's series, which had wide circulation in
Italy from an early date. The single exception is the second
print of the series, seen here, where God the Father is
represented standing, instead of seated on a rainbow as in
Dürer's print (cat. 7) and the figure of John is lying on the
ground instead of kneeling, when he 'fell as dead' at God's
feet. This interpretation was used later in Luther's September
Testament of 1522 illustrated by Lucas Cranach the Elder
(cat. 27), who depicted John in a prostrate position in
accordance with the literal reading of the text advocated by

Secunda figura

25

Luther, but Cranach did not use this print as a source. The iconography used by Vavassore has a different origin, probably taken from a drawn or printed copy of a medieval manuscript. The same source was also used in a drawing of *St John's Vision of the Seven Candlesticks* by the Venetian artist Domenico Campagnola (1500–64) in his series of twenty-two Apocalypse drawings in the Royal Collection, Windsor Castle, none of which is related to Dürer (inv. no. 7764; see A.E. Popham and J. Wilde, *Italian Drawings of the XV and XVI Centuries at Windsor Castle*, London 1949, no.161). Campagnola used the same figural positions as Vavassore, with God the Father holding keys in his left hand and stars in his right, and the prostrate figure of John turning his head upwards, as well as the same frontal display of candlesticks with four on the left and three on the right.

Vavassore was a well-known block-cutter and publisher, who also worked as a book dealer in Venice during the first half of the sixteenth century.

G.B.

26 Lucas Cranach I (1472–1553)
and Workshop

The Lives of Christ and Antichrist [*Antithesis figurata vitae Christi et Antichristi*]

J. Grunenberg, Wittenberg 1521

The Ascension of Christ and *The Descent of Antichrist into Hell*

Woodcuts from two blocks, each approx. 120 × 95mm

Watermark: bull's head and shield partly visible on some sheets

Lit: Campbell Dodgson, II, p.324, 3; F.W.H. Hollstein, *German Engravings, Etchings and Woodcuts, c.1400–1700*, Amsterdam 1954 – no. 66y and z; Karin Groll, *Das 'Passional Christi und Antichristi' von Lucas Cranach d. Ä*, Frankfurt 1990, 27–8; *German Renaissance Prints*, 181

London, British Museum 1851-8-2-2 (25) and (26)

Commonly known as the *Passional Christi und Antichristi*, this was first published in May 1521, shortly after the Diet of Worms, at which the papal bull of excommunication issued against Martin Luther was ratified by Emperor Charles V. To ensure Luther's personal safety, he was hidden under the protection of the elector Frederick the Wise of Saxony in the castle of Wartburg, near Eisenach, where he remained until the spring of 1522. The pamphlet was inspired by ideas in Luther's manifestos of 1520, although in form it is a simple elaboration of the traditional *Passional*, a prayerbook with scenes from the life of Christ, the Virgin Mary, or of the saints (see pp.109ff.). It contains twenty-six woodcuts in which scenes from the life of Christ are juxtaposed with those of the Antichrist, who is identified with the pope. The moralizing commentaries underneath each design were written by Philip Melanchthon and the lawyer Johann Schwertfeger, with Luther's approval.

By the end of the fifteenth century, the Antichrist was as common a figure of popular belief as Satan, and a Latin summary of his life appeared in nine printed editions between 1473 and 1505 (see cat. 3). His precise identification always remained vague, although the fact that his appearance was a sign that the end of the world was imminent meant that he was closely associated with interpretations of the Apocalypse. Criticism of the Church in the form of comparative texts of the life of Christ and Antichrist as seen here was not new; it had been used, for instance, by the English priest John Wycliffe (c.1320–84) in his *De Christo et suo adversario Antichristo* of c.1383/4, and comparative manuscript illustrations were produced under the influence of the Bohemian church critic Jan Hus (c.1369–1415). The importance of the *Passional Christi und Antichristi*, however, lies in the fact that it became the most influential piece of visual propaganda produced by the reformers. This is primarily to do with the much wider circulation of the printed book than manuscript text, but it is also related to the particular interest generated at that time by any publication associated with Martin Luther,

26

whose activities became the focus of wide public attention only after the Diet of Worms.

The book is open at the final pair of images, *The Ascension of Christ* and *The Descent of Antichrist into Hell*, in which Christ ascends to the Father in Heaven, while the Antichrist's efforts to imitate Christ are defeated in mid-flight and he is despatched to hell. Cranach would have been aware of the woodcut of the latter subject in the *Nuremberg Chronicle* of 1493 (fig. 6) in which, however, the identification with the pope was not made. A drawing of *c.*1538 of the *Descent of the Pope and his Followers into Hell* produced in Cranach's workshop (Bamberg, Staatsbibliothek, I. Pa.21) is a more elaborate form of Cranach's design for the *Passional*, and is probably connected with two paintings of *The Ascension of Christ* and the *Descent of the Pope into Hell* in the electoral castle at Torgau, for which Cranach was paid in 1538 (see Dieter Koepplin and Tilman Falk, *Lukas Cranach: Gemälde Zeichnungen Druckgraphik*, exh. cat., Basel, Kunstmuseum 1976, vol.2, p.512, no.360).

G.B.

27 Lucas Cranach I (1472–1553)
and Workshop

Martin Luther, *The German New Testament* [*Das Newe Testament Deutzsch*], Wittenberg, September 1522

Frontispiece and opening to the Book of Revelation, *St John's Vision of the Seven Candlesticks* (Rev. 1: 10–17)

Woodcut, 233 × 161mm

Lit: Campbell Dodgson, II, pp.330f, no.23; Hollstein, 30a; Reinitzer, 73, 74

London, British Library, C.36 g.7

Luther completed his translation of the New Testament in just under eleven weeks from December 1521, while he was in hiding in the castle of Wartburg. Due to the fact that his works were banned by the Catholic Church after his excommunication, author and publication details are never mentioned in his early bibles. It is known from other sources, however, that Melchior Lotter was the printer and that Christian Döring was the publisher of this first edition of the New Testament, known as the September Testament, for which Döring provided financial backing for 3,000 copies to be printed. It sold out so quickly that a second edition was produced in December of the same year (cat. 28). Although based loosely on Dürer's woodcuts in appearance, the twenty-one designs for the Apocalypse, the only part of the book to be illustrated, are quite different from pre-Reformation series, on account of their close link with

Die offinbarung

Luther's precise interpretation of the Revelation of St John and his insistence that images should always remain subservient to text. Luther also viewed the text as a prophecy of the history of Christianity, and considered the apocalyptic events an inevitable retribution for the abuses perpetrated by the Catholic Church. The development of the identification of the pope as the monster Antichrist stemmed from this line of reasoning, and three of Cranach's woodcuts in the September Testament, *The Two Witnesses and the Beast from the Bottomless Pit*, the *Angels Emptying Seven Vials* and the *Whore of Babylon*, show dragons and the figure of the Whore wearing three-tiered papal tiaras for the first time in connection with Reformation propaganda. The directness of this satire proved unacceptable at this early date, and a decree was issued by the elector's brother, Duke Georg of Saxony, and other princes, banning the printing of such anti-papal polemic. In the second edition of the New Testament, the blocks were altered to show non-specific two-tiered crowns. In the *Destruction of Babylon*, however, Cranach identified Babylon as Rome by adding recognizable views of the Castel Sant'Angelo and the Belvedere, details which remained unaltered. Ultimately, the powerful impact of the reformers' imagery was crucial, because Cranach's series had a more pervasive influence on book illustrations of the Apocalypse than Dürer's technically and aesthetically far superior series of 1498. Curiously, this influence was not restricted to Reformation literature, because Cranach sold the blocks of his series to Luther's rival, Hieronymus Emser (1478–1527), in 1527. A German bible for a Catholic readership, with Emser's re-worked translation and a foreword written by Duke Georg of Saxony, was published in Dresden by Wolfgang Stöckel in 1527 (see Reinitzer 111) with nineteen of the Cranach Apocalypse illustrations, and two from the series designed by Georg Lemberger (see cat. 42). By the eighteenth century it had been reprinted almost a hundred times.

Cranach's frontispiece, *St John's Vision of the Seven Candlesticks*, exhibited here, is typical of the more literal interpretation of the text advocated by Luther. In contrast to Dürer's woodcut (cat. 7), the face of God is represented as the sun rather than with a striated nimbus, the sword comes directly out of God's mouth instead of next to it, and John is shown prostrate rather than kneeling, to accord more closely with the text: 'and out of his mouth went a sharp two-edged sword: and his countenance was as the sun shineth in his strength. And when I saw him, I fell at his feet as dead' (Rev. 1: 16–17).

G.B.

145

28 Lucas Cranach I (1472–1553)

and Workshop

Martin Luther, *The German New Testament* [*Das Newe Testament Deutzsch*], Wittenberg, December 1522

Fols 76 v–77 r: *The Four Horsemen* and the *Opening of the Fifth Seal and Clothing the Elect* (Rev. 6: 1–11)

Woodcuts from two blocks, each approx. 233 × 161mm

Lit: Campbell Dodgson, II, p.331, no.24; Hollstein, 30c; Reinitzer, 77, 109

London, British Library 1562/285

The major difference to the second edition of Luther's New Testament, the so-called December Testament, is that the papal tiaras which appear in the first edition in *The Two Witnesses and the Beast from the Bottomless Pit*, the *Angels Emptying Seven Vials* and the *Whore of Babylon* were altered to represent less specific headdress. Cranach did not personally design all twenty-one illustrations to the Apocalypse, but allocated some to members of his workshop. The *Four Horsemen* exhibited here is attributed to the Master of the Zackenblätter, and in appearance is a much simplified derivation of Dürer's famous image. Significantly, the variety of figures trampled by the rider, Death, in Dürer's woodcut,

most notably the emperor in the mouth of hell, the cleric and the burgher, are not indicated here. The four figures in the lower right corner represent the lower classes. Luther considered the common man to be weak, inevitably to be overwhelmed by the forces of governmental authority, war, famine and plague. The *Opening of the Fifth Seal and Clothing the Elect*, designed by Cranach, is based on a scene in the uppermost section of Dürer's *Opening of the Fifth and Sixth Seals* (cat. 10). The idea of the martyrs being clothed by angels stems from the block-book Apocalypse, while the motif of an angel standing behind an altar distributing garments comes from the Cologne Bible.

The position of Cranach, who was court artist to the electors of Saxony and a personal friend of Luther, was of paramount importance in the dissemination of Lutheran literature. Not only did he design illustrations for Luther's work, but he also worked in partnership with Döring as publisher of the reformer's work from at least 1523 until *c.*1525–6. The two were granted a privilege in *c.*1525 by the elector's brother, Duke John I of Saxony, which gave them protection and exclusive rights to publish religious work of the reformers (see J. Flood, 'Lucas Cranach as Publisher', in *German Life and Letters*, XLVIII no.3, 1995, pp.241ff.). G.B.

28

29 Hans Holbein (1497/8–1543)

The Revelations of St John the Theologian [*Die offenbarung Sancti Joannis des Theologen*],

T. Wolff, Basel 1523

Fol.clxxxi r: *Seven Angels pouring out the Vials of God's Wrath* (Rev.16: 1–17)

Woodcut, 125 × 76mm

Lit: Reinitzer, 123; Hollstein, 49

London, British Museum 1904-2-6-59. Presented by William Mitchell

The publication of Luther's translation of the New Testament in September 1522 caused a sensation within the German-speaking world. In Switzerland the activity of the reformer Ulrich Zwingli (1484–1531) was of particular significance during the 1520s, and Luther's popularity here may be judged by the speed at which copies of his books appeared. The first pirated version of Luther's September Testament was published by Adam Petri in December 1522 (see *German Renaissance Prints*, 227), for which Holbein designed eight illustrations for the Gospels, and some initial letters; Revelation remained unillustrated. His series of twenty-one Apocalypse prints was commissioned from Holbein by Thomas Wolff, another Basel publisher, for a later version of Luther's New Testament which appeared just before August 1523. The paramount importance of Luther's text and its visual interpretation at this particular time was inevitably impressed on Holbein who, despite his international fame as an artist, produced designs which are merely notable for their subservience to the iconography established by Cranach for the September Testament. Fifteen of the designs, including *Seven Angels pouring out the Vials of God's Wrath*, were cut by Hans Lützelburger (active *c*.1514–26), the highly talented block-cutter who collaborated with Holbein on his famous *Dance of Death* (Lyons 1538).

Holbein's series of Apocalypse prints was reprinted by Wolff five times in both quarto and octavo publications, and once by Knoblauch in Strasbourg, before the end of 1524. Numerous copies or variants of the series appeared in bibles published in Paris, Antwerp and elsewhere during the 1530s, including editions of Tyndale's English New Testament of 1536 and 1537. Further evidence of the wide circulation of Holbein's series and copies of them is provided by the fact that they were used as models for the Apocalypse cycle in the monastery of St Docharíou on Mount Athos (see cat. 117).

G.B.

29

30–41 Hans Burgkmair

Twelve impressions from a series of twenty-one woodcuts of the Apocalypse, S. Otmar, Augsburg 1523

30 Hans Burgkmair (1473–1531)

The Vision of the Lamb and the Twenty-Four Elders (Rev. 4: 2–8)

Woodcut, borders trimmed, 161 × 129mm

Lit: Campbell Dodgson, II, p.422, 199; Hollstein, 8

London, British Museum 1909-4-3-28

Burgkmair's series of twenty-one Apocalypse prints was produced for a Lutheran translation of the New Testament published by Silvan Otmar in Augsburg, which appeared in four editions between March 1523 and April 1524. The demand for Luther's translation of the Bible since its first appearance in Wittenberg in September of the previous year (cat. 27) was so great that Otmar was also induced to publish an earlier, undated edition which contained only six of Burgkmair's woodcuts, presumably because the designer had not yet completed the series (see *Hans Burgkmair: Das graphische Werk*, ed. Tilman Falk *et al*, exh. cat., Augsburg, Städtische Kunstsammlungen 1973, no.145).

Hans Burgkmair was court artist to the Holy Roman emperor Maximilian I in Augsburg and the leading designer for the monumental woodcut projects commissioned by the emperor. Many of his woodcuts, particularly the single-sheet prints, are remarkable for their dramatic, innovatory style. Book illustrations were not usually produced with high artistic quality in mind, and the design of Burgkmair's Apocalypse series also suffered from shortage of time, but the artist certainly attempted a novel approach to the individual subjects. His images remain, however, fundamentally Lutheran in their close interpretation of the text, and follow the format and sequence of the December Testament. Like Cranach's series, they are smaller in size than Dürer's in order to accommodate text and image in close proximity on the page.

The Vision of the Lamb and the *Four Horsemen of the Apocalypse* (cat. 31) are the second and third prints of Burgkmair's series. The motif of the Gate of Heaven seen on the left comes from Dürer's print, but the diagonal axis of the throne of God creates a different sense of spatial awareness from the frontal view employed by both Dürer and Cranach, and is typical of the various perspectival angles Burgkmair employed throughout his series in an attempt to clarify the difficult subjects.

G.B.

30

31

32

31 Hans Burgkmair (1473–1531)

The Four Horsemen of the Apocalypse (Rev. 6: 1–8)

Woodcut, borders trimmed, 161 × 130mm

Lit: Campbell Dodgson, II, p.422, 200; Hollstein, 9

London, British Museum 1909-4-3-29

In contrast to the *Four Horsemen* of Dürer's series and that of the Wittenberg Bible in which the horsemen are represented galloping in the foreground alongside each other, Burgkmair shows them descending from clouds one behind the other. In this way the figures seem to appear literally from Heaven in front of John's eyes; he is not represented in the earlier series but is seen here watching the scene from below. Burgkmair has also moved hell to the upper part of the print, where it follows behind the last horseman, Death, in a close interpretation of the text: 'I looked, and behold a pale horse: and his name that sat on him was Death, and Hell followed with him.'
G.B.

32 Hans Burgkmair (1473–1531)

The Opening of the Fifth Seal and the Clothing of the Martyrs
(Rev. 6: 9–12)

Woodcut, upper and side borders trimmed, with two lines of lettering underneath; 154 × 130mm

Lit: Campbell Dodgson, II, p.422, 201; Hollstein, 10

London, British Museum 1909-4-3-30

This and the following woodcut are the fourth and fifth prints of the series. In treating these two subjects separately, Burgkmair has followed the example of the Wittenberg Bible rather than that of Dürer, who combined both scenes in one print (cat. 10). He has again employed a diagonal rather than the usual frontal perspective of the altar, which has the effect of increasing a sense of space, thereby providing room for the souls to be literally placed underneath the altar, as understood in the text: 'And when he had opened the fifth seal, I saw under the altar the souls of them that were slain for the word of God.'
G.B.

33

34

35

33 Hans Burgkmair (1473–1531)

The Opening of the Sixth Seal with Stars Falling (Rev. 6: 12–17)

Woodcut, 162 × 129mm

Lit: Campbell Dodgson, II, p.422, 212; Hollstein, 11

London, British Museum 1909-4-3-31

G.B.

34 Hans Burgkmair (1473–1531)

The Opening of the Seventh Seal and the Seven Trumpeters
(Rev. 8: 1–13)

Woodcut, lower and side borders trimmed, 162 × 129mm

Lit: Campbell Dodgson, II, p.422, 204; Hollstein, 13

London, British Museum 1909-4-3-33

G.B.

35 Hans Burgkmair (1473–1531)

The Star Falling into the Pit of Hell and the Plague of Locusts
(Rev. 9: 1–11)

Woodcut, 162 × 130mm

Lit: Campbell Dodgson, II, p.422, 205; Hollstein, 14

London, British Museum 1909-4-3-34

G.B.

36

37

38

36 Hans Burgkmair (1473–1531)

The Harvest of the World (Rev. 4: 14–20)

Woodcut, upper and side borders trimmed, 160×129mm

Lit: Campbell Dodgson, II, p.422, 212; Hollstein, 21

London, British Museum 1909-4-3-41

G.B.

37 Hans Burgkmair (1473–1531)

The Whore of Babylon (Rev. 17: 3–6)

Woodcut, 160×129 mm

Lit: Campbell Dodgson, II, p.422, 214; Hollstein, 23

London, British Museum 1909-4-3-43

G.B.

38 Hans Burgkmair (1473–1531)

The Destruction of Babylon (Rev. 18: 21–24)

Woodcut, borders trimmed, 161×130mm

Lit: Campbell Dodgson, II, p.422, 215; Hollstein, 24

London, British Museum 1909-4-3-44

G.B.

39 **Hans Burgkmair** (1473–1531)

The Vision of a Rider named Faithful and True (Rev. 19: 11–16)

Woodcut, borders trimmed, 161 × 129mm

Lit: Campbell Dodgson, II, p.422, 216; Hollstein, 25

London, British Museum 1909-4-3-45

Burgkmair's interpretation of the rider 'called faithful and true' extends to lettering the block *TREW UN WARHAFTIG* in a particularly close rendering of the text: 'And I saw heaven opened, and behold a white horse; and he that sat upon him was called Faithful and True, … His eyes were as a flame of fire, and on his head were many crowns; and he had a name written, that no man knew, but he himself.'

G.B.

40 **Hans Burgkmair** (1473–1531)

The Angel locking the Dragon in the Bottomless Pit for One Thousand Years (Rev. 20: 1–3)

Woodcut, borders trimmed, 162 × 130mm

Lit: Campbell Dodgson, II, p.422, 217; Hollstein, 26

London, British Museum 1909-4-3-46

G.B.

39

40

41

41 Hans Burgkmair (1473–1531)

The Vision of the New Jerusalem (Rev. 21: 9–27; 22: 1–5)

Woodcut, borders trimmed, 160 × 130mm

Lit: Campbell Dodgson, II, p.422, 218; Hollstein, 27

London, British Museum 1909-4-3-47

G.B.

42–53 Georg Lemberger

Twelve impressions from a series of twenty-one woodcuts for the *Apocalypse*, M. Lotter, Wittenberg 1524

42 Georg Lemberger (c.1490–after 1537)

The Vision of the Lamb and the Twenty-Four Elders, 1523
(Rev. 4: 2–8)

Woodcut with hand-colouring added later, 146 × 94mm

Lit: Campbell Dodgson, II, p.365, 6; Hollstein, 7

London, British Museum 1907-10-29-2

This series of Apocalypse prints by Georg Lemberger was the first of the small-scale illustrations of Luther's New Testament to appear in Wittenberg, and is in this respect similar to Thomas Wolff's pirated version which appeared in Basel the year before (cat. 29). Smaller prints meant not only more illustration to a page of a quarto publication, but also that they could be published in an octavo format. The subjects are closely derived from the set designed by Cranach and his workshop for the December Testament of 1522 (cat. 28). The series was first published by Melchior Lotter in 1524, and it was then produced with a Low German text by Hans Lufft in the same town in 1525 (see Reinitzer, op. cit. cat. 5, 86). The particular set on display here is incomplete, and comes from neither Lotter's edition of 1524 nor that of Lufft in the following year, but from an undescribed edition in which some of the woodcuts were printed on the versos of others.

Melchior Lotter had printed Luther's New Testaments of 1522 for Christian Döring, but by 1524 he had fallen out with Döring and Cranach who by this date were running a joint publishing enterprise. The rapidly increasing demand for Luther's text, however, encouraged Lotter to publish his own New Testament, with illustrations commissioned from Lemberger. This must have happened shortly before Döring and Cranach were granted exclusive rights by the duke of Saxony to publish Luther's works; by early 1525 Lotter found himself unable to work in the town because of the strong competition, and left Wittenberg for good.

Georg Lemberger probably came from Nuremberg, but by 1523 he was living in Leipzig. Earlier in his career he worked with Erhard Altdorfer's well-known brother

Albrecht Altdorfer (see cat. 56) on projects for the emperor Maximilian, and the influence of the atmospheric landscapes produced by Danube school artists is reflected in his series of Apocalypse woodcuts. Significantly, he was an active Protestant and is best known for his works on Lutheran themes, such as his large painting of the *Allegory of the Fall and Redemption of Mankind* of 1535 (Nuremberg, Germanisches Nationalmuseum). In 1532 he was expelled from Leipzig for participating in a Lutheran service, and he then moved to Magdeburg where he designed book illustrations for Melchior Lotter's brother, Michael, between 1532 and 1536.

G.B.

42

43 Georg Lemberger (c.1490–after 1537)

The Four Horsemen of the Apocalypse (Rev. 6: 1–8)

Woodcut with hand-colouring added later, 147 × 96mm

Lit: Campbell Dodgson, II, p.365, 7 II; Hollstein, 7

London, British Museum 1907-10-29-3

G.B.

44 Georg Lemberger (c.1490–after 1537)

Angels holding back the Winds and the Marking of the Elect (Rev. 7: 1–8)

Woodcut, 145 × 92mm

Lit: Campbell Dodgson, II, p.365, 8; Hollstein, 7

London, British Museum 1907-10-29-4

G.B.

45 Georg Lemberger (c.1490–after 1537)

The Star falling into the Pit of Hell and the Plague of Locusts (Rev. 9: 1–11)

Woodcut, 145 × 94mm

Lit: Campbell Dodgson, II, p.365, 9; Hollstein, 7

London, British Museum 1907-10-29-5

G.B.

43

44

45

46 Georg Lemberger (*c.*1490–after 1537)

The Four Angels of Death (Rev. 9: 13–19)

Woodcut, 145 × 93mm

Lit: Campbell Dodgson, II, p.365, 10; Hollstein, 7

London, British Museum 1907-10-29-6

G.B.

47 Georg Lemberger (*c.*1490–after 1537)

The Two Witnesses and the Beast from the Bottomless Pit (Rev. 11: 3–7)

Woodcut with touches of brown wash added later, 146 × 94mm

Lit: Campbell Dodgson, II, p.365, 11; Hollstein, 7

London, British Museum 1907-10-29-7

G.B.

48 Georg Lemberger (*c.*1490–after 1537)

The Beast with the Lamb's Horns and the Beast with Seven Heads (Rev. 13: 1–20)

Woodcut, 146 × 94mm

Lit: Campbell Dodgson, II, p.365, 12; Hollstein, 7

London, British Museum 1907-10-29-8

G.B.

46

47

48

49 Georg Lemberger (*c*.1490–after 1537)

The Adoration of the Lamb and the Fall of Babylon (Rev. 14: 1–13)

Woodcut, 144 × 94mm

Lit: Campbell Dodgson, II, p.366, 13; Hollstein, 7

London, British Museum 1907-10-29-9

G.B.

50 Georg Lemberger (*c*.1490–after 1537)

The Emptying of the Seven Vials (Rev. 16: 1–7)

Woodcut, 145 × 91mm

Lit: Campbell Dodgson, II, p.366, 14; Hollstein, 7

London, British Museum 1907-10-29-10

G.B.

51 Georg Lemberger (*c*.1490–after 1537)

The Whore of Babylon (Rev. 17: 3–6)

Woodcut, 145 × 94mm

Lit: Campbell Dodgson, II, p.366, 15; Hollstein, 7

London, British Museum 1907-10-29-11

G.B.

49

50

51

52 Georg Lemberger (c.1490–after 1537)

The Angel locking the Dragon in the Bottomless Pit for One Thousand Years (Rev. 20: 1–3)

Woodcut, 145 × 94mm

Lit: Campbell Dodgson, II, p.366, 17; Hollstein, 7

London, British Museum 1907-10-29-13

G.B.

52

53

53 Georg Lemberger (c.1490–after 1537)

The Vision of the New Jerusalem (Rev. 21: 9–27)

Woodcut, 145 × 94mm

Lit: Campbell Dodgson, II, p.366, 18; Hollstein, 7

London, British Museum 1907-10-29-14

G.B.

54 Hans Schäufelein (1480/85–1540)

The German New Testament [Jesus. Das New Testament Teutsch mit scho[e]nen figuren], H. Schönsperger, Augsburg 1524

Sig. Ee iii, *The Angel locking the Dragon in the Bottomless Pit for One Thousand Years* (Rev. 20: 1–3)

Woodcut, 233 × 158mm

Lit: Bartsch, VII, p.260, 52; Hollstein, 1050; Reinitzer, 125

London, British Museum 1949-4-11-5108. Bequeathed by Campbell Dodgson

Schäufelein designed five of the series of twenty-one illustrations to the Apocalypse for this Lutheran New Testament, first published in Augsburg by Schönsperger in 1523, the year after the first edition of Luther's translation, known as the September Testament, appeared in Wittenberg. The remaining nineteen illustrations are simplified copies of the series produced in Cranach's workshop for the September Testament, and include the three-tiered papal tiaras on the dragons in *The Two Witnesses and the Beast from the Bottomless Pit* and the *Angels Emptying Seven Vials*, and on the woman in the *Whore of Babylon*, which caused problems when they first appeared and were removed from the second edition of Luther's New Testament of December 1522 (see cats 27, 28).

Hans Schäufelein was originally from Nuremberg, where he worked in Dürer's workshop between *c*.1503 and 1508. He moved to Nördlingen in *c*.1515 and spent much of his later career working for publishers there and in Augsburg. The influence of Dürer is evident throughout his career, and the high quality of his five designs for this set of Apocalypse illustrations typically betrays a greater debt to Dürer in terms of technique and dramatic content than to the simple, more narrative style of the series produced in Cranach's workshop. The particularly fine typeface of this publication, with characteristic flourishes under some of the letters, was designed by Schönsperger's father Hans for *Der Theuerdank*, an allegorical account of the courtship of the Holy Roman emperor Maximilian and his wife Mary of Burgundy, which was commissioned by Maximilian and published in Nuremberg in 1517.
G.B.

Die Offenbarung

Das Zweintzigst

54

55

55 Anton Woensam (1493/6–c.1541)

German Old and New Testaments [Biblia beyder Alt und Newen Testaments Teutsch], Peter Schöffer, Worms 1529

Fols 70v–71r: *Four Horsemen of the Apocalypse*, 1525 (Rev. 6: 1–8); *The Opening of the Fifth Seal and the Clothing of the Martyrs* (Rev. 6: 9–12); *The Opening of the Sixth Seal* (Rev. 6: 12–17); *Angels holding back the Winds and the Marking of the Elect* (Rev. 7: 1–8); *The Opening of the Seventh Seal* (Rev. 8: 1–12)

Woodcuts, each approx. 122 × 78mm

Lit: J.J. Merlo, 'Anton Woensam von Worms, Maler und Xylograph zu Köln. Sein Leben und seine Werke: eine kunstgeschichtliche Monographie', in *Archiv für zeichnenden Künste mit besonderer Beziehung auf Kupferstecher- und Holzschneidekunst… herausgegeben von Dr Robert Naumann*, Leipzig 1864, p.185, nos 344-8; Reinitzer, 101

London, British Library 3040. g.6

This Bible contains a compilation of Luther's translations of the New Testament and the first three parts of the Old Testament, together with the first German translation of the Prophets by Ludwig Hätzer (d.1529) and Hans Denck (d.1527), which had appeared in 1527 and of which Luther highly approved, and the Apocrypha translated by Leo Jud (1482–1542), a close friend and colleague of the Swiss reformer Ulrich Zwingli.

The small scale and subjects of Woensam's twenty-one Apocalypse prints are based on the set designed by Georg Lemberger (cats 42–53), in its turn derived from the Cranach series for Luther's December Testament of 1522 (cat. 28). The date of 1525 on the *Four Horsemen* implies that the series may have first been published in a book in that year, although none is recorded. It seems that not many impressions were issued, perhaps because they appeared shortly before Luther's revised preface to his New Testament of 1530, which altered the iconography of the Apocalypse illustrations. The last time Woensam's prints appeared was probably in the German translation of the New Testament by D. Johannem Dietenberger, published by Quentel in Cologne in 1556.

Anton Woensam was the son of the painter Jaspar Woensam, who moved from Worms to Cologne in *c*.1510. Anton probably trained as a painter with his father, but seems to have made his living primarily from designing book illustrations, the majority of which were published in Cologne. His most famous work is a monumental woodcut view of Cologne, which was published by Quentel and presented to the Holy Roman emperor Charles V on his entry into Cologne in 1531.
G.B.

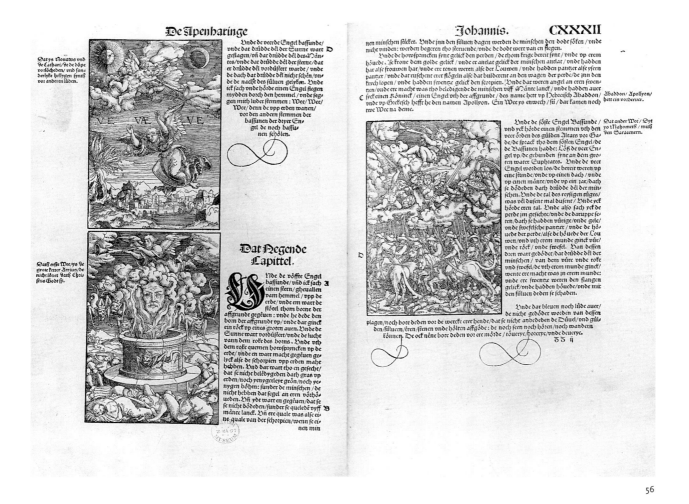

56

56 Erhard Altdorfer (c.1485/7–c.1561)

The Bible [De Biblie vth den vthleggin- ge Doctoris Martini Luthers yn dyth du[e]desche vlitich vthgesettet, mit sundergen vnderrichtingen alse men seen mach], Ludwig Dietz, Lübeck 1533–4

Fols 131v–132r: *The Fourth trumpeting Angel and the Angel crying Woe* (Rev. 8: 12–13); *The Star falling into the Pit of Hell and the Plague of Locusts* (Rev. 9: 1–11) and fol. 132r: *The Four Angels of Death* (Rev. 9: 13–19)

Woodcuts, each approx.133 × 90mm

Lit: Campbell Dodgson, II, p.378, 1; Reinitzer, 96; Hollstein, w.68–w.70

London, British Library, 2.d.11

This set of twenty-six Apocalypse prints was first executed for a north German dialect version of Luther's Bible, published in Lübeck six months before Luther's complete German Bible was published by Lufft in Wittenberg in 1534 (cat. 57). It was produced with the collaboraton of Johannes Bugenhagen (1485–1558), the vicar of Wittenberg and a close friend of Luther, who introduced the Reformation to a number of north German towns, including Hamburg,

Hildesheim and Lübeck, and also the duchies of Schleswig-Holstein and Pomerania. This version was also used for the first Danish translation of the Bible, commissioned by King Christian III and published by Dietz in Copenhagen in 1550.

Altdorfer's designs are essentially derived from the series of twenty-one produced by Cranach and his workshop for the New Testaments of 1522 (cats 27, 28) but, like the series designed by the Monogrammist MS for the Lufft Bible of 1534, an extra five scenes are included to reflect Luther's revised introduction to Revelation written for his 1530 edition of the New Testament, which was published by Lufft in Wittenberg with illustrations by the Monogrammist AW (see Reinitzer 85). During the turbulent political and social events of the 1520s, Luther concluded that the notion of the history and downfall of the Catholic Church being reflected in Revelation was in need of greater clarification. He realized that more specific use could be made of parallels with the Old Testament prophecies of Daniel and Ezekiel, as well as with early Christian history and recent topical events. The main differences caused by Luther's revisions lie in the illustrations to Revelation 8, which is now represented by five scenes, compared with one. The first four trumpeting angels, who appear when the seventh seal is broken, heralding successive disasters, are shown in separate scenes and linked by Luther with early heresies. Thus the fourth trumpeting angel shown here represents the Roman priest Novatian, who founded a rigorous heretical sect in the third century, known as the 'pure ones', and who was considered by Luther to be a particularly evil heretic. *The Four Angels of Death* with their cavalry mounted on lion-headed horses, seen here on the facing page, were associated by Luther in his 1530 introduction with the invasions of Mohammad, the founder of Islam, and the Saracens in the seventh century. The riders wear Turkish turbans and scimitars, because Luther equated the Saracens with all contemporary Muslims of the Middle-Eastern world.

One entirely new subject appeared as the penultimate print of the series, *The Destruction of Gog and Magog* (Rev. 20: 7–10) (fig. 9), the evil forces that are let loose when Satan is released after one thousand years of imprisonment: 'And they went up on the breadth of the earth, and compassed the camp of the saints about, and the beloved city: and fire came down from God out of heaven and devoured them.' Luther links the subject with the flight of the Turks after the siege of Vienna of 1529, and Altdorfer's print follows the illustration by the Monogrammist AW in the identification of the 'beloved city' as Vienna, with views of the cathedral of St Stephen and the church of St Maria am Gestade.

Erhard Altdorfer was the younger brother of the well-known Albrecht Altdorfer (*c*.1482/5–1538) of Regensburg, by whom he was much influenced. The particular interest in landscape which dominates the work of both artists even emerges in the unearthly scenes of Erhard's Apocalypse prints, such as the view of mountains in the background of *The Fourth Trumpeting Angel* seen here.
G.B.

Fig. 9 (London, British Museum).

57, Fol. 188v

57, Fol. 189r

57 The Monogrammist MS

(active c.1530–c.1551)

*Bible: the complete Holy Scriptures translated by Martin Luther
[Biblia, das ist, das gantze Heilige Schrifft Deudsch. Mart. Luth.
Wittemberg. Begnadet mit Kürfurstlicher zu Sachsen freiheit]*, Hans
Lufft, Wittenberg 1534

Fols 188v–189r: *The Second Trumpeting Angel and the Burning
Mountain in the Sea* (Rev. 8: 8); *The Third Trumpeting Angel and the
Star Wormwood falling from Heaven* (Rev. 8: 10–11) (not illustrated);
The Fourth Trumpeting Angel and the Angel crying Woe (Rev. 8:
12–13)

Woodcuts with hand-colouring, each approx. 108 × 148mm

Lit: Campbell Dodgson, II, p.404, 1; Reinitzer, 97, 97a

London, British Library 1b.10

This was the first complete High German bible to be issued
entirely in Luther's translation. The illustrations throughout
were commissioned from the Monogrammist MS, an
unidentified artist of possibly Saxon origin who probably
worked in Cranach's studio and who was influenced by
Danube school artists. His designs for the Apocalypse were
inspired by details from Cranach's series, notably in the
reappearance of the papal tiara in *The Two Witnesses and the
Beast from the Bottomless Pit* (Rev. 11: 3–7), *The Emptying of
the Seven Vials* (Rev. 16: 1–7) and *The Whore of Babylon* (Rev.
17: 3–6) as they were used in the September Testament (cat.
27). The Monogrammist MS introduced a landscape format to
the subjects, however, which gave some variety to the
designs and removed them entirely from Dürer's sphere of
influence. The dense application of hand-colouring to this
particular work also adds an atmospheric mood which
provides further contrast with Dürer's dramatic figure
compositions.

There are twenty-six illustrations to the Apocalypse in
this edition which, like Altdorfer's set for the Lübeck Bible
(cat. 56), reflect Luther's revised introduction to his New

Testament of 1530. Revelation 8 is illustrated with five
separate scenes, of which the second, third and fourth
trumpeting angels are displayed here. Luther interpreted the
second angel and the burning mountain as the Manichaean
sect of the second-century Gnostic heretic Marcion, and the
bitterness of the star Wormwood, accompanying the third
angel, as the allegorical writings of Origen, the third-century
theologian whose influence Luther considered responsible
for the deterioration of the study of the Holy Scriptures in
universities. Curiously, the Monogrammist MS designed one
print in which he consciously deviated from Luther's
interpretation: *The Destruction of Babylon* (Rev. 18: 21–4). It
is represented as the German city of Worms, instead of Rome
which Cranach had shown in the 1522 New Testament, as
had Altdorfer in the Lübeck Bible of 1534, to accord with
Luther's analogy of the subject with the Sack of Rome of
1527 made in his revised introduction of 1530. The
'destruction' of Worms seen here probably symbolizes the
Diet of Worms of 1521, at which the emperor Charles V
confirmed the papal bull of excommunication and banned
Luther's publications from the Holy Roman Empire. The
uncomplicated, somewhat naive style of the Monogrammist
MS particularly appealed to Luther, because with only one
exception these designs illustrated all the Lutheran bibles
issued in Wittenberg up to the reformer's death in 1546.

There exists a broadsheet showing a 'heavenly sign' over
Wittenberg, dated 1551, with text underneath by Philip
Melanchthon, which has also been attributed to the
Monogrammist MS (Berlin, Kupferstichkabinett; M. Geisberg,
*Der deutsche Einblatt-Holzschnitt in der ersten Hälfte des 16.
Jahrhunderts*, Munich [1927] xxiii, no.946). Such meteo-
rological occurrences were commonly viewed as portents of
impending doom, in much the same way that the reformers
interpreted the disasters of the Book of Revelation as retri-
bution for the venal behaviour of the Catholic Church.
G.B.

58 Sebald Beham (1500–50)

Illustrations to John's Apocalypse [*Typi in Apocalypsi Ioannis Depicti vt clarivs vaticinia Ioannis intelligi possint*], C. Egenolph, Frankfurt 1539

Sig. Bii v–Biii r: *The Third Angel sounding a Trumpet and the Burning Star, Wormwood* and *The Fourth Angel sounding a Trumpet* (Rev. 8: 10–12)

Woodcuts, 67 × 70mm, 67 × 71mm

Lit: Gustav Pauli, *Hans Sebald Beham: Ein kritisches Verzeichniss seiner Kupferstiche, Radierungen und Holzschnitte*, 2 vols, Strasbourg 1911, 83–58 (1st edition); Campbell Dodgson, II, p.443, 28

London, British Museum 1934-11-27-4

The iconography of Beham's set of twenty-six Apocalypse prints is based on Luther's revised New Testament of 1530, and many of the designs were influenced by the corresponding scenes produced by the Monogrammist MS for the Lufft Bible of 1534 (see cat. 57), although the papal tiaras worn by the Whore of Babylon and two of the dragons are omitted. Other prints relate to the series designed by Dürer in 1498, and by Cranach and his workshop for the first Lutheran New Testament of 1522. For example, in his frontispiece, *St John's Vision of the Candlesticks*, Beham has taken the standing figure of God from the Cranach series and the kneeling figure of John from Dürer, although by including eight rather than seven candlesticks, he was curiously inattentive to the text.

In terms of function, however, Beham's work responds more directly to Dürer's publication than to the moralizing texts of the reformers. Although the scenes are much smaller in scale and interpreted in a quite different manner, there are similarities. Like Dürer's series, Beham's set did not constitute a small part of a large bible or New Testament volume, but was issued on its own. There is a similar emphasis on contemplation of the images, as opposed to the textual dominance of Luther's approved publications. The text in Beham's Apocalypse is not even given in full; instead, each page is devoted to one illustration, described in a short Latin caption underneath with reference to the relevant chapter of Revelation. Beham did not attempt to convey the drama of Dürer's compositions; his interest lay in creating small-scale, intimate versions of the subject, which would have been appropriate for private devotional use, and which he has achieved in the illustrations on display here with particularly evocative landscape backgrounds.

Sebald Beham was born in Dürer's home town, Nuremberg, but moved to Frankfurt in *c*.1532. Many of his early prints were closely based on Dürer's work and he was one of the most prolific printmakers of his generation. He excelled in the design of small-scale engravings and woodcuts, for which a collectors' market developed during the sixteenth century. This edition of the Apocalypse is the first of five produced by Frankfurt publishers up to 1558; the final two editions included the set as part of complete bibles. G.B.

58

59 Matthias Gerung (c.1500–70)

Forty-eight woodcuts of the *Apocalypse and Satirical Allegories on the Church*, 1544–8, in a leather-bound album lettered on the cover: APOCAL: GRVNE/WALT/ 1637

The Destruction of Babylon, 1547 (Rev. 18: 1–24)

Woodcut, 232 × 162mm

Watermark: tower (similar to Piccard I, XI, 138)

Lit: Hollstein, 32; Petra Roettig, *Reformation als Apokalypse: die Holzschnitte von Matthias Gerung im Codex germanicus 6592 der Bayerischen Staatsbibliothek in München*, Bern 1991, 22a; *German Renaissance Prints*, 167

London, British Museum 1911-7-8-145

Gerung's woodcut series of the Apocalypse is one of the most important documents of Reformation propaganda, but due to its rarity, and the fact that the series was never published as a book with text, it has been little understood. By 1637, when this album was compiled, the designer was forgotten and the prints attributed to the well-known Mathis Grünewald (c.1480–1528) on account of Gerung's MG monogram. Gerung's identity was later re-established, and the iconography of the prints fully elucidated through Roettig's publication of a manuscript of a German translation of Sebastian Meyer's polemical commentary on the Apocalypse, illustrated with Gerung's woodcuts (Munich, Bayerische Staatsbibliothek, Cgm.6592). Sebastian Meyer was a reformer in Bern, whose anti-papal commentary on the Apocalypse was published in Latin in Zurich in 1539. In 1544 Gerung's patron, the Palatine Count Ottheinrich, who had converted to Protestantism in 1541, commissioned Laurentius Agricola (1497–1564; a follower of the Swiss reformer Ulrich Zwingli) to translate Meyer's commentary into German, and Gerung to design woodcuts for it. Gerung had designed fifty-nine woodcuts for the series by 1558, but they were never completed or published, perhaps because of Ottheinrich's death in 1559.

The design of Gerung's Apocalypse prints reveals a debt to the famous series of Cranach and Dürer where the subjects correspond, but not only is Gerung's series much longer, which allows little-known parts of Revelation to be illustrated, but also the nature of Count Ottheinrich's commission makes the interpretation of the series quite different. The arrangement of Gerung's woodcuts in the Munich manuscript shows that he designed each illustration to the Apocalypse with a corresponding satire on the Catholic Church or the Turks as the Muslim infidels on the facing page. This type of visual parallel had been popularized by Cranach's *Passional Christi und Antichristi* of 1521, in which each opening compared a scene from the life of Christ with one from the life of Antichrist (cat. 26). Gerung's *Destruction of Babylon*, seen here, shows a detailed interpretation of the text: merchants, clerical figures and Turks are in a prominent foreground position lamenting the destruction of Babylon and its riches. It is shown as a

59

burning medieval town in the background, the flames of which take up most of the upper half of the print (Rev. 18: 9–20). The angel crying 'Babylon the great is fallen' and the angel hurling a millstone into the sea (Rev. 18: 2, 21) are in the upper right corner, with St John seated on a cloud in the upper left corner.

G.B.

60 Matthias Gerung (c.1500–70)

The Destruction of the Catholic Church, c.1547

Woodcut, 234 × 164mm

Lit: Campbell Dodgson, II, p.217,10; Hollstein, 51; Roettig, 22b

London, British Museum 1867-7-13-107

60

This print is shown on the page facing the *Destruction of Babylon* in the manuscript copy of Meyer's commentary to the Apocalypse in Munich (see cat. 59). The identification of Babylon as Rome had become a traditional part of the reformers' language since Cranach displayed the buildings of Castel Sant'Angelo and the Belvedere in his *Destruction of Babylon* in the September Testament of 1522. By using two separate woodcuts, Gerung's imagery takes this interpretation a step further, because he is able to show the fall of Babylon on one page, which would then appear as a precursor for the fall of the Roman Church seen opposite. A group of clerics and princes looks up in horror as, in parallel with the millstone hurled by the angel at Babylon, the book of the Gospels is thrown at a Gothic church, causing it to collapse into a pile of rubble with ornaments, artefacts and figures associated with Catholicism lying underneath. In his commentary, Sebastian Meyer makes it clear that he considers God's destruction of the Catholic Church inevitable, on account of the sacrilegious behaviour of the clergy in seducing all lay rulers into the ways of evil.

Gerung lived in Lauingen from 1525, where he worked for the Palatine Count Ottheinrich and was also employed from 1531 to 1567 as the town inspector of weights and measures. He probably trained with the well-known woodcut designer Hans Schäufelein (1480/5–1540) (cat. 54), who worked on commissions for the emperor Maximilian, but Lauingen was an artistic backwater and Gerung developed an idiosyncratic style without reference to the major German artists of the period, or to the current vogue for Italianate motifs. Among other work for Ottheinrich, he illuminated the New Testament and Apocalypse of a fifteenth-century Bible commissioned in 1530–1 before the count's conversion to Protestantism (Heidelberg, Kurpfälzisches Museum, Hs.28). The difference in approach between this Catholic commission and Gerung's illustrations to Meyer's commentary is emphasized by the fact that the seventeen miniatures illustrating the Apocalypse of the former commission are essentially derivations of earlier series, and give no indication of Gerung's creative talent in terms of satirical imagery, so amply demonstrated here.
G.B.

61 Matthias Gerung (*c.*1500–70)

Pope and Turk as Demons drag their Followers into Hell, c.1545–8

Woodcut, 234 × 164mm

Lit: Campbell Dodgson, II, p.217,11; Hollstein, 67; Roettig, 23b

London, British Museum 1895-1-22-45. Presented by William Mitchell

Gerung designed this woodcut for Meyer's commentary as a satirical counterpart to *The Fall of the Whore of Babylon* (Rev. 19: 11–21; see fig. 10). Two diabolical monsters are seated on the edge of the abyss, one crowned with the papal tiara and the other with a sultan's turban. They are firmly bound together with each other's tails and are in the process of dragging into the furnace below a group of Catholic clergy and monks on the right, and various Muslim figures on the left. On a plateau above, Christ is surrounded by followers of the true faith, with two angels who despatch two false believers off the edge into the abyss below. The characterization of pope and Turk as agents from hell, in the pope's case as Antichrist, is a constant motif throughout the commentary and Gerung's prints; it was readily understood by the reformers and their public as the major contemporary source of evil prefigured by the Whore of Babylon from the Book of Revelation.

Impressions from Gerung's series of Apocalypse woodcuts are rare. It is worth mentioning as a footnote to the literature that there is a previously unrecorded group of seventeen in the Hessische Landesmuseum, Darmstadt, which correspond to: Roettig 5b, 6a, 6b, 7a, 8a, 9a, 10a, 10b, 11b, 12a, 12f, 13a, 14b, 15a, 19a, 21a and 23b. A selection of these was exhibited in Darmstadt in 1996 (see Wolfgang Glüber, *Das Ende der Welt. Drei Apokalypsefolgen des 15. und 16. Jahrhunderts aus eigenem Bestand*, exhibition pamphlet, Darmstadt, Hessisches Landesmuseum 1996).

G.B.

Fig. 10.

61

62 **Matthias Gerung** (c.1500–70)

The Birth of Antichrist, c.1544–58

Woodcut within an ornamental border, lettered in a cartouche above with title and four lines of Latin verse, and in a cartouche below with the title and verse in German; woodcut 212 × 170mm, border 328 × 240mm

Lit: J. Rowlands, *Burlington Magazine*, cxviii 1976, p.257; Carsten-Peter Warncke, *Die ornamentale Groteske in Deutschland 1500–1650*, 2 vols, Berlin 1979, 504; Roettig, pp.245f, n.896

London, British Museum 1976-1-31-3

The story of Antichrist first appeared in medieval manuscripts and fifteenth-century block-books, and was first published in the *Compendium of Theological Truth* in 1473 (see cat. 3). The mother of Antichrist is shown here giving birth in the normal manner, unlike the depiction of the scene in block-books, in which Antichrist is born by Caesarean section with the consequent death of his mother. The attendant devils are, however, a traditional part of the iconography.

G.B.

62

63 Matthias Gerung (c.1500–70)

The Baptism of Antichrist, c.1544–58

Woodcut within an ornamental border, lettered in a cartouche
above with title and four lines of Latin verse, and in a cartouche
below with the title and verse in German; woodcut 210 × 170mm,
border 323 × 236mm

Lit: J. Rowlands, p.257; Warncke, 505; Roettig, pp.245f, n.897

London, British Museum 1976-1-31-2

Together with the *Birth of Antichrist* (cat. 62), this print was
unrecorded when it was acquired by the British Museum in
1976. They may be dated to the same period as Gerung's
Apocalypse prints, but belong to a different series of prints
illustrating the life of the Antichrist, the false Messiah who
was usually equated with the Beast from the Sea of
Revelation 13, and whose activities were closely linked in
Protestant propaganda with those of the papacy following
the publication of the best-selling *Passional Christi und
Antichristi* (cat. 26). The infant in Gerung's *Baptism* already
wears a papal tiara on his head. These impressions of the
Birth and *Baptism of Antichrist* come from a later edition of
*c.*1565, at which time the ornamental borders, designed by a
different artist, were added with the explanatory verses.
According to the verses in the first woodcut, the birth of
Antichrist was so slow and painful that the devils could
continue to bathe in the Acheron, the river of hell. In the
second woodcut, the verses inform us that true baptism frees
mankind from the threat of the Last Judgement and that the
sign of the Cross reveals the true nature of false religion. The
design of the borders overlaps, indicating that the series
could be joined together and displayed as a frieze.

A third print which appears to belong to the same series
as the *Birth* and *Baptism of Antichrist* is Gerung's woodcut of
Revelling Catholic Clergy (Hollstein 68), of which the only
recorded impression is in the British Museum (1910-4-18-4;
fig. 11). It is the same size to within a few millimetres, and is
closely comparable in terms of style and subject. Antichrist
is the clerical figure escorted into the scene of debauchery by
two devils on the left, his identity established by the papal
tiara held over his head by a third devil.
G.B.

63

Fig. 11.

Apocalypse Illustration during the Second Half of the Sixteenth Century

64–81 Jean Duvet

Sixteen plates from a series of twenty-three engravings of the Apocalypse, 1555

64 Jean Duvet (c.1485–1561)

Frontispiece of the Apocalypse: Jean Duvet as St John the Evangelist, 1555

Engraving, trimmed along the side edges, 301 × 215mm

Lit: Colin Eisler, *The Master of the Unicorn. The Life and Work of Jean Duvet*, New York 1979, 65 II

London, British Museum 1842-8-6-108

Duvet's series of Apocalypse prints is remarkable for its idiosyncratic style which, although conceived with reference to Dürer's cycle, stands alone in its imaginative interpretation of the subject. Duvet was born in Dijon but spent most of his life in Langres, and was court goldsmith to the French kings François I and Henri II. The earliest engraver in France to emerge with a clear artistic personality, he shows an eclectic style characterized by a lack of interest in perspective, an obsession with background pattern and detail, particularly of architecture and ornament, which reflects his occupations as a goldsmith and an architect, and an interest in Italian Renaissance figures, with the prints of Marcantonio Raimondi (*c.*1480–*c.*1534) as his main source of influence.

The vivid narrative of Revelation appealed to Duvet's temperament, and his densely packed compositions are among the most memorable of Apocalypse imagery. Unlike Dürer, who started his career with the publication of his Apocalypse at the age of twenty-seven, Duvet engraved his set over a period of time at an advanced age, with this frontispiece produced at the end in 1555. He followed Dürer's example, however, in viewing the series as a sequence of independent images, and several sets were issued in this way. The series was later published as a book entitled *L'Apocalypse figurée*, with French text interspersed between the engraved sheets and a royal privilege, by J. de Tournes in Lyons, 1561. Only seven recorded books are known to have survived intact (Eisler's edition cited in the British Museum is, in fact, in the British Library, C.18. e.10).

Duvet's frontispiece to the series is one of the most personal documents ever to be produced by an artist in connection with the Apocalypse. He represented himself as his patron saint, St John, the author of Revelation, an elderly man surrounded by emblems of death and triumphant in the completion of a great work. In order to emphasize the dual nature of the portrait he inscribed the plate extensively in Latin: on the copper plate in front of him, 'Jean Duvet,

64

goldsmith of Langres, aged seventy has completed these histories in 1555'; on an open book nearby, 'Book of the Apocalypse of St John the Apostle'; in the lower left corner: 'The sacred mysteries contained in this and the other following tablets are derived from the divine revelation of John and are closely adapted to the true letter of the text with the judgement of more learned men brought to bear'; on the right, just above a swan that has broken its chain and swims towards the old man, bearing an arrow in its beak: 'The Fates are pressing, already the hands tremble and the sight fails, yet the mind remains victorious and the great work is completed'. This engraving is one of Duvet's most successful compositions. The bizarre contrast between naturalistic detail, expressed in the dog, cat, birds and plants in the foreground, and the total disregard for three-dimensional perspective, as in the strange juxtaposition of desk, clouds and boats in the centre of the composition, is characteristic of Duvet's art.
G.B.

65 Jean Duvet (c.1485–1561)

St John's Vision of the Seven Candlesticks (Rev. 1: 12–20)

Engraving, 301 × 214mm

Lit: Eisler, 40

London, British Museum 1842-8-6-110

G.B.

66 Jean Duvet (c.1485–1561)

St John Kneeling before Christ and the Twenty-Four Elders, and the Worship of the Lamb (Rev. 4: 1–11; 5: 8–10)

Engraving, 301 × 215mm

Lit: Eisler, 41

London, British Museum 1868-8-22-1077. Bequeathed by Felix Slade

This engraving was acquired by the British Museum after the other prints of the series, so would not have formed part of the same set.

G.B.

65

66

67 Jean Duvet (c.1485–1561)

The Clothing of the Martyrs and the Star Falling into the Pit of Hell
(Rev. 6: 9–11; 9: 1–11)

Engraving; late impression, with reworked outlines, trimmed along side and lower edges;

304 × 216mm

Lit: Eisler, 43 II

London, British Museum 1842-8-6-113

Duvet has disregarded the chronology of Revelation here, and selected two episodes from different chapters, in much the same way that Dürer combined elements from Chapters 7 and 14 in his *Hymn in Adoration of the Lamb* (see cat. 18). The upper scene represents the Roman martyrs being clothed in white robes from Chapter 6. Below, the star that unleashes the plague of monstrous locusts at the sounding of the fifth trumpet, in Chapter 9, has landed on the crowned figure of Satan on the right, who brandishes the key to hell in his right hand. The writhing figures below represent those who have not been sealed with a cross (see cat. 68) being tormented by human-headed locusts who emerge from hell.
G.B.

68 Jean Duvet (c.1485–1561)

Four Angels Holding back the Winds and the Marking of the Elect
(Rev.7: 1–8)

Engraving, 299 × 211mm

Lit: Eisler, 44

London, British Museum, 1842-8-6-114

Duvet's densely packed composition of this subject gives a totally different impression from other interpretations, because he has boldly attempted to convey the idea of a multitude of people. The text states that 144,000 people were elected to be saved, and an angel in the foreground is seen marking their foreheads with a cross. Those waiting to be marked recede far into the mountains in the background on the left.
G.B.

67

68

69 **Jean Duvet** (*c*.1485–1561)

The Opening of the Seventh Seal (Rev. 8: 1–12)

Engraving, 302 × 220mm

Lit: Eisler, 46

London, British Museum 1842-8-6-116

G.B.

70 **Jean Duvet** (*c*.1485–1561)

The Sixth Trumpet and the Four Angels of Death (Rev. 9: 13–19)

Engraving, 298 × 211mm

Lit: Eisler, 47

London, British Museum 1842-8-6-117

G.B.

69

70

71 Jean Duvet (*c*.1485–1561)

St John eating the Book (Rev. 10: 1–11)

Engraving; late impression, with some outlines reworked;
299 × 215mm

Lit: Eisler, 48 II

London, British Museum 1842-8-6-118

G.B.

72 Jean Duvet (*c*.1485–1561)

The Measurement of the Temple; the Slaying of the Two Witnesses
(Rev. 11: 1–14)

Engraving; late impression, some lines reworked, lower corners
made up; 305 × 220mm

Lit: Eisler, 49 II

London, British Museum 1842-8-6-119

St John is shown in the upper left corner, holding the reed
given to him by the angel, with which he is about to measure
the temple of God. The two witnesses, who receive divine
rays from the mouth of God above, kneel beneath the figure
of John. In the foreground the witnesses are killed by the
beast 'that ascendeth out of the bottomless pit' and in the
background Duvet has represented the city, one tenth of
which is destroyed by earthquake when the witnesses are
resurrected.

G.B.

71

72

73 **Jean Duvet** (*c*.1485–1561)

St Michael fighting the Dragon (Rev. 12: 7–9)

Engraving, trimmed along left edge, 298 × 210mm

Lit: Eisler, 51

London, British Museum 1842-8-6-121

G.B.

74 **Jean Duvet** (*c*.1485–1561)

The Whore of Babylon (Rev. 17: 3–6; 18: 21)

Engraving, made up in the lower right corner, 303 × 215mm

Lit: Eisler, 55

London, British Museum 1842-8-6-125

The extensive degree of detail of the buildings seen here, and in much of the series, may indicate the engraver's activities as an architect and military engineer. The city of Babylon burns in the background, while the admirers of the Whore appear to be anxiously aware of her fate.
G.B.

73

74

75 Jean Duvet (c.1485–1561)

The Destruction of Babylon; the Descent of the Whore into Hell (Rev. 18: 21–4)

Engraving, 300 × 211mm

Lit: Eisler, 56 II

London, British Museum 1842-8-6-126

Duvet produced more prints to illustrate the later chapters of the Book of Revelation than the earlier ones, and this print overlaps with the *Whore of Babylon* (cat. 74) in his treatment of the narrative. The millstone hurled by the angel at Babylon in the upper section of the preceding print is seen again here striking dead the figure of a king in the right foreground. The most dominant feature of this composition is the monumental figure of the Whore, who falls in a strikingly unusual inverted pose, with the seven heads of her beast below lending her a Medusa-like appearance. G.B.

76 Jean Duvet (c.1485–1561)

The Rider Faithful and True on a White Horse (Rev. 19: 11–16)

Engraving, trimmed along left edge, 301 × 216mm

Lit: Eisler, 57 II

London, British Museum 1842-8-6-127

G.B.

75

76

77 Jean Duvet (c.1485–1561)

The Angel locks up the Dragon for One Thousand Years (Rev. 20: 1–3)

Engraving, trimmed along left edge, 302 × 216mm

Lit: Eisler, 59

London, British Museum 1842-8-6-129

Duvet frequently betrays a medievalist approach to narrative in his Apocalypse prints by representing the same figures more than once in a single image. The middle section here shows the angel with a chain and a key holding Satan fast from verses 1–2, while underneath the angel is represented again, this time casting Satan into the bottomless pit for one thousand years (verse 3).
G.B.

78 Jean Duvet (c.1485–1561)

The Angel shows St John the New Jerusalem (Rev. 21: 9–27)

Engraving, trimmed along side edges, 302 × 215mm

Lit: Eisler, 60

London, British Museum 1842-8-6-130

G.B.

77

78

79 Jean Duvet (c.1485–1561)

The Angel shows St John the Fountain of Living Water (Rev. 22: 1–5)

Engraving, trimmed along side edges, 297 × 212mm

Lit: Eisler, 61 II

London, British Museum 1842-8-6-131

Duvet ends his series with an additional view of the New Jerusalem, thereby giving himself a further opportunity to create an imaginary architectural scene. The angel grasps St John by the shoulder and points towards the New Jerusalem: 'And he shewed me a pure river of water of life, clear as crystal, proceeding out of the throne of God and of the Lamb'.

G.B.

80 Jean Duvet (c.1485–1561)

The Martyrdom of St John the Evangelist

Engraving, 298 × 209mm

Lit: Eisler, 38 II

London, British Museum 1840-6-27-130

This and the following print of *The Revelation of St John* are not part of the Apocalypse series as they appeared in the book edition of 1561, although they are clearly related in terms of subject and format. Instead of the reference to the corresponding chapter of Revelation which appears on the main series, Duvet gives longer inscriptions in Latin on these two engravings to explain their context. The inscription on the lower edge here reads: 'In Rome, by order of Emperor Domitian, the apostle John, placed in a vat of boiling oil, leaving it safe and sound, was sent to the island of Patmos, where he wrote the Apocalypse'.

The subject of the martyrdom of St John was included by Dürer at the beginning of his series of Apocalypse woodcuts and was also seen on the title-page of Revelation in the Bible published by Dürer's godfather, Anton Koberger (p.104, fig. 2, cats 4, 6). It is also represented on a reliquary of St John in the cathedral of Duvet's home town of Langres.

G.B.

79

80

81 Jean Duvet (*c.1485–1561*)

The Revelation of St John the Evangelist

Engraving, reworked, notably in the lower left corner; lower right corner made up in black ink; 293 × 207mm

Lit: Eisler, 39 II

London, British Museum 1842-8-6-109

This subject was traditionally represented with a scene of John on Patmos, writing his Revelation (see cats 22–4), but Duvet's interpretation is, typically, more complex. It shows John in a dream-like trance receiving divine inspiration for all three of his written works, the Gospel, the Epistle and Revelation, at the same time. He is in a church interior with the three empty books open in front of him, and a trumpet blowing in his right ear: 'I was in the spirit on the Lord's day, and heard behind me a great voice, as of a trumpet' (Rev. 1: 10). The Trinity is represented above him as three male figures united by a cope knotted together and jointly holding the Book of the Apocalypse with its seven seals. Beneath John, a figure of Satan falls into an abyss (Rev. 12). The first words of John's Gospel are inscribed in a book open on his lap; and the inscription in the aureole surrounding the Trinity relates to the Epistle according to John, 'Three equal persons are a single God, beginning and end of all, as John testifies' (see I John 5: 7). The inscription on a pedestal underneath the statue of Noah on the left also relates to John's Gospel: 'Saint John apostle, under prince Pertinax, delivered from exile, returned to Ephesus where he wrote a Gospel, the last of all, which he began with the birth of Christ in order to refute the bad heresy of the Ebionites'. The statue on the pedestal on the right of the print represents Abraham.

The representation of the Trinity in the form of three male figures is quite common in French fifteenth-century art, and the emphasis on John as an advocate of Trinitarian doctrine, with a setting reminiscent of the cathedral at Langres, emphasizes that this print, and by extension perhaps all of Duvet's Apocalypse series, was produced for a conservative Catholic market.

G.B.

81

82 Virgil Solis (1514–62)

Illustrated New Testament [*Biblische Figuren des Neüwen Testaments gar künstlich gerissen. Durch den weitberhümpten Vergilium Solis Maler und Kunststecher zů Nürnberg*], S. Feyerabend, Frankfurt am Main 1562

Angels Emptying the Seven Vials of God's Wrath (Rev. 16: 1–13) and *The Whore of Babylon* (Rev. 17: 1–18)

Woodcuts, with ornamental borders, 118 × 149mm, 120 × 152mm

Lit: A. Andresen, 'Die Holzschnitte des Virgil Solis', *Archiv für zeichnende Künste*, ed. R. Naumann, 1864, x, pp.316ff., no. 1, 212–13; *Tobias Stimmer 1539–1584*, exhib. cat., eds D. Koepplin, P. Tanner *et al.*, Kunsthistorisches Museum, Basel 1984, 75

London, British Museum 1870-6-25-373 and 374

This and cat. 95 are examples of the so-called picture bibles, in which illustrations were accompanied by short lines of verse or abbreviated references to the text. Picture bibles belong to the tradition of religious popular prints exemplified by fifteenth-century block-books (see cats 2–3), and became fashionable in northern Europe during the sixteenth century. The ideas of the reformers stimulated a wider iconography of biblical images after the first Lutheran bibles appeared from 1522 onwards and, during the second half of the century, increasing numbers of print publishers in all major cities commissioned thematic series of prints, which naturally included the Bible. Well-known examples that have survived in large numbers from the first half of the sixteenth century are the Old Testament illustrated by Sebald Beham in 1533 (Egenolph, Frankfurt am Main; Pauli, op. cit. cat. 58, 277–356), reprinted at least twenty-five times before 1600, and the *Icones* by Hans Holbein II in 1538 (Trechsel, Lyons), produced in at least nine editions before 1551, including ones with French, Spanish and English text, and extensively copied (see *German Renaissance Prints*).

Virgil Solis was a painter and prolific designer of book illustrations from Nuremberg. This volume contains 116 woodcuts of biblical scenes, including two title-pages to introduce the Old and New Testaments. His compositions of the scenes from Revelation are based on the Lutheran bibles, but the decorative ornamental frames, with their playful figures of children, animals and fruit, decisively lessen the impact of the dramatic subjects. The frames were printed from separate blocks, and are two of about thirty different designs used throughout the publication.

G.B.

82

83–94 Gerard van Groeningen

Series of twelve plates of *The Apocalypse*, c.1565–71

Watermark: circle or shield surmounted with a five-petalled flower and with a small circle suspended beneath; present in all sheets, most legible in A. 1369 (cat. 87)

83 Gerard van Groeningen

(active 1561–c.1575/6)

St John's Vision of the Seven Candlesticks (Rev. 1: 10–16)

Etching and engraving, 270 × 249mm

Lit: Hollstein, 2 III

Amsterdam, Rijksprentenkabinet, Rijksmuseum A.1365

Gerard van Groeningen's set of twelve Apocalypse prints was issued in Antwerp in *c*.1565–71. Despite his imaginative compositions, which are largely independent of either Dürer's series or the sets illustrating the Lutheran bibles, his series is little known. Van Groeningen was a Netherlandish artist working as a glass-painter and designer of prints in the Italianate style which was particularly fashionable in northern Europe during the mid-sixteenth century. His name quickly fell into obscurity, however, since very few of his prints are signed. The rarity of his Apocalypse series may also be explained by its decorative function, because the prints, which were originally issued with an arched top, were adapted in the second state to suit a wall decoration.

A framework of partly represented pilasters and arches was added in such a manner that the prints could be joined together to form a continuous frieze. Related passages from the Book of Revelation, in German, Latin and French, were also added in the second state, so the series was obviously aimed at an international market. Since van Groeningen was primarily involved in the production of designs for glass-paintings, it has been suggested that his Apocalypse prints, together with his series of the *Fall and Redemption of Mankind* (Hollstein 159–70), also designed within a framework of pilasters and arched tops, may have been used for such paintings.
G.B.

83

CANDELABRA ATQVE STOLA GRANDÆVVM CERNIS AMICTVM.

84 Gerard van Groeningen

(active 1561–*c*.1575/6)

The Vision of the Lamb and the Twenty-Four Elders (Rev. 4: 2–8)

Etching and engraving, 269 × 246mm

Lit: Hollstein, 3 III

Amsterdam, Rijksprentenkabinet, Rijksmuseum A.1366

G.B.

85 Gerard van Groeningen

(active 1561–*c*.1575/6)

The Four Horsemen of the Apocalypse (Rev. 6: 1–8)

Etching and engraving, 270 × 249mm

Lit: Hollstein, 4 III

Amsterdam, Rijksprentenkabinet, Rijksmuseum A.1367

G.B.

86 Gerard van Groeningen

(active 1561–*c*.1575/6)

The Breaking of the Sixth Seal (Rev. 6: 12–17)

Etching and engraving, 272 × 249mm

Lit: Hollstein, 5 III

Amsterdam, Rijksprentenkabinet, Rijksmuseum A.1368

G.B.

84

85

86

ANGELICI CÆTVS STANT MVNDI AD QVATTVOR ORA. *Apoca. 7.*

87

87 Gerard van Groeningen

(active 1561–*c*.1575/6)

Angels restraining the Four Winds, while the Elect are marked with a Cross (Rev. 7: 1–8)

Etching and engraving, 269 × 248mm

Lit: Hollstein, 6 III

Amsterdam, Rijksprentenkabinet, Rijksmuseum A.1369

G.B.

88 Gerard van Groeningen

(active 1561–*c*.1575/6)

The Opening of the Seventh Seal, Angels sounding the First Five Trumpets (Rev. 8: 1–12)

Etching and engraving, 273 × 246mm

Lit: Hollstein, 7 III

Amsterdam, Rijksprentenkabinet, Rijksmuseum A.1370

G.B.

89 Gerard van Groeningen

(active 1561–*c*.1575/6)

The Plague of Locusts (Rev. 9: 1–11)

Etching and engraving, 268 × 247mm

Lit: Hollstein, 8 III

Amsterdam, Rijksprentenkabinet, Rijksmuseum A.1371

G.B.

88

89

IGNEM FLAMMIVAGVM SPECTAS CVM THVRE SABÆO. *Apoca. 8.*

AVDITVR TVBA, DE CELO TERRAM QVOQVE STELLA. *Apoca. 9.*

90 Gerard van Groeningen

(active 1561–c.1575/6)

The Four Angels of Death and their Lion-Headed Cavalry (Rev. 9: 13–19)

Etching and engraving, 268 × 247mm

Lit: Hollstein, 9 III

Amsterdam, Rijksprentenkabinet, Rijksmuseum A.1372

G.B.

91 Gerard van Groeningen

(active 1561–c.1575/6)

St John receives the Book from the Angel (Rev. 10: 1–11)

Etching and engraving, 268 × 250mm

Lit: Hollstein, 10 III

Amsterdam, Rijksprentenkabinet, Rijksmuseum A.1373

G.B.

92 Gerard van Groeningen

(active 1561–c.1575/6)

The Beast of the Bottomless Pit slaying the Two Witnesses (Rev. 11: 7–13)

Etching and engraving, 268 × 246mm

Lit: Hollstein, 11 III

Amsterdam, Rijksprentenkabinet, Rijksmuseum A.1374

G.B.

90

91

92

93 **Gerard van Groeningen**

(active 1561–c.1575/6)

The Woman Robed with the Sun and Crowned with Twelve Stars (Rev. 12: 1–6)

Etching and engraving, 267 × 244mm

Lit: Hollstein, 12 III

Amsterdam, Rijksprentenkabinet, Rijksmuseum A.1375

G.B.

94 **Gerard van Groeningen**

(active 1561–c.1575/6)

The Whore of Babylon and the Destruction of Babylon (Rev. 17: 3–6; 18: 21–4)

Etching and engraving, 265 × 247mm

Lit: Hollstein, 13 III

Amsterdam, Rijksprentenkabinet, Rijksmuseum A.1376

G.B.

93

94

ORNATVR MVLIER PHÆBO LVNAQVE DECORE. *Apoca .12 .*

POCVLA SPVRCITIÆ GENETRIX HÆC AVREA MONSTRAT. *Apoca. 17 .*

95 Tobias Stimmer (1539–84)

New Illustrated Bible [*Neue künstliche Figuren Biblischer Historien grüntlich von Tobia Stimmer gerissen*], T. Gwarin, Basel 1576

St John receiving the Book (Rev. 10: 1–11) and *The Slaying of the Two Witnesses* (Rev. 11: 7–12)

Woodcuts, with ornamental borders, each approx. 158 × 134mm

Lit: Reinitzer, 153, 153a; Stimmer, 66

London, British Museum 1848-12-9-350

Tobias Stimmer was the leading Swiss painter and draughtsman of the later sixteenth century, and he designed numerous book illustrations for publishers in Strasbourg and Basel. This picture bible contains woodcuts illustrating 135 scenes from the Old Testament and 34 from the New Testament. The rhyming couplets composed by Johann Fischart (1546/7–90), a leading evangelical writer from Strasbourg, have more in common with emblem books than with traditional bibles. Stimmer was much influenced by Hans Holbein's *Icones* of 1538 for the designs of the Old Testament in this work. The subjects in the central panels throughout the book, however, are virtually overwhelmed by the large decorative frames, of which there are eight designs in the book, and which appeared only in the first edition. The idea of using standing figures in imitation of sculptured relief in the ornamental frames was also taken from Holbein, who frequently employed them in his designs for title-pages. A number of the subjects of the Old Testament were copied in pen and ink drawings by Peter Paul Rubens (1577–1640), who was apprenticed to Stimmer during the 1590s (see Stimmer, op. cit. cat. 82, pp.201ff).

Similar picture bibles, or sets of religious woodcuts, were issued in Paris during the 1560s by the publishers of rue Montorgueil. They also have ornamental frames in a French Renaissance style, and relevant quotations, often in Spanish as well as French, on panels within the image (see *The French Renaissance in Prints from the Bibliothèque Nationale*, exhib. cat., ed. K. Jacobson, Grunwald Center for the Graphic Arts, Los Angeles 1994, no.144). One particularly influential engraved picture bible published soon after Stimmer's was the *Thesaurus veteris et novi Testamenti*, Gerard de Jode, Antwerp 1585 (see H. Mielke, *Zeitschrift für Kunstgeschichte*, XXXVIII, 1975, pp.29ff). The twenty-five prints illustrating the Book of Revelation were engraved after designs attributed to Gerard de Jode's son-in-law, Jan Snellinck (1549–1638). There is a copy of the *Thesaurus*, with contemporary hand-colouring, in the British Museum (reg. no.1968-10-18-1).
G.B.

95

Michelangelo's Last Judgement

96 Giulio Bonasone

(*c*.1510–after 1576), after Michelangelo (1475–1564)

The Last Judgement, second half of 1540s

Engraving, 580 × 446mm (trimmed)

Lit. Bartsch XV.80; Stefania Massari, *Giulio Bonasone*, exhib.cat.,
Istituto Nazionale per la Grafica, Rome 1983, p.71, pl. 79a and b; *La
Sistina Riprodotta*, ed. Alida Maltedo, exhib. cat., Istituto Nazionale
per la Grafica, Rome 1991, no.10

London, British Museum 1866-7-14-721

Knowledge of Michelangelo's monumental fresco of the *Last
Judgement* was primarily spread through prints, since access
to the Sistine Chapel in the Vatican Palace was restricted at
first to the papal curia and a select number of the laity.
Nevertheless, exceptions must have been made for illustrious
visitors and for a number of artists, who came to study
Michelangelo's frescoes on the vault and the altar wall. The

Last Judgement was completed in 1541 and by the early
seventeenth century more than a dozen printmakers had
produced their versions of the mural.

Giulio Bonasone's engraving of the late 1540s was among
the earliest copies of the fresco, proving so popular that parts
of the copper plate had to be recut during the lifetime of its
first publisher, Salamanca. However, some contemporaries,

96

for example the Dutch humanist Lampsonius, considered the print of such inferior quality as to have tarnished the reputation of Cardinal Alessandro Farnese, to whom it was dedicated.

The *Last Judgement* was unveiled on 31 October 1541, close to the Feast of All Souls (2 November), for which the mass includes the *Dies Irae*. Its subject relates to the doctrine of the Second Coming of Christ as told in the Gospel of St Matthew and the Book of Revelation, and the fresco itself is often interpreted as a visual response to apocalyptic currents of thought prevailing in Italy after the Sack of Rome of 1527, when the destruction and looting of the city by imperial troops was seen by some as divine retribution for the corruption and sexual immorality of its inhabitants. Like Luca Signorelli and other artists before him, Michelangelo combined Christian iconography with images from Dante's *Divine Comedy*. In particular, Charon, who stands in a boat beneath Christ and threateningly raises an oar, and Minos, the nude in the lower right corner encircled by a snake, are similarly described in the *Inferno*.

The publication of the first prints after the *Last Judgement* appears to have been linked to the famous volte-face of Pietro Aretino (1492–1556), the rebarbative writer whose attitude towards the fresco changed from admiration to invective. He claimed to fear the scandalous effect of the nudity of the figures upon Lutheran sensibilities and, above all, attacked Michelangelo's arrogance in valuing artistic expression to the detriment of religious truth. The work thus threatened to undermine the faith of the wider audience who would have access to the printed reproductions. (See Bernardine Barnes, *Michelangelo's Last Judgement. The Renaissance Response*, Berkeley and London 1998, pp.74–93.) Soon after the Council of Trent in 1563, which decreed that images should be easily understandable, Daniele da Volterra, Michelangelo's disciple and friend, was appointed to repaint all the objectionable areas. Printmakers continued to produce copies of the fresco in its uncensored state, for which there was clearly a market (cats 97–8).

In general, the more elaborate and extended treatment of apocalyptic themes was closely associated with the Protestant reform movement and few cycles of illustration were made in Catholic countries from the sixteenth century onwards. An album of twenty-two drawings illustrating the Apocalypse at Windsor Castle represents a rare exception. It is attributed to the Venetian painter and draughtsman Domenico Campagnola, who worked in the first half of the

sixteenth century, yet the naïveté of the presentation suggests that the series is based on some earlier medieval prototype (cat. 25). The Portuguese painter Francisco de Hollanda, a student of Michelangelo, drew twenty-two scenes from the Book of Revelation as part of a larger series of 152 Bible illustrations which were executed in Portugal between 1545 and 1573, bound together under the title of *De aetatibus mundi imagines* (Madrid, Biblioteca Nacional; I am grateful to Elena Santiago for drawing our attention to the series); their imagery is clearly indebted to Dürer's woodcuts. Furthermore, a drawing in the Louvre, thought to be a copy after an original design by Raphael, suggests that earlier in the century one of the walls of the Vatican *stanze* – in all likelihood the Judgement wall of the Stanza della Segnatura – was intended to show a scene of the Father giving the seven angels the trumpets which announce the Last Judgement (Revelation 8, 2). More personal are Leonardo's series of drawings known as the Deluge series, as well as a sheet of studies at Windsor Castle showing scenes from the end of the world, with fire raining from Heaven, a boiling sea and skeletons rising from the earth (inv. no. 12388). The sources for these disturbing images appear to be the version of the coming judgement given in the Second Letter of Peter 3:10: 'On that day the heavens will disappear with a great rushing sound, the elements will disintegrate in flames, and the earth with all that is in it will be laid bare. ... that day will set the heavens ablaze until they fall apart, and will melt the elements in flames' or in Revelation 8: 7–9: 'The first angel sounded, and there followed hail and fire mingled with blood, and they were cast upon the earth: and the third part of trees was burnt up, and all the green grass was burnt up. ... a great mountain burning with fire was cast into the sea...'.

The most famous heir to Michelangelo's dynamic conception of the Last Judgement was Rubens, whose painting of 1614–16 (Munich, Alte Pinakothek) was in turn widely disseminated through printed versions. More common than representations of the *Last Judgement* as a whole in the years after the Council of Trent was the closely related subject of the *Fall of the Rebel Angels*, for which the descent of the damned in Michelangelo's and Rubens's compositions provided the main source of inspiration (cat. 109). The popularity of the subject in Catholic iconography lay in the fact that together with the figure of the victorious St Michael, it came to be understood as a symbol of the triumph of the Roman Catholic church over Protestant heresy. R.E.-P.

97 Martino Rota (*c*.1510–83)
after Michelangelo

The Last Judgement, 1569

Engraving, 312 × 234mm (trimmed)

Lit: Bartsch, XVI, 28; *La Sistina Riprodotta*, no. 21

London, British Museum 1868-8-22-68

More than any other copy after Michelangelo, this engraving, which was published in two editions, served to spread his influence. Very weak late impressions attest to the excessive use of the plate. In addition, the print itself served as the prototype for four further engravings, respectively by Leonard Gaultier, an anonymous artist 'M', usually identified as Matthias Greuter, a further sixteenth-century anonymous engraver and Jan Wierix (see cat. 98).

Though usually thought to have been made after 1565 (one recent scholar, however, proposed a date of pre-1564), when Daniele da Volterra and his assistants had repainted the previously unclothed figure of St Catherine and had supplied some of the other figures with drawers to cover their nudity, Rota's engraving and nearly all the later prints after the fresco reproduce its original state.

Rota himself used the composition for a further print of the same subject (Bartsch, XVI, 30).
R.E.-P.

97

98 **Jan Wierix** (1549–c.1618)
after Martino Rota

The Last Judgement, 1573

Engraving, 313 × 231 mm

Lit: Marie Mauquoy-Hendrickx, *Les estampes des Wierix conservées au Cabinet des estampes de la Bibliothèque royale Albert Ier*, 4 vols, Brussels 1978–83, 393 VI; *La Sistina Riprodotta*, p. 102, fig. 21e

London, British Museum 1874-8-8-1539

This engraving is one of four made by different printmakers after Martino Rota's copy of Michelangelo's *Last Judgement* (cat. 97). It is unlikely that Wierix, who had probably never been to Italy, would have known the original fresco. With the exception of the sixth state, which was published by Hans de Beeck in Cologne, the engraving was probably published in the Netherlands.

As early as 1565, in a letter to Giorgio Vasari, Lampsonius refers to the need to complement with printed reproductions of high quality the dissemination of knowledge of works of the masters through Vasari's *Lives*. Elsewhere, he suggests that an excellent Flemish engraver, possibly Cornelis Cort, ought to be entrusted with this task. It seems, however, that the idea never came to fruition and that Wierix, who came from a family of Flemish engravers (see cat. 101), was the first northern artist to reproduce the *Last Judgement*.
R.E.-P.

98

Political Polemic and Religious Satire: Images of the Apocalypse in War and Peace in the Sixteenth and Seventeenth Centuries

99 Attributed to Hans Brosamer (c.1500–54)

Caricature of Martin Luther with Seven Heads, 1529

Woodcut, two lines of lettering above, beginning: *Septiceps Lutherus, ubiq[u]e sibi, suis/scriptis*, 178 × 135mm

Lit: Campbell Dodgson, II, p.413, 10 (anon. Saxon school); Reinitzer, 11; *German Renaissance Prints*, 182

London, British Museum 1880-7-10-592

This woodcut of Luther as the seven-headed monster who appears to the Woman Clothed with the Sun (Rev. 12: 1–6), the traditional symbol of the Church, is one of the most famous caricatures of the reformer. The seven heads, which are labelled to represent the different faces of Luther, or in other words various threats to Catholicism, include a Turk to represent the infidel; Barabbas, the robber released by Pilate instead of Christ; and a fanatic with his hair on end surrounded by hornets. The print served as a title-page to a pamphlet written by Johann Cochleus (1479–1552), one of Luther's most vociferous opponents, in response to a

99

broadsheet of 1529 which represented the pope as the seven-headed monster, with text written by the famous cobbler and master singer of Nuremberg, Hans Sachs (1494–1576).

Johann Cochleus also played a significant part in the history of the English Bible. In 1525 he was responsible for betraying to the Catholic council of the city of Cologne the attempt of William Tyndale to publish the first translation of the New Testament in English. Only 3,000 copies of the first ten sheets were secretly printed, probably by Peter Quentel in Cologne, when Tyndale and an English monk working with him were obliged to flee to Worms and begin afresh. The work was eventually published in 1526. Tyndale's New Testament was influenced by Luther's New Testament of 1522, and in its turn had profound influence on all subsequent English translations of the Bible. Cochleus describes the chain of events in his *Commentaria de actis et scriptis M. Lutheri*, 1549. (See David Daniell, *William Tyndale. A biography*, New Haven and London 1994, pp.109–11.)
G.B.

100 Anonymous German

Heavenly Apparition over Nuremberg [*Was zu Nürnberg am Himel dises Tausendt fünffhundert zwey und sibenzigsten jars im Januario den 17. In der nacht gesehen worden ist*] Herman Gall, Nuremberg 1572

Woodcut with hand-colouring, two columns of letterpress; whole sheet 377 × 280mm, woodcut 166 × 256mm

London, British Museum 1880-7-10-319

Meteorological occurrences were a common subject for broadsides in the sixteenth century. They were frequently interpreted as portents of impending doom or the last days, and their imagery was closely linked with the dramatic events described in Revelation. The text on this print describes the appearance on a clear starlit night, on 17 January 1572, of a bright cloud which emanated rays of lightning like fire. The sky was lit up for two hours, during which time rainbows also briefly appeared. It was witnessed by many people in the country around Nuremberg, 'without causing any injury'.

Like the broadsheet of a battle in the heavens issued by Georg Merkel in 1554 (fig. 5, p.108), a link is made in the title of the print with the Second Coming of Christ, 'Also wirdt auch sein die zukunfft des Menschen Son', with reference to Matthew 24 which describes various signs of Christ's coming. Other biblical references are given in the text below. The way in which the occurrence is described is particularly close to Matthew 24: 27, 'For as the lightning cometh out of the east and shineth even unto the west; so shall also the coming of the Son of Man be'. The event depicted would probably be recognized today as an *aurora borealis*.
G.B.

Was zu Nürnberg am Himel dises Tausendt fünffhundert zwey
vnd sibenzigsten Jars / im Januario den 17. in der nacht gesehen worden ist.

Matthei. am 24.
Gleich wie der Blitz außgehet vom Auffgang / vnnd scheinet biß zum Nidergang / Also
wirdt auch sein die zukunfft des Menschen Son. etc:

IM 1572. Jar / den 17. Januarij / welcher war der tag Antonij. In desselben tages nacht / wurd es von zwey vhr auß fast biß in die mitte nacht so liecht / als wenn der Mon hell schiene / welcher doch dazumal am himel nicht leuchten kundte / sintemal. Den 15. Januarij. Zunot ein Newes gewesen / vnd wurde diese nachtleuchtung so hell / das man hette gelt auff der Erden sehen / vnd kennen mügen. Da man sich nun vmbsihet / wo solch Liecht herkommen möchte / Sihe / da findet man gegen dem Morgen in die mitnacht an dem Himel / der doch sonst vberal herumb one gewülck / vnd schön gestirnet war / ein herrliche Liechte wolcke / vnnd die etwas wol niderstehen / Auß oder hinder welchem gewölcke man etliche Stralen vnd Blitzer / als wenn Fewer von Büchsen / die man abschiest / blicket nach vnd vbereinander hauffen weiß auffschiessen / sich außbreiten / vnd gen Himel steigen sahe / vnd das so scheinlich vñ bereit / das einen daucht er wolte solches schiessens knallen hören / aber nichts gehöret wurde. Es waren aber solche stral / vnd derselbigen blitze / nicht Geel / nicht Rott / noch Fewer farb / sondern bleych vnd hell anzusehen / allein wenn sie in die höhe kamen / sich etwas anbreunneten / vnd dick wurden. Es begab sich auch / das biß weilen sich solches schiessen / vnnd Blitzen inn der wolcken legt / vnd still wurde / aber bald widerumb mit gewalt auff war / auffure / vnd gen Himel eilet. Man hat auch zwischen solcher zeit etliche stück / hin vnd wider / neben vnd ineinander von Regenbogen gesehen / wiewol dieselben nicht lang gestanden / sondern bald verblichen. Solch Blitzen vnd leuchten derselbigen Liechten wolcken / (hat die obgemelte stunde) biß fast in mittenacht geweret / vnd von vielen menschen hie in der Stat / auff der Vesten / auch auff dem Landt / vnnd vber viel meil von anderer ort einwonern nicht one sondere verwunderung vnd entsitzung gesehen worden.

Das aber nun sich leut finden / die auß solchem Gottes werck ein Brunst / so in den orten gegen dem Morgen ergangen / machen wöllen / da laß man sie hin machen. So auch etliche sagen wolten / da diese nachtleuchtung gleich kein Brunst angezeiget hett / dennoch nichts vnglücklichs der Christenheit Propheceyen mügen / lassen wir auch mit Jrem warsagen dahin faren / als gute Epicurische gesellen / die den leuten inn

iren sünden vnnd vnbußfertigem leben / in diser grund suppen / der welt noch dazu küsse vnd Pölster vnterlegen / vnnd nemen die warnung des Propheten zu hertzen / der da saget / Mein Volck / deine Tröster verfüren dich / vnd zustören den weg / da du gehen solt / denn sie sagen von friede / da doch kein friede ist. [Ezech. 13.] [Esaie. 3.]

Wie aber solche nachtliecht vor viel hundert Jaren gedeutet / vnd was sie mit sich gebracht / vnd daraufferfolget / werden andere auß den Historien / wie ich verhoffe / wol anzeygen / vnd weisen.

Josephus der Juden Geschicht schreiber erzelet ein solche Geschicht / Vor dem Krieg / spricht er / vnd der zerstörung Jerusalem / da das volck auff das fest der süssen Brodt zusamen kam / begab sichs am 8. tag des Monats Xanthici / welcher vnser April ist / bey der nacht / vmb 9. vhr / das ein solcher glantz den Tempel vnd altar vmbzoge / vnd vmbleuchtet / das menniglich meinete / es wer der helle Liechte tag / vnnd stund solches Liecht bey einer halben stund / Vnerfarne vnd vnuerstendige Leut daucht es ein gut zeichen sein / aber den Schrifftuerstendigen / vnd andern frommen lerern / war es nicht verborgen / was solch liecht bedeutet / Nemlich das es were ein exitiale portentum, Das Jerusalem vñ den Tempel in ein liecht Fewer setzen / vnd darinn gen Himel schicken würde. [Iose..li.7.]

Wir lassen aber dise nachtleuchtung auch ein frölich gut zeichen sein / welches vns vnter andern wunderwercken / den Jüngsten tag mit seinem vniuersalfewer / welches dann nicht auß holtz oder anderer brennenden Materi allein / sondern vbernatürlich vnd vom himel sol angeflaiset werden vñ leuchten / vns offenbaret / in welchem der himel zergehen / vnd die Elament von hitze zerschmeltzen werden, [2. pet. 3.]

Wöllen derhalben auffsehen / vnd vnsere heupter auffheben / vnd vnser Seelen mit gedult fassen / in diser grossen not auff erden / vnd in solchem zorn des Herren. Denn es knospet vnd blüet daher / vnd wil schier Sommer werden / er ist nahe vor der thür / vnd vnser erlösung nahet sich. Es mag in des die Welt hin spotten / vnd in jren kolhauffen hin faren / darinn alle geschlecht auff erden heulen werden / vnd werden sehen kommen des Menschen Sohn / in den wolcken des Himels / mit grosser krafft vnnd Herrligkeit. Amen. [Luc. 21.] [Matt. 24.]

Gedruckt zu Nürmberg / durch Herman Gall /
Brieffmaler inn der Braiten gassen.

100

101 Attributed to Jan Wierix

(1549–*c*.1618) after Maarten de Vos (1532–1603)

Tree of Peace, 1577

Engraving, 362 × 424mm

Lit: Mauquoy-Hendrickx, 1651 II; Hollstein, 1333 II

Amsterdam, Rijksprentenkabinet, Rijksmuseum FM 723 Aa

This is one of a series of five allegorical prints on the re-establishment of peace in the Netherlands published by Pieter Baltens after the Peace of Ghent. The Protestants in the Netherlands, led by William the Silent of Orange, had been in open revolt since 1566 against their ruler, King Philip II of Spain, and his rigorous policy of religious persecution. The Peace of Ghent was signed on 8 November 1576 by the deputies of the provinces of the Netherlands and ratified by Don Juan, the governor of the Netherlands, on 12 February 1577, and by King Philip on 7 April 1577. An allegorical Tree of Peace is represented, with Charity on the left branch and Divine Order on the right, with the arms of Philip II in the centre. In the left foreground a figure of Faith tramples on Deceit, and on the right, Concord brandishes a caduceus in triumph over Discord. A cord with the arms of the seventeen United Provinces unites the four virtuous figures. In the background various monsters, representing the preceding period of war and upheaval and reminiscent of the beasts of the Apocalypse, are chased away by avenging angels. Despite the evident desire for reconciliation expressed in this print, peace was short-lived; there proved to be irreconcilable differences between the Catholic and Protestant provinces. After the appointment in 1578 of Alessandro Farnese, duke of Parma, as governor-general of the Netherlands, the Spanish initiated further attempts to reconquer the region.

Jan Wierix (see cat. 98) came from a Flemish family of engravers, and together with his brothers Hieronymus (see cats 102, 103) and Anton Wierix (*c*.1555/9–1604) was as famous for his disorderly behaviour as for the high quality of his work.

G.B.

101

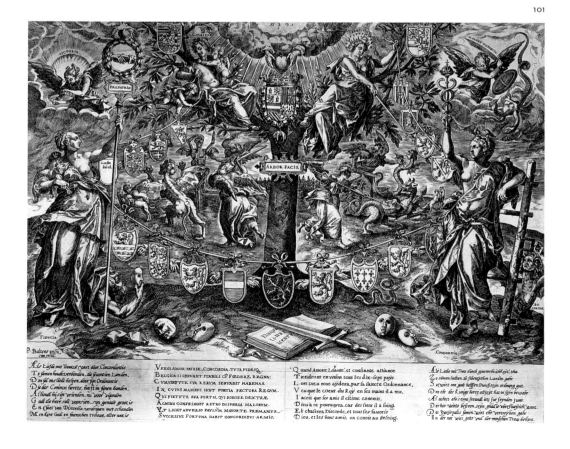

102 Hieronymus Wierix (1553–1619) after
Maarten de Vos (1532–1603)

The Battle of the Christian Knight, c.1580s

Engraving, 301 × 396mm

Lit: Mauquoy-Hendrickx, 1470; J.F. Heijbroek and M. Schapelhoumann, *Kunst in kaart*, exh.cat., Rijksmuseum, Amsterdam p.48; P. Barber, *The Map Collector*, 1990, no.52, pp.8ff.; Hollstein, 1199 II

London, British Museum 1870-10-8-2868

This complex allegory illustrates the true Christian in terms of a warrior, and the sheet is covered with quotations from the Old and New Testaments which elucidate this visual message. The main theme of the Christian Knight comes from Paul's Epistle to the Ephesians (6: 10–20), in which much emphasis is laid on the need to fight for the defence of the faith: 'Put on the whole armour of God, that ye may be able to stand against the wiles of the devil. For we wrestle not against flesh and blood, but against principalities, against powers, against the rulers of the darkness of this world, against spiritual wickedness in high places.' The iconography of the subject has medieval origins, and one of the earliest illustrations of it is in a manuscript made for a Dominican friar in c.1250 (see Ch. 3, cat. 8). The theme also

appeared in fifteenth-century woodcuts before it found its most famous expression in Dürer's masterly engraving of 1513, *The Knight, Death and the Devil* (see E. Panofsky, *The Life and Art of Albrecht Dürer*, Princeton 1955, pp.151ff).

The Knight is shown in the centre of the print, trampling a female figure representing the sins of the flesh ('Caro'). He defends himself from, on the right, the Devil and Death ('Diabolus' and 'Mors') and on the left, Sin, a monstrous half-woman, half-serpent ('Peccatum'). The richly attired figure on the left, identified by the orb on her head as Lady World, is a clear reference to the Whore of Babylon from Revelation 17. She vainly offers the chalice containing the sins of the world to the Knight, in an attempt to lure him away from the narrow path of virtue which leads to the New Jerusalem, seen in the upper left corner of the print.

Wierix's print was copied for an apparently propagandist purpose, in a decorative border of a map of the world engraved and published by Jodocus Hondius in 1596–7 (Hollstein, 51). The title of the print was altered to imply that the battle enacted in the allegory was actually taking place in the world depicted. Furthermore, the facial characteristics of the Knight were altered to resemble those of King Henri IV of France. Officially entitled 'The Most Christian King', Henri during the early 1590s had been leader of the Huguenot faction in France, and was for a while a popular Protestant hero in his battle against Philip II of Spain. In this case, the Knight becomes a defender of the Protestant faith against Catholicism, and Lady World, holding the chalice of the Whore of Babylon, would represent the papacy, as she always did to ardent Protestants.

The most famous literary evocation of the Christian Knight occurs in Book I of Edmund Spenser's *The Faerie Queen* (1590), which is profoundly indebted to the Book of Revelation. The chief protagonist, the Red Cross Knight, is an allegorical representation of England, progressing from the corrupt faith of Catholicism embodied in the figure of Duessa, for whom the Whore of Babylon is a prototype, to the true faith of the Protestant Church in the form of Una, who refers both to 'the Woman Clothed with the Sun' and to Elizabeth I, 'the Faerie Queen' herself. (On the subject of the Reformation and prophetic poetry in England, see David Norbrook, *Poetry and Politics in the English Renaissance*, London 1984).

G.B.

102

103

103 Hieronymus Wierix (1553–1619) after

Maarten de Vos (1532–1603)

St Michael triumphing over the Devil, 1584

Engraving, 284 × 200mm

Lit: Mauquoy-Hendrickx, 1260 I; Hollstein, 1127 I

London, British Museum 1868-6-12-551

A related drawing of the figure of St Michael by de Vos, dated 1583, is in the Louvre, Paris (inv. no. 20.595). Maarten de Vos was among the most important religious painters in Antwerp during the 1590s. He was a prolific draughtsman, and most of his 500 surviving drawings were designs for prints. This example is typical of the refined engraving technique at which the Wierix brothers excelled.
G.B.

104 Jan Sadeler I (1550–c.1600)

after Joos van Winghe (c.1544–1603)

The Twenty-Four Elders and the Elect kneeling before a Vision of the Holy Lamb (Rev. 5: 7, 14), 1588

Engraving, 403 × 322mm (trimmed)

Lit: G. Poensgen, *Pantheon*, xxx 1972, p.45, no.25; Hollstein, 340

London, British Museum 1868-6-12-505

Untrimmed impressions of this devotional print are lettered along the lower edge with a dedication to the ecclesiastical authorities in Würzburg. The motets engraved over the emblems representing the four beasts are clearly legible as a song for four voices, signed by the Flemish composer Andreas Pevernage (1543–91). Its function as a song-sheet gives a clue to the elaborate appearance of this print, which combines two musical scenes from different parts of the Apocalypse. In the upper section, the twenty-four elders with harps and bowls of incense surround God, who holds the book with the seven seals. The lower section of the print shows the Adoration of the Lamb from Revelation 7, in which a great multitude dressed in white robes with palms in their hands stand before the Lamb. It also refers to the adoration of the Lamb on Mount Sion from Revelation 14: 'I heard a voice from heaven, as the voice of many waters, and as the voice of a great thunder: and I heard the voice of harpers harping with their harps: And they sung as it were a new song before the throne, and before the four beasts, and the elders: and no man could learn that song but the hundred and forty and four thousand, which were redeemed from the earth' (Rev. 14: 2–3). The combination of different parts of Revelation for this subject was also used by Dürer (see cat. 18).

Joos van Winghe came from Brussels and worked in Italy during his early years. He emigrated to Frankfurt in about 1585, probably on account of the religious and political turmoil in his own country, which he made the subject of one of his paintings described by van Mander, *Belgica freed from Tyranny*. He acquired citizenship in Frankfurt in 1588, the year in which this print was engraved and published by his compatriot Jan Sadeler, who had also acquired citizenship in the same city the previous year. Van Winghe was a major exponent of Italianate mannerism in the North, but few of his paintings have survived and the influence of his figure compositions, which demonstrate a dramatic use of light and shade, has been chiefly conveyed through engravings by Jan Sadeler, his brother Raphael Sadeler (c.1560–1632) and others.

Pevernage, the composer of the motets, was choirmaster of the cathedral in Antwerp from 1585. Concerts were often held in his Antwerp home, and he was in close touch with prominent artists of his time, as well as the printer Christoph Plantin (c.1520–89), who published work by leading Netherlandish engravers. Motets composed by Pevernage appear in four other devotional engravings

104

by Sadeler, including *David Playing the Harp*, also after Joos van Winghe and published in Frankfurt (Hollstein, 126), and two prints after Maarten de Vos, the *Annunciation to the Shepherds* of 1587 and the *Song of Solomon* of 1590 (de Vos, Hollstein 528 and 132). Picture motets were a unique phenomenon of late sixteenth-century engraving in Antwerp. The music was conceived not so much for performance in this world but as an imitation of what might be sung in the next (Willem Elders, *Composers of the Low Countries*, trans. Graham Dixon, Oxford 1991, pp. 74–6).

G.B.

105

105 Jan Sadeler I (1550–c.1600) after Christoph Schwarz (1548–1592)

The Last Judgement (Rev. 20: 11–15), *c.*1590–4

Engraving, 406 × 455mm (oval)

Lit: Hollstein, 260

Amsterdam, Rijksprentenkabinet, Rijksmuseum OB 5337

The Last Judgement relates to the Second Coming of Christ, which will end the millennium of his reign on earth and occur just after the final battle with Satan. There are numerous scriptural references to it in addition to Revelation; the reference given for this print is to the Sibylline book, seen in the lettering above, *libr.Sibyll: orat.viii*, and relates to the prophetic Sibyls of antiquity, twelve of whom had been accepted by the Western Church as foretelling the story of Christ.

The inscription below dedicates the print to Duchess Renata, wife of Duke William V of Bavaria, for whom Schwarz worked extensively from 1581 as court painter, decorating the interior of the duchess's private oratory at the Residenz in Munich. Jan Sadeler, who came from a family of Flemish engravers active throughout Europe, worked in Munich from 1588 to 1595. The composition of the print is related to two small panels of the *Last Judgement* by or after Schwarz, sold in Cologne in 1895 (Heberle, 14 June 1895, nos 216, 217).
G.B.

106 Hendrick Hondius (1573–1650)

The Papist Pyramid, 1599

Engraving, with two columns of text in French and Latin below,
332 × 183mm

Lit : Ger Luijten *et al.*(ed.), *Dawn of the Golden Age: Northern
Netherlandish Art 1580–1620*, exhib. cat., Rijksmuseum,
Amsterdam 1993, p.188; Hollstein, 38 I

London, British Museum 1992-1-25-16

This virulent anti-Catholic satire is composed of a pyramid of
snakes, each wearing a clergyman's headdress to indicate an
ascending hierarchy of the Catholic clergy, with the snake at
the top of the pile wearing a papal tiara. The title, *Den
Antechrist sit inden Tempel Gods* ('Antichrist sits in God's
temple'), refers to the 'son of perdition' worshipped
mistakenly as God in St Paul's second Epistle to the
Thessalonians (II Thess. 2: 4). This is the most important of
the very few references in the Bible to Antichrist (see cat. 3).
Other quotations on the print reinforce the theme: on the left
edge is a reference to Daniel's vision of one 'like the Son of
Man, to whom was given dominion, and who was
worshipped by all people' (7: 25), also interpreted as the
Antichrist; along the upper and right edges are references to
the Whore of Babylon from Revelation (Rev. 17, 18).

Hendrick Hondius had a long career as the chief print
publisher in The Hague; he held an influential position in the
city, which at this period was involved in much political and
religious turmoil. In 1599, the same year that this print was
published, he issued a series of fifty-one prints of *Celebrated
Reformers and Men of the Religion*, which was used to
illustrate a Dutch edition of Verheiden's *Praestantium aliquot
theologorum*, The Hague 1603. The *Papist Pyramid* must have
been produced in response to the Peace of Vervins of 1598
between the great Catholic powers of France and Spain, for
which Pope Clement VIII was largely responsible. Hondius's
Protestant beliefs did not, however, affect the subject-matter
of his prints: the following year he engraved the five-plate
View of Rome after Hendrik van Cleef, with verses praising
Pope Clement VIII on the occasion of his jubilee year in 1600.
G.B.

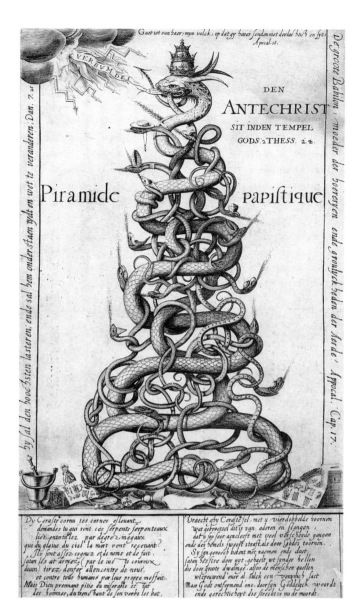

106

107 Claes Jansz. Visscher (1586/87–1652)

Illustration and Comment on the St George of Cleves [*Verthooninghe ende verclaringhe van den Cleefschen S. Joris*], 1615

Etching, with four columns of Dutch letterpress; whole sheet 310 × 372mm, etching 168 × 372mm

Lit: W. Harms *et al.*, *Deutsche illustrierte Flugblätter des 16. und 17. Jahrhunderts*, Tübingen, vols 1–4, 7, 1985–97, 2, 105; Hollstein, 25

Amsterdam, Rijksprentenkabinet, Rijksmuseum FM 1301

This broadsheet refers to one of many episodes fraught with religious tension that arose in Europe at this period. Ambrogio, marquis of Spinola, the Spanish enemy of the Dutch, is cast in the role of the Whore of Babylon, his seven-headed beast wearing a papal tiara and other Catholic headdresses. He is fighting Moritz of Nassau, the leader of the United Provinces, in the guise of St George protecting a woman who represents the Duchy of Cleves. The allegorical battle refers to the disputed succession of the duchy, which lay just to the east of the newly created United Provinces. At the same time that a peace treaty at The Hague was being concluded between the Netherlands and Spain, a crisis emerged when Johann Wilhelm, duke of Cleves, Jülich and Berg, died childless in March 1609. The duchy was traditionally Catholic, but the Dutch were anxious that their new neighbour should be Protestant, while the Spanish wished to maintain a route into the Netherlands and therefore required the successor to be Catholic. The two main Protestant contenders for the succession, Johann Sigismund, elector of Brandenburg, and Wolfgang Wilhelm, the heir to the Palatinate, soon invaded and jointly occupied the duchy, except for the city of Jülich which remained Catholic.

A change in the balance of power after the assassination of the French king Henri IV in May 1610 meant that Jülich soon afterwards fell into Protestant hands; but the situation remained unresolved, because in 1613 Wolfgang Wilhelm converted to Catholicism. Both contenders were by this time financially constrained, and resorted for aid to the greater powers of Spain and the United Provinces. The Spanish general, the marquis of Spinola, occupied Aachen and other

107

Verthooninghe ende verclaringhe van den Cleefschen S. Joris

towns on the Rhine, and Moritz of Nassau moved his troops to protect the United Provinces, but no battle between the two ever actually occurred. A peace negotiated at the Treaty of Xanten in November 1614 divided the duchy, Jülich and Berg going to Wolfgang Wilhelm, Cleves to Johann Sigismund.

This broadsheet was also issued with German text (see J.R. Paas, *The German Political Broadsheet 1600–1700*, Wiesbaden 1985–, I, P-212; Harms II, 106) and was clearly intended for a Protestant audience. The Protestant town of Cleves is identified on the left behind Moritz of Nassau and the Catholic stronghold, Cologne, is in the background behind Spinola. In the middle distance the Tower of Babel is under construction, watched by leading figures of the Catholic hierarchy. The Tower of Babel refers to man's vain attempt to build a tower that would reach Heaven, and God's creation of a multitude of languages as punishment (Gen. 1: 11). In the context of this print, it probably refers to the confused interpretation of the treaty of The Hague in 1609; no sooner was peace agreed than tension in the duchy of Cleves threatened a renewal of hostilities.

G.B.

108 Anonymous German

The Seven-headed Calvinist Phantom [Der Sibenköpffige Calvinisten Geist], 1619

Engraving with seven verses in letterpress; whole sheet 274 × 371mm, engraving 99 × 152mm

Lit: J.R. Paas, *The German Political Broadsheet 1600–1700*, Wiesbaden 1985–, P-475

London, British Museum 1880-7-10-840

This anonymous caricature of a follower of the Protestant reformer Jean Calvin (1509–64) attacks the duplicity of Calvinists in a similar way to the condemnation of Martin Luther in the print attributed to Hans Brosamer (cat. 99). It was issued during the Thirty Years War, by which time Calvinism had taken hold in much of Europe. Few caricatures of the leading reformers have survived, and they are mild in tone compared with the virulent and more numerous prints issued against the Catholic clergy, particularly the Jesuits, during this period.

G.B.

108

PHILIPPO IIII. HISPANIARVM REGI CATHOLICO INDIARVM MONARCHÆ   Humill. Lucas Vorſtermin Sculptor D.D.

P.P. Rubens inuent   Cum priuilegio Regis Chriſtianiſſimi, Principum Belgarum et Ord. Batauæ. Aᵒ 1621.

109

109 Lucas Vorsterman I (1595–1675)
after Peter Paul Rubens (1577–1640)

St Michael fighting the Rebel Angels, 1621 (Rev. 12: 7–9)

Engraving, 563 × 430mm

Lit: Hollstein, 92 1

London, British Museum R.3–4. Bequeathed by the Rev. C.M. Cracherode, 1799

The print is dedicated by the engraver, Lucas Vorsterman, to King Philip IV of Spain. The composition is taken from a painting by Rubens which was probably executed for the Jesuit church in Lille, and destroyed by fire in 1740. There is a copy of the painting in the collection of John Blondel, Mont-sur-Rolle (see H. Vlieghe, *Corpus Rubenianum Ludwig Burchard* II, London and New York 1973, 134). A preparatory drawing for the print in Stockholm (inv. NM 1964/1863) has been tentatively attributed to Anthony van Dyck, who sometimes worked as an assistant for Rubens from *c*.1616 to 1620 (see A.-M. Logan, *Master Drawings* XV, 1977, p.416).

Rubens worked in Antwerp after travelling in Italy from 1600 to 1608, and was the most influential and prolific Baroque artist in northern Europe. The subject of this powerful design of the Fall of the Rebel Angels is related to his vast compositions of the Last Judgement, in which he excelled at dramatic interpretations of struggling figures vainly attempting to resist their descent into hell (Munich, Alte Pinakothek, inv. nos 611 and 890; related drawings in the British Museum, reg. nos 1895-9-15-1052, 1994-5-14-33 to 36, Oo-3-9 and 1885-5-9-51). At an early point in his career, Rubens recognized the potential profits to be made from reproductive prints, and took on Lucas Vorsterman to train for this purpose from *c*.1617 to 1618. Vorsterman became one of the finest engravers of his master's work, and developed a sophisticated tonal technique, which involved accumulating layers of lines engraved to different depths, in order to express Rubens's highly coloured paintings.

The two artists were initially close friends, but they were both highly ambitious and during the early 1620s conflict developed between them, with the engraver demanding credit for privileges and dedicatory inscriptions, such as the one seen on this print. Hostility between the two grew to such an extent that in April 1622 Vorsterman made an attempt on Rubens's life. He departed for England soon afterwards, where he worked for Thomas Howard, earl of Arundel; and although he returned to Antwerp later in his career, he never worked with Rubens again. Rubens later returned to the Book of Revelation for his painting of *The Woman of the Apocalypse* of 1624–5, which was commissioned for the high altar of the cathedral in Freising (Munich, Alte Pinakothek, inv. no.891).
G.B.

110 Anonymous German

The Town of Augsburg under Siege [Die betrangte Stadt Augsburg], 1632

Etching, with two columns of letterpress, damaged along lower edge, hole in the centre; whole sheet 335 × 287mm, etching 167 × 283mm

Lit: Harms, II, 265; Paas, P-1736

London, British Museum 1875-7-10-4372

This piece of Protestant propaganda refers to a period of intense re-Catholicization throughout the Holy Roman Empire from 1629 to 1632. The imperial Edict of Restitution, proclaimed in 1629, was a major achievement of the Counter-Reformation. All Catholic lands which had been under Protestant control since 1552 were forced to re-convert to Catholicism. Despite opposition in strongholds such as Augsburg, there was little effective resistance at the time because there was no Protestant prince capable of mounting a campaign against the emperor, Ferdinand II. Protestant ministers lost their jobs in scores of imperial free cities, Hanseatic towns and small parish churches. In Augsburg, around 8,000 Protestant citizens left the city. This print shows an imaginative use of traditional apocalyptic imagery within a specific setting: two huge monsters representing the beasts from Revelation 13 are seated on hills overlooking Augsburg, which has two of its churches and the town hall identified with inscriptions. The seven-headed beast on the

110

left symbolizes the papacy and throws up various Catholic clerics into the town; the beast with the lamb's horns on the right, wearing a Jesuit's hat, disgorges numerous Jesuits. The text, addressed to 'dear reader', states that the two monsters 'spewed up their brood' in August 1629, taking over the Protestant churches, schools and libraries in the town; it reports on the misery and persecution suffered by many in the city. The print was issued in 1632, either shortly before or at the same time as its pendant, cat. 111.
G.B.

III Anonymous German

Augsburg Liberated by the Grace of God [*Die durch Gottes Gnad erledigte Stadt Augsburg*],1632

Etching, with two columns of letterpress, whole sheet 361 × 289mm, etching 151 × 289mm

Lit: Harms II, 266; Paas, P-1737

Darmstadt, Hessische Landes- und Hochschulbibliothek Gü 8045, 57

This was designed as a sequel to the preceding print, and represents Gustavus Adolphus as the Christian knight who liberated Augsburg from the oppression of Catholic forces, depicted as apocalyptic monsters. Gustavus Adolphus (1594–1632) was the Swedish king whose rapid success as

the leader of Protestant forces in Germany during the early 1630s culminated in his entry into Augsburg on 24 April 1632. Not only was this a victory of great military and political significance, but it also had considerable symbolic importance as the liberation of the place where the Augsburg Confession, the articles of Lutheran faith, had been promulgated in 1530. On the left of this print, underneath the dead monster's tail, which snakes through Freising and Munich into the mountains in the background, the Catholic clergy are seen leaving Augsburg, while on the right, Protestants are returning to the city.

The survival of a comparatively high number of broadsheets representing Gustavus Adolphus as the saviour of German Protestantism at this period attests to a significant propaganda campaign. The Swedish king started using local printers for this purpose soon after he invaded Pomerania in the summer of 1630, and continued to take control of printers' workshops as he occupied towns further south. One particularly successful print that was frequently reprinted and copied was *The Swedish Deliverance of the Christian Church*, engraved by Lucas Schnitzer and first published in 1630. It represents the king as a lion stepping ashore from a boat to fight the papacy, shown as the seven-headed monster from the Apocalyse (see Harms II, 217, and Münster 1998, p.362, no.1031).
G.B.

111

II2 Stefano Della Bella (1610–64)

Death on Horseback, with a Trumpet, 1640s

Etching with engraving, second of three states, 190 × 150mm

Lit: *Stefano Della Bella. Catalogue raisonné Alexandre De Vesme with Introduction and Additions by Phyllis Dearborn Massar*, 2 vols, New York 1971, 87; *Stefano Della Bella 1610–1664*, exhib. cat., Musée des Beaux-Arts, Caen 1998, no. 23

London, British Museum 1871-5-13-648

In 1639 the etcher and engraver Stefano Della Bella travelled to Paris in the entourage of the Florentine ambassador to the French court. During his Parisian sojourn, which lasted at least until 1650, Della Bella made a set of four upright oval engravings portraying Death abducting a victim, included here as cats 113–15. Two further oval prints on this theme were probably created around 1662, during Della Bella's later years (De Vesme/Massar 91–2; Anna Forlani Tempesti, 'Un libro su Stefano Della Bella', *Paragone* XXIV, no. 279, May 1973, pp.54–76); one of them was completed after the artist's death by Giovan Battista Galestruzzi (De Vesme/Massar 92). Drawings by Della Bella preparatory to the engravings are in the Hermitage, St Petersburg; Stanford University Art Museum; Albertina, Vienna; Ashmolean Museum, Oxford; Bibliothèque Nationale, Paris; Gabinetto Nazionale delle Stampe, Florence; and in a private English collection (Caen 1998, pp.74–6).

112

The series appears to have been inspired by the famous representation of the Dance of Death or *danse macabre*, painted in 1424–5 on the walls of the cemetery adjoining the Church of the Holy Innocents in Paris. Though the murals were destroyed in 1669 when the cemetery walls were pulled down to accommodate a wider road, a set of woodcuts published by Guyot Marchand in Paris in 1485 is believed to be a good copy. The cycle consisted of a procession or dance in which skeletons were paired with living persons of different social classes, from the pope and emperor down-wards. Moralizing inscriptions in the form of a dialogue between Death and each living companion accompanied the scenes (Hellmut Rosenfeld, *Der mittelalterliche Totentanz*, 2nd edn, Cologne 1968, *passim*). Of the many representations of the Dance of Death that followed in the wake of the Paris *danse macabre*, still considered the earliest example of this genre, two mural cycles in Basel of the late fifteenth century and a series of woodcuts by Hans Holbein, published in Lyons in 1538 (Alexander Goette, *Holbeins Totentanz und seine Vorbilder*, Strasbourg 1897, *passim*), are probably the most famous. The subject was most popular in the fifteenth

century (pp.58–9; Ch. 3, cat. 24), and was then revived in the nineteenth and twentieth centuries (see Ch. 6, p.271, cats 9c., 15). The medieval cycles functioned as a *memento mori* and, like apocalyptic announcements of the coming of the Antichrist and the end of the world, they called the viewer to repentance and devotion. The connection between the Apocalypse and the painted figures must certainly have been felt by a certain friar who is known to have delivered apocalyptic sermons from a pulpit hard by the Dance of Death at the Innocents in Paris.

The subject of the Dance of Death had already fascinated Della Bella in his youth, as is demonstrated by a group of his drawings now in the Albertina, Vienna (inv. nos 11243–9; Veronika Birke and Janine Kertész, *Die italienischen Zeichnungen der Albertina, Generalverzeichnis*, 4 vols, Vienna, Cologne and Weimar 1992–7, III, pp.1706–11), which copy motifs from Holbein's famous woodcuts. In his own variation on the theme, Della Bella transposes the subject more strongly into a contemporary context. Thus the present example may be seen against the background of the Thirty Years War which ravaged Europe until 1648. The population suffered tremendously at the hands of the pillaging armies, from famine and the plague. The following three entries, two of which locate the scene at the Cemetery of the Innocents, reflect perhaps the high infant mortality in the seventeenth century, when every second child died before reaching adulthood, often taking its mother to the grave as well during childbirth.

Here Della Bella evokes the vision of the Fourth Horseman as described in the Apocalypse, where, after the opening of the fourth seal, the narrator beholds '… a pale horse: and his name that sat on him was Death, and Hell followed with him. And power was given unto them over the fourth of the earth, to kill with sword, and with hunger, and with death, and with the beasts of the earth' (Rev. 6: 8). Death brandishes in a sword-like manner the attribute of the seven angels, a trumpet (Rev. 8), and the fact that one of the horse's hooves projects beyond the oval boundary adds to the figure's immediacy. The accoutrements of the group of skeletons climbing the hill at right – the processional cross, from which hangs a cardinal's hat, the crowns, and the breastplate held up like a military standard – seem directed against the three institutions most heavily involved in warfare at the time. Besides representing the ravages of war, the skulls in the middle ground, visible beneath the belly of the horse, recall the contemporary custom, as practised at the Cemetery of the Innocents, of disinterring the dead and stacking their remains in charnel houses to make room for newcomers.

R.E.-P.

113

II3 Stefano Della Bella (1610–64)

Two Skeletons, Each carrying an Infant, 1640s

Etching with engraving, second of three states, 187 × 151mm

Lit: De Vesme/Massar, 88; Caen 1998, no. 23

London, British Museum 1871-5-13-649

The setting for this and the following catalogue number, which both show Death carrying off children, is the Cemetery of the Innocents in Paris, whose name refers to the biblical story of the infants massacred on Herod's orders. On the left is the Church of the Innocents, at right stand the Croix Glatine and Tour Notre-Dame des Bois.
R.E.-P.

114

115

114 Stefano Della Bella (1610–64)

Death Carrying a Child on his Back, 1640s

Etching with engraving, second of three states, 182 × 151mm

Lit: De Vesme/Massar, 89; Caen 1998, no. 23

London, British Museum 1871-5-13-650

The monuments at left are the Croix Glatine and the Tour Notre-Dame des Bois. In the background are seen the arcades of the charnel house of the Innocents, where the famous painted Dance of Death was located.
R.E.-P.

115 Stefano Della Bella (1610–64)

Death carrying a Young Woman, 1640s

Etching with engraving, third of four states, 188 × 152mm

Lit: De Vesme/Massar, 90; Caen 1998, no. 23

London, British Museum 1871-5-13-650

R.E.-P.

116 Stefano Della Bella (1610–64)

Death Riding Across a Battlefield, 1646/7

Etching, third of four states, 220 × 293mm

Lit: De Vesme/Massar, 93; Caen 1998, no. 24

London, British Museum X.5-13

This print was once thought to have been made in 1663, but recent scholarship agrees that it was etched earlier, in around 1646, at approximately the same time as the four previous catalogue entries. A preparatory drawing belongs to the Albertina, Vienna (inv. no.961; Birke and Kertész, I, pp. 496–7). Like cat. 112, this is a version of the theme of Death on a Pale Horse (Rev. 6: 8), the elegant plumed cap making a particularly grotesque contrast to the skeleton on the skeletal horse. In this instance, however, warfare is explicitly referred to in verses appearing beneath the image, of which the first two lines read: 'Here Death triumphs among the obsequies. His most favoured promenades are battlegrounds.' Callot's so-called *Large Miseries of War*, a set of eighteen etchings published in Paris in 1633, provided a source of inspiration for Della Bella's print and themselves reflect the ills of the Thirty Years War (Klaus Bussmann and Heinz Schilling (eds), *1648 – War and Peace in Europe*, exhib. cat., and two vols of essays, Münster and Osnabrück 1998–9, pp. 158–9).
R.E.-P.

116

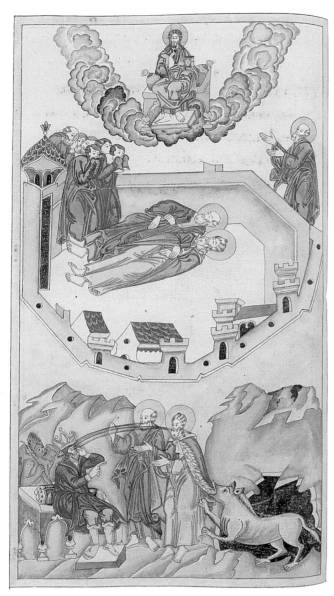

117, Fol. 115v

117   The Apocalypse in Russia

The Revelation of St John with the Commentary of Archbishop Andrew of Caesarea

Russian Church Slavonic

Old Believer Apocalypse, after 1812

Manuscript on paper with A. Goncharov watermarks dated 1812. 428 × 260mm; image size 298 × 164mm; 242 leaves. 74 full-page illustrations in pen and ink and watercolour, with each one appearing on the verso of a blank recto apart from f.3bis r which is an inserted leaf.

Fol 115v: Antichrist and the Two Witnesses below; above are the bodies of the slain witnesses lying 'in the street of the great city which is allegorically called Sodom and Egypt, where their Lord was crucified' (Rev. 11: 7–11)

Fol.122v: The Dragon standing before the Woman clothed in the Sun with her child caught up unto God (Rev. 12: 3–5)

Oslo and London, The Schøyen Collection MS 2623

The Book of Revelation was not accepted into the canon of the Eastern Church until the early fourteenth century, but despite the prohibition maintained in Constantinople, interest developed in Cappadocia where the commentary of Andrew of Caesarea of *c*.613 was an early attempt to rehabilitate the text. Once it had achieved canonical status, illustration of the Apocalypse did not evolve until the fifteenth century, some of the earliest recorded representations being those in a Greek manuscript of 1422 (Bibliothèque Nationale, Paris), a fresco of 1415 in the Cathedral of the Annunciation in the Kremlin in Moscow and a fifteenth-century icon also in the Kremlin (see *The Art of Holy Russia. Icons from Moscow 1400–1600*, Royal Academy, London 1998, p.188). The iconography was given considerable impetus by the dissemination of western graphic cycles, starting with those by Cranach of 1522 (cat. 27) and Holbein of 1523 (cat. 29), which were reflected in frescoes in the monasteries of Sts Dionysius and Docharíou on Mount Athos, for example, and in manuscript illumination. (See Paul Huber, *Apokalypse Bilderzyklen zur Johannes-Offenbarung in Trier, auf dem Athos und von Caillaud d'Angers*, Düsseldorf 1989.)

    Peter the Great's cultural revolution in Russia during the period 1689–1725 systematically introduced European imagery through imported prints and printmakers; the latter, of Dutch, German, French and Italian origin, were brought in to establish the necessary skills and technology for the reproduction of western imagery. The arrival of the printed medium did not wholly supersede manuscript illumination, which continued until the twentieth century due to the high cost of printing, the state monopoly of printing facilities and censorship, and the provincialism of Russian society (see S. Michalski, *The Reformation and the Visual Arts: The Protestant Image Question in Western and Eastern Europe*, New York 1993, p.70).

Printing was also resisted as a symbol of detested Tsarist authority by the Old Believers, whose opposition stemmed from the liturgical reforms instigated in the mid-seventeenth century under Tsar Alexis I (1645–76). The draconian nature of the Petrine reforms, involving a population census as a prelude to levying a 'soul tax', and prohibitions on the wearing of beards and traditional Russian dress, further conspired to encourage a mood of apocalypticism. From 1667, the official date for the schism in the Russian Church, the Old Believers were often ruthlessly persecuted, at least until the mid-nineteenth century. The corollary of their identification of the Tsar with Antichrist and of the Russian Patriarch with the Beast of the Apocalypse, coupled with their doctrine of Moscow as the third Rome whose fall from grace would signal the end of time, was a refusal to conform to secular edicts. (See Michael Cherniavsky, 'The Old Believers and the New Religion', *Slavic Review* Vol.XXV, 1966, pp.1–39, and Will Ryan, 'The Number of the Beast' in *The Bathhouse at Midnight: An Historical Survey of Magic and Divination in Russia*, Stroud 1999, pp.6–8.)

The Old Believers were responsible for a proliferation of apocalyptic tracts and illuminated manuscripts, some of high quality as in the case of the one described here, which was probably made for a wealthy merchant in Moscow. Its link to the Old Believers is apparent from the sign of blessing made with two fingers and further indicated by the use of the Russian three-barred cross. However, the imagery contains none of the more blatant propaganda to be found elsewhere among Old Believer material. The artist was certainly aware of Western precedents – for example, the Whore of Babylon is shown wearing a papal tiara, a feature borrowed from Protestant iconography – but he has largely adhered to a Byzantine-Slavonic tradition which is apparent in the scenes illustrated here. Antichrist in the bottom left of f.115v may be intended to be identified by his crown as the Tsar, who has made himself the mirror image and antithesis of God in Heaven.

Another Old Believer Apocalypse of *c*.1818–26, with seventy-two full-page miniatures, is in the Fitzwilliam Museum in Cambridge (MS 7-1972, see Ralph Cleminson, *A Union Catalogue of Cyrillic Manuscripts in British and Irish Collections*, London 1983, no.3); though similar in format and iconography, the script and the illuminations are inferior in quality. (I would like to thank Dr Will Ryan of the Warburg Institute for his advice on this entry.)
F.C.

117, Fol. 122v

5 The English Apocalypse

David Bindman

I n the mid-seventeenth century, the period of the Civil War, radical dissenters – Levellers, Fifth-Monarchy men and others – were defined by a
conviction that the bloody internecine conflicts of the day were the fulfilment in actuality of the prophecies of the Books of Revelation and Daniel.
For them the Antichrist, the Beast and the Whore of Babylon were a real presence in the world, bringing about the end of material life as a stage on the way
to the redemption of mankind, or the Holy City of Jerusalem as described in
Ezekiel and Revelation. The belief, widespread among the poor, but by no
means confined to them, that the world could end imminently in the destruction of evil-doers and the achievement of universal redemption threatened all
forms of authority. Rulers such as Oliver Cromwell, especially in his later years
when he failed to fulfil the hopes of radicals, Catholic monarchs, the pope,
Anglican bishops, merchants and judges, could be perceived as agents of, or
indeed be themselves, Antichrist. Activities detrimental to the poor, like the
imposition of law and the accumulation of wealth, were readily seen as the work
of the Beast under the guidance of the Dragon who was Satan.

If there were many in seventeenth-century England who believed in
impending Apocalypse, even those with reservations, from the barely literate to
the most educated, would have been steeped in the Bible, and familiar with the
Book of Revelation in normal discourse. The literature of the period – one need
only mention John Milton and John Bunyan – is suffused with apocalyptic
imagery, but so also was the emerging discourse of science. A printer could
replace the date of 1643 on a broadside by the words: 'Printed in the yeere
wherein Antichrist is falling',[1] and in literary and visual satire the evil powers
figuring in Revelation could be applied as part of a standard repertoire of negative associations to foreign or religious enemies, as they had been in the Reformation and during the religious wars in Germany (1618–48) and the Netherlands
(1568–1648). In satire the Dragon, the Beast, the Whore of Babylon and
Antichrist could merge, separate, reveal themselves coyly, or be interchangeable;
indeed, the frequency of the use of such imagery by nonconformists could turn

them into objects of satire, like Ben Jonson's character Zeal-of-the-Land in *Bartholomew Fair* of 1614. The elaborate frontispiece to William Prynne's *The Second Tome*, 1665,[2] contrasting the benign constitutionality of Charles II's rule as Protestant Defender of the Faith with the despotism of the pope, invites us to see the pope as the Great Red Dragon or Satan, giving power to the tyrants of the earth: 'and all the world wondered after the beast. And they worshipped the dragon which gave power unto the beast' (Revelation 13: 4).

In a much simplified version dating from the constitutional and dynastic crisis of 1688, *Babel and Bethel: or the Pope in his Colours*[3] (cat. 5), the pope has now become 'Rome's scarlet *whore*', the Whore of Babylon receiving homage from the earth's rulers while martyrs are burned in the background. A broadsheet of 1682, referring to the 'Popish Plot' of 1678, with a woodcut illustration of the Whore of Babylon, reveals similar associations in its title: *Romes Thunder-Bolt, Or, Antichrist displaid, Being a brief Character of the Sordid Ignorance of the Church of Rome, called in Scripture Mistry Babylon the Great*.[4] Such imagery tends to disappear from English satire after 1688, and the Antichrist, in Christopher Hill's words, 'disappeared into the nonconformist underworld',[5] though the Dragon or Beast may appear occasionally to signify taxation or a threat to the state. In a print of the time of the Excise Crisis of 1733 (cat. 6) the Great Beast of Revelation is reduced to a many-headed dragon, identifiable also as the one defeated by St George, blocking the way of Sir Robert Walpole's state coach, to show popular feeling against the excise tax.[6]

The Book of Revelation was a book for troubled times, but in the relatively peaceful course of the eighteenth century in England it lost much of its immediacy, until the advent of the French Revolution. Many in the seventeenth century had already questioned the motives and sanity of those who eagerly awaited the Apocalypse, but in the eighteenth century the Book of Revelation itself became identified, not altogether unjustly, with not only the uneducated but the insane.[7] Even so, as a canonical yet highly problematic book and as a work of vivid imagination, it remained of profound interest to poets such as William Blake and Samuel Taylor Coleridge,[8] and to 'learned provincial clergymen', of the type of Mr Casaubon in George Eliot's *Middlemarch*, who continued to immerse themselves in its problems of interpretation throughout the nineteenth century. Early in the eighteenth century the Book of Revelation could still be the subject of analysis by Anglican men of science like Sir Isaac Newton (see Chapter 3) and his eccentric successor as professor of mathematics at Cambridge, William Whiston, who in the tradition of the early seventeenth-century Cambridge scientist Joseph Mede, author of the *Clavis Apocalyptica*, 1627, believed it to be evidence of God's providence. Mede had, like many others, studied mathematics before Divinity; indeed the prestige of mathematics in the seventeenth century was due in part to its ability to calculate the dates of the phases of Apocalypse and the meaning of the Number of the Beast.[9]

Between 1688 and the outbreak of the French Revolution in 1789, despite the lack in Britain of political or natural upheaval, there were always prophets and seers who could see in thunderclaps, comets and eclipses portents of universal destruction and ultimate redemption. For millennialists, those rationally persuaded of the broad truth of the prophecy of Revelation,[10] Jerusalem was a city created by knowledge and improvement, to be designed by architects and built either literally or metaphorically brick by brick. Millenarians, on the other hand, tended to see wars and natural disasters as the Opening of the Seals, leading to universal cataclysm and the destruction of material life. In practice, however, prophetic writings very often retain both senses; Jerusalem might appear as if in a sudden vision, yet it still needed to be built by toiling hands. Millennialist intellectuals, like Richard Price and Joseph Priestley who were also Dissenting ministers, could be caught up in the excitement of events like the Fall of the Bastille and be persuaded that Apocalypse was indeed imminent;[11] millenarians, on the other hand, could show astonishing resilience in the face of prophets who turned out to be false, thrones that failed to topple, and the continued dominance of the Beast and Whore of Babylon in the face of seemingly unavoidable portents.

Attitudes towards the Book of Revelation depended crucially upon beliefs about the nature of the Bible itself. A belief in the truth, or the relative truth, of the Bible as history meant that its record of mankind's past could be projected into the future through its prophecies. The truth of past history and future prediction was relative to the authorship and date of each book of the Bible, the authenticity of the text, and its relation to the political realities of its time, on the understanding that if its prophecies had worked in the past they would continue to work in predicting the future. Even so there was an enormous gulf between those who applied scholarly method to the Bible and saw Apocalypse as a slow unfolding over the centuries, and those who saw it as an imminent possibility, given the fallen nature of the world, though there were unconventional scholars such as William Whiston whose investigations into the geological history of the world and mathematical calculations persuaded him that Apocalypse could happen in the immediate future.[12]

Blake's famous colour print of 1795 of Isaac Newton (Tate Gallery, London) represents the great scientist as a narrow rationalist, whose 'single vision' confined him to the arid contemplation of the material universe.[13] But Newton, in writing on the Books of Daniel and Revelation, argued that they were, if understood properly, a rational and truthful account of the history of the world subsequent to their writing, and beyond the present times. The ultimate ambition of the clergy and bishops of the Church of England in the eighteenth century was, like Newton, to prove that the world is governed by Providence by confirming the veracity of the prophets of the Old Testament.[14] If the prophets had demonstrably predicted the first incarnation of Christ then their prophecies of the Second Coming and Revelation must also be verifiable. If the prophecies of Daniel and Revelation could be shown to have predicted accurately events between their own and more recent times, then on their authority the Last Days could be placed in the certain future, at a time open to mathematical and historical calculation. Eighteenth-century theological scholarship, so often satirized as dreary pedantry, was in reality driven by a passionate quest for the proofs of Revelation to be found in the correct reading of disputed texts.

Newton, in his *Observations upon the Prophecies of Daniel, and the Apocalypse of St John*, 1734, sought to convert the language of those books into demonstrable propositions, invoking what he calls 'the analogy between the world natural, and an empire or kingdom',[15] by which natural events or catastrophes can be taken to refer to political events and the relations between nations and peoples. By natural analogy in the Book of Revelation, Heaven and earth refer to thrones and people; 'ascending towards Heaven and descending to the earth, are put for rising in power and honour';[16] the sun is the king and the moon is the body of the common people; the sea, river and flood refer to 'the several nations', and so on. If it is understood that Daniel and Revelation refer to the politics of the early Christian period, then it is possible to identify the Great Red Dragon, the two Beasts and the Whore of Babylon as representing the great nations and empires of the world in that period, with the Roman empire and its successor the papacy pre-eminent. However, even the standard assumption that a biblical day equalled a year required complex scholarship and mathematics to make the dates indicated in Revelation fit a plausible chronology, and there was the question of how far the biblical text might have become corrupted over the ages.

For nonconformists and antinomians[17] the notion that the Bible stood in need of proof was abhorrent. For them the Bible was *ipso facto* true, and the prophecies of Revelation in the Old Testament and the Book of Revelation would surely come to pass. On the other hand, the Bible could also be regarded as fable, a series of stories that contained moral and spiritual meaning, if read in what Swedenborg called 'the spiritual sense'.[18] Apocalypse could be enacted not only in the future of mankind, but in the life history of an individual whose personal fall is redeemed according to the promise of Revelation. Apocalypse thus becomes a psychomachia: man struggling with his own Beast and Whore to find redemption within himself. In Blake's words, applied to his watercolour of *The Last Judgment* (National Trust, Petworth House) (cat. 35), 'whenever any Individual Rejects Error and Embraces Truth a Last Judgment passes upon that Individual'.[19]

Despite Newton's authority the Book of Revelation was treated with wariness by protagonists of the 'reasonableness' of Christianity from Locke onwards, and by clergymen like Wesley. Its association with seventeenth-century antinomianism discouraged its use as a subject for painters, but there were in any case few painted biblical cycles in the eighteenth century. Protestant unease about the danger of idolatry was strong enough even in 1773 to prevent the painters of the Royal Academy from decorating St Paul's Cathedral.[20] Benjamin West's *Revealed Religion* cycle for Windsor Castle was unique in its ambition and the grandeur of its intended setting; there is nothing in the period to compare with it in scope, except for Blake's biblical designs for Thomas Butts (and they were private works). Apocalyptic designs were more often to be found among popular prints or were the work of theologically radical engravers such as William Blake. 'Respectable' painters, like respectable clergymen, were wary of the Book of Revelation's association with popular belief.

The Road to Bedlam: Benjamin West's Apocalyptic Paintings

From the start in the late 1770s Benjamin West's project for a cycle of large paintings for the Royal Chapel at Windsor Castle, dedicated to *Revealed Religion*, was firmly conceived within the framework of an historical approach to the Bible.[21] The initial subjects of the paintings and the overall scheme were negotiated in detail by a commission of bishops advising George III, including Dr Richard Hurd, who had been closely associated with the completion of William Warburton's *The Divine Legation of Moses, In nine Books*, 1754. The scheme was described as 'displaying a pictorial illustration of the history of revealed religion', and the chapel was to be decorated with 'the great events in the history of religion'.[22] The eventual fate of the paintings was confused and unhappy. Because of George III's eventual loss of enthusiasm the scheme was never completed and the finished pictures were dispersed, despite West's own thirty-year commitment to the project and his desperate attempts to reorder the series for at least one different location in Windsor Castle. Detailed architectural drawings, probably drawn in collaboration by West and the architect William Chambers, give a good idea of an early scheme, almost certainly designed for the Royal Chapel. Scenes from the Book of Revelation, making up the final Dispensation, take up five oblong spaces above the windows on the south wall (Royal Library, Windsor Castle).[23] These were reduced to four in one of the last attempts, in August 1801, to give a coherent order to the paintings, in a hand-drawn diagram which makes it clear that the Royal Chapel was no longer their intended setting.[24] The Revelation group represents a final Dispensation, foreshadowed in the *Antediluvian and Patriarchal*, *The Mosaical*, and *Gospel Dispensations*.

Though the Revelation subjects in West's scheme were selected by clergymen of unimpeachable orthodoxy, such subjects took on a different coloration as the project continued into the 1790s, the period of the Terror in France and its aftermath. The king is reported to have claimed that the Royal Academy under West's presidency in spring 1794 was 'under the Stigma of having many Democrats in it'.[25] His suspicions were also directed towards West himself, who in the years 1796 to 1798 exhibited at the Royal Academy a total of five paintings of Revelation subjects. The most sensational, *The Opening of the Four Seals*, was exhibited in 1796 (fig. 1), and it was followed in the subsequent years by sketches for a group of four Revelation subjects for William Beckford's 'Revelation Chamber' at Fonthill.[26]

Such a display of subjects at this time, with unavoidable connotations of revolution, is at first sight surprising. West, as president of the Royal Academy and King's Painter, despite his American birth, always professed his loyalty to

George III, and had kept his royal position even through the American War of Independence. The sublime mode of *The Opening of the Four Seals*, however, brings it close to the work of the more 'democratic' history painters of the time or a little earlier, like John Hamilton Mortimer (who died in 1779), Philippe de Loutherbourg, James Barry, Henry Fuseli and even William Blake; of these five painters all but one, James Barry, made paintings, at one time or another, in illustration of the Book of Revelation.[27] West may have been anxious to make a gesture in the direction of the more radical spirits in the Academy in the hope of keeping them on board, but there is also evidence that he was becoming increasingly disaffected with the king's hostility towards his Windsor Castle project. West declared openly to his Royal Academy colleagues in the later 1790s his desire to return to the United States, and he and his son Raphael were involved in property speculation in New York State at the time.[28] George III's famous remark, reported in 1804 when the *Revealed Religion* project was finally abandoned, that 'the pictures which West had painted for the Chapel at Windsor should not be put up, except the Altar piece, & *that* should not be a *Bedlamite scene from the Revelations*',[29] can be read with hindsight as an astute comment on West's potentially 'unsound' attitudes.

West's involvement with William Beckford, by repute the richest man in England on the basis of his West Indian plantations, is also suggestive of disaffection with the king. Beckford had become a social pariah after a publicly revealed homosexual episode, and he reciprocated by being openly contemptuous of society.[30] He lived briefly in Paris in the early phase of the French Revolution, with which he sympathized, and was treated with honour by the revolutionary government. Beckford was one of the very few wealthy men of the time to offer serious patronage to Royal Academy painters, though the

Fig.1. Benjamin West (1738–1820), *The Opening of the Four Seals* ('Death on a Pale Horse') (1796). Oil on canvas. Detroit Institute of Arts, Founders Society Purchase, Robert H. Tannahill Foundation Fund (see cat.24).

Academy itself was uncertain whether to encourage him or not.[31] The exhibition of West's *The Opening of the Four Seals* at the Royal Academy in 1796 may have encouraged him to commission the artist to make four paintings from the Book of Revelation for his abortive Revelation Chamber in Fonthill, the great 'Gothick' house he was then beginning. West exhibited all four paintings at the Royal Academy in 1797 and 1798,[32] and the openness of his involvement with Beckford and the 'Bedlamite' nature of the scheme hint at the depth of his alienation from the court in the 1790s. Yet he still protested his loyalty to the Crown, retaining hopes of a completion of the Windsor Castle scheme, until 1804 when it was finally ended by George III.[33]

The People's Apocalypse: the French Revolution and the Last Days

George III's awareness of the 'Bedlamite' qualities of Revelation subjects might have been heightened by the fact that the assassin James Hadfield, who had wounded him with a pistol shot in 1800, was a millenarian who justified his action on the grounds that 'our saviour's second advent, and the dissolution of all human things, were at hand'.[34] Prophesying the end of the world had been identified by Robert Burton, in *The Anatomy of Melancholy* of 1621, as a 'Symptome of Religious Melancholy', and madness had been imputed by Church of England clergy to religious 'enthusiasts' from at least as early as the period of the Civil War.[35] In the early eighteenth century memories would have been alive of seventeenth-century millenarianism; there was also awareness of the dramatic activities of the 'French Prophets', who had arrived from the Cévennes after the Edict of Nantes of 1685, and were notorious for 'extravagant enthusiasm' which involved convulsions, speaking with tongues, and preparations for the imminent destruction of the world.[36] The French Prophets, despite support in respectable quarters, faded fairly quickly from attention, but individual prophets and prophetesses were there to greet John Wesley when he began to preach to the common people in the provinces in the late 1730s,[37] and Joanna Southcott in the early nineteenth century was a late example of the rural type.

Such prophets or prophetesses rarely had any interest in expressing their visions in visual form. One who did was 'Poor Adam', the author of a series of woodblock prints produced shortly after 1760, consisting mainly of meditations on the coming Apocalypse with coarse illustrations from Revelation, text and design hand-carved on to the block and relief-printed[38] (cat. 9a.–c.). In a few cases the text is in letterpress, and on one the publisher is given as A.Toppin of York, presumably Poor Adam's surname, though he also seems to have spelled it 'Topham' elsewhere. He tells us that he was born in 1701, and the prints were made after 1760, for many of them are dedicated to George III. He had worked for the well-known York family, the Fairfaxes, at their home in Toulston, Tadcaster, and he was a parish constable.

Poor Adam frequently cites as a source a book on Revelation by John Tillinghast, published in 1701, the year of his own birth, though the edition must have been a reprint, for Tillinghast had died in 1655.[39] Tillinghast was a Fifth-Monarchy man, believing that under Cromwell the 'fifth monarchy', following the fall of Rome and the previous three empires, would inaugurate the reign of Christ and the saints. Poor Adam had difficulty achieving clear legibility in his block prints because of the grain of the wood, so neither text nor design is easily readable, and the prints are obsessively repetitive in content. They give none the less an example of the transforming power of the Book of Revelation upon those of limited education, and in their combination of self-conscious technical innovation and apocalyptic content, foreshadow in some essential respects Blake's illuminated books, though it is unlikely that he would have known of their existence.

Many such prophets were drawn towards Methodism, despite its equivocation towards millenarianism, and attempts were made to find common ground between the two.[40] The anonymous print of *The Tree of Life* (cats 10, 11), which contains both Methodist and millenarian elements, first appeared in engraved versions in London in the 1770s; it was repeated by popular publishers, and then in cheap woodcut versions by Catnach and others until late in the nineteenth century. It is in the form of a 'Hieroglyphick' print, a type that can be traced back at least to the sixteenth century, carrying with it connotations of ancient Egyptian hieroglyphics, believed to be repositories of the mysteries of the Ancients.[41] Such prints are arcane in meaning at first glance, and demand from the viewer a process of decipherment by working through biblical passages. The central motif is of Christ crucified on the Tree of Life, in Genesis described as growing in the Garden of Eden and in the Book of Revelation as planted within the walls of the New Jerusalem. The foreground of the print, before the walls, represents 'this present Evil World' filled with carousing figures engaged (somewhat decorously) in 'Chambering & Wantoness', with only the Methodists, Wesley and Whitefield, and an unidentified preacher to offer the possibility of salvation.

The Fall of the Bastille in 1789, the subsequent collapse and abolition of the French monarchy, the American Revolution of the previous decade, and the imminence of the century's end[42] created precisely the circumstances for the hope of Apocalypse across the whole spectrum of belief. For many the French Revolution was the fulfilment of prophecies made in previous ages, and the scale of its impact seemed potentially universal as it spread across borders and continents. The most influential of the English prophets to identify the French Revolution with the final Apocalypse was Richard Brothers, a former seaman.[43] He made the claim in *A Revealed Knowledge of the Prophecies & Times*, 1794, that the book was 'wrote under the direction of the LORD GOD, And published by His Sacred Command',[44] and that he had been charged by God to fulfil the prophecy of Revelation by taking over the government of the world. Brothers claimed to have already rendered the nation great service by dissuading God from destroying London, 'the other SPIRITUAL BABYLON', in his wrath at its luxury. This was signalled by a clap of thunder at the beginning of January

1791, fulfilling Revelation 18.[45] On another occasion 'The thunder that was heard in the Evening of the Third of August, 1793, was the Voice of the Angel mentioned in the Nineteenth Chapter of the Revelation, standing in the Sun',[46] that would destroy the monarchy and all social injustice.

Brothers was reluctant to proclaim equality or advocate a republic, despite his belief that the French were granted a revolution by the favour of God. As 'the temporal representative of the Almighty' he insisted that everyone follow him in his mission of leading the Jews back to Jerusalem 'by the year 1798', in order to rebuild it as the Holy City. Brothers's literal-mindedness made him predict the date of the Apocalypse very precisely and see the prophecy of Revelation as being fulfilled to the letter; as 'Prince of the Hebrews' he was commanded by God to rebuild Jerusalem exactly according to the regular scheme laid down in Ezekiel and Revelation[47] (see cat. 17). *Revealed Knowledge* made a dramatic impact on its appearance in 1794, and provoked two brilliant satires by James Gillray (cats 18 and 19). It also attracted the attention of the Privy Council, alarmed at the possibility that treason might lurk behind the façade of prophecy. Brothers was arrested on 4 March 1795 and after being charged with treason was incarcerated as a lunatic, remaining in an asylum until 1806.[48]

If madness was frequently imputed to millenarians, as it had been earlier in the century to Methodists, it was only in the late eighteenth century and beyond that it became habitual to incarcerate them in Bedlam or another asylum.[49] It was already commonplace in the 1790s to refer to artists who displayed extremes of feeling or drama, whether apocalyptic or not, as insane. Horace Walpole, for instance, described Fuseli's painting of 1785 of *The Mandrake* as 'Shockingly mad, madder than ever, quite mad',[50] while Fuseli himself noted in conversation with Farington in 1796 that 'Blake has something of madness abt. him'.[51] Fuseli's 'Gothicism' was part of a careful strategy, and he kept a distance from the plebeian millenarianism attributed to Blake and others, but his own imputation to Blake of madness is surely a euphemism for millenarian beliefs. He is at pains in the same conversation, as was Farington, to emphasize Blake's humble social position as 'Blake, the Engraver' who 'married a maid servant'. Madness, on the other hand, could also be a protection; by the beginning of the nineteenth century it could be a defence even against a charge of sedition,[52] and those judged to be harmless if of unsound mind like Joanna Southcott were not incarcerated at all.

Brothers made a particularly strong impact upon radical artisans in London, and a number of reproductive engravers became involved with him, including the much-admired William Sharp.[53] Sharp was an enthusiastic political radical who was called before the Privy Council in 1794, but released without charge. He was instantly captivated by Brothers' *Revealed Knowledge*, and a little over a month after Brothers's arrest and incarceration he published a print of Brothers dated 16 April 1795, showing him with his head bathed gently in heavenly rays, inscribed 'RICHARD BROTHERS PRINCE OF THE HEBREWS. Fully believing this to be the Man whom GOD has appointed; I engrave his likeness, William Sharp'.

As a skilled engraver Sharp was familar to his contemporaries as a type of artisan who sought consolation from mechanical labour in mental speculation.[54] Yet, sharing Brothers' literal-mindedness, he did not attempt to engrave anything from his own invention, though he did make portrait engravings of his own company of the elect. These, of himself, Brothers and later Joanna Southcott, have a striking directness; only the Brothers portrait, with its hint of divine illumination and the extraordinarily large winged cravat, suggests a metaphysical dimension. A manuscript obituary of Sharp, first published as recently as 1977,[55] gives an insight into his fierce independence and credulity that led him to follow one seer after another; the obituary lists John Wright and William Bryan among his mentors, and he was to be one of the most devoted followers of Joanna Southcott. He usually became rapidly disillusioned with his idols, but in each case the devotion he gave was total:

> So firmly was he prepossessed with the opinion that the Millenium [*sic*] was at hand, and that Brother's rod was to be turned into a Serpent he actually made preparations for his Journey to Jerusalem; for which purpose he ordered a Coat with particularly large pockets to serve him for carrying his shirts and cravats and to serve him on his journey through the deserts of Arabia; also he ordered some particular strong Shoes to be made, his belief was that they should Journey on foot over France to the Holy Land.[56]

The engraver and minor print and book publisher Garnet Terry, unlike Sharp, did make a number of millenarian prints.[57] At some point, probably in the mid-1780s, Terry was 'rescued' by the former coal heaver, the Rev. William Huntington S.S. (for Sinner Saved) of the Providence Chapel, a millenarian as notorious in his day as Brothers.[58] Terry set himself up as a 'printer and publisher in divinity' to publish Huntington's works, and to republish seventeenth-century apocalyptic texts. Huntington, like Brothers, was politically a loyalist, who believed that social justice would have to be deferred to the Last Days, but Terry, like others in the Providence Chapel congregation, was more radical; in Huntington's words, 'the same in religion as he is in politics – a leveller and for all things common'.[59] He then appears to have moved towards Brothers, agreeing with him in identifying the French monarchy with the Beast of Revelation.

The first of Terry's two known large-scale engravings, *An Hieroglyphical Print of the Church of God in her Five-Fold State* (cat. 15), engraved by Terry after a design by Huntington and a painting by the fashionable and well-connected painter E.F. Burney, is essentially a version of the *Tree of Life* type, with a 'scriptural Exhibition of the numerous Artists, Mechanicks, and Manufacturers, Engaged in their Respective Pursuits For promoting the various Branches of Natural Religion'. These reprobates are shown outside the city of Jerusalem which is represented as a pastoral paradise within four regular walls, surrounding an enclosure in which there is a figure of the enthroned Christ. Above, held aloft by angels, is the Jerusalem of the Saints, with the Holy Lamb on the altar, and the Tree of Life ending in the Seven Candlesticks before it.

The second print, *An Hieroglyphical Print of Daniel's Great Image, or Mystical Man*[60] (cat. 16), folded within a pamphlet, is of a single figure of a strangely Buddhist cast with a mandorla. It also recalls, in the labels attached to every part of the body, early medical illustrations and satirical prints by caricaturists of the period such as William Dent and James Gillray. The prophetic nature of the image is confirmed by the title-page to the pamphlet, for 'Daniel's Great Image of the Mystical Body of Babylon' shows 'the approaching Destruction of Antichrist, the Beast, the Whore, and the False Prophet… confirmed by the Signs of the Times'. The vision in fact combines two figures from Daniel, the man made of four metals with feet of iron and clay in Chapter 2, and the figure made up of four beasts in Chapter 7. The commentary on the figure makes frequent reference to Revelation and other biblical texts, but avoids the French Revolution and contemporary politics, making slighting allusions to commerce and materialism. The figure is a kind of Moloch, a gigantic monument to materialism that faces destruction in the pending or impending Apocalypse.

William Sharp's theological progress led him to early support of the rustic millenarian Joanna Southcott, who emerged in Devon at the beginning of the nineteenth century, claiming to be a vehicle for the holy spirit and identifying herself as the Woman Clothed with the Sun.[61] She asserted that England's current catastrophes – bad harvests, the war with France – were visited by God as punishments for the clergy's disbelief and neglect of the poor. Her transition from village prophetess to leader of a nationwide following was a consequence of her exploitation of the printed word, her semi-literacy paradoxically reinforcing the authenticity of her claims to speak from spiritual communication.[62] Her movement spread northwards, following poverty and industrial unrest, making her a worry to the authorities as the threat of the French invasion intensified in the years 1803–5. Joanna's vision of invasion was apocalyptic; she urged a spiritual rather than a military response towards Napoleon and Satan, producing 'seals' that would act as a defence against them.[63] Implicit in these prophecies was the imminence of the Second Coming and the instrumental role of Joanna as the Second Eve who would become the Bride of Christ, the Second Adam, in an 'England as happy nation… first redeemed'.

Sharp played a vital role in making Southcott a national rather than a provincial figure. In 1804 he wrote to a bishop that 'the whole tendency of her writings proves that the millenium [*sic*], or Kingdom of Christ, is at hand',[64] claiming also that if people were to think 'upon what has happened within the period of the last thirteen years [i.e. from Joanna's conversion in 1792] they must conclude, that some GREAT and MIGHTY change is about to take place'. He was a believer to the last in Joanna's putative child, the fruit of her union with Christ, to be named Shiloh, who would return after her death to lead the Jews back to Jerusalem and prepare the way for the Second Coming. Even at the end, when the autopsy proved that Joanna had not been pregnant after all, Sharp was touchingly stoical, as *The Times* reported:

> Mr Sharpe [*sic*] was the only one that held out to the rest the balm of consolation. Life, he observed, was involved in mystery. His mind had been so often turned to the investigation of the works of the Deity, to discover evidence for the existence of the soul, that he was satisfied of the existence of a *God* and of a *soul*: that he was in hopes, by this woman, something would be revealed; but now he felt greatly disappointed, and all he could say was, that he was in the same state with respect to his knowledge of God, as before he saw this woman.[65]

The visual fruits of the Southcottian movement are sparse – Sharp's masterly portrait of Joanna and some visionary paintings by a follower, Joseph Prescott[66] – but she did have the misfortune to attract an unusual amount of visual satire[67] (cats 21, 22). Inevitably the promised birth of Shiloh gave the opportunity for ribald jokes at the expense of doctors and the credulous. The father of Shiloh was in some prints scurrilously presumed to be the Rev. William Tozer, the preacher at the Duke Street Chapel and Southcott's general factotum, or to be Satan, with her as a False Prophet. Her pregnancy proved to be a phantom one, and the doctors are shown in a number of caricatures to be colluding with her presumed deception through venality or stupidity. An anonymous print of 7 September 1814,[68] entitled *A Paradice for Fools – A Nocturnal Trip – or – The Disciple of Joanna benighted*, a narrative series of three episodes, lampoons the credulity of her rural followers. It shows a country wife who unwisely follows a 'Holy Angel' on a donkey, and tells her husband he has been 'sent by Joanna Southcott to conduct your sealed Spouse to the Mansions of bliss!!' After being abandoned in the country she returns to her family to find herself rejected by her husband who believes his wife to have 'gone to Heaven on one of Joanna's spiritual donkeys'.

The link between Apocalypse and radical politics in England was largely severed by the early nineteenth century, partly as a consequence of repression, but also because of the transformation of France in popular belief, from scourge of Catholicism and tyranny under the Revolution to 'atheist' power under Napoleon, at war with the common people of England.[69] Millenarianism tended instead to focus wrath not on kings or nobility but on the bishops, whose presumed worldliness had left their flock bereft of spiritual leadership.[70]

William Blake: Prophet and History Painter

Several recent commentators on Blake have pointed out how much of his work, particularly in the 1790s, echoes the message and language of contemporary self-proclaimed prophets. Edward Thompson and Jon Mee,[71] in exploring in depth Blake's connections with the artisan religious and social cultures of

London, have approached him from the viewpoint of 'history from below'. This can, however, lead to an undervaluing of the other world he inhabited, mentally at least: that of the professional painters and sculptors around the Royal Academy, struggling to uphold the cause of high art in an uncertain marketplace.

Though a profound millenarianism pervades almost everything Blake wrote or designed, he seems to have kept a certain distance from Richard Brothers and William Sharp, and other self-proclaimed prophets in the age of the French Revolution.[72] His proclaimed heroes from youth were Milton, Raphael and Michelangelo, and the contemporaries he singled out as mentors or exemplars were almost all senior members of the Royal Academy under the presidency of Benjamin West in the 1790s: James Barry, Professor of Painting at the Royal Academy (expelled 1799); Henry Fuseli, his successor as Professor of Painting from 1799, and the sculptor John Flaxman, a Royal Academician from 1800, and from 1810 Professor of Sculpture.

Blake's watercolours and tempera paintings, as distinct from his illuminated prophecies, belong visually and generically within the orbit of the Royal Academy, where he was partly trained and at which he exhibited on many occasions.[73] In the 1790s he attracted the admiration, even if mixed with condescension, of some senior Academicians, and the disdain of others. Farington records a discussion on 19 February 1796 in which '[Benjamin] West, [Richard] Cosway & [Ozias] Humphry spoke warmly in favour of the designs of Blake the Engraver, as works of extraordinary genius & imagination'.[74] It is probable that the designs that they saw were those 'I printed for Mr. [Ozias] Humphry… a selection from the different Books [i.e. illuminated books] of such as could be printed without the Writing, tho' to the loss of some of the best things. For they, when Printed perfect, accompany Poetical Personifications & Acts, without which Poems they could never have been executed'.[75] This is almost certainly copy A of *A Small Book of Designs* (British Museum), which contains a series of dramatic images taken from pages of illuminated books, superlatively colour-printed to heighten their sublimity. West according to tradition owned a copy of Blake's *America* (copy K, Yale University Library), though the date of acquisition is unknown.[76] It is a handsomely coloured copy, probably printed about 1794, and it may have been given to West by Blake himself.

On the basis of Blake's known hatred for the institutions of church and state, one might expect Benjamin West to appear to him as in thrall to worldly power and kingship; but for Blake the true artist was always forced into internal exile, obliged to preserve an acquiescent façade while covertly weaving prophetic meanings into his work.[77] The designers of the cathedrals and Michelangelo were subject to the Catholic Church, but they none the less created works that transcended their ostensible purposes.[78] Blake himself adopted the persona of an artist forced to hide the true meaning of his art in a society hostile to the spirit. His older contemporaries James Barry and Fuseli, by the same token, suffered attempts to suppress their greatest work by 'the gang of hired thieves' around Sir Joshua Reynolds, prompting Blake to ask of a supposed attempt to suppress Fuseli's *Milton Gallery*, 'Is Satan troubled at his exposure?'[79]

Blake did not, however, mention West as belonging to that revered company, and his own watercolour illustrations to the Book of Revelation, made for Thomas Butts as part of an ongoing biblical series in the years 1800–9,[80] suggest a more equivocal attitude towards the President of the Royal Academy. Blake's Revelation watercolours do not form a coherent series and they were made at different times within the decade. Even so, all but one are close in subject-matter to the six Revelation paintings West exhibited at the Royal Academy in the years 1796–8, which Blake could not have failed to see. It is possible to see in Blake's watercolours an implied critique of West's Revelation paintings, especially in the contrast between their versions of *The Great Red Dragon and the Beast from the Sea*. West's painting (McCormick Coll.; von Erffa and Staley no. 409, exhibited 1798), an oil study for Beckford's Revelation Chamber at Fonthill, has preserved the natural scale of the identifiable creatures that make up the Dragon and Beast, emphasizing their physical substantiality and making them appear to be of the same order of reality as the cowering human family on the beach. In Blake's watercolour of *c*.1803–5 (National Gallery of Art, Washington) (cat. 30), on the other hand, the Dragon and Beast are creatures on a sublime scale. This is evident also in a companion watercolour, *The Number of the Beast is 666* (Rosenbach Museum and Library, Philadelphia) (cat. 31), in which innumerable tiny figures prostrate themselves before the ram on the altar. If West follows literally the animal-like character of the Dragon and Beast in Revelation, Blake resolutely emphasizes their degenerate humanity.

Blake's *Great Red Dragon and Beast from the Sea* and *The Number of the Beast is 666* are part of a narrative sequence of four watercolours, clearly made at the same time, probably between 1803 and 1805, that tell the story of the Dragon and his failed attempt to suborn the Woman Clothed with the Sun. The Dragon as Satan is depicted not as wholly demonic but as a classically ideal body from which grow a serpentine tail, bat wings, scales, and small heads like malignant growths. The Beast, on the other hand, is the excremental product of the Dragon-Satan's fall from grace. The watercolours, even in their present faded state, evoke a limitless space, humanity and sea united in their contrasting smallness and immensity.

Equally telling is a comparison of West's and Blake's conceptions of the Woman Clothed with the Sun. West's version (von Erffa and Staley no. 405) is clearly based on an Ascension of the Virgin with attendant angels, the Dragon reduced to an ineffectual Leviathan on the shore. Blake's Dragon, in his version of the subject (The Brooklyn Museum) (cat. 28), is by contrast, with his scaly back, tail and wings, a figure of monumental terror, presenting the Woman Clothed with the Sun with a threat from which she is fortunate to escape. In the second of the sequence of four watercolours, *The Great Red Dragon and the Woman Clothed with the Sun: 'The Devil is come down'* (National Gallery of Art, Washington) (cat. 29), the drama is watched by tiny human figures in the sea, establishing the scale of the two protagonists and the helplessness of humanity in observing the titanic struggle.[81]

The imaginative richness of Blake's Revelation watercolours sets them apart from West, yet as interpretations of specific texts and narrative moments, however personal, they remain framed within a discourse set by traditional history painting.[82] In Blake's summative prophecy *Jerusalem: The Emanation of the Giant Albion*, 1804–20 (cat. 36), a book of 100 plates, as in his other prophecies, the Book of Revelation is an unavoidable but usually indirect presence in both text and design.[83] *Jerusalem* is made up of a series of interwoven myths; of the artist as creator, embodied in the figure of Los, and of humanity and nation, fallen and finally redeemed, represented by the divided figure of Albion. Albion's fallen and agonized body remains throughout the text and designs, impervious to interventions by the Saviour and by Los until the last pages, when he rises in an ecstatic vision of eternal and universal unity. Albion, the founding father of all false religions and perversions of Christianity, is also the rationalistic spirit of the Britain of his own time.[84] Albion exists in division from his 'emanation' Jerusalem, who is, as in Revelation and the prophecies, both city and woman. As woman she is an outcast, rejected by Albion, and as city she is London longing to be rebuilt as the Holy City. Because in Blake's myth Britain was the seat of patriarchal religion, London was the site of ancient Jerusalem before the destruction of the Temple; hence London-as-Jerusalem represents the ancient Golden Age of Britain and humanity, but was also the scene of Satan's first victory. In one of *Jerusalem*'s narratives the Holy City is to be built through the agency of art; it is a 'Continuing City' to be striven for, and Golgonooza, the city of art, drawn from the fourfold city of Jerusalem in Ezekiel and Revelation.[85] Golgonooza is the meeting-point of the myth of the artist and Apocalypse, for art keeps open mankind's perception of the divine. Yet there is also in *Jerusalem* the possibility of Apocalypse as an historical and an imaginative event, the present time as ripe for the gathering of the final harvest; Albion might wake at any moment to the spirit and enter into eternity. Blake is thus both millennialist and millenarian; the millennium is a state of mind and yet the object of perpetual toil.

If Jerusalem is London's redemptive state, modern London is Babylon; the children of Albion, or the British people, did 'build Babylon because they have forsaken Jerusalem';[86] in thrall to the rationalist religion of Bacon, Locke and Newton, they have expunged London's past as Jerusalem and its future as Holy City. The most prominent of Albion's children are named for Blake's enemies in the years of *Jerusalem*'s composition. Hand, based probably on the three brothers Hunt, is a kind of perverted artist, 'a demonic parody of Los' in Paley's words,[87] and on plate 26 (cat. 36b.) he is identified as Antichrist wreathed in serpentine flames, his arms mimicking the crucified Christ, with the marks of the stigmata on his hands.[88] The crowned, three-headed male figure from which female figures emanate, seated on the cliffs of Dover in plate 50 (cat. 36c.), can be identified as Hand, but also suggests the domination of the Beast over the island of Britain. This figure, a tailpiece to the second section, is echoed in the tailpiece to the third on plate 75 (cat. 36e.), where two crowned females are intermingled with a group of seven serpents, all joined together as one body. This figure is clearly the Whore of Babylon, riding on the 'scarlet covered beast… having seven heads and ten horns', but it encompasses also the 'male females' of history who are the great leaders of institutional religion from Abraham to Luther, expressing the seductiveness and menace of power while also ridiculing it.

If the ghastly spectres of the Beast and Whore hover around the body of Albion, so Jerusalem in all her forms, like the Woman Clothed with the Sun, keeps alive the hope of redemption. Plate 76 (cat. 36f.), as the frontispiece to the final apocalyptic section of *Jerusalem*, shows Albion before a radiant vision of Christ crucified on a tree with hanging fruits.[89] Albion opens his arms in exultation before a Christ whose body is the main source of illumination. The tree is the Tree of Life which in Revelation 22: 2 'bare twelve manner of fruits, and yielded her fruit every month: and the leaves of the tree were for the healing of nations'. Blake's image refers back to the popular print *The Tree of Life*, discussed on page 215, where the tree is seen growing within the walls of the Jerusalem described in Ezekiel and Revelation.

Blake was a private artist not by choice but by circumstance; his aim for all his work, and especially his prophecies, was to find a universal audience, however unwilling it might be to hear his message of redemption.[90] Yet, paradoxically, Blake's self-published prophetic works, like *Jerusalem*, were issued in small numbers (only five copies are recorded) while his watercolours for Butts belong formally within typologies established by the Royal Academy. The former, though demanding upon their readers and evidently unattractive to the wider public, were designed to make universal the warnings of prophecy; the latter, though deploying the public forms of history painting, were made for a private individual with no part in public life.

Destroying Babylon and Building Jerusalem: the Martin Brothers and the City

> Mark, my kind readers, the hand of God in a poor humble cot. God has raised of us four brothers; my oldest brother He has made a Natural Philosopher, my youngest an Historical Painter; his drawings and engravings have made Kings and Emperors to wonder… But I, the unworthiest, God has given to me the gift of prophecy, which is the best of all, for I feel that God is with me.[91]

John Martin's large paintings and mezzotints made in the 1820s and 1830s, of cities in the process of destruction, are self-evidently millenarian in spirit, but it was surprisingly little remarked at the time. Contemporaries tended to focus on their sublimity and marvel at their spectacular effects and archaeological accuracy, while more fastidious critics found them showy and ill-drawn, designed for a popular rather than a discriminating audience.[92] In the years 1826–8 he painted and exhibited most of his very large paintings of sublime biblical subjects, in which the Lord unleashes destruction upon masses of sinful humanity. In *Belshazzar's Feast*, first engraved 1826 (cat. 38b.), the prophet Daniel spreads terror among the banqueters as he warns Belshazzar of divine displeasure; in the distance the multitudes of revellers are heedless of events. In *Joshua Commanding the Sun to Stand Still*, engraved 1827 (CW 77), Joshua commands the sun to stand still, with God's consent, so that he can have more daylight to complete the destruction of his enemies, the Amorites. *The Deluge*, 1828 (CW 78), is notable for the carefully differentiated groups of sinners facing destruction in the foreground. In May of the same year Martin exhibited in London a large picture of *The Fall of Nineveh*, where it was seen by some 2,500 members of 'the nobility and gentry',[93] but the mezzotint was not begun until 1829 (CW 82) and not fully completed until well into 1830. Martin was at particular pains to deflect all connotations of radicalism from his earlier apocalyptic paintings, by emphasizing their archaeological accuracy and by dedicating the prints after them to European royalty, some of whom became personal friends. The first plate of *Belshazzar's Feast* was dedicated with permission to George IV; the *Joshua Commanding the Sun to Stand Still* to his friend Prince Leopold of Saxe-Coburg; *The Deluge* to Nicholas I of Russia; and the large mezzotint of *The Fall of Nineveh*, with Sardanapalus surrounded by his concubines, apparently without irony, to the fervently reactionary king of France 'his Most Christian Majesty Charles X… as a humble tribute of the Artist's grateful feeling for the high honour his most Christian Majesty has been graciously pleased to confer upon him'.[94]

The artist also revealed an avid practical interest in the mundane matter of city improvement; he produced as many as fifteen serious pamphlets between 1827 and 1849 on, among other things, the purification of London's water supply and the recycling of sewage and human waste.[95] Yet arguably such concerns are perfectly compatible with the images of destruction in his paintings and with millenarianism; they express once again the tension between the Holy City as vision and as a real city that needed to be built in its ideal form by careful thought and efficient practice. Martin's concerns with cleaning and purifying London were at one level a way of rebuilding Babylonish London as Jerusalem, as a city of pure air, clean water and stately buildings, according to the ambitions of urban improvers of the day. It is only in his last works, the series of three huge paintings in the Tate Gallery[96] completed in 1853, that he gives an image of the New Jerusalem. The Heavenly City appears in the background to *The Last Judgment* painting (fig. 2) and the engraving after it (cat. 41), conventionally represented by ranks of white-robed saints, and its orderliness is contrasted implicitly with chaotic aspects of the modern industrial world, represented by two trains; one in the middle distance hurtles out of control with passengers yelling at each window into the abyss opening up before them, while the second, some distance behind the first, is pulled by a fire-breathing monstrous locomotive. The abyss is about to swallow them and all the Powers of the World, including the Whore of Babylon, as the temporal world comes to an end.[97]

Despite John Martin's success his hard-won respectability was continually under threat from the notoriety of two of his older brothers. William, the eldest (b. 1772), was a highly eccentric inventor who styled himself 'The Philosophical Conqueror of All Nations',[98] wearing in the streets of Newcastle a hat made of a conch-shell. Jonathan (b. 1782) was a religious fanatic who set fire to and seriously damaged York Minster in 1829. Following a sensational trial that attracted national attention, Jonathan was declared insane and incarcerated in Bedlam where he died in 1838.[99]

John Martin's shadowy apocalypticism and verbal parsimony are counterpointed by Jonathan's fervent hatred of worldliness and his incontinent literary productivity. Jonathan left a number of painfully self-revelatory texts, including an autobiography, *The Life of Jonathan Martin, Tanner*, by Himself, 1826; four warning letters to the clergy of York Minster; a brief deposition at his trial, and often barely legible but highly revealing and passionate texts scribbled on his few surviving drawings,[100] filled with prophetic warnings and millenarian rhetoric. The burning of York Minster was seen by him as an act of warning, threatening ruin upon the bishops of the Church of England. In letters

Fig. 2. John Martin (1789–1854), *The Last Judgement* (c.1850–3). Oil on canvas. London, Tate Gallery (see cat.40).

written in the weeks before the dread act of arson, 'the Job' as he called it, he warned the clergy 'to fly from the roth to cum you who are bringing a Grevus Cors upon the Land you blind Gieds and Decever of the Peopeal',[101] and 'to repent and cry for marcy for the Sorde of Justes is at Hand and your Gret Charchis ans Minstaris will cume rattling down upon your Giltey Heads'. The avenging angel is identified as 'the Sun of Boney', or Napoleon's son, the Duke of Reichstadt, who would come as an avenging angel at the head of a French army, and after defeating English resistance at a battle, burn London. Only repentance could prevent it.

The bishops are described by Jonathan according to the traditions of Protestant vituperation, but with a distinctively English ribaldry recalling the satires of James Gillray and Richard Newton. On 6 January 1829 he wrote, 'you blind clergymen, you who are pricking for for your bottles of wine, and roast beef and plum puddings and your loaves and fishes', and ten days later on 16 January, 'you blind Hypocrits, you Serpents and vipers of Hell, you wine bibbers and beef eaters, whose eyes stand out with fatness'.[102] The trigger to burning the minster was a dream, as he recounted to the trial judge, of

> a wonderful thick cloud [that] came from the heavens, and rested upon the cathedral... I was told by the Lord that I was to destroy the cathedral, on account of the clergy going to plays and balls, playing at cards, and drinking wine. I thought I heard a voice inwardly speak, informing that the Lord showed me the vision of the dark and thick cloud to point out the proprity of setting the cathedral on fire.... I found the Lord was determined to have me show this people a warning to flee the wrath to come.[103]

Jonathan Martin, then, claims the burning of the minster not as an act of destruction but as a prophetic warning, evoking the images of destruction unleashed in the Book of Revelation and Old Testament prophecies. The John-Martinesque quality of the dream is obvious, and the connection between Jonathan's sensational act of destruction and his brother's apocalyptic designs is made explicit in Jonathan's largest surviving drawing, *London's Overthrow* of June 1830 (Bethlem Royal Hospital Archives and Museum) (cat. 41), made shortly after he was incarcerated in Bedlam after his trial.[104] It is plainly based on John's *Fall of Nineveh* mezzotint (CW 82), to which it is very close in size, and Jonathan is most likely to have known it from a proof impression that John might have shown him on a visit to Bedlam, for the print was not finally published until 1 July 1830.[105] On the back of the drawing Jonathan has written, among dense calculations of what the king owed him for loss of work during his imprisonment, 'If I had sought the whole creation round A better subject than my brother's downfall [of Nineveh] I could not have found; to help me to paint sad London's overthrow, when in my dream I saw the awful scene; the inhabitants in great distress; an horrid sight to see them tearing each other's flesh.' The drawing itself has the columns of Nineveh in the background but otherwise is set in London with Westminster Abbey and St Paul's in the background, the former evidently surmounted (the perspective is unclear) by a black cloud like the one that hung over York Minster in Jonathan's portentous dream. The scene is a curious mixture of elements from the disturbed banquet in his brother's mezzotint and elements that relate to Jonathan's obsessions: the carousing bishops in the foreground, gambling and drinking, presided over by a bishop, 'Behold the drunken sot he has got the back of the Book towards him/ Lord save us from the Sword fire and famine and/ Send us more wine roast Beef and plum pudding'. In the centre background is a large one-legged lion, 'The Lion is an Emblem too/ That England stands but on one foot/ And that has lost one Toe/ Therefore long it cannot stand/ For Foreign Troops shall invade our Land'. The attack on Nineveh/London is carried out by endless columns of French troops, led from the top of a cliff on the left by a Napoleonic figure who must be the duke of Reichstadt.

John Martin's apocalyptic designs clearly gave a shape to Jonathan's fevered imaginings in the period in which he was contemplating the destruction of York Minster; they also make it clear that, despite their very different

Fig. 3. J.M.W. Turner (1775–1851), *The Angel Standing in the Sun* (1846). Oil on canvas. London, Tate Gallery.

circumstances and fates, the two brothers shared something of the same mental world. In Martin's epic biblical scenes of the later 1820s, and in his brother's destruction of the minster, there can be discerned an abhorrence towards a decadent civilization engaged in worldly pursuits, without heed to divine wrath. However much John sought to distract attention from the millenarian import of his images of destruction, it remains the common thread that binds his eclectic concerns as a scientific 'improver' to his visions of urban cataclysm, together with the demented impulses that made his brother set on fire, with great deliberation, the second cathedral church in the land.

The tragic career and public trial of Jonathan Martin linked together Apocalypse and insanity in the public mind, but evidently did not diminish the extraordinary influence of his brother John's apocalyptic designs, not only in England but also in France and the United States, reaching even as far as the early films of D.W. Griffith.[106] There were contemporary painters like Francis Danby who sought to emulate the sublime effect of Martin's paintings in an attempt to match the former's financial success[107] (cat. 42). Samuel Colman, also of Bristol, on the other hand, was a sincere dissenter, whose heavily populated paintings clearly reflect Martin's influence but are more overtly apocalyptic.[108] The most suggestive mid-nineteenth century meditation on Revelation, how-ever, is surely Turner's late painting *The Angel Standing in the Sun* (fig. 3), exhib-ited in the Royal Academy in 1846, accompanied by a quotation from Revelation 19: 17–18, and an extract from a poem by Samuel Rogers: 'The morn-ing march that flashes to the sun;/The feast of vultures when the day is done'.[109] It shows the 'kings, captains and mighty men' whose flesh will be eaten by 'the fowls that fly in the midst of heaven' in the Last Days.[110] This painting, one of Turner's last invocations of transcendent light, has perhaps some echoes of the Martinesque sublime, but it is essentially an inward conception of Revelation, hinting at the ultimate supremacy of the artistic spirit over the mundane world of hostile critics. The Christian vision of the ultimate destruction and redemp-tion of humanity is now subordinated to a transcendental vision of art.

NOTES

1 Anon., *A Spirituall Song of Comfort*, 1643 (Tomason Tracts, vol. 12, p. 47).

2 *The Second Tome of an exact Chronological Vindication and Historical Reconstruction of our British, Roman, Saxon, Danish, Norman and English Kings Supream Ecclesiastical Jurisdiction*, 1665 (*Catalogue of Personal and Political Satires preserved in the Department of Prints and Drawings in the British Museum*, later vols ed. D.M. George (BM Sat.), 1029).

3 BM Sat., op. cit. (n.2), 1076.

4 'Printed by H.B. for J. Conyers at the sign of the black Raven in Duck Lane, 1682'. British Library C.40.m.11, p. 93.

5 Christopher Hill, *Antichrist in Seventeenth-Century England*, London 1990, p. 159.

6 BM Sat.1937.

7 See Christopher Burdon, *The Apocalypse in England: Revelation Unravelling, 1700–1834*, Basingstoke 1997. For the connections between the French Revolution and the sense of *fin de siècle* see Hillel Schwartz, 'The Napoeozoic era: Revolution and the 1790s', in *Century's End: An Orientation manual towards the Year 2000*, New York and London 1996, pp.102f.

8 For the former see pp. 219f.; for the latter, Morton D. Paley, 'Apocalypse and Millennium in the Poetry of Coleridge', in *Apocalypse and Millennium in English Romantic Poetry*, Oxford 1999, pp. 24–34.

9 Hill, op. cit. (n.5), p. 25.

10 I have followed here the convention of calling those who believed in a gradual progress towards redemption 'millennialists', and those who believed in the destruction of the world before redemption 'millenarians' (see J.F.C. Harrison, *The Second Coming: Popular Millenarianism, 1780–1850*, London 1979, pp. 4f.).

11 For Priestley's belief in the imminence of Apocalypse see Jack Fruchtman Jr, 'The Revolutionary Millennialism of Thomas Paine', *Studies in Eighteenth-Century Culture*, 1984, p. 67; and 'Politics and the Apocalypse: The republic and the millennium in late eighteenth-century English political thought', *Studies in Eighteenth-Century Culture*, 1981, pp. 153–64.

12 G.S. Rousseau, 'Wicked Whiston and the English wits', in *Enlightenment Borders*, Manchester 1991, pp. 323–41.

13 See D. Bindman, *William Blake: His Art and Times*, London 1982, p. 118.

14 'The event of things predicated many ages before, will then be a convincing argument that the world is governed by providence…. The Event will prove the Apocalypse; and this Prophecy, thus proved and understood, will open the old Prophets, and all together will make known the true religion, and establish it;… but the time is not yet come for understanding them perfectly, because the main revolution in them is not come to pass' (Sir Isaac Newton, *Observations upon the Prophecies of Daniel, And the Apocalypse of St. John*, London 1734, pp. 251–2.

15 Newton, ibid. p. 16.

16 Newton, ibid. p. 18.

17 Antinomians believed that they were not subject to the constraints of the moral law, but justified themselves by their faith.

18 'Not a few have laboured in explaining the Apocalypse, but as the spiritual sense of the Word had hitherto been unknown, they could not see the mysteries which lay concealed within it, for these can only be unfolded by the spiritual sense. Expositors have therefore formed various conjectures, most of them applying its contents to the affairs of empires, blending them, at the same time, with ecclesiastical matters. The Apocalypse, however, like the rest of the Word, in its spiritual sense treats not of worldly but of heavenly things, thus not of empires and kingdoms, but of heaven and the church' (Emanuel Swedenborg, *The Apocalypse Revealed*, trans. of 1766 edn, n.d., iii).

19 G.L. Keynes, *The Complete Writings of William Blake*, London 1966, p. 613.

20 The scheme was prevented by the then archbishop of Canterbury and the bishop of London (see Joshua Reynolds's letter to Lord Hardwicke, 16 Oct. 1783; F.W. Hilles, *Letters of Sir Joshua Reynolds*, Cambridge 1929, pp. 37–8.)

21 West's *Revealed Religion* series has been much written about. Among those consulted is Jerry D. Meyer, 'BW's Chapel of Revealed Religion: A Study in Eighteenth-Century Protestant Religious Art', *Art Bulletin*, LVII 1975, pp. 247–65.

22 Helmut von Erffa and Allen Staley, *The Paintings of Benjamin West*, New Haven and London 1986, pp. 579–80.

23 Reproduced von Erffa and Staley, ibid. p. 578.

24 Reproduced in diagrammatic form in Nancy L. Pressly, *Revealed Religion: Benjamin West's Commissions for Windsor Castle and Fonthill Abbey*, exhib. cat., San Antonio 1983, p. 18, fig. 7.

25 Kenneth Garlick and Angus Macintyre (eds), *The Diary of Joseph Farington*, 16 vols and index, New Haven and London 1978–96, 28 Dec. 1799, IV, p. 1334.

26 von Erffa and Staley, op. cit. (n.22), nos 403, *The Opening of the Four Seals*, exhib. 1796; 404, *A Mighty Angel Standeth upon the Land and upon the Sea*, exhib. 1797; 405, *The Woman Cloathed with the Sun*, exhib. 1798; and 409, *The Beast Riseth out of the Sea*, exhib. 1798 (408 and 415, of St Michael and Thomas à Becket, both exhib. 1798, are designs for stained-glass windows at Fonthill).

27 For Mortimer's *Death on a Pale Horse* engraving see cat. 23; both Loutherbourg and Fuseli made paintings for the Macklin *Holy Bible*, commissioned in 1796 and published as engravings in 1800, the former *Death on the White Horse* and the latter *St John's Vision of the Seven Candlesticks*. For Blake's illustrations to Revelation see cats 26–35.

28 'West told Williams – go to America if cd get £16,000 paid' (Farington Diary, op. cit. (n.25), 24 March 1798, III, p.994); 'West has signified that if He could obtain payment from the King of the great demand on him, He would quit England for America' (Farington Diary, op. cit. (n.25), 8 December 1798, III, p. 1106).

29 The king said this to Lysons. Farington Diary, op. cit. (n.25), 1 December 1804, VI, p. 2461.

30 Boyd Alexander, *England's Wealthiest Son*, London 1962, pp. 67–8 *passim*.

31 Farington reported the frosty reception of a proposal by James Wyatt to invite Beckford to the annual Royal Academy dinner: 'A dead silence. West then spoke of the intention of Beckford to patronize the Arts, and that an invitation be sent it would not be accepted but [taken] as a compliment.' The invitation was dropped after discussion (Farington Diary, op. cit. (n.25), 14 April 1797, III, p. 821).

32 See n.26 above.

33 For West's plea for George III's support to finish the project in 1801 see Pressly, op. cit. (n.24), p. 19.

34 Roy Porter, *Mind-Forg'd Manacles*, London 1990, p. 116.

35 Porter, op. cit., pp. 19f.

36 See Hillel Schwartz, *The French Prophets in England: a social history*, London 1974.

37 Harrison, op. cit. (n.10), pp. 27f.

38 The works of 'Poor Adam' appear to be entirely unpublished. They are known at present from two collections, in the Huntington Library, San Marino, California (call no. RB 289719), formerly in the Dyson Perrins collection; and the Yale Center for British Art, New Haven, Conn. I am grateful to Sheila O'Connell for introducing me to these works.

39 This was possibly a reprint of Tillinghast's *Generation-work*, 1654, which contains expositions of passages in Revelation (BL 1471.e.44). The British Library has no copy of a 1701 edition.

40 As late as 1829 Jonathan Martin (see pp. 225ff.) claimed to be a Methodist (see Thomas Balston, *The Life of Jonathan Martin Incendiary of York Minster*, London 1945, pp. 21f.).

41 D. Bindman, 'William Blake and popular religious imagery', *Burlington Magazine* CXXVIII, Oct. 1986, pp. 713–14.

42 See Hillel Schwarz, op. cit. (n.7).

43 Jon Mee, *Dangerous Enthusiasm: William Blake and the Culture of Radicalism in the 1790s*, Oxford 1992, *passim*.

44 Richard Brothers, *A Revealed Knowledge of the Prophecies & Times… Wrote under the direction of the LORD GOD, And published by His Sacred Command, it being the first sign of warning for the benefit of all nations; containing, with other Great and Remarkable Things, Not Revealed to any Other Person on Earth, The Restoration of the Hebrews to Jerusalem, By the Year 1798, under Their Revealed PRINCE and PROPHET*, London 1794.

45 Brothers, op. cit., p. 37.

46 Brothers, op. cit., pp. 44–5.

47 See Richard Brothers, *A Description of Jerusalem; its houses and streets, squares, colleges, markets, and cathedrals, etc., etc.*, London, printed for George Diebau, Bookseller to the King of the Hebrews, London 1801.

48 Morton D. Paley, 'William Blake, The Prince of the Hebrews, and The Woman Clothed with the Sun', in Morton D. Paley and Michael Phillips (eds), *William Blake: Essays in Honour of Sir Geoffrey Keynes*, Oxford 1973, pp. 261–7.

49 A study of admissions to Bedlam made in 1810 made 'Religion and Methodism' the fourth highest cause of insanity after 'Misfortunes, Troubles, Disappointments, Grief', 'Family and Heredity' and 'Fevers' (cited in Porter, op. cit. (n.34), p. 33).

50 Eudo Mason, *The Mind of Henry Fuseli*, London 1951, p. 70.

51 Farington Diary, op. cit. (n.25), 24 June 1796, II, p. 589.

52 Porter, op. cit. (n.34), p. 80.

53 For Sharp see Mee, op. cit. (n.43), pp. 48–9. He also makes frequent appearances in the literature on Blake.

54 'Flaxman is… a profound mystic. This last is a characteristic common to many other artists in our days – Loutherbourg, Cosway, Blake, Sharp, Varley, &c. – who seem to relieve the literalness of their professional studies by voluntary excursions into the regions of the preternatural, pass their time between sleeping and waking, and whose ideas are like a stormy night, with the clouds driven rapidly across, and the blue sky and stars gleaming between!' (William Hazlitt, *The Plain Speaker*, London 1826, I, pp. 223–4).

55 In A.W. Exell, *Joanna Southcott at Blockley and the Rock Cottage Relics*, Blockley Antiquarian Society, Blockley, Gloucs., 1977, pp. 75–9.

56 Exell, op. cit., p. 76.

57 A number of good if unexceptional political satires were engraved and designed by Terry in the 1770s, and as a small publisher he took on engraving commissions and issued books of cyphers and 'Allegorical Hair-devices' (list of publications

58 For Huntington see Mee, op. cit. (n.43), pp. 61–4.

59 Mee, op. cit. (n.43), p. 63.

60 The pamphlet is entitled: *A Description accompanying an Hieroglyphical Print of Daniel's Great Image, or Mystical Man*, London 1793. See D. Bindman, op. cit. (n.41), p. 717, and Mee, op. cit. (n.43), pp. 63–5.

61 For Southcott see James K. Hopkins, *A Woman to Deliver Her People: Joanna Southcott and English Millenarianism in an Era of Revolution*, Austin, Texas, 1982.

62 Hopkins, ibid., p. 33f.

63 For the seals see Hopkins, ibid., pp. 103–7.

64 Hopkins, ibid., pp. 184–5.

65 *The Times*, London, Monday 9 January 1815.

66 Hopkins, op. cit. (n.61), pp. 128–31.

67 The British Museum has many prints satirizing Southcott, for example BM Sat.12329–36 and 12624.

68 BM Sat.12331.

69 Napoleon was not infrequently identified with the Antichrist.

70 William Blake maintained a connection between radicalism and belief in Apocalypse well into the nineteenth century. In his 1810 exhibition he showed two paintings, *The Spiritual Form of Nelson guiding Leviathan* and *The Spiritual Form of Pitt guiding Behemoth* (Tate Gallery). Blake's description of the second painting identifies the scene with Revelation 14: 14–19 and Pitt with the Destroying Angel: 'and upon the cloud one sat like unto the Son of Man, having on his head a golden crown, and in his hand a sharp sickle'. He directs the angels to reap the harvest of the earth to 'cast it into the great winepress of the wrath of God'. The war with France, directed by Pitt and carried out by Nelson, is explicitly identified with the Last Days and with the events leading up to the final confrontation between the righteous and the forces of Satan at Armageddon. By 1805–10 then the process of Apocalypse is presumed to be well under way and the final battle imminent. The paintings in the medium of 'Portable Fresco' were essentially modelli for large-scale public paintings that might go in 'Westminster Hall, or the walls of any other great Building'. Their public function was neither to celebrate nor condemn Nelson or Pitt but to depict them as the instruments of the divine will, locating them within the prophecies of the Bible that have been fulfilled. They are neither heroes nor villains but sent to carry out the destruction required to cleanse the world in preparation for the Second Coming.

71 E.P. Thompson, *Witness against the Beast: William Blake and the Moral Law*, Cambridge 1993, and Mee, op. cit. (n.43).

72 There is an anecdote, told by John Flaxman and reported by Henry Crabb Robinson in his diary for 30 Jan. 1815, about Sharp's attempt to recruit Blake to the cause of Brothers (see G.E. Bentley Jr, *Blake Records*, Oxford 1969, p. 235).

73 Blake exhibited at the Royal Academy in the years 1780, 1784, 1785, 1799, 1800, 1807 and 1808.

74 Farington Diary, op. cit. (n.25), II, p. 497.

75 Letter to Dawson Turner, 9 June 1818. (G.L. Keynes, *The Letters of William Blake*, 3rd edn 1980, no.133).

76 There are no marks of West's ownership on the volume, but the tradition is certainly a nineteenth-century one, and it is not in any way implausible that of all his books he should have given West *America*. For the volume provenance see G.L. Keynes and E. Wolf, *William Blake's Illuminated Books: A Census*, New York 1953, p. 46.

77 In *The [first] Book of Urizen*, 1794–5, this is expressed in the

added to copy of Robert Fleming's *Apocalyptic Key*, 1793, author's collection).

complex relationship between Los, the eternal artist-creator, and the Jehovah-like figure of Urizen. Los's eternal role is to give form to the inchoate forces governing the universe before the creation of the material world, but in so doing he becomes captive to his own autocratic creation.

78 See Blake's print *Joseph of Arimathea among the Rocks of Albion* in R. Essick, *The Separate Plates of William Blake*, Princeton 1983, no.I.

79 See Blake's annotations to Reynolds in Keynes, op. cit. (n.19), p. 445.

80 All reproduced and fully catalogued in Martin Butlin, *The Paintings and Drawings of William Blake*, 2 vols, New Haven and London 1981.

81 Blake's version of the appearance of the Angel to St John, '*And the Angel which I saw lifted up his Hand to Heaven*' (Metropolitan Museum of Art, New York), is not part of the same sub-group as the four watercolours, but it is closely related to the painting for Beckford by West exhibited in 1798, *A Mighty Angel Standeth upon the Land and upon the Sea* (von Erffa and Staley, op. cit. (n.22), 404). In Blake's watercolour West's influence is mediated by a memory of Dürer; he has included a tiny figure of St John on Patmos, giving the monumental vision a statuesque substantiality in keeping with his belief in the reality of vision. Other watercolours for Revelation in the Butts series, with the exception of *Michael and Satan* (Fogg Museum, Harvard University), which corresponds in subject, if not in treatment, with a painting for Beckford exhibited in 1797, and *The Whore of Babylon* (British Museum), dated 1809 and in a tighter and more linear style than the others, are concerned with the redemptive aspects of Revelation, not featured in the Beckford Revelation paintings. *The Four and Twenty Elders Casting their Crowns before the Divine Throne* (Tate Gallery) is a luminous and atmospheric representation of the saints before the throne of God, while *The River of Life* (Tate Gallery), though ruinously faded, gives a vision of the post-millennium Jerusalem as a paradise of innocent pastoral enjoyment rather than a teeming city.

82 It could, of course, allow for a personal interpretation of the text; the Dragon's fearful apprehension of his own doom in *The Number of the Beast is 666*, for example, is Blake's own gloss.

83 The literature on *Jerusalem* is immense: see Morton D. Paley, *The Continuing City: William Blake's Jerusalem*, Oxford 1983, and William Blake, *Jerusalem, The Emanation of the Giant Albion*, Morton D. Paley (ed.), in the series *Blake's Illuminated Books*, William Blake Trust/Tate Gallery, I, 1991.

84 Paley, *Continuing City*, ibid, pp.196–210.

85 Paley, *Continuing City*, ibid, pp.136–43.

86 *Jerusalem*, pl. 24, l.30.

87 Paley, *Continuing City*, op. cit. (n.83), p.218.

88 The stigmata are visible only in uncoloured copies.

89 See D. Bindman, op. cit. (n.41), pp. 714–16.

90 See the prospectus *To the Public*, 10 Oct. 1793 (Keynes, op. cit. (n.19), p. 207).

91 Jonathan Martin, *The Life of Jonathan Martin*, Tanner, 3rd edn, Lincoln 1829, title-page.

92 For positive comment see W. Feaver, *The Art of John Martin*, London 1975, pp. 190–4.

93 M.J. Campbell, *John Martin: Visionary Printmaker*, York 1992 (catalogue by M.J. Campbell and J. Dustin Wees: cited as CW), p. 102.

94 CW, ibid., p. 102.

95 Feaver, op. cit. (n.92), pp. 114–29.

96 Feaver, op. cit. (n.92), pp. 190–4.

97 The railway as a vehicle for destruction in the metaphorical as well as the literal sense was a popular motif, used, for example, by Nathaniel Hawthorne in his short story *The Celestial Railroad* of 1843, which is a variation on the theme of *The Pilgrim's Progress*.

98 He handed out pamphlets of an extremely eccentric nature, claiming to be an 'anti-Newtonian'. He claimed among many other things to have anticipated Davy's invention of a safety-lamp.

99 John Martin was solicitous of his brother, paid his trial expenses, took in his disturbed son, and visited him in Bedlam. For further accounts of Jonathan Martin see Balston, op. cit. (n.40); J.M. MacGregor, *The Discovery of the Art of the Insane*, Princeton 1989, ch. 4, pp. 45–66, 'Jonathan Martin of Bedlam'.

100 Most of the drawings are in the collection of the Royal Bethlem Hospital.

101 Balston, op. cit. (n.40), p. 56. The poor spelling appears to have been a consequence of his agitated mental state at this point; when less agitated he could spell perfectly well.

102 Balston, op. cit. (n.40), p. 57.

103 Balston, op. cit. (n.40), p. 58.

104 I am grateful to Patricia Allderidge for her help with Jonathan Martin and his time in Bedlam. This spectacular drawing and the others in the Bethlem Hospital collection were unknown to Thomas Balston when he wrote his biography of Jonathan Martin.

105 CW, op. cit. (n.93), p. 102.

106 Bernard Hanson, 'D.W. Griffith: Some Sources', *Art Bulletin* 54, Dec. 1972, pp. 493–511.

107 The cynical spirit in which he conceived his painting of *An Attempt to Illustrate the Opening of the Sixth Seal*, exhibited at the Royal Academy, 1828, is revealed in a letter: 'I agree with you in quite disliking the class of pictures which I am now painting… [the painting is a response to] the rage for novelty in the public' (Francis Greenacre, *The Bristol School of Artists*, City Art Gallery, Bristol 1973, p. 65).

108 For Samuel Colman, a relatively recent rediscovery, see Greenacre, op. cit. (n.106), pp. 203–9; Ronald Parkinson, *Samuel Colman: Four Apocalyptic Themes*, Tate Gallery pamphlet, n.d.

109 Martin Butlin and Evelyn Joll, *The Paintings of J.M.W. Turner*, 1984, no.425; John Gage, *Colour in Turner*, London 1969, pp. 145–6.

110 Rev. 19: 17–18, quoted by Turner in the RA catalogue accompanying the painting.

The Seventeenth Century and after: Political Apocalypse

In the seventeenth century the Book of Revelation was a prophecy available to all Christians, and the grotesque figures of the Dragon, the Beast, and the Whore of Babylon were, as they had been in the Reformation, a staple of religious and political satire. There are fewer examples in the eighteenth century, but the many-headed Beast could still be part of the satirist's armoury, and was revived during the period of the French Revolution and the rise of Napoleon.

1 Joseph Mede (1586–1638)

The Key of the Revelation, 2nd edn, 1650

Printed book, 350 × 405mm (fold-out diagram of the process of Revelation shown)

Lit: C. Burdon, *The Apocalypse in England,* Basingstoke 1997, pp.34–5

London, British Library 1508/1565

First published in 1627 in Latin as *Clavis Apocalyptica.* Joseph Mede as an Anglican and royalist stands firmly at the rational end of the interpretation of the Book of Revelation. A mathematician before he studied divinity, Mede assumes the Book of Revelation to contain a mathematically precise system under the direct authorship of the Holy Spirit. Hence his Key can be expressed in diagrammatic form, leading from the beginning of Apocalypse and continuing through the epochs of the Seals and Trumpets to the phase in which 'The Kingdoms of the World are become our Lordes and his Christes'. Mede is the prime forerunner of Isaac Newton's enquiries into Revelation (see p.211), and they shared not only a belief that it could really be used to predict the redemption of mankind, but also that the Beast was to be identified with the papacy.

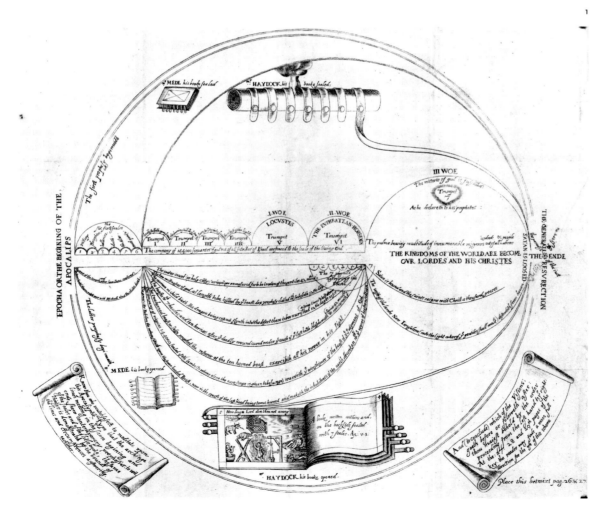

2

2 Anon., pub. William Peake,

text by John Vicars

The Pope Seated on the Seven-Headed Beast of Rome, 1643

Broadside with letterpress and engraving, image 184 × 268mm, sheet 352 × 292mm

Lit: *Catalogue of Personal and Political Satires preserved in the Department of Prints and Drawings in the British Museum* (cited as BM Sat.), 378

London, British Library 669, f.8/29 (Thomason Coll., no.68)

The pope is represented as the Whore of Babylon or 'Rome's Whore', uttering 'Babylonish blasphemies', riding on the seven-headed Beast of Rome. Though the pope is the ostensible subject it would have been read, in this early stage of the Civil War, as an attack on the court and Church of England. This high-quality print shows knowledge of earlier German and Netherlandish prints, and may have been made by a Dutch or Flemish engraver.

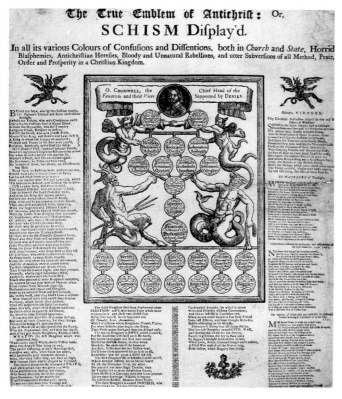

3

4

3 Anon.

The True Emblem of Antichrist: Or, Schism Display'd. In all its various Colours of Confusions and Dissentions, both in Church and State, Horrid Blasphemies, Antichristian Heresies, Bloody and Unnatural Rebellions, and utter Subversions of all Method, Peace, Order and Prosperity in a Christian Kingdom (Genealogy of Oliver Cromwell), *c.*1654–5

Broadside, letterpress and woodcut; sheet 403 × 340mm, image 243 × 187mm

Lit: BM Sat.819

London, British Museum 1868-8-8-3257

Oliver Cromwell is 'the Chief Head of the Fanaticks and their Vices Supported by Devils'. The idea that Cromwell was False Prophet or Antichrist was common among royalist supporters during the Civil War and the Protectorate, and was held also by dissenters disillusioned by his rule, like the Fifth-Monarchy men (see pp.214–15). Cromwell is represented as the head of a family of fanatical sects and social and personal vices. For a redemptive view of Cromwell see cat. 4 below.

4 After Francis Barlow

The Embleme of Englands Distractions ('Oliver Cromwell between two Pillars'), 1658

Engraving, 562 × 422mm

Lit.: Antony Griffiths, *The Print in Stuart Britain,* London 1998, no.115

London, British Museum 1848-9-11-242

This print, published shortly before Cromwell's death in September 1658, takes the opposite view from cat.3. It shows the Lord Protector standing triumphant, one foot upon the corpse of the Whore of Babylon and the other on Discord represented by the two serpents of Error and Faction. The hybrid nature of the imagery is reflected in the suggestion that Cromwell has piloted the ship of state through Scylla and Charybdis (top right), but has come to rest like the ark on Mount Ararat (top left). The use of an image from Revelation suggests the 'further expected Freedome, & Happines[s]', and the New Jerusalem being built under Cromwell's godly rule. Such imagery, however, was readily adaptable to different political circumstances as demonstrated by the subsequent use of the plate in 1690, when the head of William III was substituted for that of Cromwell.

5 Anon.

Babel and Bethel: or the Pope in his Colours, 1679

Broadsheet, letterpress and engraving; sheet 464 × 365mm, image 174 × 294mm

Lit: BM Sat.1076

London, British Museum 1849-3-15-35

Produced at the time of the Popish Plot of 1679, this print is derived from a section of the earlier and much more elaborate frontispiece to William Prynne's *The Second Tome of an exact Chronological Vindication and Historical Reconstruction of our British, Roman, Saxon, Danish, Norman and English Kings Supream Ecclesiastical Jurisdiction*, 1665. However, in the latter the pope is identified as the Beast who is given power by the Dragon or Satan, and in turn asserts that power over the world; in the present print the pope is 'Rome's *Scarlet* whore' or the Whore of Babylon, leading men to luxury and the burning of Protestant martyrs. In both cases papal power is contrasted with the benign rule of Charles II.

5

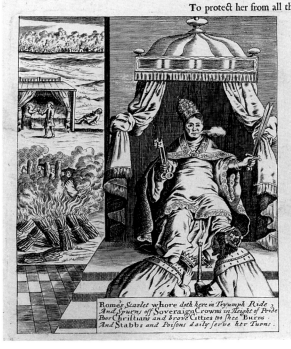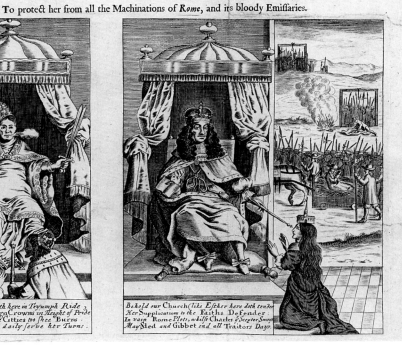

BABEL and BETHEL: or, The POPE in his Colours.

WITH

The Church of *E N G L A N D's* Supplication to his Majesty, our gracious Soveraign, the true Defender of the Faith;

To protect her from all the Machinations of *Rome*, and its bloody Emissaries.

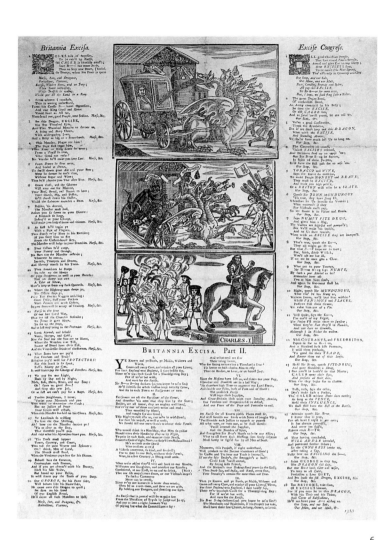

6 Anon.

Britannia Excisa, Part II, 1733

Broadsheet with woodcut; sheet 483 × 345mm, image 296 × 152mm

Lit: BM Sat.1937

London, British Museum 1868-8-8-3556

This is a characteristic eighteenth-century use of the Dragon of Revelation as a satirical trope representing the excise tax; it is also identified as the dragon slain by St George. The Dragon is seen leading the coach of the Prime Minister, Sir Robert Walpole, pouring the people's hard-earned money into his hand, until slain by the political opposition. Walpole's campaign for an augmented excise tax in 1733 was ferociously attacked by the opposition, making him vulnerable to such propaganda.

7 Thomas Rowlandson (1756–1827)

The Champion of the People, 1784

Etching, hand-coloured, 216 × 328mm

Lit: BM Sat.6444

London, British Museum 1851-9-1-138

Charles James Fox, the Whig political leader, seeks to cut off the heads of the Dragon which, again with its multiple heads, is both the Dragon of Revelation and of St George.

6

8 Thomas Rowlandson (1756–1827)

Downfal[l] of Monopoly in 1800, 14 August 1800

Etching, hand-coloured, 337 × 450mm

Lit: BM Sat.9546

London, British Museum 1948-2-14-607

The central image of Death on horseback, here identified with those seeking to monopolize trade, refers unmistakably to Benjamin West's apocalyptic design usually called *Death on a Pale Horse*, which was exhibited at the Royal Academy as a drawing (cat. 24) in 1784 and as a painting in 1796, and perhaps also to Mortimer's version of the subject (cat. 23). Death here chases the monopolizers out of the kingdom in the direction of hell, where the devil awaits them. With the monopolizers sent packing, a new age begins as the country rejoices in prosperity and social justice, in the benign presence of a large statue of Britannia with an overflowing cornucopia.

THE CHAMPION OF THE PEOPLE.

7

8

DOWNFAL OF MONOPOLY in 1800

The People's Millennium

If the Book of Revelation seldom made an appearance in paintings or 'high' art, its imagery continued to have a resonance in cheap religious engravings and woodcuts throughout the eighteenth century. It had a more general revival in the 'dangerous times' of the French Revolution and of Napoleon Bonaparte.

9 'Poor Adam' (Adam Toppin)

(1701–after 1760)

a. *Adam his Picture*; b. *Prophesies Fulfilled the Signs of Poor Adam*; c. *The Methodists Formalists Confounded*, c.1760s

Woodcut broadsides, hand-coloured; a. 304 × 151mm; b. 220 × 205mm; c. 286 × 162mm

New Haven, Connecticut, Yale Center for British Art, Paul Mellon Collection

a. Adam Toppin in his uniform of 'petty constable', proclaiming himself to be 'a good soldier of Jesus Christ'.
b. A characteristically apocalyptic image of Christ and the apostles marching joyfully to confront the devil. The text is full of exhortations to heed the Book of Revelation, ending with 'God bless King George the III'.
c. One of the few plates to be printed from letterpress, though very amateurishly, as well as from a woodblock, it is important in identifying 'Poor Adam' as Adam Toppin, and his residence in North Street in York. Here he claims to be 'The Inventer of the new Bloc-Print that some Cal's the Saxon's Hand where it is to be sold, so buy these Paper's or keep them clean till call'd for'.

9a

9b

The works of 'Poor Adam' have evidently never been published before, and to date they are known only from two collections, in the Huntington Library, San Marino, California, and the Yale Center for British Art, New Haven. They are all, except for a few that include letterpress printing, in a distinctive technique of woodcut applied to both text and design. They are passionately apocalyptic in imagery, deriving, we are told, from a book by George Tillinghast, a Fifth-Monarchy man (see pp.214–15), who at first welcomed Cromwell as a true prophet, but later saw him as Antichrist. Though most of the texts and illustrations repeatedly illustrate the Book of Revelation, a few pages in the Yale group give glimpses of Poor Adam himself. His name appears to have been Adam Toppin (or possibly Topham),

and he was a servant in the household of the Fairfax family outside Tadcaster near York, where he was a member of the watch. He was born in 1701 and the dedication of a number of the pages to George III dates them after 1760, though they are unlikely to have been made much after that date. He appears to have been something of a public character in York, running at one point a Punch and Judy show, and practising as a musician. There is an intriguing possibility that he might have known Thomas Gent, a millenarian printer and publisher also in York, who wrote *A History of the Great Eastern Window*, 1762, highlighting the apocalyptic imagery in the Great East Window of York Minster, and speculating on the date of the coming Apocalypse (Ch.3, fig.9).

9c

239

The TREE of LIFE.

10

10 Bowles and Carver pub.

The Tree of Life, 1780s

Engraving, hand-coloured, 352 × 248mm

Lit.: D. Bindman, 'William Blake and popular religious imagery', *Burlington Magazine* CXXVIII, Oct. 1986, p.714

London, British Museum, *Bowles and Carver Album*, III, p.51

On the basis of the many reprints and copies in engraving and woodcut that have survived, mainly from popular printsellers like Bowles and Carver, and Catnach (see cat. 11), some dating as late as the second half of the nineteenth century, *The Tree of Life* can claim to have been the most popular of all such images. It is a 'Hieroglyphic' print, requiring close scrutiny and recourse to the Bible to decipher its true meaning. The Tree of Life set in the redeemed Jerusalem is derived from the Book of Revelation, but it is also the Tree of Life from Genesis, where it is contrasted with the Tree of the Knowledge of Good and Evil (see cat. 12 below). The scenes of revelry or 'Chambering & Wantoness' below are interrupted ineffectually by three preachers, two of whom are identifiable as Wesley and Whitefield, while the presence of the Gate of Hell, attended by the Whore of Babylon, does little to spoil the party. The 'brands plucked

from the fire', or the few redeemed souls, make their way along the Narrow Way (as opposed to the Broad Way that leads to the mouth of hell) to the door in a wall leading into the New Jerusalem. While the Tree of Life with its 'twelve manner of fruits' is described in Revelation 12: 2, the figure of Christ crucified upon it is not. This motif has medieval precedents in St Bonaventura and Meister Eckhart, but earlier visual representations, mainly from the German Reformation, usually show the branches formed into a cruciform shape.

We may assume such Hieroglyphic prints to have had, if one takes into account all the different versions, enormous print runs, available to those outside metropolitan networks. They would, therefore, have done much to keep millenarian ideas alive in the country at large. The presence in the earliest known printings of the two most famous Methodist preachers suggests that the design was first conceived around the middle of the eighteenth century, not necessarily by a Methodist but by one of the many who saw common ground between Methodism and millenarianism (see p.215).

11 J. Catnach pub.

The Tree of Life, c.1830s

Woodcut and letterpress, hand-coloured, 490 × 352mm

Lit: T. Gretton, *Murders and Moralities: English catchpenny prints, 1800-60*, 1980, pl.82

London, British Museum 1992-1-25-32. Presented by Antony Griffiths

This print is evidence of the popularity of *The Tree of Life* well into the nineteenth century. Catnach was the most famous of the popular broadside publishers who inhabited the area around Seven Dials, Monmouth Street, near Covent Garden in London. The design was also popular in America, and a lithographic version was made by Currier and Ives.

Tree of Life.

SON of God! thy blessing grant,
Still supply our ev'ry want,
Tree of Life thine influence
    shed,
With thy sap our spirits feed!

Tend'rest branch, alas! am I
Wither without thee, and
    die;
Weak as helpless infancy—
O confirm our souls in thee!

Un-sustain'd by thee we fall!
Send the strength for which
    we call!
Weaker than a bruised reed
Help we ev'ry moment need.

All our hope on thee depend,
Love us! save us to the end!
Give us the continuing grace,
Take the everlasting praise!

CHRIST

Worshipped by all his Creatures.

YE servants of God,
    Your Master proclaim,
And publish abroad
    His wonderful Name,
The Name all victorious
    Of Jesus extol;
His Kingdom is glorious,
    And rules over all.

God ruleth on high,
    Almighty to save,
And still he is nigh,
    His presence we have.
The great congregation
    His triumph shall sing,
Ascribing salvation
    To Jesus our King.

Salvation to God,
    Who sits on the throne:
Let all cry aloud,
    And honour the Son.
Our Jesus's praises
    The angels proclaim,
Fall down on their faces,
    And worship the Lamb.

Then let us adore,
    And give him his right,
All glory and pow'r
    And wisdom and might;
All honour and blessing,
    With angels above,
And thanks never ceasing,
    And infinite love.

GIVE to the Father praise,
Give glory to the Son,
And to the Spirit of his grace
Be equal honour done.

HYMN OF THE OMNIPOTENT.

LORD of universal na-
    ture,
God of every living creature,
Light of morning—shade of
    even—
King of ocean, earth, and
    heaven;
Whilst I prostrate bow be-
    ore thee,
Teach my spirit to adore
    thee.

Soul of love—and source of
    pleasure,
Mine of ev'ry richer treasure;
King of tempests, storm, and
    shower,
Ruler of each secret power:
Whilst for favour I implore
    thee,
Teach my spirit to adore
    thee!

Spring of river, lake, and
    fountain,
Piler of the rock and moun-
    tain,
Breath of animal creation,
Life of varied vegetation—
Whilst I prostrate bow before
    thee,
Teach my spirit to adore
    thee!

First and last Eternal Being
All-pervading, & all-seeing;
Centre of divine perfection—
Whence the planets learn
    subjection—
Whilst for favour I implore
    thee,
Teach my spirit to adore
    thee!

CHRIST

The Believer's Refuge.

IN ev'ry trouble sharp and
    strong,
My soul to Jesus flies,
My anchor-hold is firm in him
When swelling billows rise.

His comforts bear my spirits
    up,
I trust a faithful God,
The sure foundation of my
    hope,
Is in a Saviour's blood.

Loud hallelujahs sing my soul
To thy Redeemer's name,
In joy, in sorrow, life and
    death,
His love is still the same.

THE TREE OF LIFE.

Which bear twelve manner of Fruits, and yielded her Fruits every Month, and the Leaves of the Tree were for the healing of the Nations.--- *Rev.* ch. xxii. v. 2.
Likewise a View of the New Jerusalem, and this present Evil World, with the industry of Gospel Ministers in endeavouring to pluck Sinners from the wrath to come.---*Mat.* ch. vii.

A Prospect of Heaven
MAKES DEATH EASY.

THERE is a land of pure delight,
    Where saints immortal reign;
Infinite day excludes the night
    And pleasure banish pain.

There everlasting springs abides,
    And never with'ring flow'rs;
Death like a narrow sea, divides
    This heav'nly land from ours.

Sweet fields beyond the swelling flood
    Stand dress'd in living green,
So to the Jews old Canaan stood
    While Jordan roll'd between.

O could we climb where Moses stood
    And view the landscape o'er,
Not Jordan's stream, nor death's cold
    flood,
    Should fright us from the shore.

DISMISS as with thy blessing,
    Lord,
Help us to feed upon thy Word:
All that has been amiss, forgive,
And let thy truth within us live.
Tho' we are guilty, thou art good,
Wash all our works in Jesu's blood
Give ev'ry fetter'd soul release,
And bid us all depart in peace

finish'd—was his latest voice;
    These sacred accents o'er,
He bow'd his head, gave up the ghost
    And suffer'd pain no more.
'Tis finish'd—The MESSIAH dies
    For sins, but not his own;
The great redemption is complete,
    And Satan's pow'r o'erthrown.

'Tis finish'd—All his groans are past;
    His blood, his pain, and toils,
Have fully vanquished our foes,
    And crown'd him with their spoils.
'Tis finish'd—Legal worship ends,
    And gospel ages run;
All old things now are past away,
    And a new world begun.

THE CRUCIFIXION.

BEHOLD the Saviour on the
    A spectacle of woe! (cross,
See from his agonizing wound
    The blood incessant flow;
Till death's pale ensigns o'er his cheek
    And trembling lips were spread;
Till light forsook his closing eyes,
    And life his drooping head

J. Catnach,

Printer, 2, Monmouth-court, 7 Dials, London.

Travellers supplied with Sheet Hymns, ornamented
with Cuts, the finest of England; also, Ships,
and Pattern, Cheaper than at any other
Shop in London.

O MAY the grave become to me
    The bed of peaceful rest,
Whence I shall gladly rise at length,
    And mingle with the blest!
Cheer'd by this hope, with patient mind
    I'll wait Heavens high decree,
Till the appointed period come,
    When death shall set me free.

12

13

12 J. Bakewell

Hieroglyphics of the Natural Man, 1780s

Engraving, hand-coloured, 350 × 245mm

London, British Museum, *Bowles and Carver Album*, III, p.52

This print was frequently issued as a companion to *The Tree of Life* and to the next print. The 'Natural Man' in this context is the man of the world or believer in Natural Religion, who pursues material and sensual desires without regard for salvation. The tree is barren, abandoned by birds and foliage; it is also the Tree of the Knowledge of Good and Evil from Genesis, which harboured the serpent who tempted Eve. It is watered here by Satan and Death. J. Bakewell may have been a clergyman who provided the design for an engraver.

13 J. Bakewell

Hieroglyphics of a Christian, 1780s

Engraving, hand-coloured, 349 × 248mm

London, British Museum, *Bowles and Carver Album*, III, p.53

This tree, by contrast with the previous one, is the Tree of Life, rooted in Faith and Repentance, and growing from the strong trunk of Hope and Love. If the previous print represents the material world then this is the promise of redemption in which Satan is finally cast out.

14 G. Kirkham   after Charlotte Reihlen

The Broad and Narrow Way, 1883

Lithograph, 570 × 475mm

Lit: J.M. Massing, 'The Broad and Narrow Way From German Pietists to English Open-Air Preachers', *Print Quarterly*, V 1988, pp.257–67

London, British Museum 1999-4-25-13. Presented by David Bindman and Frances Carey

Despite this print's visual similarity to *The Tree of Life* prints above, this design was devised as late as 1862, by Charlotte Reihlen, founder of the Deaconess Institute in Stuttgart and a member of a Pietist community, though it seems to have been based on eighteenth-century prototypes (Massing 257). The design was brought to England by an open-air evangelist, Gawin Kirkham, in a Dutch version that was then translated into English. Kirkham had it copied as a large painting, using

it and further versions as a mainstay of his open-air preaching, taking it abroad on several occasions. The success of the English version of the print, first published in 1883, was phenomenal, and it was continually reprinted up to recent times. The allegory is explained in detail in a pamphlet that may have been sold with it, *Explanation of the Picture 'The Broad and the Narrow Way', Translated from the German*, London 1885. A copy of the fourth edition is in the British Library (4372.i.4).

In accordance with the Sermon on the Mount (Matthew 7: 13–14) the viewer is offered the Broad Way to perdition and the Narrow Way to salvation. Unlike the *The Tree of Life* the two ways run parallel, and once through the Narrow Gate the believer still has a rocky road to the New Jerusalem. The reprobate eventually reaches the flames of destruction along a broad path with several attractions on the way, laid out with small buildings like a modern theme park.

14

THE BROAD AND NARROW WAY.

Matthew VII., 13, 14.

The French Revolution as the Fulfilment of Prophecy

The outbreak and progress of the French Revolution had the effect of revitalizing the popular apocalyptic tradition, and many large-scale prints were produced claiming, openly or by implication, that the events of the present time fulfilled the prophecy of Revelation. The revival of popular millenarianism by self-proclaimed prophets such as Richard Brothers and Joanna Southcott goaded satirists into spectacular displays of ridicule.

15 Garnet Terry (active 1770–1800) and E. F. Burney (1760–1848)

after W. Huntington

An Hieroglyphical Print of the Church of God in her Five-Fold State, 1791

Engraving, 591 × 411mm

London, British Museum 1849-5-12-858

This print was originally accompanied by another 'containing the Ground Plot of the Heavenly City', with an explanatory key to the two, though copies of neither are known to the present author. The key would be helpful, for there are intriguing scenes around the Holy City in which, according to the caption, 'Artists, Mechanicks, and Manufacturers, [are] Engaged in their Respective Pursuits for promoting the various Branches of Natural Religion'. The attack on Natural Religion allies the standpoint of the print more with Blake's rejection of materialism than with the excoriation of sin represented by the previous group of prints (cats 10–14). The humorous language of the scenes is a reminder that Garnet Terry had an earlier practice as a political satirist. The print was a joint venture of the preacher William Huntington S.S. and his follower, the publisher and engraver Garnet Terry (see p.217). The role of the painter Edward Francis Burney is puzzling, but he may have been brought in only to make a painting on Huntington's instructions, either as a model for engraving or perhaps as an aid to preaching. The vision of the Heavenly City floating over the more earthly one bears a resemblance to a much earlier print by Nicholas Cochin after Stefano Della Bella, *La Carte du Royaume des Cieux*, produced originally in Paris *c*.1650–70.

15

An HIEROGLYPHICAL PRINT of the CHURCH of GOD in her FIVE FOLD STATE, INCLUDING THE HOLY JERUSALEM Together with

16 Garnet Terry (active 1770–1800)

An Hieroglyphical Print of Daniel's Great Image, or Mystical Man,
1793

Printed pamphlet with large fold-out engraved plate, 560 × 380mm

Lit: Bindman 1986, p.717; J. Mee, *Dangerous Enthusiasm: William
Blake and the Culture of Radicalism in the 1790s*, Oxford 1992,
pp.63–5

Altadena, California, Collection Robert N. Essick

This illustrates Daniel's vision of the figure with a head of
gold and feet of iron and clay, standing for Babylon and the
kingdoms of the world, which in the prophecy will be
smashed and replaced by the eternal kingdom. In a second
title-page to the accompanying pamphlet it is described as
'Daniel's Great Image of the Mystical Body of Babylon,
shewing the approaching Destruction of Antichrist, the
Beast, the Whore, and the False Prophet; According to Rev.
xix, 20. Demonstrated from the Prophecies of Daniel, and
confirmed by the Signs of the Times'. The image derives the
labelling of body parts from either medical illustration or
popular satirical prints, like those produced by William Dent
(see BM Sat.6257 and 8271). Though the figure is elegantly
engraved, the caption 'Hieroglyphics' places it within the
popular tradition represented by *The Tree of Life* prints (see
cats 10–13).

17 Richard Brothers (1757–1824) and Wilson Lowry (1762–1824)

A Description of Jerusalem, 1801/2

Printed book with two coloured fold-out plans (plan of Jerusalem
shown)

Lit: M.D. Paley, 'William Blake, The Prince of the Hebrews, and The
Woman Clothed with the Sun', in Morton D. Paley and Michael
Phillips (eds), *William Blake: Essays in Honour of Sir Geoffrey
Keynes*, Oxford 1973, pp.260–94

London, British Library 1509/1344

Richard Brothers, self-proclaimed 'Prince of the Hebrews
and Nephew of the Almighty'(see p.215), had a literal-
minded conception of the New Jerusalem, which was to be
built by himself and his followers, including the Jews whom
he was to lead in person to the Holy Land (see p.216).
According to Paley his plan was 'a beatific vision of a city as
it might have been laid out by a heavenly town-planner of
the period'. Everything was based on a grid and upon exact
measurements. The plan is signed by 'Lowry'. This is almost
certainly Wilson Lowry, one of the foremost technical
engravers of the day. He was well known to John Linnell and
John Varley, and very probably to William Blake, whose
conception of Jerusalem was very different (see p.222). For
Gillray's cynical response to Brothers see cats 18 and 19
below.

16

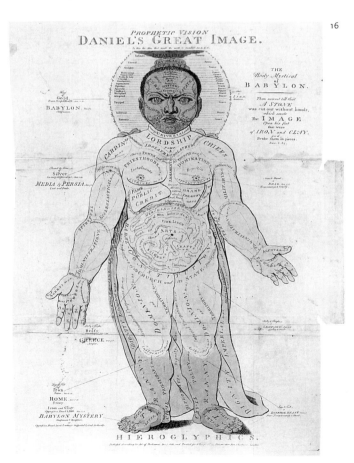

17

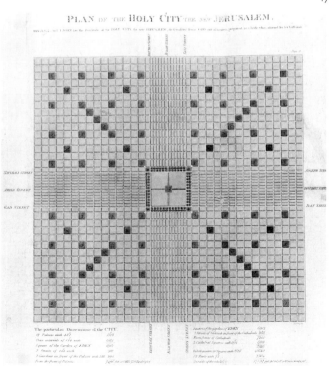

The PROPHET of the HEBREWS, — the PRINCE of PEACE, conducting the JEWS to the PROMIS'D-LAND.

18

18 James Gillray (1756–1815)

The Prophet of the Hebrews, – The Prince of Peace – Conducting the Jews to the Promis'd Land, 5 March 1795

Etching, hand-coloured, 260 × 360mm

Lit: BM Sat.8627

London, British Museum 1868-8-8-6470

Despite the humorous references to Richard Brothers the print is as much a satire on the Whig opposition led by Charles James Fox. Brothers, depicted as a ragged and demented revolutionary, tramples on the Beast of Revelation with its crowned and tiaraed heads as he leads the Jews, with an elderly pedlar in front and including a supporter, Isabella Wake, towards Jerusalem. On Brothers's back is the 'Bundle of the Elect' among whom can be recognized the familiar profiles of Fox and his colleagues. In his left hand

Brothers carries a flaming sword and a copy of the Book of Revelation which he uses as a guide on his journey past the ruins of London's monuments, including St Paul's, but the Gate of Jerusalem at the end of a steep climb is also a gibbet awaiting him. The bundling together of Fox and Brothers is a consequence of their regard for revolutionary France and their support of a peace treaty with the French Directory, vehemently opposed by Edmund Burke.

19 James Gillray (1756–1815)

Presages of the Millenium [sic]; – with The Destruction of the Faithful, as Revealed to R: Brothers the Prophet, & attested by M.B. Hallhead Esq., 4 June 1795

Etching with aquatint, hand-coloured, 330 × 378mm

Lit: BM Sat.8655

London, British Museum 1851-9-1-736

This satire on William Pitt and the opposition led by Charles James Fox shows the Prime Minister as Death on a pale horse, his bottom being kissed by a diminutive figure of the Prince of Wales who has recently received a generous settlement, while Charles James Fox, clutching a peace petition, is kicked by the pale horse on to a heap of his allies. The apocalyptic vision is described in the caption as the

fulfilment of Richard Brothers's recent sensational prophecy (see pp.215–17), but the composition is clearly based upon Benjamin West's so-called *Death on a Pale Horse*. The question is: which version of West's design? It is certain that Gillray would have seen the Royal Academy drawing in the present exhibition (cat. 24), when it was exhibited at the Royal Academy in 1784. There is also the intriguing possibility that Gillray saw in West's studio the painting of the same subject West must have been working on at the time, and which was exhibited at the Royal Academy the following year, in 1796 (fig. 1).

The pigs are presumably Burke's 'Swinish Multitude', or the common people, a name adopted ironically by radicals such as Thomas Spence and Daniel Eaton. Burke himself is the last creature flying in the wake of the tail.

19

20 J. Cooke pub. Obadiah Prim

The Representative of a Great Nation, 1799

Etching, hand-coloured, 644 × 513mm (trimmed)

Lit: BM Sat.9349

London, British Museum 1868-8-8-13705

A complete impression of the print (Musée de la Révolution Française, Vizille) has the address line claiming it to be published by 'Obadiah Prim, for the Increase of Voluntary Contributions', and it is dated 23 February 1799. The profusion of inscriptions might suggest a French origin, but it was published in London and it does include Charles James Fox and the Whig opposition as collaborators with the French Directory, which governed France between the fall of Robespierre in 1794 and the advent of Bonaparte later in 1799. The monstrous figure in the foreground, with a '5' on his forehead and the words 'Roi de Paris' and '200' and '500' in each eye, must stand for the Directory and the number of members of the two Councils beneath them. The prominence of gold around the figure's head suggests a comparison with the prophet Daniel's vision of a man with a head of gold and feet of iron and clay, standing for the tyrannies that will be destroyed by God in the fulfilment of Apocalypse (see cat. 16). 'Obadiah Prim' is presumably a *nom-de-plume*, and the print may have originated in the French émigré community in London, among those worried about 'Jacobin' tendencies in the Directory.

21 Thomas Rowlandson (1756–1827)

Joanna Southcott the Prophetess excommunicating the Bishops, 20 September 1814

Etching, hand-coloured, 274 × 438mm

Lit: BM Sat.12334

London, British Museum 1868-8-8-12801

Joanna Southcott and her devoted supporter the Rev. William Tozer putting to flight the bishops who had refused to accept her claims to divine inspiration (see p.219). Despite the date of 20 September 1814 the print evidently makes no reference to her sensational declaration of pregnancy in October 1813, so it is probably a reprint of an earlier one.

22 Mayhew

Preparations for the Humbug, 1814

Etching, hand-coloured, 252 × 350mm

Lit: BM Sat.12330

London, British Museum 1868-8-8-8170

One of a veritable flood of ribald satires that greeted Joanna's declaration in October 1813 that in her sixty-fifth year she had been impregnated by the Holy Spirit (see p.219), an event, her followers believed, that made the descent of the Messiah imminent. Joanna died three months later on 27 December 1814; she had not been pregnant. The print implies that Joanna's pregnancy is a cunning plot to deceive, aided by the Rev. William Tozer, and that a real baby was to be smuggled in to act as 'Shiloh'. The gullibility and mendacity of the doctors are also satirized, for seventeen out of twenty-one physicians who examined her in the summer believed her to be pregnant. The artist, Mayhew, is otherwise almost unknown.

21

22

'Bedlamite Scenes': Art and Revelation

John Hamilton Mortimer was instrumental in bringing Revelation imagery back into British art with the exhibition of his *Death on a Pale Horse* in 1775. The subject, in one form or another, was taken up by a number of artists, and it began to take on particular resonance after the outbreak of the French Revolution in 1789. Other Revelation subjects were also taken up in the context of biblical cycles by Benjamin West and William Blake. For the controversies surrounding the former see pp.212–14.

23 J. Haynes after John Hamilton Mortimer (1740–79)

Death on a Pale Horse, 1784

Etching, 687 × 476mm

Lit: J. Sunderland, *John Hamilton Mortimer: his Life and Works*, Walpole Society, LII 1988, no.100a

London, British Museum 1865-5-20-866

Mortimer's *Death on a Pale Horse* was first exhibited as a finished drawing at the Society of Arts in 1775, apparently paired with a drawing illustrating I Corinthians 15: 55, 'O Death where is thy sting? O Grave where is thy victory?' (Sunderland, no. 101), but its influence dates largely from its publication as an engraving, paired with an engraved version of 'O Death where is thy Sting?', published by his widow Jane on 1 January 1784. Mortimer, who died in 1779, had a difficult relationship with the Royal Academy, but was revered by younger artists like Blake, who saw him as a radical opponent to Sir Joshua Reynolds and the more academic artists in the Royal Academy.

23

Death on a Pale Horse

24 Benjamin West (1738–1820)

Death on a Pale Horse, dated '1783, retouched 1803'

Pen, pencil and wash, 570 × 1120mm

Lit: H. von Erffa and A. Staley, *The Paintings of Benjamin West*, New Haven and London 1986, no. 402

London, Royal Academy of Arts

This finished drawing was exhibited in the Royal Academy in 1784 as 'The triumph of Death, from the Revelations, a design for a picture for his Majesty's chapel in Windsor-castle'. It was intended as part of the culmination of West's great scheme for a biblical cycle for George III, which was never completed (see pp.212–14). It is the first of three major versions of the subject, which is strictly speaking not *Death on a Pale Horse*, but *The Opening of the Four Seals*, for the other Horsemen of the Apocalypse are also included. The second version, an oil painting (Detroit Institute of Arts; see fig. 1), was exhibited at the Royal Academy in 1796 as 'a sketch, for His Majesty's Chapel, Windsor', and the final version is the colossal painting in the Pennsylvania Academy of the Fine Arts, Philadelphia (von Erffa and Staley no. 401), painted after the final collapse of the Windsor project,

between 1815 and 1817, when West was seventy-nine years old. As discussed on pp.212–14, the composition, by the time the first oil version was exhibited in 1796, had become controversial, despite being conceived within an eminently orthodox context, because of the millenarian and politically radical implications of the subject. The presence of this and other Revelation subjects in the Windsor Castle scheme seems to have alarmed George III and led to the eventual curtailment of the project, to West's great distress. A composition drawing of the subject in the Pierpont Morgan Library, attributed to Benjamin West (R. S. Kraemer, *Drawings by Benjamin West*, New York 1975, no.39, pl.24), appears to be by his son Raphael, and another, certainly by Raphael West, but severely damaged, is in a private London collection.

24

25 William Blake (1757–1827)

Designs for Edward Young's *Night Thoughts*, 1797

Pen and watercolour around letterpress

Lit: David V. Erdman *et al.* (ed.), *William Blake's Designs for Edward Young's Night Thoughts*, Oxford 1980

London, British Museum

Edward Young's *Night Thoughts* was one of the most popular of eighteenth-century long poems, on the subject of death and the consolation of Christianity. Blake was commissioned by the bookseller Richard Edwards to make an extensive series of illustrations in 1795, with the intention of using them as the basis for an engraved edition, but in the end only the first four of the nine 'Nights' with forty-three illustrations were published. Blake made a total of 537 watercolours for the project (all in the British Museum), all painted around pages of letterpress taken from a printed copy of the book.

Young, an Anglican clergyman, was neither millenarian nor millennialist, and there is a conspicuous avoidance of reference to the Book of Revelation in the text. It is striking that Blake has made unmistakable allusions to Revelation on two of the title-pages, though they are not warranted by Young's text, perhaps as a veiled criticism of its limitations.

In the twentieth century Young's poem and the work of Blake were both admired by the Surrealists; Philippe Soupault's monograph of 1928 included fourteen of Blake's illustrations to *Night Thoughts*.

a. Title-page to Night III, *Narcissa*

420 × 325mm

1929-7-13-40

Narcissa, the tragic heroine whose virtue does not prevent her from dying young, is seen by analogy as 'The Woman Clothed with the Sun', seeking to avoid the clutches of the Dragon, as in Revelation 12: 1 (see cats 28–30 below).

b. Title-page to Night VIII, *The Beast of Revelation*

420 × 325mm

1929-7-13-174

This Night tells of the Christian's answer to 'The Man of the World': 'the love of this life: the Ambition and Pleasure, with the Wit and Wisdom of the World' are pictured by Blake as the Whore of Babylon riding the Beast of Revelation, the former as pleasure or luxury, and the latter as ambition or power, represented by heads signifying the ecclesiastical and political powers of the world (cf. cat. 34 below).

25a

25b

26

frontispiece to the Book of Revelation. The motif and scale of the figures make it closest to Mortimer's conception of the subject (cat. 23). Blake had a particular admiration for Mortimer.

27 William Blake (1757–1827)

The Angel of Revelation (Rev. 10: 1–6), *c.*1805

Pen and watercolour, 393 × 262mm

Lit: Butlin no.518

New York, Metropolitan Museum of Art, Rogers Fund, 1914, 14.81.1

An illustration to Revelation 10: 1–6, where John sees a vision of a 'mighty angel [who] lifted up his hand to Heaven'. The angel is given a little book, here still in his hand, which John swallows to 'prophesy again before many people, and nations, and tongues, and kings'. In this scene and in most of his Revelation watercolours Blake creates an astonishing disjunction of scale between the human figures and those who belong to the great cosmic drama.

26 William Blake (1757–1827)

Death on a Pale Horse (Rev. 6: 8), *c.*1800

Pen and watercolour, 393 × 311mm

Lit: M. Butlin, *The Paintings and Drawings of William Blake*, 2 vols, New Haven and London 1981, no.517

Cambridge, Fitzwilliam Museum, Acc. No. 0765

The subject is the opening of the fourth seal of the Book of Revelation (note the three seals remaining on the scroll carried by the angel behind): 'And I looked, and behold a pale horse: and his name that sat on him was Death, and Hell followed with him'. Death is represented as a medieval warrior-king with a beard like Blake's Jehovah-like creation Urizen, wreaking justice on humanity, quite without the skeletal form usually used to depict Death but borrowing elements of the description of the first of the riders, on a white horse (Rev. 6: 2). This watercolour might well have been the first illustration to Revelation to have been made by Blake for his patron Thomas Butts, who commissioned from him an extensive series of watercolour illustrations to the Bible, following a series of tempera paintings. The Butts watercolour series may have been begun around 1800 with the intention of providing single illustrations to each book of the Bible; only later does it appear that separate series, like the later Revelation watercolours, were contemplated. This watercolour, then, may have originally acted as the

28 William Blake (1757–1827)

The Great Red Dragon and the Woman Clothed with the Sun
(Rev. 12: 1–4), *c.*1805

Pen and watercolour, 435 × 345mm

Lit: Butlin no.519

New York, The Brooklyn Museum of Art, Gift of William Augustus White, Acc. No. 15.368

This is the first of a group of four watercolours that form a well-defined sub-series within the Butts Revelation watercolours (see cats 29, 30 and 31 below). The episodes are tightly connected to each other and tell the story of the emergence of the Great Red Dragon and the Beast, and their aggressive confrontation with the Woman Clothed with the Sun, who manages to elude their clutches while they impose their rule upon mankind, from whom they extract abject submission. In Revelation 12, there appears 'a great wonder in heaven, a woman clothed with the sun, and the moon under her feet, and upon her head a crown of twelve stars'. As she cries aloud in the pain of childbirth there now appears the Great Red Dragon, waiting to 'devour her child as soon as it is born'. The Dragon was subsequently identified as Satan, and the Woman Clothed with the Sun as the mother of the Redeemer.

29 William Blake (1757–1827)

*The Great Red Dragon and the Woman Clothed with the Sun:
'the Devil is come down'* (Rev. 12: 12–17), *c.*1805

Pen and watercolour, 408 × 337mm

Lit: Butlin no.520

Washington, DC, National Gallery of Art, Rosenwald Collection, 1943, Acc. No. 1943.3.8999

In Revelation 12, the Dragon pursues the Woman Clothed with the Sun, spewing out a flood to carry her away, but the earth opens up to swallow the flood and save her, leaving the Dragon 'to make war with the remnant of her seed, which keep the commandments of God, and have the testimony of Jesus Christ'. Note the first appearance of human figures who appear as the flood subsides.

28

30 **William Blake** (1757–1827)

The Great Red Dragon and the Beast from the Sea (Rev. 13: 1–2, 7), *c.*1805

Pen and watercolour, 401 × 356mm

Lit: Butlin no.521

Washington, DC, National Gallery of Art, Rosenwald Collection, 1943, Acc. No. 1943.3.8997

In Revelation 13 the Beast emerges from the sea 'having seven heads and ten horns, and upon his horns ten crowns, and upon his head the name of blasphemy'. The Beast normally represents temporal power, under the direction of the Dragon who is Satan. He is an enemy to Christianity but is worshipped by humanity: 'And they worshipped the dragon which gave power unto the beast, saying, Who is like unto the beast? Who is able to make war with him?' The Dragon here gives power in the form of the sword and sceptre 'to make war with the saints'. Though many of the heads are crowned Blake does not connect them explicitly with the powers of the world, as he does in the *Night Thoughts* watercolour (cat. 25b).

31 **William Blake** (1757–1827)

The Number of the Beast is 666 (Rev. 13: 18), *c.*1805

Pen and watercolour, 412 × 335mm

Lit: Butlin no.522

Philadelphia, Rosenbach Museum and Library, Acc. No. 54.11

In the final scene of the group of four watercolours, the Beast is worshipped by abject ranks of humanity, deceived by the gigantic lamb-like beast who represents False Prophecy. The Dragon, however, appears startled, hearing an intimation of his own doom in the 'voice from heaven' telling of the power of the true God and the fate of Babylon; in the triumph of Satan is the sign of his ultimate defeat.

30

31

32 William Blake (1757–1827)

The Four and Twenty Elders Casting their Crowns before the Divine Throne (Rev. 4: 2–10), *c.*1803–5

Pen and watercolour, 354 × 293mm

Lit: Butlin no.515

London, Tate Gallery, National Gallery of British Art, N.05897/B515

Though possibly finished about the same date, this watercolour does not appear to belong with the same group as the four above. It is smaller and differs in handling. It illustrates Revelation 4: 2–10 in which John is transported in spirit to Heaven, where he sees four and twenty elders before the throne of God. Blake has painstakingly reconstructed the imagery in the text but suffused the scene with divine radiance.

32

33

33 William Blake (1757–1827)

The River of Life (Rev. 22: 1–2), *c.*1805

Pen and watercolour, 305 × 336mm

Lit: Butlin no.525

London, Tate Gallery, National Gallery of British Art, N.05887/B525

Blake's only Revelation design to represent mankind redeemed in the New Jerusalem, this is a pastoral vision, with the Tree of Life on the left, in a setting of musical celebration, peace and elevated conversation. In Revelation 22: 1–2 the river of life proceeds 'out of the throne of God and of the Lamb'. The role of the figures in the river is less clear. The figure guiding the two children has often been identified as Jesus but this is uncertain. The angel descending could be the angel sent by Jesus 'to testify unto you these things in the churches' (Rev. 22: 16), but the female figure to the right, apparently carrying a knife, is unexplained.

34

34 William Blake (1757–1827)

The Whore of Babylon (Rev. 17: 1–4), 1809

Pen and watercolour over pencil, 266 × 223mm

Lit: Butlin no.523

London, British Museum 1847-3-18-123

This watercolour with its precise penwork is quite different in style from the previous Revelation illustrations; it reflects Blake's assertion in his *Descriptive Catalogue* of the same year, 1809, of the necessity of a firm outline, and his preoccupation at the time with line engraving in the large *Canterbury Pilgrims* plate. Blake here emphasizes the interconnection between worldliness and the senses, represented by the Whore of Babylon, and war, represented by the Beast of Revelation.

35 William Blake (1757–1827)

The Vision of the Last Judgment, 1808

Pen and watercolour, 510 × 395mm

Lit: Butlin no.642

Petworth House, Sussex, National Trust

Like the prophetic book *Jerusalem* Blake's various compositions of the *Last Judgment* (Butlin nos 639–46) are a kind of summation of the history of the human spirit, much indebted to prints after Michelangelo (see cats 96–8). The Petworth version, the most elaborate except for the lost tempera version with 'upward of a thousand figures', partly combines the imagery of two earlier watercolours, *The Fall of Man* (Victoria and Albert Museum), and *A Vision of the Last Judgment* (Glasgow, Pollok House) to bring together all biblical prophecies of the redemption of man, the Last Judgement, and the final binding of Satan, with a particular emphasis on the account in Revelation. According to an accompanying letter of explanation, written to his friend the painter Ozias Humphry (G. L. Keynes, *Complete Writings of William Blake*, Oxford 1957 and subsequent editions, p.443), 'Beneath [the] Earth is convulsed with the labours of the Resurrection – in the Caverns of the Earth is the Dragon with Seven heads & ten Horns chained by two Angels & above his Cavern on the Earth's Surface is the Harlot seized & bound by two Angels with chains while her Palaces are falling into ruins & her councellors & warriors are descending into the Abyss in wailing & despair'.

35

36 William Blake (1757–1827)

Jerusalem: The Emanation of the Giant Albion, 1804–20

Eight relief etchings, with pen and wash, from a volume of 100 plates

Lit: Keynes and Wolf, copy A (see n.76, p.230); M.D. Paley (ed.), *Jerusalem*, Blake's Illuminated Books, vol.1, London 1991 (facsimile of copy in Yale Center for British Art, Paul Mellon Collection)

London, British Museum 1847-3-18-93, except for d., which is Cambridge, Fitzwilliam Museum, Keynes Collection. Acc. No. P.709-1985, pl. 51

Jerusalem is the summation of Blake's prophetic enterprise, occupying a large part of his later career. It now exists in only five complete copies, of which only one is coloured (see lit. above), and a coloured copy of twenty-five plates. If the group of watercolour designs for the Book of Revelation shown above (cats 26–34) illustrates the biblical text, then *Jerusalem* should be seen as a conscious equivalent to the Book itself, a visionary work that defies easily apprehended structures, and is filled with astonishing imagery in rapidly shifting registers and time sequences. *Jerusalem* is in the fullest sense an apocalyptic work, telling the story of the fall and captivity of mankind, ending with a vision of ultimate redemption (see pp.222–3). The story is of the archetypal figure Albion, both mankind and Britain, whose fall is in his separation from his emanation Jerusalem, with whom he must reunite to achieve redemption. Albion is in a fallen state in this world, but the book ends with an apocalyptic vision of the redeemed state when divisions are healed in the unity of all things. The following eight plates have been chosen not to provide a summary of the work but to illustrate aspects of

36a

36b

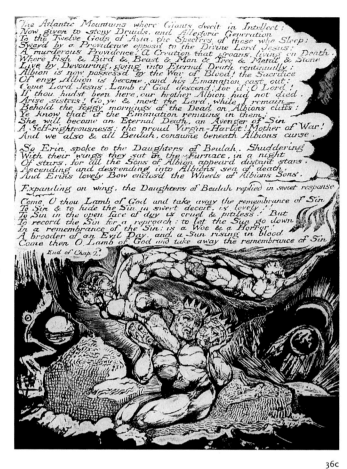

36c

Jerusalem's relationship to the Book of Revelation.

a. Frontispiece, 223 × 161mm. The 'author' Los, epitomizing prophetic poetry and representing Blake's spiritual self, in the guise of a watchman (associating him with the prophets Ezekiel and Isaiah) enters the tomb to bring back to humanity its secrets. Like John the Evangelist the author of *Jerusalem* takes in the word of God: 'I see the Saviour over me/Spreading his beams of love, & dictating the words of this mild song'.

b. Plate 26, 162 × 222mm. In this plate, which acts as a frontispiece to the second of the four books of *Jerusalem*, the figure of Hand is shown as a False Prophet or Antichrist, adopting the cruciform posture and even the stigmata, but walking with pride, bearing a serpent and enfolded in flames. The figure of Jerusalem looks on him apparently in horror. Hand, based on the brothers Hunt who had ridiculed Blake's art, links the biblical world with the present world when artists, the true heirs to prophecy, are reviled.

c. Plate 50, 226 × 164mm. This image, the tailpiece to the second book of *Jerusalem*, is a re-imagining of the Beast of Revelation, seen as ever-proliferating, associated not with the biblical past but with the present-day island of Britain.

d. Plate 51, 162 × 223mm. A proof plate with the names of three figures inscribed beneath. Vala, Hyle and Skofeld were, with Hand, the powers of the world and, as Albion's children, of Britain. Vala broadly represents nature, Hyle materialism and Skofeld warlike brutality, and their despair represents the state of Britain in the early nineteenth century, cut off from the world of the spirit.

36d

And Rahab Babylon the Great hath destroyed Jerusalem
Bath stood upon the Severn with Merlin & Bladud & Arthur
The Cup of Rahab in his hand: her Poisons Twenty-seven-fold

And all her Twenty-seven Heavens now hid & now reveald
Appear in strong delusive light of Time & Space drawn out
In shadowy pomp by the Eternal Prophet created evermore
For Los in Six Thousand Years walks up & down continually
That not one Moment of Time be lost & every revolution
Of Space he makes permanent in Bowlahoola & Cathedron.

And these the names of the Twenty-seven Heavens & their Churches
Adam. Seth. Enos. Cainan. Mahalaleel. Jared. Enoch.
Methuselah. Lamech; these are the Giants mighty Hermaphroditic
Noah. Shem. Arphaxad. Cainan the Second. Salah. Heber.
Peleg. Reu. Serug. Nahor. Terah; these are the Female Males:
A Male within a Female hid as in an Ark & Curtains.
Abraham. Moses. Solomon. Paul. Constantine. Charlemaine.
Luther. these Seven are the Male Females: the Dragon Forms
The Female hid within a Male; thus Rahab is reveald
Mystery Babylon the Great: the Abomination of Desolation
Religion hid in War; a Dragon red, & hidden Harlot
But Jesus breaking thro the Central Zones of Death & Hell
Opens Eternity in Time & Space; triumphant in Mercy

Thus are the Heavens formd by Los within the Mundane Shell
And where Luther ends Adam begins again in Eternal Circle
To awake the Prisoners of Death; to bring Albion again
With Luvah into light eternal, in his eternal day.
But now the Starry Heavens are fled from the mighty limbs of Albion

All Human Forms identified even Tree Metal Earth & Stone. all
Human Forms identified, living going forth & returning wearied
Into the Planetary lives of Years Months Days & Hours reposing
And then Awaking into his Bosom in the Life of Immortality.
And I heard the Name of their Emanations they are named Jerusalem

The End of The Song
of Jerusalem

e. Plate 75, 224 × 162mm. The tailpiece to the third book of *Jerusalem*: the image seems to represent the Whore of Babylon in an embrace with the Beast of Revelation, the embrace of power and luxury. It may be seen as a counterpart to plate 50 above.

f. Plate 76, 222 × 161mm. As the frontispiece to the fourth and final part of *Jerusalem* this plate anticipates the great vision of redemption that brings the work to a close. Albion in an exultant gesture of affirmation worships the body of Jesus on a tree, which can be taken to be the Tree of Life (see cat. 10). If so the scene represents Albion's first understanding of the meaning of Christ's sacrifice, anticipating the redeemed state when he will throw off materialism and the powers of the world, and enter fully into the New Jerusalem.

g. Plate 99, 225 × 154mm. A vision of redemption as an act of apprehension and exultation, when all divisions shall be subsumed in the unity of all things. The two figures can be read at several levels of reconciliation: God the Father and Christ the Son; Imagination and Reason; matter and spirit; male and female.

h. Plate 100, 145 × 224mm. *Jerusalem* ends not with exultant vision but with the work of the poet, in his eternal form as Los, building the New Jerusalem out of ancient artefacts with painful labour. The apocalyptic vision of *Jerusalem* can, paradoxically, be instantaneous yet must also be worked for.

37 William Blake (1757–1827)

Beatrice on the Car, Matilda and Dante, from Dante's *Divine Comedy* (Purgatory, canto 29), 1824–7

Pen and watercolour over pencil, 367 × 520mm

Lit.: Butlin no.812 (87)

London, British Museum 1918-4-13-5

This is one of the latest in the sequence of 100 watercolours to *The Divine Comedy*, made by Blake in his last years and left unfinished on his death. Dante's *Divine Comedy* is itself profoundly apocalyptic in structure, content and imagery, as were Blake's prophetic books, but it was framed by medieval Catholicism, towards which Blake was antipathetic. Blake's illustrations in some cases subtly highlight his differences from Dante, and on some of the less finished pages there are written expressions of distaste for Dante's vision. This is particularly evident in the scenes in Purgatory where Paradise is anticipated, such as the present one, and in Paradise itself.

The extraordinary radiance of the scene is, therefore, deceptive. It shows Dante's first glimpse of Beatrice, who for Dante represents the Catholic Church and redemption, but for Blake she is a negative principle: the Church as the restriction of imagination, the worship of nature, and the ceremonial and ritual that veiled the true meaning of Christ's first incarnation. At another level she has aspects of the

37

Whore of Babylon exacting submission from mankind, here represented by Dante, who in this and the next watercolour in the sequence (Tate Gallery, Butlin no. 812 (88)), is shown in supplication. The connection with the Whore of Babylon is made more explicit in the next watercolour (National Gallery of Victoria, Melbourne, Butlin no. 812 (89)), where she is shown embracing the Giant or temporal power, in a kind of parody of Beatrice on her chariot.

Apocalypse and the City

The Book of Revelation is a tale of two cities, or rather of two alternative visions of the city: Babylon and Jerusalem. With the alarming growth of London as a metropolis in the early nineteenth century the idea of London as a Babylon that might be regenerated as Jerusalem became a powerful one. It was already expressed in Blake's Jerusalem, but it is also an underlying theme in the extraordinary images of the destruction of cities produced by John Martin and others. At the same time attempts were made to represent Apocalypse as a form of natural and geological cataclysm.

38a

38 John Martin (1789–1854)

a. *The Fall of Babylon*, 1831

Mezzotint on steel, with etching, image 470 × 923mm

Lit: M. J. Campbell, *John Martin: Visionary Printmaker*, York 1992 (catalogue by M. J. Campbell and J. Dustin Wees; cited as CW), 88

London, British Museum M.M.10-6

b. *Belshazzar's Feast*, 1832

Mezzotint on steel, with etching (second plate), image 474 × 718mm

Lit: CW 89

London, British Museum M.M.10-1

The force and drama of these images lie in their marriage of an apocalyptic vision of destruction, prophesied in both the Book of Daniel and of Revelation, with an image of the modern city. The sinfulness that would bring down divine wrath on humanity, and destroy it in preparation for judgement and redemption, is collective and not individual as in Blake. Though Martin does not state it explicitly, and

indeed distances himself from such an interpretation (see p.224), there is a clear implication that the fate of Babylon could be visited upon London, and for the same reasons.

These plates were based on large-scale paintings by Martin, and they brought him fame and success; a. is dedicated to Henry Philip Hope of Deepdene House and b. to King William IV.

38b

39 John Martin (1789–1854)

The Angel with the Book, 1837

Lithograph, 270 × 375mm

Lit: CW 127

Collection of Michael J. Campbell

This remarkable lithograph, despite the difference in
treatment, illustrates the same passage in Revelation 10: 1–5
as Blake's watercolour of *The Angel of Revelation* (cat. 27).
John is seen on a rocky outcrop of the island of Patmos, while
the Angel is an immense figure rising from the horizon line.
The translucency of the Angel suggests that the vision is the
product of an imagination stimulated by natural effects, in
this case an unusual cloud formation.

39

40

40 John Martin (1789–1854), engr. Charles Mottram

The Last Judgement, published January 1857 by Thomas McLean

Engraving, image 704 × 1055mm; platemark 801 × 1134mm

Lit: CW XV

Collection of Michael J. Campbell

This print, along with two others, *The Great Day of his Wrath* and *The Plains of Heaven*, was engraved and published by Thomas McLean after Martin's death in 1854, after three enormous paintings (Tate Gallery) all dating from his last years, though he had contracted for them to be engraved. The engravings were also published in New York, perhaps to take advantage of the exhibition of the three paintings in the United States.

If Martin's millenarianism was less than overt in his earlier years, in these works, his final testament, it is now fully expressed. *The Great Day of his Wrath* shows the destruction of Babylon and the material world by natural cataclysm, while *The Last Judgement* shows the casting out of the Whore of Babylon and the Beast in the form of the powers of the world. The world in the process of dissolution is plainly the modern one, for there are two trains in the background on the right: one is led by a demonic fire-

breathing engine, and the other is a long train filled with passengers yelling out of the windows as they hurtle into the abyss opening up before them. As a consequence of the Last Judgement, on the left there is Elysium with the great men of all ages, based on James Barry's painting in the Royal Society of Arts (Adelphi, London), contrasted with sinful humanity on the other side of the abyss, scourged by an avenging angel. Behind there is the Holy City, and floating above a scene of Christ enthroned in judgement with saints and angels around him. Though in style it could hardly be further from Blake's *Vision of the Last Judgment* (cat. 35), it shares with it a desire to encompass all the phases of judgement and redemption described in Revelation within one composition.

A contemporary reworking of Martin's composition is Glenn Brown's *The Tragic Conversion of Salvador Dali*, exhibited at the Jerwood Gallery, London 1999.

41 Jonathan Martin (1782–1838)

London's Overthrow, 1832

Pen and ink drawing, 660 × 980mm

Lit: John M. MacGregor, *The Discovery of the Art of the Insane*, Princeton 1989

Beckenham, Kent, The Bethlem Royal Hospital Archives and Museum

The tragic career of John Martin's brother Jonathan, his burning of York Minster and his subsequent confinement in Bethlem Hospital from 1829 until his death in 1838 are described on pp.225–7. This drawing, the most elaborate of his few surviving drawings, shows the destruction of London by the armies of 'the son of Bonaparte'. The foreground is occupied by carousing bishops, whose iniquity and pursuit of vice have incurred the descent of apocalyptic wrath. In the background are Westminster Abbey and St Paul's Cathedral apparently under a black cloud, as was York Minster in the dream that provoked Jonathan to attempt to burn it down (see p.227). Among the more peculiar symbols is that of the one-legged lion in the background, signifying that

England stands but on one Foot
And that has lost one Toe
Therefore long it cannot stand
For Foreign Troops shall invade our Land.

The resemblance to his brother's paintings of cities in the process of destruction is not fortuitous; he wrote on the back of the drawing:

If I had sought the whole creation round
A better subject than my brother's downfall [of Nineveh] I could not have found; to help me
to paint sad London's overthrow.

It is indeed close to the large painting of the subject that John exhibited in London in 1828, but it is unlikely that Jonathan could have seen it in London; it is more likely that John brought him a proof impression of the mezzotint (CW 82) on one of his many visits to his brother in Bethlem Hospital.

The verso of the drawing is covered with dense calculations of the money owed him for false imprisonment, and there are verses of varying degrees of lucidity on both recto and verso. (Transcripts have been kindly provided by the Bethlem Hospital curator, Patricia Allderidge.)

41

42 Francis Danby (1793–1861), engr. G.H. Phillips

The Opening of the Sixth Seal, 1828

Mezzotint, proof impression, 489 × 689mm

Lit: E. Adams, *Francis Danby: Varieties of Poetic Landscape*, London 1973, no.26 (painting)

London, British Museum 1872-1-13-844

Inscribed on published state: 'Engraved by G.H. Phillips, from the Original Picture by F. Danby A.R.A. in the Collection of William Beckford Esq.ʳᵉ', with verses 12–17 of the Book of Revelation 6. Danby's opportunism in exploiting the fashionability of John Martin's apocalyptic paintings is fully revealed in his letters (see p.228), yet it is a powerful exercise in the sublime, expressing the apocalyptic destruction of 'the great day of his wrath' in terms of a natural catastrophe. William Beckford's purchase of the painting is significant given his patronage of Benjamin West's Revelation paintings in the 1790s (see p.213).

42

6 *The Apocalyptic Imagination: between Tradition and Modernity*

Frances Carey

T he preceding chapters have described the enduring legacy of the Book of Revelation as a source for metaphor and symbol both within a system of belief and as a paradigmatic form of narrative fiction. Despite the many alterations to belief and fiction during the modern period, from realism to existentialism, symbolism to semiotics, the apocalyptic mode has proved infinitely adaptable, demonstrating 'the ubiquity of the apocalyptic imagination... in the disenchanted heart of twentieth-century avant-garde movements'.[1] The same comment may be applied to the previous century, notwithstanding the impact of scientific enquiry which began by questioning the physical origins of the earth in relation to the biblical scheme: 'No vestige of a Beginning – no prospect of an end'(James Hutton, 1790).[2] Apocalyptic terms of reference are so deeply ingrained in Western culture that they have taken on an archetypal function. Science and technology, politics and art have been variously co-opted as part of 'manifest destiny' or perceived as providing a surrogate form of eschatological purpose, promising renewal as well as calamity, the principle of hope required for the fulfilment of a redemptive plan for history. Even where that vision has failed, the language, motifs and mood of the Apocalypse have survived, though without the belief in redemption its original meaning is destroyed.

The greatest threat to the redemptive vision has come from cultural pessimism and social alienation, creating a metaphysical void or what 'a modernist would call... the sensation of the abyss'.[3] It has been central to the modern experience of personal crisis whether extolled in Baudelaire's *Les Fleurs du Mal* (1857) or in Francis Ford Coppola's film *Apocalypse Now* (1979). At 'the heart of darkness' Colonel Kurtz (Marlon Brando) reads aloud from T.S. Eliot's *Hollow Men* (1925), which closes with 'This is the way the world ends/This is the way the world ends/This is the way the world ends/ Not with a bang but a whimper.'[4] Jim Morrison's line 'cancel my subscription to the Resurrection' (from 'When the Music's Over'; another track, 'The End', was chosen as the closing music to *Apocalypse Now*) represents a nihilism that has been as alarming to established Christian morality as the most uncompromising views of scientific positivists or historical materialists: 'There is nothing more contrary to God, and his proceedings, than annihilation'.[5]

That such pessimism became a quintessential form of modernism is to a large degree attributable to the influence of Charles Baudelaire; his 'satanic verses' and evocations of sensual indulgence and death as an alternative to the ennui of mundane existence, or as part of a sacrilegious quest for the ideal, became the *sine qua non* of artistic revolt, whether in *fin-de-siècle* Paris or among the Beat poets and musicians of California in the mid-twentieth century. Baudelaire's imagery of death drew upon his knowledge of engravings of anatomical subjects and of other compositions such as the print of 1784 after John Hamilton Mortimer's *Death on a Pale Horse* (Ch. 5, cat. 23), which he took as his point of departure for *A Fantastic Engraving*:

> This ghastly skeleton, bone-bare, on ghostly nag,
> Gallops through space. No spurs, no whips...
> And yet his steed pants toward Apocalypse,
> Nostrils a-snort in epileptic fit.
> Headlong they rush, athwart the infinite,
> With rash and trampling hoof. The cavalier,
> His flashing sword aflame, slashes – now here,
> Now there – amongst the nameless slaughtered horde;
> Then goes inspecting, like some manor-lord,
> The charnel-ground, chill and unbounded, where,
> Under a bleak sun's pallid, leaden glare,
> History's great sepulchered masses lie,
> From ages near and ages long gone by.[6]

In his play upon the theme of the *danse macabre* in a poem of this title, Baudelaire's immediate source was one of the sculptures exhibited at the Salon of 1859,[7] but he was also familiar with the subject's long tradition through publications such as Hyacinthe Langlois, *L'Histoire des danses macabres* (Rouen 1852), as well as graphic series such as Alfred Rethel's *Auch ein Todtentanz aus dem Jahre 1848* (Dance of Death for the Year 1848), to which he gave qualified praise in his essay on 'Philosophic Art'. Baudelaire, writing in the light of Rethel's insanity, to which the artist succumbed in 1852, praised the 'satanic, Byronic quality and the feeling of desolation' in the series, whose true originality lay in 'the fact that it appeared at a moment when practically the whole of European humanity had rushed headlong, with eyes open, into the follies of revolution'[8] (fig. 1). Encouraged by the huge success of this series, Rethel went on to produce two further single-sheet prints that plagiarized the work of Dürer and Holbein more literally, *Death as a Strangler* and *Death as a Friend* (1851). *Auch ein Todtentanz* was not the only work of art to take inspiration from the sixteenth century in order to strike a cautionary note in relation to the 1848 revolutions. Meyerbeer's opera *Le Prophète*, which had its première at the Paris

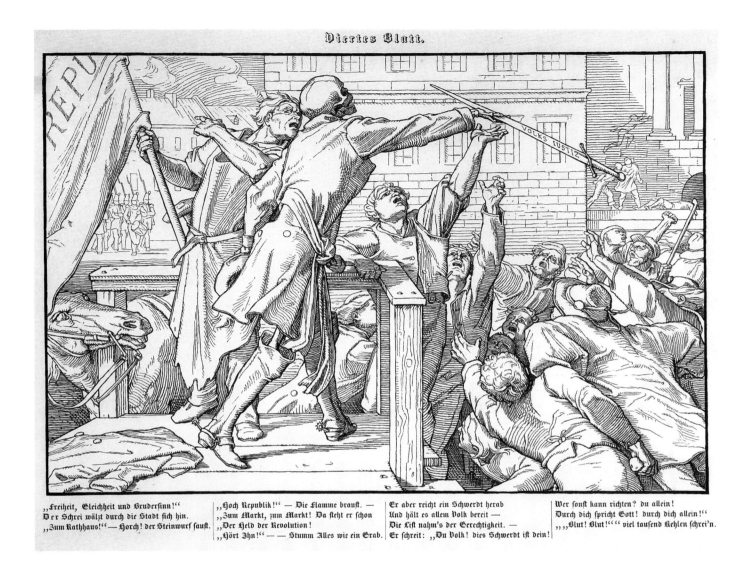

Viertes Blatt.

„Freiheit, Gleichheit und Brudersinn!"
Der Schrei wälzt durch die Stadt sich hin.
„Zum Rathhaus!" — Horch! der Steinwurf saust.

„Hoch Republik!" — Die Flamme braust. —
„Zum Markt, zum Markt! Da steht er schon
„Der Held der Revolution!
„Hört Ihn!" — — Stumm Alles wie ein Grab.

Er aber reicht ein Schwerdt herab
Und hält es allem Volk bereit —
Die List nahm's der Gerechtigkeit. —
Er schreit: „Du Volk! dies Schwerdt ist dein!

Wer sonst kann richten? du allein!
Durch dich spricht Gott! durch dich allein!"
„„Blut! Blut!"" viel tausend Kehlen schrei'n.

Fig.1. Alfred Rethel (1816–59), Plate 4 from *Auch ein Todtentanz aus dem Jahre 1848* (Leipzig 1849). Wood engraving. London, British Museum.

Opéra on 16 April 1849, showed the dangers of sedition and demagogy in the form of the story of the Anabaptists in Münster who attempted to establish a Kingdom of the Saints under the leadership of the apocalyptic figure of Jan of Leiden in the mid-1530s.[9]

If Baudelaire's poetry was one conduit for pessimism, Dante's was another, rendered all the more concrete to the popular imagination by Gustave Doré's illustrations for the *Inferno*, first published in Paris in 1861, followed by an English edition in 1865. His work enjoyed considerable success, although critics like John Ruskin recoiled in distaste from what he regarded as the diabolic nature of the paintings that followed the illustrations, when they were shown in London at the Doré Gallery from 1869 onwards. It was this very quality, their graphic sensationalism, that later captivated the young Cecil B. DeMille, who drew upon his early fascination with Doré's Bible subjects in the creation of epic cinema (see pp.323–4).[10] Dante was the eschatological poet of the secular world and his narrative became the paradigm for many a modern psychodrama. The

British poet James Thomson, in thrall to alcohol as well as Dante, wrote *The City of Dreadful Night* (1874), a contemporary journey through the 'doleful City', which is the antithesis of the redemptive pattern of Christian eschatology, Dante's *Inferno* without the prospect of *Paradiso*. It concludes with a literary paraphrase of Dürer's engraving of *Melencolia* (1514, fig. 2), one of the 'inescapable works of art' (see p.8) of the nineteenth century used by Michelet in his *Histoire de France au seizième siècle* of 1855 to exemplify at one and the same time 'the genius of the Renaissance'[11] and a discordant despair awaiting the musicality engendered by Lutheranism to restore harmony to the world.

The *Inferno* supplied the motif for Auguste Rodin's most ambitious project, the *Gates of Hell*, the doorway originally intended for the new Musée des Arts Décoratifs in Paris, for which he received the commission in 1880. The choice of subject was meant to reflect the troubled soul of modern society, a counterpart to Ghiberti's *Gates of Paradise*, the bronze doors to the Baptistery in Florence, and provided an opportunity for Rodin to create a sculptural equivalent to Michelangelo's *Last Judgement*. Rodin admired Dante's ability to give form to his imagination: 'Dante is not only a visionary, but also a sculptor. His expression is lapidary in the good sense of the word',[12] but he was equally indebted to Baudelaire, whose *Fleurs du Mal* he read and re-read innumerable times, inscribing passages on to the base of some of the figure studies for the main composition.

Dante and Baudelaire were again among the precedents for the notable dramatizations of the modern artist's predicament in the autobiographical works by Arthur Rimbaud, *Une Saison en Enfer* (1874), and August Strindberg, *Inferno* (1898). Strindberg's *Inferno* was a voyage through paranoia and despair, reaching its climax amidst the intolerable heat of the summer of 1896, which he wrote upon his return from Paris to Sweden in 1897; the Dance of Death, later used for the title of his play published in 1900, also appears in the *Inferno* in the guise of a story of a woman dressed as a bride who dances incessantly because she believes Death has come to claim her.[13]

Ruskin knew 'most of the Apocalypse, every syllable by heart' thanks to the evangelical fervour of his mother, who made him read the Bible programmatically from one end of the year to the other, placing particular emphasis on committing to memory the fifth and sixth chapters of Revelation, which describe the vision of the Lamb and the Book, followed by the opening of the seven seals.[14] Despite his 'unconversion' from the evangelicism of his upbringing in 1858, the tenor of Ruskin's scriptural grounding informed his own apocalyptic vision of the 'storm cloud of the nineteenth century', a 'plague-wind'

Fig.2. Albrecht Dürer (1471–1528), *Melencolia* (1514). Engraving. London, British Museum.

273

compounded from climatic change, industrial pollution, social and political unrest and personal crisis, which he first witnessed in 1871:

> Blanched Sun, – blighted grass, – blinded man. – If, in conclusion, you ask me for any conceivable cause or meaning of these things – I can tell you none, according to your modern beliefs; but I can tell you what meaning it would have borne to the men of old time. Remember, for the last twenty years, England, and all foreign nations, either tempting her or following her, have blasphemed the name of God deliberately and openly; and have done iniquity by proclamation.... Of states in such moral gloom every seer of old predicted the physical gloom, saying, 'The light shall be darkened in the heavens thereof, and the stars shall withdraw their shining.'[15]

The initial impression made by this sinister vapour was evoked by Ruskin in the Dantesque terms of 'dead men's souls – such of them as are not yet gone where they have to go', which he associated with the Franco-Prussian War, 'especially horrible to me, in its digging, as the Germans should have known, a moat flooded with the waters of death between the two nations for a century to come'.[16]

For those who see the First World War as the great climacteric or watershed in modern history, it is worth remembering the trauma of the 1870–1 campaign, whose devastation through foreign conquest and civil war brought forth its own brand of apocalyptic despair. Zola, anatomizing the Second Empire in terms of the family history of the Rougon-Macquart, published his series of twenty novels between 1871 and 1893. The penultimate one, *Le Débâcle* (1892), devoted to the Franco-Prussian War and the ensuing Paris Commune, was an instant success; its final chapter begins with the dreadful spectacle of Paris burning, set alight by the Communards, 'Babylon in flames' as a young Prussian soldier sees it, secure in the conviction that 'Paris was burning as a punishment for centuries of wickedness, for the long tale of its crimes and debauches. Once again the Germanic tribes would save the world and sweep away the last remains of Latin corruption.'[17] An earlier novel in the series, *L'Oeuvre* (1885), and the one most completely devoted to art, culminates in the funeral of the painter Claude Lantier. Amidst a scene of urban and human detritus, to the accompaniment of the shriek of passing locomotives and a gathering pall of smoke from the coffins smouldering to make way for new inhabitants of the ground, the author's alter ego, Sandoz, enters upon a soliloquy that is concerned with the spiritual malaise soon to be characterized as *fin-de-siècle*:

> It was inevitable. All our activity, our boastfulness about our knowledge was bound to lead us back again to doubt. The present century has cast so much light on so many things, but it was bound to end under the threat of another wave of darkness.... And that is the root of our troubles. We have been promised too much and led to expect too much, including the conquest and the explanation of everything; and now we've grown

impatient. We're surprised things don't move more quickly. We're resentful because, in a matter of a hundred years, science hasn't given us absolute certitude and perfect happiness. Why then continue, we ask, since we shall never know everything and our bread will always be bitter? The century has been a failure. Hearts are tortured with pessimism and brains clouded with mysticism for, try as we may to put imagination to flight with the cold light of science, we have the supernatural once more in arms against us and the whole world of legend in revolt, bent on enslaving us again in our moment of fatigue and uncertainty.... I'm no more sure of things than anyone else; my mind, too, is divided. But I do not think that this last shattering upheaval of our old religious fears was only to be expected. We are not at an end; we are a transition, the beginning only of something new.... And it's that sets my mind at rest, and somehow encourages me: to know we are moving towards rationality and the firm foundations that only science can give.... Unless of course madness makes us come a cropper in the dark and we end up like our old friend sleeping there in his coffin, strangled by our own ideals.[18]

The exemplification of a 'heart tortured by pessimism' and a 'brain clouded by mysticism' was Des Esseintes, the solipsistic anti-hero of *A Rebours* (Against Nature), published the year before *L'Oeuvre* by Zola's erstwhile protégé, Joris-Karl Huysmans. In the character's aestheticized existence, pride of place is given to the work of Redon among the paintings and watercolours of Gustave Moreau, the prints of Jan Luyken, Goya and Bresdin:

> Filled with an indefinable sense of unease by these drawings, just as he was by certain of Goya's *Proverbs* which they recalled, and just as he also was by reading Edgar Allan Poe, whose hallucinatory phantasms and terror-inducing effects Odilon Redon seemed to have transposed into a different art form, Des Esseintes would rub his eyes and rest them upon a radiant figure of Melancholy seated on some rocks before the disk of the sun, in an attitude of despondency and gloom.[19]

The figure of Melancholy (the charcoal and pastel drawing of 1876 belongs to the Art Institute of Chicago) was Redon's homage to the Dürer print, a reproduction of which he kept pinned to his studio wall and whose resonance was apparent throughout his career. *A Rebours* very much governed the reception of his work thereafter, identifying him as 'an artist who is an absolute master in the realm of the fantastic and the ideal, a creator of forms more sinister than the Caprichos of Goya and more mystical than the Apocalypse of Albrecht Dürer'.[20] Redon's homage to the latter series was to be his final suite of lithographs, published in 1899 by Ambroise Vollard (cat. 1). The Catholic literary revival of the 1890s encouraged a mystical religiosity to which Redon's images lent themselves as readily as they did to satanic occultism. His earlier mentor, Huysmans, moved from the exploration of the latter in *Là-Bas* (1891)[21] to a position of didactic Catholicism in his novel of 1898, *La Cathédrale*. In the preface to a new edition of *A Rebours* in 1904, Huysmans explained the shift in his beliefs from the 'Theory of Pessimism' embraced by Des Esseintes:

> I never dreamt that from Schopenhauer... to Ecclesiastes and the Book of Job was but a step. The hypotheses about pessimism are the same, only, when it is time to reach a conclusion, the philosopher makes himself scarce. I liked his ideas on the horror of existence, on the absurdity of the world, on the cruelty of destiny; I also like them in the Holy Scriptures; but Schopenhauer's remarks lead nowhere; he leaves you, so to speak, in the lurch, in a word, his aphorisms are nothing but a herbarium of barren plants; the Church, on the other hand, elucidates origins and causes, points to conclusions, offers remedies.[22]

Baudelaire and Schopenhauer were joined in their position of central importance to the 'disenchanted heart' of the avant-garde by Nietzsche, who played a commanding role in relation to the early twentieth century. During the 1880s, prior to his final collapse in 1889 (he died in 1900 after prolonged mental illness), Nietzsche adumbrated his rejection of metaphysical belief, questioning all values and the whole idea of eschatology. From the pronouncement 'God is dead' he moved swiftly to the resolution of this dilemma in the form of the Superman who is the epitome of self-mastery and the will to power, as described in *Also sprach Zarathustra*, which he wrote in 1883–5 (published 1892). A direct assault on Christianity, with special opprobrium reserved for Luther and the German Reformation, followed in *The Anti-Christ* (1888, published 1895), one of his final works, where he 'exposes' 'the concepts "Beyond", "Last Judgement", "immortality of the soul", the soul itself: they are instruments of torture, they are forms of systematic cruelty by virtue of which the priest has become master, stays master'.[23] For all his professed scepticism and the repudiation of his Lutheran background, Nietzsche borrowed the clothes of apocalyptic rhetoric; through the prophetic figure of Zarathustra he articulated a secular form of messianism that trespassed on the divine. Jung seized upon this apparent contradiction in *Psychology and Religion* (1938–40): 'The tragedy of *Zarathustra* is that, because his God died, Nietzsche himself became a god; and this happened because he was no atheist. He was of too positive a nature to tolerate the urban neurosis of atheism. It seems dangerous for such a man to assert that "God is dead": he instantly becomes the victim of inflation.'[24] Of all the books in the Bible, Revelation was perceived as the most 'Nietzschean' by D.H. Lawrence among others, when he later condemned it in his own work on the Apocalypse (see p.20): 'For Revelation...is the revelation of the undying will-to-power in man and its sanctification, its final triumph.'[25]

Nietzsche's intense individualism, belief in self-realization and 'intoxication of the will which demands artistic expression',[26] proved enormously compelling to artists and writers of the early decades of the twentieth century. Paul Klee as a student in Munich in 1899 referred to 'Nietzsche in the air. Glorification of the self and the instincts. Boundless sexual drives', and Kandinsky felt 'as if a great earthquake had erupted in the soul'.[27] The image of the 'bridge' which occurs repeatedly in *Zarathustra*, as in 'man is a bridge and not a goal; counting himself happy for his noontides and evenings, as a way to new dawns',[28] provided a collective name for the pioneering group of German Expressionist artists in Dresden in 1905. 'Bridges' are also concepts, like 'Good' and 'Evil', but these are not fixed absolutes; they are subject to change by 'he it is who creates a goal for mankind and gives the earth its meaning and future; he it is who *creates the quality of good and evil in things*'.[29] To the creative intelligence, Nietzsche appeared to offer an infinity of promise: 'as poet, reader of riddles, and redeemer of chance, I taught them to create the future, and to redeem by creating – all that *was past... this did I call redemption, this alone did I teach them to call redemption*'.[30] Marinetti's Futurist manifesto of 1909 and *War, the World's only Hygiene* of 1911–15 were imbued with Nietzschean rhetoric, whose influence was given even greater potency by the actuality of war. *Zarathustra*, which had been part of Max Beckmann's formative reading, accompanied him during his service as a medical orderly from 1914 to 1915;[31] Franz Marc, while away on active duty, was recommending his wife to read *Beyond Good and Evil* and *The Anti-Christ* in 1915,[32] and Otto Dix was indebted to Nietzsche's ideas throughout his career.[33] Beckmann, Marc and Dix were all artists who accepted the necessity of war, at least at the outset, but Nietzsche was equally attractive to a vehement pacifist such as Hermann Hesse, who in 'Zarathustra's Return. A Word to German Youth. 1919' appealed to the spirit of Nietzsche to rebuild a Germany based on 'courage and solitude' and the dictates of individual conscience as opposed to 'the herd outcry'.[34]

The fragile balance between fear and hope represented by the Apocalypse and Last Judgement was part of the fabric of life in Russia, from the time of the liturgical schism of the later seventeenth century with the ensuing persecution of the 'Old Believers' (Ch. 4, cat. 117), who identified the Tsar and westernizing influences with Antichrist, to the utopian and revolutionary political movements of the nineteenth and early twentieth centuries. In recalling her childhood in St Petersburg in the mid-1890s, the ballerina Tamara Karsavina described the powerful association of word and image in her experience of the Apocalypse:

> After the Epistles I came to the reading of Revelation. Its symbolic meaning I could not grasp. The flamboyant vision of the Last Judgement filled me with an agony of awe. I had seen before, under the arcades of the old Nikolsky Market, the frescoes of the Last Judgement. I was even then drawn by their terrible fascination, but the whole of their meaning was now revealed to me. The last trump of the Archangel, the sea and earth giving up their dead, in the gaudy imagery of an obscure master, entered into my vision, there to grow and torment with ever-increasing terror.[35]

Tolstoy and Dostoevsky, both profoundly interested in eschatology and its relationship to contemporary spiritual and sociological crisis, were, together with

Nietzsche and Strindberg, part of that pantheon of prophetic mentors whose impact was keenly felt in Central Europe in the years immediately before and during the First World War. In 1906, the Munich publisher Reinhard Piper inaugurated an edition of the collected works of Dostoevsky. Beckmann was one of many artists to acknowledge his inspiration, with typical hubris equating Dostoevsky's importance to himself with that of Dante to Michelangelo.[36] The Russian people represented on the one hand an ideal of simple, incorruptible piety, as admired by Rilke in his *Book of Monastic Life*, the poem inspired by his journey to Moscow in 1899 which he published in 1905 as part of *The Book of Hours*;[37] on the other hand they embodied the moral and political upheaval of a society in process of rapid change, torn between 'Asiatic' and Western influences. Dostoevsky's friend, the poet Apollon Maikov, was working on a new verse translation of the Apocalypse while he was engaged with the composition of *The Idiot* (1868), which has an apocalyptic momentum of its own, focused on the redemptive role of the 'Holy Fool' in the form of the Idiot himself. Images of the 'star that is called Wormwood' and the 'drying up of the waters of life' are invoked by one of the characters to suggest moral plague, a parallel that was resurrected in 1986 in connection with Chernobyl, whose name is Russian for 'Wormwood', the star that fell from Heaven when the third angel blew his trumpet, poisoning a third of the waters (Revelation 8: 10–11).

The zenith of apocalypticism in Russia was reached during the period from the 1890s to the Bolshevik Revolution and its aftermath, which offered rich possibilities for evidence of the activity of Antichrist. The principal context for this apocalypticism was that of the Symbolist movement and the mystical writings of the philosopher Vladimir Solovyev (1853–1900), a friend of Dostoevsky, and Dimitri Merezhovsky (1865–1941), the author of a trilogy of historical novels, *Christ and Antichrist*, that appeared between 1895 and 1905, the final part telling the story of Peter the Great from the perspective of the Old Believers. Its most vivid literary expression occurs in the work of Andrei Bely (1880–1934), who published an essay on *The Apocalypse in Russian Poetry* in 1905, becoming an acolyte of Rudolf Steiner from 1912 (Steiner's lecture on the Apocalypse had been published in 1908). The most important and influential of all Bely's 'apocalyptic' creations is *Petersburg*, the novel set in October 1905 which he wrote during 1912, but which did not appear in book form until 1916. Throughout the elliptical, fragmented narrative, pregnant with foreboding, the Book of Revelation is both tacitly acknowledged and directly invoked in images which express the sense of psychic and physical rupture pervading Eastern and Western Europe at this juncture.[38] Such was the association between Russian mysticism and the Apocalypse that a fictitious Russian philosopher called Tchernoff was the character chosen to introduce the leitmotif of the novel by Blasco Ibañez, and the subsequent film *The Four Horsemen of the Apocalypse* (1921, see pp.325–7).

A similarly apocalyptic intuition of living on the brink of a new era suffused the language and the visual imagery of Kandinsky, of whom Marc wrote in 1914: 'He belonged in a high degree to a foreign race and merely wore the mask of a "West European"'.[39] 1910 was the year of his first painting of an overtly eschatological subject, *The Last Judgement* (Städtische Galerie im Lembachhaus, Munich). He had already written his treatise *Über das Geistige in der Kunst* (On the Spiritual in Art), which was published in 1912. This was followed by the anthology of essays that he edited with Marc, *Der Blaue Reiter* [Blue Rider] *Almanac* (1912), whose prospectus contained the famous clarion call: 'Today art is moving in a direction of which our fathers would never have dreamed. We stand before new pictures as in a dream, and we hear the apocalyptic horsemen in the air. There is an artistic tension all over Europe.'[40] Mankind was on the threshold of 'the epoch of great spirituality' which Kandinsky described in terms that were ultimately indebted to Joachim of Fiore's Trinitarian scheme (see p.23): 'Today is the great day of the revelations of this world.... Here begins the epoch of the spiritual, the revelation of the spirit, Father-son-Spirit.... Art is like religion in many respects....Its development consists of sudden illuminations.'[41] The route to attainment of this epoch was through new forms of artistic perception. The horse and rider motif was not automatically to be associated with the Apocalypse, since the 'Blue Rider' could be interpreted as a latter-day St George or 'the Christian knight of art which will shape the future'[42] (see Ch. 3, cat. 8, Ch. 4, cat. 102 for the antecedents of this iconography), but the correspondence to the horsemen of the Apocalypse was made perfectly explicit in other instances. The direction in which the horsemen of these compositions and their related subjects were moving was that of non-objectivity, a dissolution of form appropriate to the apocalyptic content.

If Symbolism provided one vehicle for imagining and imaging apocalyptic ideas, there were other, more strident languages, notably Futurism and Expressionism, to create a vocabulary that could approximate to the experiences of the First World War. They anticipated those experiences, helped to articulate them at the time, and, particularly in the case of Expressionism, played an important role in subsequently memorializing them. Futurism espoused a secular Apocalypse, abrogating time and space through 'a perpetual dynamism of thought',[43] while Expressionism provided a spiritual dimension, drawing upon biblical imagery from the Old and New Testaments, especially Job, the Prophets and Revelation. Whether viewed as an event breaking into history and thereby giving it meaning, or as part of a providential scheme advancing towards a necessary goal, or in a despairing light as 'the abridgement of hope',[44] the First World War became the crucible for all manner of apocalyptic and messianic apprehensions; 'the apocalyptic scheme of the war appeared right at the beginning. *Dies irae, dies illa* (4 August).'[45] Henri Focillon's interpretation of the anxieties focused on or close to the year 1000 (see p.6), in terms of a fissure in the 'moral geology' of society that momentarily laid bare the primordial layers of belief,[46] might well be applied to the whole period from 1914 to 1945. Its relevance is underlined by the context for Focillon's study *L'An Mil*, on which he worked in America until his death in 1943, doubtless aware of the parallels to be made with the contemporary state of Europe.[47]

The foundations of a world of reinvigorated myth had been laid prior to the actual outbreak of hostilities when both participants and onlookers drew upon every kind of precedent from classical, Jewish and Christian sources to frame the 'fierce imaginings their dark souls lit'.[48] Personal and collective crisis were conjoined in the experience of figures such as C.G. Jung, for whom the period 1913–14 proved to be a breakthrough in the development of his distinctive form of psychoanalytical theory, the concept of archetypes as images of ideas within the collective unconscious.

> In October [1913], while I was alone on a journey, I was suddenly seized by an overpowering vision: I saw a monstrous flood covering all the northern and low-lying lands between the North Sea and the Alps. When it came up to Switzerland I saw that the mountains grew higher and higher to protect our country. I realized that a frightful catastrophe was in progress. I saw the mighty yellow waves, the floating rubble of civilization, and the drowned bodies of uncounted thousands. Then the whole sea turned to blood. This vision lasted about one hour.... Two weeks passed; then the vision recurred, under the same conditions, even more vividly than before, and the blood was more emphasized.[49]

The meaning of these visions, with their reference to the seven angels with the seven trumpets in Revelation, and of those that followed in the spring and summer of 1914 of a world frozen into a new ice age, culminating in one of a tree whose leaves had been transformed into sweet grapes full of healing juices, 'my tree of life, I thought' (see Ch. 5, cats 10–11), was fully revealed to Jung on 1 August when war broke out between Germany and Russia: 'Now my task was clear: I had to try to understand what had happened and to what extent my own experience coincided with that of mankind in general.'[50]

The prior intimations of decline, death and destruction, of the passing of one age and possibly the dawn of another, proliferated in the literature of the German-speaking world, represented by the work of Jakob von Hoddis (1887–1942), whose poem *The End of the World* was published in 1911, and Georg Heym (1887–1912), a devotee of Baudelaire, with *War* and *The Everlasting Day* in 1911, followed by *Shadow of Life* (1912), in which he used the image of a comet to signify impending doom, perhaps reflecting alarmism over heavenly portents in the popular press.[51] Among the early casualties of the war was the Austrian Georg Trakl (1887–1914), driven to despair and possibly suicide by drug addiction and his experiences as a medical orderly in Galicia, who called his inner life 'an infernal chaos of rhythms and images';[52] his prose poem *Revelation and Fall* (unpublished until 1947) became the basis for Peter Maxwell Davies's musical dramas of the same name composed in 1965–6.[53] Carl Hauptmann (1858–1921) wrote the play *War, a Te Deum* in 1913 (published 1914), on the theme of apocalyptic destruction and regeneration, including among his cast of characters 'The European Reckoner', 'The Archangel in Armour' and 'The Great Power Beasts', while the lyrical, symbolic style of

Stefan George (1868–1933) shifted to a prophetic, apocalyptic tone in the three books of poetry called *The Star of the Covenant* (1913).[54]

Ludwig Meidner was the foremost visual artist to identify with 'the new pathos' of contemporary literary expression. 1912 was the year of his epiphany, when exposure to the hectic, kaleidoscopic paintings of Delaunay and the Futurists exhibited at the Sturm Gallery in Berlin, to Expressionist literature, and to a resurgent Jewish spirituality that the philosopher Martin Buber (1878–1965) was investing with Nietzschean language, stimulated Meidner's explosive outpouring of apocalyptic compositions. Under the effects of the heatwave in Berlin from April to September 1912, reminiscent of Nietzsche's reference to 'intoxication under certain meteorological influences',[55] Meidner worked as one possessed, producing images of bombardment, revolution, conflagration, devastation and chaos. 'Vision of the Apocalyptic Summer', one of the texts in his volume *September Shout* (*Septemberschrei*, written in 1917 but published 1920, cat. 4), describes how amidst an extremity of psychic and bodily discomfort, conjoined with the most exiguous means of life, Meidner came to paint the canvases which he exhibited at the Sturm Gallery in November 1912 with titles such as *Decline of the World*, *Cosmic Landscape I with Comet*, and *Apocalyptic Landscape* (fig. 3):

> A painful urge led me to break the vertical, the straightforward. To strew ruins, debris and ashes on to the landscapes. On my rocks I built ruins, wretchedly fissured, with the dismal wail of the bare trees tearing through the creaking skies above. Mountains looming in the background like warning voices; the comet laughed hoarsely and aeroplanes glided like infernal dragonflies in the yellow night-storm. My brain bled with frightful visions. I could see nothing but a thousand skeletons dancing in a ring. Graves and burnt cities writhing across the plain.[56]

What struck his contemporaries was the sheer energy of these compositions. They were among those seen by the future Dadaist Hugo Ball in Munich in 1913, when he observed in his diary that pictures by Meidner, Jawlensky and Rousseau had 'achieved total expression of life without a detour through the intellect.... The energy in the pictures was so intense that they seemed almost to burst out of their frames. Great things seemed imminent...'.[57]

Meidner's prodigious output, in colour and in black and white, continued until his military call-up in 1916. The final painting in the apocalyptic series (the title of apocalyptic landscapes was not applied to them as a whole until his exhibition at Paul Cassirer's gallery in 1918) was *The Last Day* of 1916 (Berlinische Galerie), although there are one or two slightly later drawings. His religious imagery changed to that of prophets and sibyls, aspects of his own self-projection, which was otherwise expressed in his self-portraiture.

Meidner's apocalyptic vision was concentrated on the city, which for him became the 'pathetic fallacy': the idea that the human condition is reflected by the natural or, in this case, man-made environment. The promotion of the city

Fig.3. Ludwig Meidner
(1884–1966), *Apocalyptic
Landscape* (1912). Oil on canvas,
Private Collection.

as a key subject for modernism was scarcely new, the tone having been set by
the Futurist Manifesto of 1909, which was translated into German for the exhibition at the Sturm Gallery in 1912 and echoed in Meidner's *An Introduction to
Painting Big Cities* of 1913.[58] Writers from Baudelaire to Walter Benjamin
extolled the world city and the image of the crowd; the city was the culmination
of history, essential to the modern artist, but could also be the nemesis of Western civilization and the site of its ultimate disintegration. Georg Heym's poetic
cycle *Berlin I-VIII*, which appeared between 1910 and 1912, and Andrei Bely's
novel *Petersburg* (p. 278) from the same period, were but two examples of works
dominated by 'the haunting presence of a threshold city, the end of history's
road or the place where all paths converge as history prepares for eschatological
change'.[59]

The First World War endowed this idea with greater urgency, recalling
Georg Trakl's image of 'the city's madness when at nightfall/The crippled trees
gape by the blackened wall/The spirit of evil peers from a silver mask' from *To
the Silenced*;[60] Trakl, when advised in 1914 to leave the town for the country
where he would be closer to nature, responded, 'I have no right to remove
myself from Hell.' George Grosz wrote of Berlin in 1915: 'How right Sweden-

borg was... when he said that Heaven and Hell exist here on earth side by side.'[61] His frenzied city scenes (cat. 5) of 1917–18, which were much influenced by Meidner, are populated with the degenerate types described by Oswald Spengler in *The Decline of the West* (1918): 'In place of a type-true people, born of and grown on the soil, there is a new sort of nomad, cohering unstably in fluid masses, the parasitical city dweller, traditionless, utterly matter-of-fact, religionless, clever, unfruitful, deeply contemptuous of the countrymen.'[62] Preoccupation with the effects of city life as manifested in undue nervous excitement, the volatility of both the individual and the crowd and the tension between the two, became constant motifs in literature and the cinema.[63] The polarities of Babylon and Jerusalem, St Augustine's City of Man and City of God and (more particularly for the English-speaking world) Bunyan's City of Destruction or Vanity Fair and the Celestial City, together with Sodom and Gomorrah and Dante's City of Dis, repeatedly underscored the real and fictive characterization of the modern metropolis. Central to T.S. Eliot's apocalyptic vision in *The Wasteland* (1922) was the 'Unreal City,/Under the brown fog of a winter dawn,/A crowd flowed over London Bridge, so many,/I had not thought death had undone so many' (based on Dante's *Inferno*, Canto IV: 25–7); 'What is that sound high in the air/Murmur of maternal lamentation/Who are those hooded hordes swarming/Over endless plains, stumbling in cracked earth/Ringed by the flat horizon only/What is the city over the mountains/Cracks and reforms and bursts in the violet air/Falling towers/Jerusalem Athens Alexandria/Vienna London/Unreal.'[64]

The Bible, Dante and Bunyan were as pertinent to the vistas of war as they were to urban imagery; the 'dark wood', 'abomination of desolation' and the 'Valley of the Shadow of Death' were everywhere to be seen on the Eastern and Western Fronts, which seemed like the end of the terrestrial world or the beginning of an infernal one, bearing no relation to any landscape hitherto experienced by those present.[65] On the German side it was memorably captured in the etchings that comprised Otto Dix's series *Der Krieg* (War) of 1924 (cat. 9), partly based on his wartime drawings. Beckmann, serving as a medical orderly in East Prussia, then in Flanders from 1914 to 1915, thrilled to the experience of travelling at night with the darkness relieved only by illuminating flares and 'the wonderfully apocalyptic tone of the cannon'.[66] He was excited by the visual possibilities of war, intent upon the realization of artistic vision come what may: 'I would drag myself through all the sewers of the world, through every conceivable humiliation and abuse in order to paint. That I have to do. All the forms I imagine and that live within me must be wrung out of me to the last drop, then I will be glad to be rid of this damned torture'.[67] The Second Battle of Ypres in May 1915 was a turning-point for him; on 24 May he referred to having 'another dream about the end of the world. Probably my twentieth',[68] then a few months later he suffered the breakdown which effectively removed him from all further service, leaving him to concentrate on capturing 'the aspects of life which cannot be spoken of'.[69]

The concept of the artist as prophet and spiritual leader promulgated by Nietzsche was reinforced through Wilhelm Worringer's *Formprobleme der Gotik* (Form in Gothic), first published by Reinhard Piper in 1912. Worringer believed in mysticism as the outcome of a process of individualization which he associated with a modern, essentially northern and German sensibility: 'It is the history of modern sensibility, the history of modern art, which begins with mysticism.'[70] The 'transcendental pathos' of that sensibility is to be found in 'true Gothic', the style of a specific historical period, and in 'latent Gothic' running throughout northern art, both before and after its 'true' counterpart.[71] Grünewald, one of the artists whom Beckmann expressly admired in 1917 for their 'masculine mysticism', was identified in the 1919 edition of Worringer's book as the archetypal visionary artist.

The early German and Flemish masters assumed a heightened emotional significance under the impact of war, remaining a powerful influence thereafter. The situation was rather as Joseph Koerner has described 'the archaism of 1500', when 'artists turned to the generation of 1420 for examples of authority and visionary power'.[72] For Germans during the First World War and its aftermath, the northern artists of the fifteenth and sixteenth centuries, painters and sculptors, reinforced a sense of national identity and provided a visual simulacrum for suffering and sacrifice. Grünewald's Isenheim Altar became the supreme symbol in this context, an object of pilgrimage from 1917 to 1919 when it was displayed in the Neue Pinakothek in Munich, and the subject of constant remark by those who had either seen it, whether in Colmar or Munich, or knew it in reproduction. Hugo Ball, who came across a pamphlet in Bern in 1917 on *Grünewald, the Romanticist of Pain*, was reminded of the impact made by his own visit to the altarpiece in Colmar in 1913.[73] Dix, who knew the work through reproductions, constantly drew upon it for inspiration in his postwar recapitulations of the wartime 'apocalypse', most notably in the controversial triptych *The Trench* of 1923, and in some of the plates for *War* (cat. 9) published the following year. In 1945 he was a prisoner in Colmar, where he painted a triptych for the chapel in the camp, once again paying homage to Grünewald.

The Isenheim Altar's iconographical scheme, which included panels of the Temptation of St Anthony, the Annunciation and Resurrection, as well as the most striking image of all, the Crucifixion with its predella of the Lamentation over the dead Christ in the Tomb, was understood as a configuration of Judgement and the end of the world. It was one of those 'nets' (see p.9) which served to 'catch' people's experiences and provide them with a point of reference for both private and public agony. Elias Canetti, visiting Colmar in 1927,

> spent an entire day in front of the Grünewald altar. I didn't know when I had come, and I didn't know when I would leave. When the museum closed, I wished for invisibility, so that I might spend the night there.... The thing that people had turned away from, horrified, in real life, could still be grasped in the painting: a memory of the dreadful things that

people do to one another. Back then, in February 1927, war and gassings were still close enough to make the painting more credible.[74]

The work quite literally provided a background for the composition of his Faustian and 'apocalyptic' masterpiece, *Die Blendung* (The Blinding, 1935, published in English as *Auto-Da-Fé*), which he wrote in a room that he occupied in Vienna from 1928 to 1934 'as soon as the reproductions of Grünewald hung around me', perhaps referring to the large portfolio of forty-nine reproductions that Piper had published in 1923. Walter Benjamin was equally drawn to the work, whose impact can only be compared with that of Picasso's *Guernica* for the middle years of the twentieth century. Picasso himself executed a suite of drawings in 1932 that were published in the first issue of *Minotaure* (June 1933), where they were described as being 'after Grünewald's *Crucifixion* in Colmar'.[75]

1932 was the year in which Hindemith broached the idea of composing an opera on the same subject. The symphonic version of *Mathis der Maler* was completed and first performed in March 1934, consisting of three movements related to panels in the Isenheim Altarpiece: 'Angelic Concert', 'Entombment' and 'Temptation of St Anthony'. The opera itself, in seven episodes, was eventually finished between July and November 1934 (bar the final orchestration) against the background of mounting Nazi opposition to Hindemith's music, the fate of which was sealed by the publication of the opera's libretto. Set at the time of the Peasants' War of 1524–5, the opera is an allegory of the artist's dilemma in a society in turmoil; the painter abandons his altarpiece to join the revolutionary cause, but eventually returns to serve God through his art before a final renunciation in anticipation of death.[76]

The year 1916–17 was a critical juncture in attitudes to the war on the main continent of Europe, with 337,000 German dead during the course of 1916 alone. That year had seen the terrible slaughter of Verdun, Passchendaele and the Somme on the Western Front, where French casualties were even higher. Meidner's endorsement of German militarism had survived the early death of his friend, the poet Ernst Wilhelm Lotz (1890–1914), which provided the impetus for the series of drawings done in 1914 and published nearly ten years later as a reproductive portfolio entitled *Krieg*. None the less he was considerably changed by his experience of service in a prisoner-of-war camp in 1916–17. In *September Shout* (cat. 4), Meidner recounted how hollow his earlier values now appeared; his emphasis shifted towards an internationalist outlook and belief in the benefits of 'brotherly love', a utopian socialism that would unite his artistic and religious views; these were articulated in a rhapsodic prose style heavily indebted to the Psalms and the Lamentations of Jeremiah.

Henri Barbusse's celebrated anti-war novel, *Le Feu* (Under Fire, 1916), sold more than 200,000 copies between the beginning of 1917, when it was published in book form, and the end of the war, Wilfrid Owen and the film director Abel Gance (see p.325) being among its many avid readers. It described a landscape submerged by a universal flood, 'a vast and waterlogged desert',[77] not unlike Jung's vision of northern Europe in 1913 (p.280), hell being neither 'the flame of shells' nor 'the suffocation of the caverns which eternally confine us... Hell is water'.[78] The narrative ends with an apocalyptic vision of the 'flayed and martyred fields' on which the soldiers under fire, 'the Cyranos and Don Quixotes' still 'struggling against victorious spectres',[79] gradually begin to understand the war as it really is, a recognition of truth which 'not only invests them with a dawn of hope, but raises on it a renewal of strength and courage'.[80] The German translation of 1918 was banned in Austria and Germany for the duration of the war but proved to be of considerable consequence to Otto Dix; Barbusse wrote an introduction to accompany the book edition of Dix's *War* in 1924, some of whose images recall the detailed descriptions of carnage and desolation in *Under Fire*, just as Dix's prints were acknowledged as an inspiration by Erich Maria Remarque for passages in his anti-war novel of 1928, *All Quiet on the Western Front*, which in turn influenced Dix's triptych *Der Krieg* of 1932. Two years later, after the Nazis had come to power, Dix executed the painting *Flanders* with the subtitle *After Henri Barbusse 'Le Feu'*[81] in homage to the French author, who had become a fervent Communist – he died in 1935 while on a visit to Moscow.

Stefan Zweig published his pacifist play *Jeremias* in 1917 from Switzerland, where he, and others of internationalist views, gathered in Bern, Zurich and Geneva. Walter Benjamin, Ernst Bloch and Hugo Ball all spent time in Berne, the political centre of the German community in exile, together with Gershom Scholem, the historian of Jewish messianism, and Hermann Hesse. The Flemish artist Frans Masereel was another of those to make his way to Switzerland, where he embarked in earnest upon his career as one of the most prolific and influential of twentieth-century graphic artists. As well as contributing illustrations to the anti-war newspapers *Les Tablettes* and *La Feuille* in Geneva, and to books by other authors, Masereel was executing woodcuts for use within his own distinctive genre, the 'novel without words', on which he principally established his reputation. Many of these had both overt and implicit eschatological themes, from *Debout les Morts: Résurrection infernale* (1917), *25 Images de la Passion d'un homme* (1918) and *Mon Livre d'Heures* (My Book of Hours, 1919), to the series of drawings he did for reproduction at the time of the Second World War, *Danse Macabre* (1941), *Destins* (1943) and *Die Apokalypse unserer Zeit* (not published until 1953, cat. 11). Stefan Zweig became a close friend, publishing the first monograph on Masereel in Berlin in 1923, while Thomas Mann, a fervent nationalist during the First World War who later 'converted' to liberal democratic views, became another admirer of Masereel's work, writing the introduction to a new edition of *My Book of Hours* in 1926. Masereel's wordless narratives of modern man's fall and redemption are enacted within an urban context. In describing one such series, *La Ville* (1925), Mann placed the artist's style within a tradition stretching from the earliest form of printed imagery to the most contemporary visual medium:

He has depicted the brutal fantasy of modern life, grotesque and horrible in its inexorable vulgarity. It is crowded with contradictions, contradictions of the diabolical and the damned. As you thumb through this German-Flemish 'block-book' brought up to date, you pass in review all the coarsest aspects of the present. It is a present that has been tried and convicted by a graphic artist who is himself so much a part of the present that in the impact of his art he is closely akin to one of the most characteristic products of our times. For is not the play of black and white on a movie screen a democratic pleasure.... The wood-block in which this Fleming silhouettes his plastically drawn figures against broad surfaces of light is akin to the small white screen of the cinema. We expect so little of that narrow screen as we sit down in front of it; yet we marvel at the way in which life seems to open out.[82]

The cinematic quality of Masereel's technique was noted by others, including the prominent French pacifist writer Romain Rolland, whom Masereel met in Geneva. In 1921 the two of them collaborated on text and illustration for a proposed film scenario entitled *La Révolte des Machines*, which Rolland characterized as a 'psychocinematic art... a psychological film, entirely introspective,... a tragedy of humanity',[83] making it clear that he expected Masereel not merely to supply the images for the book edition but to be involved in the project's cinematic realization. This did not, however, come to pass and the book, though published in Paris in 1921, was kept from public circulation until 1947.

Another, even more fantastic contemporary 'cinematic' idea of truly apocalyptic content was Blaise Cendrars's *La Fin du Monde filmée par l'Ange N.-D.* (The End of the World filmed by the Angel of Notre-Dame), accompanied by Léger's drawings and published in Paris in 1919 by Éditions de la Sirène, the imprint founded by Cendrars and Jean Cocteau. The extraordinary trajectory of the life and self-invention of Cendrars (1887–1961) almost defies description, from his roots in a Swiss family of French Anabaptist and Scottish origin, his adventures among anarchists and terrorists in St Petersburg at the time of the 1905 revolution, a period in New York in 1911–12 followed by *La Prose du Transsibérien*, the simultaneist book in a folding format decorated with the designs of Sonia Delaunay which he wrote in Paris in 1913, to wartime service with the French Foreign Legion, the loss of his right arm at the Battle of the Marne in September 1915, and his friendship with Apollinaire, whose surreal funeral he attended in November 1918.[84] The idea for *La Fin du Monde*, which was conceived as early as 1916, came to fruition in 1918–19 when he had begun to write on the cinema as well as participating in Abel Gance's visionary epic of the First World War, *J'accuse* (p.325). Cendrars's narrative revolves around the conceit of a venal and entrepreneurial God the Father, who travels to 'Mars'; determined to capitalize further on the war, which has already yielded a vast crop of souls with its attendant income from offices for the dead, he intends to open a cinema in which to show the best war films. The Old Testament prophets, called in as advisers, prove too factious, so the trumpeting angel from between the towers of Notre-Dame is charged with setting in motion and recording the end of the world, which can be made to work forwards and backwards. After the cataclysmic destruction of man-made civilization, climatic changes reinstate primeval vegetative and geological conditions, ending in the darkness and chaos before the earth existed; no sooner has this been achieved, however, than the reel is rapidly rewound and the whole process reversed.[85]

Emancipation from the past became the most difficult state of mind to achieve in the immediate post-war period. Franz Marc, who died at Verdun in March 1916, wrote in 1915 of 'the artistic logic of having painted such works [*The Fate of the Animals*, 1914] *before* the war, rather than their being stupid reminiscences *after* the war. At that point one will have to paint *constructive*, future paintings, not memories as is mostly the habit.'[86] The First World War, however, became the most intensely memorialized conflict of all time, but in so doing rendered the present and the future captive to the past. The preoccupation with death was scarcely surprising after a conflict in which 'death had undone so many', but even the scale of wartime casualties was dwarfed by that of the worldwide influenza epidemic of 1918–19, in which thirty million people are estimated to have died (Apollinaire was one). This phenomenon, curiously, went largely unnoticed as far as its contribution to myth-making was concerned, but one writer, at least, was conscious of apocalyptic imagery in the subsequent fictionalization of her own near-death experience in Denver, Colorado. For much of America, the impact of the First World War was felt more acutely through the epidemic than by any other means, with 150,000 people dying at its height in October 1918. *Pale Horse, Pale Rider* (1936) by Katherine Anne Porter (1890–1980) begins with the heroine riding a favourite horse in a dream accompanied by a pale stranger, Death. She knows she must 'outrun Death and the Devil', a reference to the Dürer engraving of *The Knight, Death and the Devil* (1513), which appears in another of Porter's stories, *Old Mortality* (1939).

The traditional iconography of death, personified in motifs such as the Dance of Death, Death and the Maiden and the Grim Reaper, helped to anchor the experience within an established frame of reference both during and after the war. The Russian film *Danse macabre* appeared in 1914/15, directed by Alexander Wolkow and intended to be accompanied by Saint-Saëns's symphonic poem of the same title (1874), while at least nineteen graphic series on the Dance of Death appeared in Germany between 1914 and 1924, as well as numerous variations of individual motifs.[87] The

Fig.4. 75-Pfennig banknote, issued in Kahla, Germany, 1921. London, British Museum, Dept. of Coins and Medals. The inscription reads: 'New Year's Eve 1921–1922 German spook in Paris'. Small-denomination notes issued in German towns during and immediately after World War I often carried stark wartime propaganda. In this example, the skeletal spectre of Germany is stalking the streets of Paris, inscribing a pillar with the biblical warning from Belshazzar's feast: 'thy days are numbered...'.

same subjects were exploited for crude propaganda purposes on all sides, along with images of the resurrected dead returning to exhort their countrymen to further sacrifice. Other sources for the dramatization of death were found in the frescoes in the Campo Santo in Pisa (pp.57–8); in Ruskin's description of those by Giotto in the Arena Chapel which inspired Stanley Spencer's *Resurrection of the Soldiers* and the other frescoes he painted in the chapel at Burghclere (1928–32); and in Bruegel's painting of *The Triumph of Death* in the Kunsthistorisches Museum in Vienna. The last had a great influence on Elias Canetti, who was chiefly impressed by the sheer 'vitality of the dead' as depicted by Bruegel; the painting became an allegory for Canetti of the struggle against fascism which formed the subject of his book *Masse und Macht* (Crowds and Power, 1960):

> I haven't found anyone *tired* of life in this painting. The dead wrest away from each person something he refuses to surrender voluntarily. The energy of this resistance, in hundreds of variations, flowed into me; and since then, I have often felt as if I were all these people fighting against death.... It is true that death triumphs here. But the struggle doesn't seem like a battle that has been fought once and for all. It keeps on being fought, again and again; and whatever the outcome here, by no means will it necessarily always be the same.[88]

Another of Canetti's most vivid experiences from the 1920s was the spectacle of Karl Kraus performing the ultimate apocalyptic drama, his 800-page play *Die letzten Tage der Menschheit* (The Last Days of Mankind), first completed in 1922. Kraus (1874–1936), variously described as 'the Isaiah of decaying old Europe or at least the Jewish Swift of Vienna',[89] was editor and sole author of *Die Fackel* (The Torch) from 1899 until his death. The play's flavour was captured by Walter Benjamin in 1931:

> In old engravings there is a messenger who rushes toward us crying aloud, his hair on end, brandishing a sheet of paper in his hands, a sheet full of war and pestilence, of cries of murder and pain, of danger from fire and flood, spreading everywhere the latest 'news'. News in this sense, in the sense that the word has in Shakespeare, is disseminated by *Die Fackel*. Full of betrayal, earthquakes, poison and the fire from the *mundus intelligibilis*.[90]

The Last Days of Mankind was written from the vantage-point of a mordant satirist for whom integrity of moral purpose could only be served by integrity of expression; he had ample command of Shakespearian and biblical rhetoric, with a delivery to match:

> When he read aloud from it, you were simply flabbergasted. No one stirred in the auditorium, you didn't dare breathe. He read all parts himself, profiteers and generals, the scoundrels and the poor wretches who were the victims of the war – they all sounded as genuine as if they were

standing in front of you. Anyone who had heard Kraus didn't want to go to the theater again, the theater was so boring compared with him; he was a whole theater by himself.[91]

But Kraus offered no hope for the future; in response to Adolf Loos's statement that Kraus 'stood at the frontier of a new age', Walter Benjamin countered: 'Alas by no means. He stands at the threshold of the Last Judgement.'[92]

'The apocalypse's re-inscription in modern ideological forms'[93] was one possibility for those who looked to drastic cultural and political change as a way forward, for which the Russian Revolution provided a kind of affirmation: 'Novels become reality. The leader of the revolutionary Navy Ministry is Rop-shin, the author of "The Pale Horse". He is the one who distributed 10,000 guns to the Maximalists.'[94] Much of the language and imagery, however, remained rooted in the past, even on the radical left; Ernst Bloch assumed a deliberately prophetic manner in his gestures and appearance, concluding his book on *The Spirit of Utopia* (1918), written in exile in Switzerland, with a chapter entitled 'Karl Marx, Death and the Apocalypse'. In 1921 followed Bloch's paean of praise to Thomas Müntzer, the early sixteenth-century Anabaptist rebel and leader of the Peasants' War, who was widely admired as a prophetic precursor of modern communism. His importance as an adversary to Luther and an exponent of a type of primitive Christianity was also seized upon by the left at a time when the legacy of the Reformation was being attacked as the culprit responsible for Prussian militarism and the worst aspects of bourgeois society in Wilhelmine Germany. Hugo Ball, one of the main detractors of the Protestant Reformation (he reverted to being a practising Catholic in 1920), recorded in 1917 how he 'had already written about Münzer in 1914 in Berlin. Since then I carry the engraving of him with me everywhere I go, and it is hanging in front of me as I write.'[95]

Germany's military defeat became the Apocalypse essential for cultural redemption. The final stage in the political radicalization of the *Jugendstil* artist and decorative designer Heinrich Vogeler was prompted by the negotiations leading up to the Treaty of Brest-Litovsk between Germany and the Russian Bolshevik government in March 1918. Vogeler was interned for two months in a lunatic asylum in Bremen after writing to the Kaiser in protest against the punitive conditions imposed on Russia, where he began work on his most overtly Expressionist work, the etching of *The Seven Vials of Wrath* (cat. 8). He took an active part in the November Revolution and in the short-lived Bremen Spartacist Republic in early 1919, subsequently turning his house in the artists' community at Worpswede into a workers' commune, then a home for the children of persecuted Communists after 1923, when he spent increasing amounts of time in Russia.

Attempts to ally Expressionist art with political revolution were pursued well into the postwar era by artists associated with the Novembergruppe in Berlin and its offshoot in Dresden, in which Meidner and Otto Dix were briefly involved. The playwright Ernst Toller (1893–1939) wrote his apocalyptic and redemptive drama from 1917 to early 1918 when he was confined to a military prison for his anti-war activities. *Transfiguration* was the expression of a fiercely committed political radicalism which condemned the author to several further years of imprisonment after the suppression of the Communist government in Bavaria at the end of the war. The play's satirical visions of 'the barracks of the dead' where the skeleton figures of 'Death by War' and 'Death by Peace' converse, and of a dance by the skeletons in No-man's Land, are eventually superseded by one of humanity vitalized and redeemed by love:

> The great cathedral of mankind arise;
> Through doors flung wide
> The youth of every nation marches singing
> Towards a crystal shrine.
> Dreams dazzle me –
> No misery, no war, no hatred left on earth.[96]

It was a vision that was cruelly traduced by events of the 1930s. Toller eventually committed suicide in America in 1939.

Lyonel Feininger's woodcut *Cathedral* was chosen by Walter Gropius in 1919 for the title-page of the programme for the Bauhaus in Weimar, because of its associations with utopian idealism. But Expressionism and utopian idealism were equally discredited in the eyes of others, who turned to irony and the absurdity of Dada to counter the spurious authority of a rhetorically inflated view of history and art. In Berlin, to which Dadaism was translated by Richard Huelsenbeck in 1917, it acquired an overtly political form of expression, particularly through the publishing house of Malik Verlag, run by Wieland Herzfelde and his brother John Heartfield, with which George Grosz was closely associated. Grosz himself denounced the 'old trappings of pious fraud: God and the Saints, plenty of cosmos and metaphysics, and some hefty blasts on the Trump of eternity'. 'To this day, some artistic revolutionaries are still depicting Christ and the Apostles, at a time when it is our duty to redouble our propaganda to purge the world of supernatural powers.'[97]

At its outset, though, in Zurich in 1916, Dadaism was a very eclectic affair and performances at the Cabaret Voltaire might unite 'all the styles of the last twenty years'.[98] One of the programmes in February 1916 described by Hugo Ball included poems by Kandinsky, the *Thundersong* by Wedekind and a 'Dance of Death' with the assistance of a revolutionary chorus. A month later, however, Hans Arp was attacking Franz Marc's bulls as 'too fat; Baumann's and Meidner's cosmogonies and mad fixed stars remind him of the stars of Bölsche and Carus.... He recommends plane geometry rather than painted versions of the Creation and Apocalypse.... He wants to purify the imagination and to concentrate on opening up not so much its store of images but what those images are made of.'[99]

Surrealism, with its species of 'profane illumination',[100] and predisposition in favour of primordial myth, revelation and esoteric knowledge, provided another medium for apocalyptic intimations (cat. 10). Among the many anti-rational approaches favoured by those who gravitated to Surrealism, albeit to challenge its assumptions further, was that of Georges Bataille, philosopher and librarian in the Cabinet des Médailles at the Bibliothèque Nationale in Paris. His article on one of the most famous Beatus manuscripts (see Ch. 3, cats 4–5), the Apocalypse of Saint-Sever, appeared in 1929 in *Documents*, the journal he directed for those 'excommunicated' from mainstream Surrealism by André Breton. In it he described 'the almost senile beatitude' of the figures in the face of unimaginable horror as akin to the impassivity of those who slaughter animals in modern abattoirs, another of his favoured images.[101] The impact of political events of the 1930s and 1940s emerged in a variety of allusive compositions executed in Europe and then in America by the community of émigré Surrealists based in New York, such as Max Ernst's *The Barbarians* (1937) and *Europe after the Rain* (1940–2).[102]

Of all the artists who managed to evade the charge of rhetorical inflation, Paul Klee was particularly esteemed for the ironical and jewel-like quality of his work contained within such a small compass: 'In an age of the colossus he falls in love with a green leaf, a star, a butterfly's wing, and since the heavens and all infinity are reflected in them to minute details, he paints those in too.'[103] Yet it was Klee's painting of the *Angelus Novus* that inspired the most famous rhetorical description of the dilemma facing humanity throughout the period between the wars and into the Second World War itself, the ninth of Walter Benjamin's 'Theses on the Philosophy of History'. The *Angelus Novus* becomes the angel of history with his face turned to the past, unable to see anything other than the endless repercussions of one great catastrophe which he longs to repair: 'But a storm is blowing from Paradise; it has got caught in his wings with such violence that the angel can no longer close them. This storm irresistibly propels him into the future to which his back is turned, while the pile of debris before him grows skyward. This storm is what we call progress.'[104] Benjamin's 'Theses' were completed just prior to his suicide in 1940. By then he understood all too well 'the negative theology in which the apocalypse is not an event in the past or future, but a constant presence where redemption is no longer manifested in the world of human affairs',[105] and Olivier Messiaen was soon to write *Quatuor pour la Fin du Temps* (Quartet for the End of Time) in a prisoner-of-war camp in Silesia, performed on broken instruments before an audience of 5,000 inmates in 1941.

Allegory was as important for articulating the response to the Second World War as it had been for the First, uniting tradition and modernity; it was a means of evading the direct representation of 'the banality of evil' which became a central preoccupation for the second half of the twentieth century. *Dr Faustus* (1947), described by its author as 'a strange aquarium of creatures of the Last Days',[106] was one of the most powerful examples of how traditional apocalyptic imagery retained its canonical force in relation to contemporary events. Thomas Mann wrote his allegory of Germany's pact with the devil, covering the period from the beginning of the twentieth century up to 1939, between 1943 and early 1947 when he was living in Los Angeles amidst a remarkable concentration of German intellectual and artistic life. These émigrés included the philosopher and musicologist Theodor Adorno, whose expert advice was critical to the novel. The tragedy of the narrative, 'in which the downfall of Germany is counterpointed by the catastrophe that draws ever and more balefully closer',[107] unfolds against the background of the war in Europe, the dropping of the atom bomb in Japan, the author's personal struggle with ill-health and the death of close friends. The main protagonist, the composer Adrian Leverkühn, is closely identified with Nietzsche, Mann's other source material including the Book of Revelation, Luther's letters and commentary on the Apocalypse, and the Dürer woodcuts. In deference to Adorno, the author decided that the central motif of the work, Leverkühn's *Apocalypse Oratorio*,

> must include within it the whole 'apocalyptic culture' and be made a kind of résumé of all proclamations of the end.... I was struck, as the text puts it, by the fact that a raving man should rave in the same pattern as another who came before him; that one is ecstatic not independently, so to speak, but by rote.... It coincided in a way with my own growing inclination, which as I discovered was not mine alone, to look upon all life as a cultural product taking the form of mythic clichés, and to prefer quotation to independent invention.[108]

Mann's observations above and their outcome in the novel summed up the whole trajectory of apocalyptic imagery, in which key works such as the Dürer *Apocalypse* and Michelangelo's *Last Judgement* serve as both an inspiration and a kind of containment to the 'vagrant fancy'[109] of successive generations. In *Dr Faustus* Leverkühn, while working on his decisive choral composition, the *Apocalypse Oratorio*, in the summer of 1919, undergoes a creative mental torment whose visual counterpart is found in the image of St John being martyred in the cauldron of oil with which the Dürer *Apocalypse* begins (Ch. 4, cats 5–20):

> Into it [the whole tradition of eschatological literature] Adrian spun himself round like a cocoon, to stimulate himself for a work which should gather up all their elements into one single focus, assemble them in one pregnant, portentous synthesis and in relentless transmission hold up to humanity the mirror of the revelation, that it might see therein what is oncoming and near at hand... so that his work amounts to the creation of a new and independent Apocalypse, a sort of résumé of the whole literature. The title, *Apocalypsis cum figuris*, is in homage to Dürer and is intended to emphasize the visual and actualizing, the graphic character, the minuteness, the saturation, in short, of space with fantastically exact detail.... But it is far from being the case that Adrian's mammoth fresco follows the Nuremberger's fifteen illustrations in any programmatic

sense…. Leverkühn's tone-picture draws much from Dante's poem; and still more from that crowded wall, swarming with bodies, where here angels perform staccato on trumpets of destruction, there Charon's bark unloads its freight, the dead rise, saints pray, daemonic masks await the nod of the serpent-wreathed Minos, the damned man, voluptuous in flesh, clung round, carried and drawn by grinning sons of the pit, makes horrid descent, covering one eye with his hand and with the other staring transfixed with horror into the bottomless perdition; while not far off Grace draws up two sinning souls from the snare into redemption – in short, from the groups and the scenic structure of the Last Judgement.[110]

NOTES

1 Anson Rabinbach, *In the Shadow of Catastrophe. German Intellectuals between Apocalypse and Enlightenment*, Berkeley, Los Angeles and London 1997, p.6.

2 Quoted in Frank Kermode, *The Sense of An Ending*, Oxford 1967, p.167.

3 Andrei Bely, *Petersburg*, first published 1916, trans. David McDuff, Harmondsworth 1995, p.358.

4 T.S. Eliot, *The Complete Poems and Plays*, London 1970, p.86.

5 Quoted from a sermon given by John Donne in 1622 in *John Donne*, ed. John Carey, Oxford 1990, p.310.

6 The translation is by Norman Shapiro from *Selected Poems from Les Fleurs du Mal*, Chicago 1998, with engravings by David Schorr (b. 1947), much of whose work has been concerned with Aids. I am grateful to Mary Ryan of the Mary Ryan Gallery in New York for drawing this publication to my attention.

7 See *Les Fleurs du Mal*, ed. A. Adam, Paris 1970, p.390.

8 See *The Painter of Modern Life and Other Essays*, ed. and trans. Jonathan Mayne, London 1995, pp.206–7. For further information on the Rethel series see Karl-Ludwig Hofmann and Christmut Präger, 'Die Revolution als Totentanz – Alfred Rethels "Auch ein Todtentanz" von 1849', in Friedrich Kasten (ed.), *Totentanz. Kontinuität und Wandel eines Bildthemas vom Mittelalter bis heute*, Baden-Baden 1987, pp.27–41. The most recent study of the theme as a whole is Karl Guthke, *The Gender of Death. A Cultural History in Art and Literature*, Cambridge 1999.

9 Anabaptist fanaticism appeared in another guise as the subject of one of Strindberg's early plays, *Master Olof* of 1872 (it was not performed until 1881; in 1890 a verse version enjoyed considerable success), about a fictitious Swedish counterpart to Luther who is urged on to defiance of both the Catholic Church and the monarchy by an Anabaptist with the name of Gert Bookprinter; Olof eventually recants when disaster overtakes them but Bookprinter remains unrepentant.

10 See Samuel Clapp, 'Voyage au pays des mythes', in *Gustave Doré 1832–1883*, Musée d'Art Moderne, Strasbourg 1983.

11 Jules Michelet, *Oeuvres Complètes*, ed. Paul Viallaneix, Paris 1978, VII, p.303.

12 Quoted in Albert Elsen, *Rodin*, London 1974, p.35.

13 Schnitzler's controversial play *Reigen* (later made into the film *La Ronde*), written in 1897 and privately published in 1900, was another of the many *fin-de-siècle* treatments of the Dance of Death. It did not receive its first complete public performance in Vienna until 1920. For a detailed study of the genre see Franz Link (ed.), *Tanz und Tod in Kunst und Literatur*, Berlin 1993.

14 John Ruskin, *Praeterita*, London 1885, I, pp.2–3 and 49.

15 John Ruskin, *Storm Cloud of the Nineteenth Century*, London 1884, pp.61–2.

16 ibid, p.48.

17 Emile Zola, *The Debacle*, trans. Leonard Hancock, Harmondsworth 1972, pp.485–6.

18 Emile Zola, *The Masterpiece*, trans. Thomas Walton, rev. Robin Pearson, Oxford 1993, pp.421–2.

19 J.-K. Huysmans, *Against Nature*, trans. Margaret Mauldon, Oxford 1998, p.53.

20 Quoted from a review of 1884 in Ted Gott, *The Enchanted Stone: The Graphic Worlds of Odilon Redon*, National Gallery of Victoria, Melbourne 1990, p.13.

21 For a discussion of *Là-Bas* see Marjorie Reeves and Warwick Gould, 'Joris-Karl Huysmans and the Vintrasian Cult of the Paraclete', in *Joachim of Fiore and the Myth of the Eternal Evangel*, Oxford 1987, pp.186–201.

22 Huysmans, op. cit. (n.19), p.187.

23 Friedrich Nietzsche, *Twilight of the Idols. The Anti-Christ*, trans. R.J. Hollingdale, Harmondsworth 1972, p.150.

24 *The Essential Jung. Selected Writings*, introduced by Anthony Storr, London 1983, p.245.

25 D.H. Lawrence, *Apocalypse*, first published in Florence 1931; London 1981, p.10.

26 Nietzsche, op. cit. (n.23), p.74.

27 Quoted in Sarah O'Brien Twohig, 'Dix and Nietzsche', in *Otto Dix 1891–1969*, Tate Gallery, London 1992, p.41.

28 Friedrich Nietzsche, *Thus spoke Zarathustra*, trans. R.J. Hollingdale, Harmondsworth 1969, p.215.

29 ibid, p.214.

30 ibid, p.216.

31 27 March 1915, 'I cook water for myself and read a little in Zarathustra or the New Testament'. *Max Beckmann. Self-*

Portrait in Words. Collected Writings and Statements, 1903-1950, ed. Barbara Copeland Buenger, Chicago and London 1997, p.155.

32 Klaus Lankheit and Uwe Steffen (eds), *Letters from the War by Franz Marc,* trans. Liselotte Dieckmann, New York 1992, p.40.

33 Twohig, op.cit. (n.27), pp. 40–7.

34 Hermann Hesse, *If the War Goes On,* trans. Ralph Manheim, London 1985, p.77.

35 Tamara Karsavina, *Theatre Street,* London 1988, p.38. I would like to thank Jenny Stratford for mentioning this reference to me.

36 See Renata Ulmer, *Passion und Apokalypse. Studien zur biblischen Thematik in der Kunst des Expressionismus,* Europäische Hochschulschriften, 144, Frankfurt 1992, p.48.

37 *The Book of Hours* trans. Stevie Krayer, Salzburg Studies in English Literature. Poetic Drama and Poetic Theory 132, 1995.

38 For a discussion of apocalypticism in Russian fiction see David Bethea, *The Shape of the Apocalypse in Modern Russian Fiction,* Princeton, New Jersey, 1989 and Bernard McGinn's section on 'Russian Writers and Antichrist' in *Antichrist,* New York 1994, pp.263–9. See also Will Ryan, 'The Number of the Beast', in *The Bathhouse at Midnight: An Historical Survey of Magic and Divination in Russia,* Stroud 1999, pp.6–8.

39 Marc, *Letters,* op. cit. (n.32), p.15.

40 *The Blaue Reiter Almanac. New Documentary Edition,* ed. Klaus Lankheit, London 1974, p.252.

41 Quoted from *Rückblicke* (Reminiscences) of 1913 in Reeves and Gould, op. cit. (n.21), pp.39–40. On Kandinsky's idea of the Third Revelation see also Sixten Ringbom, *The Sounding Cosmos,* Helsinki 1970, pp.173–9.

42 Reeves and Gould, op. cit. (n.21), p.168.

43 'War, the World's only Hygiene' in *Marinetti. Selected Writings,* ed. and trans. R.W. Flint, London 1972, p.68.

44 Paul Fussell, *The Great War and Modern Memory,* Oxford and London 1975, p.4.

45 *Flight out of Time. A Dada Diary by Hugo Ball,* ed. John Elderfield, Berkeley, Los Angeles and London 1996, p.43.

46 Henri Focillon, *L'An Mil,* Paris 1952, pp.63–4.

47 See Stephanie Barron, *Exiles and Emigrés. The Flight of European Artists from Hitler,* Los Angeles County Art Museum 1997, p.143.

48 Isaac Rosenberg, *Dead Man's Dump,* 1917, in *The Collected Works of Isaac Rosenberg,* ed. Ian Parsons, London 1979, p.110.

49 *The Essential Jung,* op. cit. (n.24), p.77.

50 *The Essential Jung,* op. cit. (n.24), p.78.

51 Halley's Comet had appeared over parts of Germany in 1910. The significance of such phenomena was heightened, not surprisingly, during the war itself. Religious leaders in London who had announced a day of prayer for 21 August 1914 feared that the coincidence of this with an eclipse of the sun, which could be partially seen from Greenwich, might occasion panic in the doomladen atmosphere of the period immediately following the declaration of war (Thomas Crump, *Solar Eclipse,* London 1999, p.189). Franz Marc asked his wife in October 1914 whether she had observed 'the war comet' that he had seen at Strasbourg (*Letters,* op. cit. (n.32), p.9).

52 Quoted in *Georg Trakl: Selected Poems,* London 1968, ed. Christopher Middleton, p.7.

53 These were first performed in 1968. An instrumental piece of the same period was *Antechrist* (sic), based on a thirteenth-century motet.

54 On this aspect of the literary background see Michael Hamburger, *A Proliferation of Prophets. Essays in German Literature from Nietzsche to Brecht,* Manchester 1983.

55 Nietzsche, op. cit. (n.23), p.72.

56 *Ludwig Meidner. Zeichner, Maler, Literat 1884–1966,* ed. Gerda Breuer and Ines Wagemann, 2 vols, Darmstadt 1991, vol. 2 pp.334–5.

57 Ball, op. cit. (n.45), p.5.

58 *Ludwig Meidner,* op. cit. (n.56), II, p.292.

59 Bethea, op. cit. (n.38), p.45.

60 Hamburger, op. cit. (n.54), p.193.

61 Frank Whitford, *The Berlin of George Grosz. Drawings, Watercolours and Prints 1912–1930,* New Haven and Royal Academy of Arts, London, 1997, p.6.

62 Oswald Spengler, *Decline of the West,* London 1971, p.32. In 1934 Grosz provided a satirical drawing of 'Spengler: Out of the capitalistic swamp he comes' for the frontispiece to *Modern Monthly,* one of the most important publications in American Marxist circles.

63 The 1926 film *Berlin: Symphony of a City* was one notable example.

64 *The Complete Poems and Plays of T.S. Eliot,* p.62 from 'The Burial of the Dead' and p.73 from 'What the Thunder said'.

65 See Paul Fussell on the response to this landscape, op.cit. (n.44), pp.135–44.

66 *Beckmann,* op. cit. (n.31), p.155.

67 *Beckmann,* op. cit. (n.31), p.159.

68 Quoted from one of Beckmann's letters to his wife in Charles Werner Haxthausen, 'Beckmann and the First World War' in *Max Beckmann. Retrospective,* ed. Carla Schultz-Hoffmann and Judith Weiss, Munich, New York and London 1984, p.76.

69 ibid., quoted from Beckmann's *Creative Confession,* 1920, in Wolf-Dieter Dube, 'On the "Resurrection"', p.81.

70 Wilhelm Worringer, *Form in Gothic,* ed. Herbert Read, London 1927, p.178.

71 ibid., p.181.

72 Joseph Koerner, *The Moment of Self-Portraiture in German Renaissance Art,* Chicago and London 1993, p.122.

73 Ball, op. cit. (n.45), p.135.

74 Elias Canetti, *The Torch in My Ear,* London 1990, p.230.

75 ibid., p.233. On the reception of the Isenheim Altar see Andrée Hayum, *The Isenheim Altarpiece. God's Medicine and the Painter's Vision,* Princeton 1989; Ann Stieglitz, 'The Reproduction of Agony: toward a Reception-History of Grünewald's Isenheim Altar after the First World War', *The Oxford Art Journal,* 12, No.2 1989, pp.87–103, and Sylvie Lecoq-Raymond and François-René Martin, 'L'Allemagne d'Otto Dix et Grünewald. Une anthologie d'écrits de langue allemande (1891–1938)', in *Otto Dix et Les Maîtres Anciens,* Colmar 1996, pp.130–55.

76 See Geoffrey Skelton (ed. and trans.), *Selected Letters of Paul Hindemith,* New Haven and London 1995.

77 Henri Barbusse, *Under Fire. The Story of a Squad,* trans. Fitzwater Wray, London 1926, p.5.

78 ibid., p.322. See also Jay Winter, *Sites of Memory. Sites of Mourning,* Cambridge 1995, pp.178–86.

79 Barbusse, op. cit. (n.77), p.343.

80 Barbusse, op. cit. (n.77), p.344.

81 See Richard Cork, *A Bitter Truth: Avant-Garde Art and the Great War,* New Haven and London 1994, pp.306–7.

82 Frans Masereel, *Passionate Journey. A Novel told in 165 Woodcuts,* with an introduction by Thomas Mann, Harmondsworth 1988.

83 Romain Rolland, *La Révolte des Machines,* Paris 1947, p.12.

84 See Winter, op. cit. (n.78), pp.20–1.

85 The conceit of a possible film programme on 'The End of the World' appears again among the manuscripts of the lunatic Moravagine, who, in Cendrars's novel of the same name (1926), believes he has visited 'Mars'.

86 Marc, *Letters*, op. cit. (n.32), p.34.

87 See Kasten, op. cit. (n.8). In 1991 the Imperial War Museum in London held an exhibition from their own collection entitled *Dance of Death. Images of Mortality in European Graphics of the First World War*, accompanied by a leaflet. Richard Oswald's film *Uncanny Tales* (1919) and Fritz Lang's *Der müde Tod* (Tired Death, 1921) are other examples of the genre.

88 Canetti, op. cit. (n.74), pp.115–16.

89 Peter Demetz in Walter Benjamin, *Reflections*, ed. Peter Demetz, trans. Edmund Jephcott, New York 1978, p.xxxv.

90 Benjamin, op. cit., p.239.

91 Canetti, op. cit. (n.74), p.66.

92 Benjamin, op. cit. (n.89), p.254. On Kraus see also Steven Beller, 'The tragic carnival: Austrian culture in the First World War', in *European Culture in the Great War*, ed. Aviel Roshwald and Richard Stiles, Cambridge 1999, pp.150–4.

93 Rabinbach, op. cit. (n.1), p.7.

94 Ball, op. cit. (n.45), p.136. V. Ropshin (1879–1925?) published *The Pale Horse* in 1909 (Eng. trans. 1917) and became prominent in the struggle against the Bolsheviks after October 1917. *The Pale Horse*, a novel written in diary form which begins with quotations from Revelation 6: 8 and John II, 11, 'contains the tragedy of every individual conscience in Russia possessed by

the necessity of violent political action and the equally strong religious objections to it' (1917 edn p.vi).

95 Ball, op. cit. (n.45), p.138.

96 Ernst Toller, *Seven Plays*, trans. Edward Crankshaw, London 1935, p.98.

97 From texts published in 1920–1, quoted in Whitford, op. cit. (n.61), pp.34–5.

98 Ball, op. cit. (n.45), p.57.

99 Ball, op. cit. (n.45), p.53.

100 'Surrealism' (first published in 1929) in Benjamin, op. cit. (n.89), p.179.

101 *Documents* I, 1929 (1991 reprint), p.78.

102 For a discussion of these works see Sabine Eckmann, 'Surrealism in exile: responses to the European destruction of humanism', in *Exiles and Emigrés*, op. cit. (n.47), pp.148–82.

103 Eckmann, op. cit., p.103.

104 Walter Benjamin, *Illuminations*, ed. Hannah Arendt, trans. Harry Zorn, London 1999, p.249.

105 Rabinbach, op. cit. (n.1), p.9.

106 Thomas Mann, *The Genesis of a Novel*, trans. Richard and Clara Winston, London 1961, p.162.

107 Mann, op. cit., p.107.

108 Mann, op. cit., p.30.

109 Meric Casaubon, *A Treatise Concerning Enthusiasm. A facsimile reproduction of the second edition of 1656*, Gainesville, 1970.

110 Thomas Mann, *Dr Faustus*, London 1996, pp.356–8.

I Odilon Redon (1840–1916)

The Apocalypse of St John, 1899

Three plates from an album of twelve lithographs and illustrated cover, printed by Blanchard and published by Ambroise Vollard in Paris in an edition of 100

Lit: André Mellerio, *Odilon Redon*, Paris 1913, nos 173–85

London, British Museum. Bequeathed by Campbell Dodgson

The Apocalypse of St John was the last of an extraordinary run of lithographic albums executed by Redon over a period of twenty years, which had begun in 1879 with *Dans le Rêve* (Dreaming), with a view to creating a wider audience for his charcoal drawings. After the occultism with which his imagery had been closely associated throughout the 1880s, much of Redon's work in the 1890s evinced a more ethereal idealism. *The Apocalypse of St John* attempted to recapture, with only partial success, some of the dark, visionary intensity of earlier series such as the three linked to Flaubert's *Temptation of St Anthony* (1879, 1889 and 1895), but within the context of the Christian canon. The parallel with Dürer's woodcuts was quite deliberate, forming part of a pattern of reference to Redon's admired artistic forebears, of which the most notable example was his album of 1885, *Homage to Goya*. Reverence for the prints of Rembrandt and

Dürer had been instilled in Redon by his most influential teacher, Rodolphe Bresdin, of whom he wrote in *A Soi-Même*, his journal for the years 1867–1915: 'When it is properly understood, archaism is a sanction. The work of art descends directly from another work'(Paris 1961, p.167).

The commission from Vollard for *The Apocalypse* came at the zenith of the lithographic revival in Paris, yet apart from a small number of individual subjects dating from 1900 to 1908, mainly portraits, it was to be Redon's last work in this medium before he concentrated on more decorative compositions in pastel. None the less he remained assiduous in cultivating his reputation as a printmaker, entrusting the compilation of the catalogue raisonné of his prints in 1898 to André Mellerio, one of the foremost champions of original lithography, who completed the publication in 1913. Redon continued to concern himself with the promotion of his graphic work through adroitly placed gifts, an example of this being the presentation of a copy of *The Apocalypse* in 1902 to the Symbolist poet Adrien Mithouard, who was also president of the Municipal Council for Paris (see Roseline Bacou (ed.), *Lettres de Gauguin, Gide, Huysmans, Jammes, Mallarmé, Verhaeren à Odilon Redon*, Paris 1960, pp.290–1).

a. Plate III: '...and his name that sat on the Pale Horse was Death' (Rev. 6: 8)

Lithograph on chine appliqué, image size 309 × 225 mm

Lit: Mellerio 176

1949-4-11-3563

As with the albums based on Flaubert's *Temptation of St Anthony*, Redon has chosen only those subjects from the Book of Revelation that appealed to his imagination. The figure of Death, with the powerful diagonal thrust of its elongated sword, is based on Dürer's dynamic figure of St Michael spearing the dragon, in the woodcut of this subject (Ch. 4, cat. 16. See the comparison made in Ted Gott, *The Enchanted Stone: The Graphic Worlds of Odilon Redon*, National Gallery of Victoria, Melbourne 1990, nos 17 and 18, p.76).

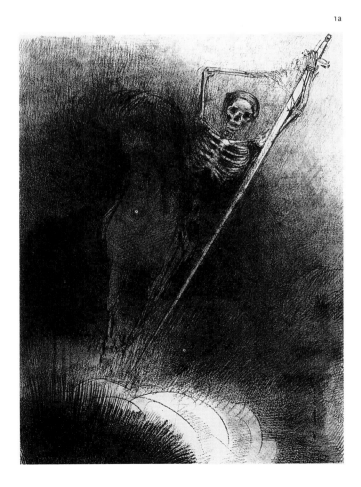

1a

b. Plate VI: '...a Woman Clothed with the Sun' (Rev. 12: 1)

Lithograph on chine appliqué, 288 × 230mm

Lit: Mellerio 179

1949-4-11-3568

The juxtaposition of a feminine head in profile against a radiance or aureole of light was one of Redon's most common motifs in the 1890s, which he has adapted for his interpretation of 'the Woman Clothed with the Sun'.

c. Plate IX: '...and bound him for a thousand years' (Rev. 20: 2)

Lithograph on chine appliqué, 299 × 210mm

Lit: Mellerio 182

1949-4-11-3571

The satanic menace of this wonderfully sinuous form is reminiscent of a lithograph of 1890, *Serpent Halo*, which was admired by Huysmans when he was working on *Là-Bas* (Down There, 1892; see pp.275–6). In both cases the imagery harks back to the artist's earlier preoccupation with satanic subjects, but with the important distinction that for *The Apocalypse* it is sanctioned by the scriptural text. Redon has chosen to emphasize the description of Satan as 'that old serpent' rather than as a dragon in the passage from Revelation. The angel who 'came down from heaven, having the key of the bottomless pit and a great chain in his hand' (Rev. 20: 1) is the subject of the preceding lithograph in the series.

1b

1c

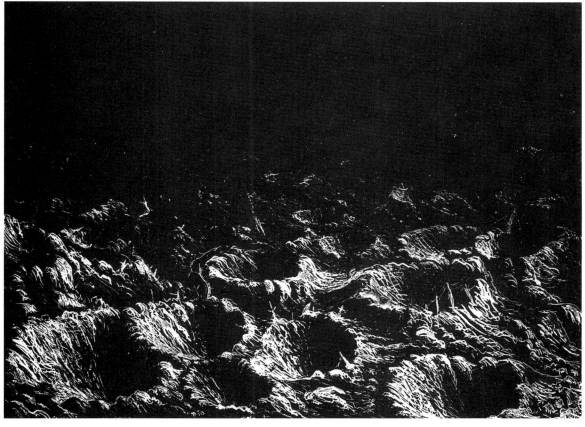

9a

9b

9 Otto Dix (1891–1969)

Der Krieg (War), 1924

Four plates from the set of fifty published in five portfolios by Karl
Nierendorf, Berlin, in an edition of seventy

Lit: John Willett, 'Dix: War', in *Disasters of War. Callot, Goya, Dix*,
South Bank Centre 1998, pp.59–75; Richard Cork, *A Bitter Truth.
Avant-garde Art and the Great War*, New Haven and London 1994,
pp.272–9; *Otto Dix 1891–1969*, Tate Gallery, London 1992,
pp.151–5, cat. 79; Carey and Griffiths, 1984 (repr. 1993), pp.183–92,
cats 157–86

London, British Museum

Dix's graphic cycle has left an indelible impression of the
horrors of war from a twentieth-century perspective,
achieving canonical status among the images that have
served to define all subsequent experience of such
phenomena. It was immediately preceded by his
controversial painting *The Trench* of 1920–3, which, after its
repudiation and return by the Wallraf-Richartz Museum in
Cologne, was lent by Dix to the touring exhibition *Never
another War* to mark the tenth anniversary of the outbreak of
the First World War. 1924 was designated as International
Anti-War Year, and Dix's publisher for *Der Krieg*, Karl
Nierendorf, was at the forefront of those who sought to
counteract the kind of sentiments with which Ernst Toller

equipped his brutish showman in *Hinckemann. A Tragedy in Three Acts* (1921–2). 'German heroism! German culture! German virility! German strength!' are supposedly embodied in the repellent spectacle of the emasculated Hinckemann devouring live rats and mice, who none the less is told: 'In that case you must see that nobody's thinking about the war. Put on a "Horrors of War" show and you won't make a penny today' (J.M. Ritchie (ed.), *Vision and Aftermath. 4 Expressionist War Plays*, London 1969, pp.175 and 191).

The shortage of capital and the collapse of the print market in Germany after the stabilization of the Mark at the end of 1923 were probably responsible for wrecking the sales of the main portfolio set of *Der Krieg*; however, it achieved widespread impact through a touring exhibition to fifteen German cities and through the book edition, which contained twenty-four reproductions, with an introduction by Henri Barbusse (see pp.285–6). 1500 of the latter were ordered by trade unions for their anti-war day in 1924, and Nierendorf circulated hundreds of copies to the press, writers, pacifists and human rights societies. In the late 1930s the work of Dix and Grosz was among the most comprehensively purged of all the artists and part of the 1937 *Entartete Kunst* (Degenerate Art) exhibition was the Berlin Print Room's complete set of *Der Krieg*.

Before embarking upon this project, Dix undertook a period of intensive study in etching techniques in order to achieve a mastery equal to the varieties of mortal and moral decay that he sought to express. The numerous Expressionist drawings made while he served almost continuously throughout the war, as an infantryman and then towards the end, in training for the air force, must have served to prompt some of the imagery that emerged in *Der Krieg*. They lacked, however, the pitiless realism of the prints themselves, which were more immediately influenced by the skulls that Dix drew in the catacombs of Palermo in the winter of 1923, and the specially enlarged photographs of disfigured corpses which were also used in Ernst Friedrich's anti-war publication, *Krieg dem Kriege* (1924). Dix's notable art-historical antecedents were, of course, in the graphic series of Callot and Goya which, among other sources, he knew from books such as Wilhelm Michel's *Das Teuflische und Groteske in der Kunst* (The Devilish and the Grotesque in Art), published in Munich by Reinhard Piper in 1911. The legacy of Dix's series continues to reverberate through the only graphic cycle of comparable ambition to have appeared in recent years, the eighty-three etchings by Jake and Dinos Chapman published in 1999 and called *The Disasters of War* after Goya (fig. 5).

a. Plate 4: *Field of Shell Craters near Dontrien lit up by Flares*
Etching printed in relief, 193 × 254mm
1982-7-24-28 (4)

Dix was much taken with the white line woodcuts of Urs Graf (1485–1527) which he saw in the collection of the Kunstmuseum in Basel. They must have influenced his choice of technique for conveying this ghostly landscape, like the surface of the moon or 'the abomination of desolation' spoken of in the Gospel of St Mark: 'But when ye shall see the abomination of desolation, spoken of by Daniel the prophet, standing where it ought not,... then let them that be in Judea flee to the mountains' (Mark 13: 14), one of the signs preceding the End, which shall be heralded by 'the beginnings of sorrows' when 'nation shall rise against nation' (Mark 13: 8).

b. Plate 16: *Corpse in Barbed Wire (Flanders)*
Etching and aquatint, 293 × 247mm
1982-7-24-28 (16)

Fig.5. Jake and Dinos Chapman, plate from *Disasters of War* (1999), set of 83 etchings. London, British Museum.

opening words of the Johannine Gospel had previously been used by Beckmann in the central panel of his *Temptation* triptych of 1936/7, in which the figure of St Anthony is equated with the artist, whose gifts confer upon him special powers of visionary understanding. The triptych was displayed at the New Burlington Galleries in 1938, when Beckmann's one and only visit to London was chiefly remarkable, from his point of view, for the William Blake material that he saw on display at the Tate Gallery.

b. Page 71: 'And God shall wipe away all tears from their eyes; and there shall be no more death, neither sorrow nor crying, neither shall there be any more pain' (Rev. 21: 4)

332 × 263 mm

This beautiful consolatory passage had inspired some of the most moving images in medieval art (see p.60). Beckmann has depicted himself as one of the recipients of divine compassion, while the view through the encircling rainbow behind the angel's head is of 'the new heaven and the new earth'.

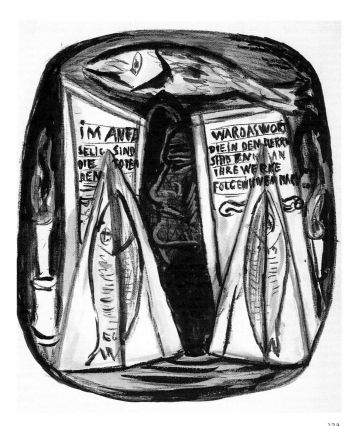

12a

12b

13 Benton Spruance (1904–67)

Riders of the Apocalypse, 1943

Lithograph, 325 × 420 mm. Signed and dated, inscribed with title and 'ed.30' (the catalogue raisonné gives the edition size as thirty-five)

Lit: Ruth Fine and Robert Looney, *The Prints of Benton Spruance*, Philadelphia 1986, p.222; Lloyd M. Abernethy, *Benton Spruance. The Artist and the Man*, Philadelphia, London and Toronto 1988

London, British Museum 1998-4-26-5

Spruance's *Riders of the Apocalypse* is one of the strongest images in a modernist idiom to emerge from the Second World War. The artist was one of a notable group of Philadelphia artists during the 1930s who chose printmaking, especially lithography, as their preferred means of expression, because of the 'democratic' nature of the medium and its relative ease of multiplication. Spruance first experimented with lithography at the Atelier Desjobert in Paris in the summer of 1928; from then on he became a tireless promoter of the medium in his capacity as an exhibiting artist and teacher, collaborating with the German-born printer Theodore Cuno, who printed his stones. His most successful compositions before the war were urban or sporting subjects, but in 1939 he executed three prints filled with a darker foreboding, known as *The Thirties*, *Windshield*, *Graduation* and *Requiem*. In the first of these the driver's view ahead through the windshield is of a landscape filled with the horror of war, while the rear mirror shows a peaceful rural scene from the past.

Spruance strongly supported American intervention in World War II and volunteeered for active service, but was

13

rejected on medical grounds. As well as *Riders of the Apocalypse*, his lithographs that made overt reference to the war include *Air Raid* (1941), *Souvenir of Lidice* (1942), *Credo 1, 2, 3* (1943) and *Fathers and Sons* (1943); the last of these shows soldiers fighting across terrain beneath which are clearly visible the skeletons of their predecessors from the First World War. By the end of the war he had abandoned his previous style, which alternated between a quasi-abstract modernism and social realism, in favour of a more metaphysical approach; this emerged in a group of five prints made in 1945–6 of subjects taken from Ecclesiastes, a modern interpretation of the vanities.

14 Edouard Goerg (1893–1969)

L'Apocalypse, 1945

Four plates from a portfolio of twenty lithographs published in Paris by Jacques Haumont in an edition of 198. The text was printed by Jacques Haumont and the images by Desjobert, completed on 25 June 1945. The British Museum's copy, which comes from the artist's estate, is numbered III from the set of forty reserved for the collaborators in the project

Each of the images measures 346 × 250mm

Lit: the only monographs are Gaston Diehl, *Edouard Goerg*, Paris

1947, and Waldemar George, *Goerg*, Paris 1947. I am grateful to my colleague Stephen Coppel for making available to me information that he has compiled from various sources, including the artist's son-in-law

London, British Museum

a. Plate III: 'And he had in his hand seven stars: and out of his mouth went a sharp two-edged sword' (Rev. 1: 16).1997-12-7-6 (3)

b. Plate XI: 'And there fell a great star from heaven, burning as it were a lamp' (Rev. 8: 10). 1997-12-7-6 (11)

c. Plate XIV: 'The beast that ascendeth out of the bottomless pit shall make war against them, and shall overcome them, and kill them' (Rev. 11: 7). 1997-12-7-6 (14)

d. Plate XX: 'And I John saw the holy city, new Jerusalem, coming down from God out of heaven' (Rev. 21: 2). 1997-12-7-6 (20)

From the mid-1930s Edouard Goerg developed a surreal, visionary style of painting and etching which was indebted to an eclectic array of influences, from the work he had seen by Bosch and Bruegel on a visit to Belgium and Holland in 1934, to Bresdin, Redon and Ensor. His most remarkable suites of prints were produced during and immediately after the war when he was appointed professor of printmaking at the Ecole des Beaux-Arts in Paris in 1946. The *Apocalypse* represented Goerg's first use of lithography, which he embarked upon during a period of acute personal difficulty between 1943 and 1945. His involvement with the Resistance

14a

14b

14c

14d

put him in a vulnerable position throughout the German Occupation of Paris (he was one of the main protagonists behind a clandestine album of anti-Nazi lithographs entitled *Vaincre*), but a much greater cause of anxiety was his wife, who on account of her Jewish birth had to remain in hiding with their daughter. She suffered from prolonged illness, eventually dying from cancer in February 1944; this precipitated a severe depression in Goerg, who resorted to a course of electric shock treatment ending in 1946.

The idiosyncratic imagery of the Apocalypse series, and the etchings that he made for the *Book of Job* from 1944 to 1946, must have reflected some of his inner despair as well as evoking, once again, the phantasmagoria associated with the artists mentioned above as among his principal sources. Another major illustrated work brought to fruition between 1943 and 1948 was the first volume of *Les Fleurs du Mal*. Thereafter he never attained the surreal intensity of either the immediately pre-war compositions or the wartime illustrations.

15

15 Jacob Pins (b. 1917)

Dance of Death, 1945

The order of subjects is as follows, starting with the central image then moving anti-clockwise from the top left-hand corner:

1. *The Horsemen of the Apocalypse*
2. *Death and the Maiden*
3. *The Murder*
4. *The Glutton*
5. *The Executioner*
6. *The Blind Man*
7. *The Dancer*
8. *The Beggar*
9. *The Angel of Death*
10. *The Sick Man*
11. *The Wrestler*
12. *The Fear of Death*
13. *The Whip of Death*

Woodcut and wood-engraving, 483 × 383 mm; signed, dated and numbered 3/20 in graphite below

Lit: *Pins: Woodcuts 1942–1985*, The Israel Museum, Jerusalem 1985, no.24

London, British Museum 1991-10-5-60

Jacob Pins emigrated from Germany to Palestine in 1936, studying in Jerusalem from 1941 to 1945 under Jacob Steinhardt (1884–1968), one of the artists associated with *The New Pathos* in Berlin (see cat. 2) who shared the exhibition of *Neo-Pathetiker* at the Sturm Galerie in Berlin in November 1912 with Ludwig Meidner and Richard Janthur. Pins has worked exclusively in the woodcut medium since 1942, printing all his impressions himself. The *Dance of Death* and the *Apocalypse* series that followed in 1946 clearly reflected his roots in the tradition of German graphic art, as well as providing an appropriate testament of the times. The series were conceived as a response to the Holocaust; in order to avoid the banality of casting them in a contemporary setting, Pins resorted instead to a deliberately allegorizing manner which evoked their sixteenth-century as well as their earlier twentieth-century antecedents. (I should like to thank the artist for information in connection with this entry.)

16 Jacob Pins (b. 1917)

The Apocalypse, 1946

Two woodcuts from a series of five, 340 × 430 mm; signed, dated and numbered 15/20 in graphite below

Lit: *Pins: Woodcuts 1942–1985*, The Israel Museum, Jerusalem 1985, nos 40.2 and 40.3

London, British Museum

a. *The Subject, 1st variation: The Plague*

1991-10-5-63

b. *2nd variation: The War*

1991-10-5-64

In the sequence of subjects, the two images shown here are preceded by *Preface – The Horses* then followed by *3rd variation: The Horse of Death* and *Conclusion: View of Apocalyptical City*. The artist has chosen to omit both the riders of the biblical narrative and one of the four horses.

16a

16b

17 Misch Kohn (b. 1916)

Death Rides a Dark Horse, 1949

Wood-engraving, 600 × 398 mm; signed and dated in graphite and inscribed with the title

Lit: Jo Farb Hernandez, *Misch Kohn. Beyond the Tradition*, Monterey Museum of Art 1998, no.132

London, British Museum 1998-11-8-17. Presented by the artist

This composition was one of the first large-scale wood-engravings that Kohn made, shortly after he had accepted a position at the Institute of Design in Chicago under the direction of Serge Chermayeff. The particular inspiration for the subject was a folksong of Flemish origin, dating from the Thirty Years War of the early seventeenth century; Kohn's wife, whose family had been among the last Jews allowed to leave Germany in 1939, had learnt the ballad in childhood and used to sing it to the accompaniment of a lute or guitar:

Death rides on a coal-black horse
He wears an invisible cap;
When the Landsknecht march into the field
He lets his horse gallop next to them
Refrain:
Flanders in misery
In Flanders Death is riding

Death rides on a light horse
Beautiful, like a cherub from heaven.
When girls march in their singing games
He goes along with them in the dance

Death can also beat the drum
You can hear the drumbeat in your heart
He drums long and he drums loud.
He drums on a skin of death
[Refrain]
When he beat the first drumbeat,

17

Blood ran off from his heart.
And when he beat the second time
The Landsknecht was carried to his grave.

The third drumbeat went so long
Until the Landsknecht received from God his blessing
The third drumbeat is soft and light
As if a mother were rocking her baby to sleep
[Refrain]
Death can ride black horses and white horses,
Death can step along smiling with the dances,
He drums hard and he drums soft.
Die, die, die you must.

(I would like to thank Lore Kohn for supplying the translation of this song and Misch Kohn and Jo Farb Hernandez for their assistance with this entry.)

When Kohn embarked upon his large-scale wood-engravings in 1948–9, his work responded to a broad swathe of traditions ranging from late fifteenth- and sixteenth-century northern European art – Grünewald, Bruegel, Bosch – to German Expressionism and the influence of the Mexican muralists, in order to convey the predicament of mankind in the immediate post-war era. He had been closely involved with the Mexican artistic community from 1943 to 1944, assisting at the radical print workshop *Taller de Grafica Popular* in Mexico City, in the reprinting of earlier woodcuts and engravings, such as those of José Guadalupe Posada

(1852–1913). Posada's name was principally connected with the satirical broadsheets or *Calaveras* (literally 'skeletons'), encapsulating the imagery of death, Apocalypse, judgement and propitiation, that was at the heart of the celebration of the Day of the Dead (fig. 6).

Kohn was greatly impressed by S.W. Hayter, whom he met both in America and in Paris in the late 1940s and early 1950s, but his subject-matter remained quite distinct from that of his mentor. Several of his other wood-engravings from the period 1949–54 are expressive of an existential concern with the state of man, in subjects such as *Prisoners* (1949); *A Season in Hell* (1951, with reference to Rimbaud); *Portrait of a Contemporary* (1951); and *Ecce Homo* (1954). They anticipated the theme of Peter Selz's renowned exhibition at the Museum of Modern Art in New York in 1959 on *New Images of Man*, for which the theologian Paul Tillich wrote a contribution. It comprised the work of artists who wanted to reclaim the image of man from the moral and physical annihilation of the Second World War, and from its artistic dissolution at the hands of abstraction. Leonard Baskin and Rico Lebrun, for example, were represented by sculptures dealing with death, in the latter case specifically connected with Dachau and Buchenwald. Baskin's apocalyptic mood was further conveyed at the same period by *The Angel of Death* (1959), one of a series of large wood-engravings which he exhibited at the São Paolo Biennale in 1961.

Fig.6. José Guadalupe Posada (1852–1913), *La Calavera de Don Quijote* (c.1910, printed c.1920s). Broadside. London, British Museum.

7 Celluloid Apocalypse

Ian Christie

The Revelation of St John is a good basis for this paper chase of horror casting.
Derek Jarman (introduction to an unfilmed script, *Neutron*, in *Up in the Air: Collected Film Scripts*, London 1996, p.147)

A world complete without me which is present to me is the world of my immortality. This is an importance of film – and a danger.
Stanley Cavell (*The World Viewed: Reflections on the Ontology of Film*, Cambridge, Mass., 1979, p.160)

The scenario is familiar, even if the décor and *dramatis personae* vary. An asteroid or an alien spaceship is fast approaching Earth; alternatively it might be a deadly infection, a long-dormant monster, some freak of nature, or nuclear retaliation. In any event, only heroism, and luck, can avert global catastrophe – and so it usually does, in a triumphant climax of salvation which sends us back into the everyday world after experiencing another of cinema's near-apocalypses. In many ways, this staple of popular cinema could be considered a continuation of the Victorian sensation melodrama that thrilled audiences at Drury Lane with its deployment of impressive stage machinery to wring maximum effect from the realistic portrayal of disaster.[1] But in spite of the routine invocation of 'Apocalypse' and 'Armageddon' in titles and publicity, does it make any sense to relate these popular entertainments to the tradition of eschatological image-making?

I will argue that it does, especially if we recall the beginnings of moving picture entertainment in the 1890s and the extent to which this in itself reflected a new climate of apocalypticism. When H.G. Wells published his landmark science-fiction tale *The Time Machine* in 1895, he was continuing a nineteenth-century tradition of apocalyptic fiction which had begun with Mary Shelley's *The Last Man* (1826) and continued with Bulwer-Lytton's *The Coming Race* (1871) and Richard Jefferies's *After London* (1885). The novelty in Wells's story was the idea of an apparatus to 'visit' different epochs, as an observer or even a tourist. Rather than invoke a quasi-biblical catastrophe, or the political revolution of William Morris's contemporary parable, *News from Nowhere*, Wells posited a Darwinian timescale and a conception of 'time travel' which related to contemporary developments in physics, as well as to a fascination with the fourth dimension common among many mystical cults of the *fin de siècle*.[2] His Time Traveller anticipates the figure invoked in Einstein's popular accounts of his Theory of Relativity some twenty years later.[3] No doubt it was this scientific underpinning which appealed to the engineer Robert Paul who, when he read Wells's story, was inspired to conceive a spectacle that would reproduce the sensation of voyaging through time:

> A novel form of exhibition whereby the spectators have presented to their view scenes which are supposed to occur in the future or past, while they are given the sensation of voyaging through time.... After starting the mechanism, and a suitable period having elapsed, representing a number of centuries, during which the platforms may be in darkness [the audience will see] a hypothetical landscape.[4]

It is unlikely, however, that this would have gone as far as Wells sent his Traveller, to satisfy a curiosity about 'the mystery of the earth's fate... more than thirty million years hence', a bleak, post-human landscape in which the figure of an eclipse stands for a Rationalist end of the world.[5]

Paul's apparatus, in any case, was not built. But within six months the projection of moving pictures in a darkened space had been demonstrated in a number of cities; and a striking feature of the rhetoric surrounding this phenomenon was its appeal to religious or metaphysical concepts. Edison envisaged his image-recording machine, the Kinetoscope, linked with his earlier Phonograph so that 'grand opera can be given at the Metropolitan Opera House at New York without any material change from the original, and with artists and musicians long since dead'.[6]

Reviews of the first Lumière Cinématographe demonstration in Paris in the same year, 1895, emphasized the same themes of resurrection and immortality.[7] And one of the most famous of all early responses, by Maxim Gorky in Russia, invoked the twilight world of Symbolist art:

> Yesterday I was in the kingdom of the shadows.
> If only you knew how strange it is to be there. There are no sounds, no colours.... This is not life but the shadow of life.
> I must explain, lest I be suspected of Symbolism or madness. I was at Aumont's café and I was watching the Lumières' cinematograph. [...]
> It is terrifying to watch but it is the movement of shadows, mere shadows. Curses and ghosts, evil spirits that have cast whole cities into eternal sleep come to mind.[8]

A similar theme was echoed by the Russian playwright Leonid Andreev fifteen years later, when he speculated on the cinema of the future taking the form of a gigantic mirror: 'Will it be [the] dead? No, because what is reflected in the mirror is neither dead nor alive: it is a second life, an enigmatic existence.'[9] In an era of pervasive Symbolism, the filmic image readily evoked a limbo world and cinema itself had an apocalyptic aura, heralding both the end of art as it had been known, and a strange new form of mechanized afterlife.

But early films could also offer more specifically apocalyptic motifs in novel form. Yuri Tsivian has shown how two English trick films appear deeply to have impressed the leading Russian Symbolist writer Andrei Bely (see p.278), prompting an 'eschatological reading'.[10] One of these was produced in 1906 by the same Robert Paul, who had meanwhile become a leading figure in the emergent film business. In *The ? Motorist*, an automobile being pursued by a policeman mysteriously drives up the wall of an inn and off into space, circling Saturn before it crashes down into a crowded courtroom. Bely interpreted this as showing that 'walls and peaceful domesticity cannot protect us from the arrival of the unknown'; while the city becomes 'just a motor car suspended in a void.... And the driver – Death in a top hat – is baring his teeth and rushing towards us'.[11] The other film, *That Fatal Sneeze*, shows a comically escalating series of sneezes which first destroy furniture, then cause havoc in the street, before the camera rocks and the film abruptly stops, suggesting, in Bely's phrase, that 'the earth begins to fall apart'. As Tsivian observes, 'For Bely, this was a perfect representation of the end of the world in its modern [i.e. unheroic, bathetic and ironic] version.'

If cinema had begun to attract the attention of modernist artists in the years before the First World War, it was also being adopted by others with a more traditional message perceived to be in need of modernization. Although the established churches were often active in opposing the 'immorality' of early cinemas and their sometimes risqué programmes, a growing number of evangelists saw great potential in the new medium. As early as 1898, a former New York lawyer and journalist, Colonel Henry Hadley, acquired a print of *Passion Play*, allegedly filmed in Oberammergau but actually shot on a roof-top on Lexington Avenue, and began to tour it as a gospel tent show, interspersed with musical performances.[12] In the same year Herbert Booth, son of the Salvation Army's founder, established a film studio in Melbourne, Australia, which eventually produced *Soldiers of the Cross* (1900), a sequence of brief tableaux portraying the Crucifixion and the Roman persecution of early Christians, linked by music and spoken exhortation, with lantern slides projected during reel changes. This format marked a continuation of the popular Victorian public lantern lecture, which combined entertainment with instruction for increasingly large audiences and, around the turn of the century, began to incorporate both recorded music and moving picture elements.[13] Lantern slides and gramophones, as well as speech and live music, would continue to play a part in many kinds of moving picture show during the early 1900s, but the culmination of this multi-media form came in 1914 with the millenarian *Photo-Drama of Creation*.

Created by the founder of the Jehovah's Witnesses, Charles Russell, this tractarian *Gesamtkunstwerk* – running for eight hours, across two evenings, in its fullest form – should perhaps be seen as an unlikely offshoot of the epic gigantism pioneered by Wagner's *Ring* that also produced such massive works as Mahler's Symphony No. 8 and Schoenberg's *Gurrelieder*.[14] Consisting of five hours' worth of slides, interspersed with three hours of film and ninety-six gramophone 'lectures' and musical items, the *Photo-Drama of Creation* offered a comprehensive interpretation of world history in relation to the biblical narrative and especially the prophecies of Daniel and Revelation. Thus a sequence on the French Revolution illustrated Daniel's prophecy, 'There shall be a time of trouble such as never was', leading to the establishment of 'Messiah's Kingdom'.[15] Similarly, the impact of printing and all the technological inventions of the nineteenth century was cited as evidence of Daniel's prediction in the same passage that 'in the Time of the End [of this age], many shall run to and fro; knowledge shall be increased'. The *Photo-Drama*'s text triumphantly concluded: 'Are we not in the midst of the running to and from which this prophecy predicted? We must therefore be living today in the period designated the Time of the End.'[16]

Only the scenario and some of the slides from the *Photo-Drama* are known to survive, so estimates of its achievement must be speculative. But there is no doubt that it was widely toured throughout the United States and Europe, and presented in prestigious venues: Jehovah's Witnesses sources claim that between eight and fourteen million attended performances of the full and condensed versions.[17] Assuming the printed illustrations were taken from the slides, these range from well-known paintings and conventional biblical illustration to scientific and contemporary photographs and emblematic composite images. Perhaps anticipating opposition to the medium, Russell claimed scriptural authority for 'the use of moving pictures in teaching Bible truths', since 'the Lord sanctioned this in parables and in the symbols of Revelation, which are word pictures'.[18]

The *Photo-Drama*'s slide-plus-film form, however, was already obsolescent in 1914. Although variable tableaux sequences persisted in religious film presentation, using the multi-part 'Lives of Christ' published by Pathé and Gaumont, continuous filmed narrative made remarkable progress from 1912 to 1913.[19] The subjects of these new spectacles were, in fact, almost all quasi-religious, drawing heavily on the vein of Roman-Christian historical fiction inaugurated by Bulwer-Lytton's *The Last Days of Pompeii*, which had already provided the basis of much pre-cinema spectacle.[20] As such, they tended towards the visually and thematically apocalyptic: Pompeii's burial by Vesuvius evoked the biblical destruction of Sodom and Gomorrah and pointed an explicit religious moral in Bulwer-Lytton's story as the Christians escaped the catastrophe; while in Pastrone and D'Annunzio's *Cabiria* (1914), the eponymous heroine is rescued by Romans from the pagan rites of Carthage just as she is about to be sacrificed to the furnace of Moloch, a figure which recurs in futuristic form in Lang's *Metropolis* (1926), fig. 1.

While D.W. Griffith and Cecil B. DeMille were laying the foundations of Hollywood's pre-eminence in popular entertainment in 1914–16 by adapting this form of spectacular melodrama, traces of the evangelical impulse clearly remain in such didactic panoramas as Thomas Ince's *Civilisation* (1915) and Griffith's own *Intolerance* (1916).[21] A similar intention can be seen in H.G. Wells's postwar crusade for popular education through his *Outline of History*

Fig.1. The new urban apocalyptic: the machine as Moloch consuming his worker-victims in Fritz Lang's *Metropolis* (1926).

(1920). But the paradigm of the new cinematic Apocalypse is undoubtedly DeMille's celebrated *The Ten Commandments* (1923), in which a modern morality tale set amid San Francisco skyscrapers is framed by the biblical narrative of Moses and the Israelites. This seems to have been influenced on the one hand by a 1906 play, *The Road to Yesterday*, which used the historical flashback to create a moral parallelism, and on the other by DeMille's shrewd awareness of the popularity of the Los Angeles evangelist Aimee Semple McPherson.[22] For all its exotic (and erotic) spectacle – much derided by modernists and cynics – the film addressed an issue that perplexed many in the hedonistic Twenties: the continuing relevance of traditional Christian morality. In its allegorical structure, the two sons of a religiously bigoted mother exemplify the extremes of vice and virtue, while the biblical set-pieces, including the destruction of the Egyptian army in the Red Sea and the orgy around the Golden Calf, are matched by a contemporary urban apocalypse as a skyscraper collapses.

Here, as in much other cinema intended for a mass audience, there is an apparent disjunction between the relatively simplistic morality-cum-theology – essentially evangelical Protestant, with overtones of mysticism – underpinning an increasingly sophisticated visual (hence more Catholic?) spectacle. The English apocalyptic painter John Martin has often been cited as an influence on DeMille, as if to imply that the latter's elaborate spectacles are both Victorian in conception and empty of anything but the ambition to impress, or titillate.[23] Yet, just as this view is to underestimate the influence of Martin's own paintings on the nineteenth-century romantic imagination, especially through their wide circulation as prints (Ch.6, cats 38–40), so it fails to recognize how cinematic spectacle emerged in the 1910s and 1920s in response to a sense of crisis experienced on a wide scale. DeMille's flashback structures in a series of films that includes *The Ten Commandments* assert a continuity between past and present that clearly spoke to the anxieties of the post-First World War world. In this connection it may be worth noting that DeMille's distinctive flashback framing begins with *Joan the Woman* (1916), one of an early group of films he made with the Metropolitan Opera diva Geraldine Farrar, in which the story of Joan of Arc is 'dreamed' by an English soldier on the Western Front.

No account of apocalyptic thought and imagery in the twentieth century can ignore the pervasive impact of the Great War, which seemed to many the loosing of Revelation's four horsemen, or in some sense 'the battle of that great day', Armageddon. Henceforth Apocalypse would be refigured in terms of the Western Front's sea of mud and labyrinth of trenches; carnage on an unimagined scale, now mechanized and with the new threat of destruction being visited from the air. Cinema began to be widely used in propaganda and to chronicle major battles (albeit by means of reconstruction), but it also produced some striking fictional images which crystallized popular responses to the war. The earliest of these appeared in Abel Gance's *J'Accuse* (1918), provocatively titled after Zola's famous pamphlet and partly inspired by Henri Barbusse's 1916 war novel *Le Feu* (p.286). The climax of the film, which carries the main thrust of its 'accusation', is the 'Return of the Dead': from a vast battlefield covered with corpses, the soldiers arise and demand to know if their sacrifice has been of any value. Their march through the countryside is shown non-naturalistically, with 'superimpositions, tracks and varying shaped masks', and is also contrasted (in horizontal split-screen) with the war's actual Victory Parade in Paris.[24] The knowledge that these were real soldiers on temporary leave from the front, and that most were later killed, added to a sense of tragic irony, removing the film from the sentimental religiosity of Ince's *Civilisation*; and according to Gance, the film met with a highly emotional response wherever it was shown.

Although it was assumed that audiences would not want to see films about the Great War immediately after its end, another exception to this rule proved an unexpected popular and commercial success in the early 1920s. Vincente Blasco Ibañez's novel *The Four Horsemen of the Apocalypse* was already an international best-seller when it was acquired by a struggling Hollywood company, Metro, in 1920 and assigned to the Irish-born director Rex Ingram.[25] Ibañez's story is a romantic variation on the theme of the family divided by war – in this case wealthy Argentine ranchers, who fight on both the French and

Fig.2.The 'resurrection of the dead' provided a symbolic climax to Abel Gance's emotional *J'Accuse* (1919), with real soldiers (many of whom would later die) challenging the film's spectators.

German sides — and is chiefly remembered today for launching Rudolph Valentino's brief but brilliant career as a screen idol. But an important feature of both novel and film, which connects these to an earlier allegorical tradition, is the motif of the 'four horsemen', linked to a recurrent prophetic figure, Tchernoff, whose name suggests a reference to the Russian mystical tradition of Theosophy or of Gurdjieff. In the film, the images of the horsemen, representing Conquest, War, Famine and Death, serve an important rhetorical function. Counterpointing the scenes of ranch life in Argentina, where the family patriarch is popularly known as 'the Centaur', they invest the European war with a mythic dimension. And in a trope repeated forty years later by Tarkovsky in *Ivan's Childhood*, Dürer's famous book of Apocalypse woodcuts is shown by Tchernoff to the hero, Julio, immediately before the horsemen appear, first singly (and vividly tinted), then superimposed as a group on rolling thunderclouds.[26] Ingram apparently took a strong personal interest in their realization, and an effective drawing of his is extant;[27] while the *New York Times* singled out this aspect for praise: 'In bringing the symbolic Four Horsemen into the photoplay, Mr Ingram again has done his work cinematographically, and with such a discerning sense of the unreal in reality that what might easily have been banal or incongruous has become a pervading and leavening part of the picture.'[28]

Fig.3. A mystic, Tchernoff (Nigel de Brulier), evokes the coming reign of the apocalyptic riders as war threatens, to Argensola (Brodwich Turner) and Julio (Rudolph Valentino, on right), in Rex Ingram's spectacular *Four Horsemen of the Apocalypse* (1921).

Fig.4. Alice Terry and Rudolph Valentino on the sheet music cover for *The Four Horsemen of the Apocalypse* (1921).

The subsequent history of films about the First World War would show a number of different concerns, reflecting the shifts in popular attitude towards an event which increasingly seemed to mark the true threshold of the twentieth century. Thus the wave of Great War films which appeared in the early Thirties – in 1930 alone, *Journey's End* (Whale), *All Quiet on the Western Front* (Milestone) and *Westfront 1918* (Pabst), followed by the Russian *Outskirts* (Barnet, 1933) and Renoir's *La Grande Illusion* (1937) – were all strikingly non-apocalyptic and avowedly realist in style, showing the war in microcosm and seeking to find in it either a moral lesson or an internationalist message of reconciliation. After the Second World War, class consciousness was the new theme of such First War films as Stanley Kubrick's *Paths of Glory* (1957) and Joseph Losey's *King and Country* (1964), before two French films, Truffaut's *La Chambre verte* (1978) and Tavernier's *La Vie et rien d'autre* (1989), both set in the Twenties, introduced an elegiac, memorializing attitude, evoking the armies of the dead as a traumatic burden for the living. More recently, alongside the therapeutic *Regeneration* (Mackinnon, 1997), there has been an intriguing instance of the postmodern apocalyptic in Terry Gilliam's *Twelve Monkeys* (1995). While the Great War is only incidental to this time-travel parable, the central character's fleeting materialization in the midst of a battle is contextualized within the film by an illustrated lecture on millennial folklore.

The end of the First World War coincided with, and of course stimulated, a new age of apocalyptic ideology, as the Bolshevik Revolution consolidated its hold on Russia, soon to be followed by Italian Fascism and eventually the German, Spanish and other totalitarian regimes, all having a distinct millennial appeal to many whose earlier beliefs had died on the battlefields of the Great War. In Russia, even before the abortive uprising of 1905, revolution had been widely associated with Apocalypse; so it was not surprising that many early artistic celebrations of the October Revolution had a distinctly mystical religious quality, from Aleksandr Blok's poem 'The Twelve' (1918), in which Christ leads a Red Guard detachment, to Kasimir Malevich's science-fiction Suprematism.[29] The radical impulse towards new forms, combined with a lack of resources, produced some fascinating hybrid works, which remain little known. A presentation of Griffith's *Intolerance* at the Comintern Congress in 1921, for instance, featured a special live prologue which pointed the film's humanist message in a Soviet version of traditional Russian utopianism:

> Four streams run down from the high old mountain of history.... From the great old mountain that we call life the familiar flows before you and, merging into the rapid change of days, leads unexpectedly to the Soviets... towards the radiant Soviets: towards our temples of labour and liberty, through which we shall resurrect everything.[30]

Earlier, an adaptation staged in 1919 of Jack London's 1908 apocalyptic novel *The Iron Heel*, in which socialists struggle against an American fascist revolution, included filmed inserts; and later came such neo-Symbolist revolutionary

Fig. 5. The apocalyptic image of a horse in the sky, however materialistically motivated, in Sergei Eisenstein's *October* (1928) provoked charges of Symbolism lurking beneath its 'Constructivist exterior'.

films as an adaptation of Poe's 'Masque of the Red Death' in *A Spectre is Haunting Europe* (Gardin, 1923) and of Lunacharsky's allegorical play *The Locksmith and the Chancellor* (Gardin, 1924).

Most striking of all was the first great science-fiction spectacle, *Aelita*, made in 1924, in part by Russians returning from exile after the Revolution, its lavish Cubo-futurist sets and costumes for the Martian episodes providing a source that has been plundered by every space-opera of the last sixty years. *Aelita* purports to be an anti-utopia, urging Soviet Russian intellectuals to forget dreams of interplanetary revolution and 'cosmism' and concentrate instead on building communism.[31] But it is also a film at least half in love with the glittering style of its futuristic fantasy.

The same theme returned in Fridrikh Ermler's 1929 film *Fragment of an Empire*, which shows the new Soviet Russia under construction, seen through the eyes of a soldier injured by the Great War and Civil War who, like Rip Van Winkle, cannot understand how everything he used to know has changed. Behind this therapeutic metaphor for revolution there is a knowing, often comic, engagement with the millennial associations still attaching to revolution in Russia: this bustling new Leningrad is a man-made New Jerusalem. Meanwhile, the most famous of the new Soviet filmmakers, Eisenstein, was widely criticized for the Symbolist trappings of his *October* (1928), prompted by the strong association between the setting of 'autocratic Petersburg' and the aesthetic which it had fostered.[32] As Tsivian has shown, the very imagery of revolutionary rupture in the film – when the bridge is raised, trapping a cart, it causes a white horse to hang in the sky – recalls traditional religious apocalyptic imagery[33] (fig.5). Subsequently, Eisenstein's two ambitious attempts at millennial pastoral, *The Old and the New* (1929) and *Bezhin Meadow* (1935), met with even greater disapproval, leading to the latter being banned.

Between making these, his voracious armchair study of myth and religion was exposed to the sensuous first-hand experience of Mexico, as he worked on what would prove to be an abortive national epic in 1931–2, *¡Que Viva Mexico!* Above all, he was fascinated by the Day of the Dead rituals, during which the skull and the skeleton become central symbols in a joyous carnival celebrating the 'interplay' of life and death, and mocking the latter.[34] Eisenstein particularly cherished the popular 'Calaveras' prints of José Guadalupe Posada, closely linked with Mexican folklore (see p.319, fig. 6): here, at last, was a joyful, blasphemous and ironic apocalypse that he could embrace. But it was not one likely to be acceptable to his Californian sponsor, the socialist writer Sinclair Lewis, nor to his ultimate master.

Eisenstein's enforced return from his Mexican paradise to Stalin's planned utopia took place shortly before H.G. Wells published an apocalyptic fantasy, *The Shape of Things to Come*, which would lead to his first major involvement with cinema.[35] With Hitler in power, Apocalypse and utopia were concepts of very real, if bitterly contested, political significance in the mid-Thirties. Having worked tirelessly since the Great War to avert its successor, Wells predicted a second devastating conflict that would return what was left of mankind to pre-industrial tribalism, from which it would only be rescued by the intervention of a new kind of authoritarian, rational leadership, which he imagined arriving from the air, like latter-day secularized angels. Under this benign dictatorship, society would make such technical and ethical progress that it would be ready to embark upon travel to the stars.

Wells's hope had been to challenge what he considered the naive melodrama of Lang's *Metropolis* (1926; fig.1). For his cautionary 'history of the future' he drew together many strands of utopian thought, starting from Plato's blueprint for the ideal *Republic*, and combined these with all three stages of the Apocalypse myth: destruction, judgement and regeneration.[36] The style is heightened and allegorical, with actors each playing several parts to emphasize their continuity as types; and Alexander Korda's ambitious production drew eclectically on many currents of modernist design to create cinema's first optimistic Apocalypse: a vision of the technological (or technocratic) sublime.[37] When the war that Wells had warned against broke out, and the film was re-issued, audiences reputedly watched the bombing of Everytown in shocked silence, as the hitherto symbolic threatened to become actual. The effect of the war on Wells himself was reflected in one of his last publications, the darkly pessimistic *Mind at the End of its Tether* (1945).

Otherwise, the Second World War produced three very different refigurations of Apocalypse, two of which would cast a long shadow over postwar cinema. The most immediate was an individual and 'metaphysical' (in the seventeenth-century sense) apocalypse, in films such as *A Guy Named Joe* (Fleming, 1944) and *A Matter of Life and Death* (Powell and Pressburger, 1946), where there is constant, reassuring contact between this world and an afterlife. Judgement and punishment are absent, or negotiable, and the dead watch over the living like true guardian angels.[38] A second was the legacy of Hitler's Holocaust: a scale of organized torment and death long considered unrepresentable, other than through documentary or personal testimony, but increasingly in recent years the focus of intense debate over the status and responsibility of cinema in such films as Claude Lanzmann's *Shoah* (1985) and Steven Spielberg's *Schindler's List* (1993). To show or not to show? To fictionalize, or only to memorialize? To the extent that the Holocaust has become for many a modern definition of 'last things' – the end of the European 'Enlightenment project' and of history itself[39] – so the issue of its representability has brought cinema back into an arena of public controversy which, as Miriam Hansen suggests, recalls the impact of *Birth of a Nation* on 'what and how a nation remembers'.[40]

The end of the war also inaugurated a new modality of Apocalypse – and indeed a new currency for the concept, as the atomic devastation of Hiroshima

Fig.6. Cautionary apocalypse: H.G. Wells adapted his 'dream of the future' as *Things to Come* (1935) for a spectacular film that inaugurated Alexander Korda's Denham Studios, and warned of imminent destruction from the air.

Fig.7. George Pal's *War of the Worlds* (1954) removed Wells's novel from Victorian England to California and streamlined the walking alien invaders into flying saucers, yet remained true to the story's original meditation on the implications of life elsewhere in the universe.

and Nagasaki evoked the Terrors of Revelation all too vividly. Henceforth there would be films about the imminence of nuclear 'mutually assured destruction', about the psychological effects of living with this threat, and about the likely aftermath of nuclear war: a whole arsenal of films devoted to this blasphemous man-made Apocalypse. Early treatments cast this in conventional suspense or thriller form, but the 1960s saw a significant new development. Stanley Kubrick had originally intended to make such a thriller, until he found himself censoring what might make the audience laugh and 'realized that these incongruous bits of reality were closer to the truth than anything else'.[41] He decided to treat the escalation of East-West confrontation beyond the point of no return as 'nightmare comedy', and the result was *Dr Strangelove, or How I Learned to Stop Worrying and Love the Bomb* (1964), a film sardonically expressing the mood of a world that had recently contemplated annihilation during the Cuban missile crisis of 1962, and had little confidence in the wisdom, or even sanity, of those responsible. Nuclear comedy moved from apocalypse to aftermath with Dick Lester's adaptation of Spike Milligan's absurdist play *The Bedsitting Room* (1969), in which desolate 'found' English locations, treated with an ironic awareness of Bosch and Breughel, provided the setting for a bizarre satire on English culture amid postnuclear mutation.[42]

Lester's film, however, is untypical of the dominant mode in which post-nuclear desolation or regeneration has been portrayed in cinema and, significantly, television. The domesticity implicit in television, typically watched by families and individuals in their own homes, lends a particular poignancy to the portrayal of mass destruction. Peter Watkins's documentary-style reportage on the likely effects of nuclear weapons on a small region of Kent, *The War Game* (1966), was withheld from British television for over twenty years on the grounds that it might terrify viewers, as Orson Welles's celebrated radio version of Wells's *War of the Worlds* had spread panic in 1938. The mid-1980s saw a return of this theme in the naturalistic American television drama *The Day After* (Nicholas Meyer) and Lynne Littman's similarly low-key *Testament* (both 1983). In these, as in a British animated version of Raymond Briggs's graphic novel *When the Wind Blows* (1987), the emphasis is on subjecting familiar characters and situations to the threat of inevitable annihilation, with no possibility of rescue or salvation. In this sense, they reflect a significant shift of sensibility away from earlier nuclear 'survivor' films, such as *On the Beach* and *The World, the Flesh and the Devil* (both 1959) – or indeed Minnelli's ill-conceived 1962 'remake' of *The Four Horsemen of the Apocalypse*, set during the Second World War – which are essentially melodramas of emblematic characters *in extremis*.[43]

The unexpected appearance of two Russian films in 1986, one made in exile by Russia's greatest modern filmmaker, the other by a former assistant benefiting from the first intimation of *glasnost* – both dealing, although in somewhat different ways, with nuclear Apocalypse – recalls how enmeshed this genre had been with the Cold War. Indeed, it has become commonplace to interpret much of American nuclear and science-fiction cinema of the 1950s and 1960s as Cold War allegory, in which aliens, monsters and catastrophes of all kinds are understood as representations of the Soviet menace.[44] And from this, it is a short step to aligning American Cold War cultural politics with Revelation's demonology of the Antichrist and its various beasts, culminating in Ronald Reagan's notorious identification of the USSR in 1983 as the 'evil empire'. Soviet Russia in turn nourished an equivalent image of the Western threat, which owed much to a pre-revolutionary messianic tradition, in which Moscow was believed to be the 'third Rome' and the eventual saviour of Christendom (see Ch. 4, cat. 117).[45]

It is against this distinctively Russian eschatological background that Konstantin Lopushansky's *Letters from a Dead Man* and Andrei Tarkovsky's *The Sacrifice* should be seen. The former shows a bleak monochrome world of post-atomic devastation, devoid of either the grim humour or 'junkyard baroque' of much Western post-nuclear cinema. The message of the film could scarcely be clearer: a scientist desperately tries to ease the pain of his dying wife but fails; then finds a final purpose in creating a Christmas ritual to prepare a group of orphaned children as potential survivors. The film was produced during the first phase of Gorbachev's liberalization, and its significance was dramatically boosted, less than a month after its release, by the Chernobyl nuclear disaster, an event itself widely interpreted in Russia as Revelation's 'star called Worm-wood' contaminating the earth (see p.278).[46] *The Sacrifice* appeared later in the same year and was inevitably drawn into the same web of prophetic specula-tion. In what would prove to be his last film, made in Sweden as a pan-European co-production, Tarkovsky was able to develop the autobiographical apocalyptic theme he had spoken of in a talk about the Book of Revelation in London.[47] In the film's strange dream-world, reminiscent of Bergman and Strindberg as well as of Chekhov and Russian Symbolism, his protagonist, a retired actor, dreams an apparently nuclear Apocalypse, and is told that he must sleep with a witch to avert this catastrophe. He does so, the world is 'saved', and Alexander makes a

Fig.8. Based on his own medieval-style morality play, Ingmar Bergman's *The Seventh Seal* (1957) evokes an anxious, millenarian world of the fourteenth century, and begins with a quotation from Revelation: 'And when the Lamb had opened the seventh seal there was silence in heaven for the space of half an hour'.

bonfire of all his possessions before being taken away in an ambulance – a martyr, a 'holy fool' and a madman. Resisting any single interpretation, the film's complex iconography includes Tarkovsky's much-quoted Leonardo, here the *Adoration of the Magi*, and a selection of Russian icons, but reaches its regenerative climax in the image of a dead tree and a child, who reiterates the film's opening words, 'in the beginning was the word'. Its underlying theme seems best understood by reference to the Russian religious philosopher Nikolai Berdyaev, who characterized Russian literature's 'thirst for expiating the sins of the world and bringing about its salvation'.[48] Berdyaev believed in a dynamic eschatology: 'The creative act of man is needed for the coming of the Kingdom of God, God is in need of and awaits it.'[49] True to the Russian apocalyptic tradition which informed so many of his Soviet-produced films, from *Ivan's Childhood* and *Andrei Rublev* to *The Stalker*, Tarkovsky's last work was his most explicit and yet most mystical statement of this belief.

Thirty years before Tarkovsky came to Sweden, Ingmar Bergman's *The Seventh Seal* (1957) created an even more explicit Apocalypse which also helped lay the foundations for what would become known in the Sixties as 'art cinema'. Although this dealt predominantly with the dilemmas of modern life, as did Bergman in most of his films, *The Seventh Seal* appeared both radically authentic in its portrayal of a brutal, superstitious medieval world, and also relevant to the concerns of an era adjusting to post-war anomie and nuclear anxiety. As in a traditional morality play, the characters are all types and the drama is explicitly framed by quotations from Revelation: symbolically, it occupies the 'space of half an hour', which occurs after the opening of the seventh seal, before the seven angels initiate the spectacular sequence of destruction (Revelation 8: 1). Between the film's elemental opening images of sky and sea, and a conclusion which combines the romantic medievalism of Carné's *Les Visiteurs du soir* (1942) with an authentically allegorical Dance of Death (fig.8), Bergman moves deftly between realism and Expressionism. His travelling players and such medieval set-pieces as a flagellants' procession and witch-burning are predominantly in *plein-air* realist style (although also recalling Carl Dreyer's 1928 *Passion de Jeanne d'Arc*), while the Knight and his chess opponent Death are figures descended from early Expressionist cinema, especially Fritz Lang's *Der müde Tod* (1921).

Bergman would develop a more contemporary sense of apocalypse in his trilogy of the early 1960s: *Through a Glass Darkly* (1961), *Winter Light* (1962) and *The Silence* (1963). Across this series of intense, harrowing studies of characters undergoing crisis runs the theme of God's absence, or 'silence'; and in the central film, the same actor who had earlier played the Knight, Max von Sydow, appears as a fisherman, obsessed with the fear that the Chinese will destroy the world with atomic bombs. When the protagonist, a pastor who has lost his faith, cannot comfort him, he shoots himself in despair. Similar concerns, with reconciling the personal and the public under the shadow of the bomb, shaped another cornerstone of the new European art cinema, Alain Resnais's *Hiroshima*

Fig.9. 'Well, *there's* something you don't see every day'. The makers of *Ghostbusters* (1984) were worried that the monstrous Stay-Puft Marshmallow Man as a manifestation of Gozer the Destructor would 'take the movie into an area of silliness that would discount everything else'. But they realized that he could be 'cute *and* terrifying' – a postmodern Terror?

mon amour (1959), which linked a French actress's attempt to comprehend Hiroshima with a personal trauma, her wartime affair with a German soldier – still very much a repressed national memory in France at that time. Thus the pattern was set for a series of films dealing with the death of emotion and difficulty of relationships in the modern world – quintessentially Michelangelo Antonioni's tetralogy *L'Avventura* (1960), *La Notte* (1961), *L'Eclisse* (1962) and *Deserto Rosso* (1964) – in what has been termed the 'quiet' or 'cool' Apocalypse: the unheralded end of the world as we knew it.[50] Later in the decade, amid growing disillusion and the revival of revolutionary ideology, this cool modernism would take a more violently apocalyptic turn in the anti-capitalist destruction that climaxes Jean-Luc Godard's *Weekend* (1967) and Antonioni's *Zabriskie Point* (1969). And yet another version of Apocalypse emerged in Pier Paolo Pasolini's exploration of myth in such films as *Edipo Re* (1967), *Teorema* (1968), *Il Porcile* and *Medea* (both 1969). In these, the veneer of classicism or civilization is ruthlessly stripped away to reveal the atavistic 'oneiric' root of myth, in a process which brings Pasolini close to the dream imagery that informs Revelation's Apocalypse myth.[51]

This essay has traced some aspects of cinema's engagement with, and consequent redefinition of, Apocalypse during this last century. It would surely be wrong to conclude that it has merely vulgarized what was once scholarly or esoteric, since Apocalypse has been traditionally populist. D.H. Lawrence believed that 'Down among the uneducated people you will still find Revelation rampant. I think it has had and perhaps still has more influence... than the Gospels or the great Epistles.'[52] If Revelation speaks the language of 'power lust', as

Fig.10. A gigantic Samurai leads the Forces of Darkness in a dream sequence from Terry Gilliam's *Brazil* (1985), which combines kitsch and debris in a striking post-industrial apocalyptic.

Fig.11. Biblical and mythological motifs recur in Andrei Tarkovsky's last film, *The Sacrifice* (1986), which frames a mysterious apocalyptic dream.

Fig.12. 'In the last minutes of *The Last of England*, Tilda [Swinton] blown by a whirlwind of destruction, becomes a figure of strength; she is able to curse the world of the patriots' (Derek Jarman). Her dress evokes Blake's image, borrowed from Revelation, of Jerusalem as a bride.

Lawrence claimed, then apocalyptic cinema has become the fantasy of power. It has also played an important part in the processes of secularizing and modernizing Apocalypse, in the ways that Sir Frank Kermode outlined in *The Sense of an Ending*.[53] The feelings of crisis, decadence and transition characteristic of modernism have been powerfully relayed by cinema, far beyond the audience for literary or painterly modernist art; while the Terrors have been intensified and amplified to an extraordinary level by spectacle cinema. In an increasingly secular and globalized society, it could be argued that any shared sense of eschatology now results from the broad following for such cycles of popular fantasy cinema as *Planet of the Apes*, *Star Wars*, *Star Trek*, *Mad Max* and Romero's *Dead* trilogy. These have become the syncretic mythology of our time.

However true this may be, it runs the risk of seeming banal. From the point of view of Kermode's 'clerkly sceptics', with their demand for 'constantly changing, constantly more subtle, relationships between a fiction and the paradigms',[54] modern cinema can offer also more challenging apocalypses. Consider, for instance, Hans-Jurgen Syberberg's massive, phantasmagoric *Hitler: a Film from Germany* (1977) which, according to Susan Sontag, 'tries to say everything' in over seven hours.[55] Or two irreverent, slapstick variations on apocalypse from the 'new' Hollywood: Ivan Reitman's *Ghostbusters* (1984), which vacuums up all the residual ghosts and spirits adrift in Manhattan before unleashing a grotesque combination of apocalyptic Beast and giant breakfast cereal monster; and Harold Ramis's *Groundhog Day* (1993), in which time mysteriously repeats itself until the callow hero attains self-knowledge and humility. Or the popular genre of the apocalyptic thriller, from *The Seventh Sign* (1988) to *Se7en* (1995), following in the footsteps of Chesterton's theological detective story *The Man Who Was Thursday*. Or, among a flowering of the neo-apocalyptic in British filmmaking, Derek Jarman's anti-Thatcher polemic *The Last of England* (1987), which Anthony Kinik has analysed in terms of very specific allusions to seventeenth-century English apocalypticism, including the sequence of Tilda Swinton's *danse macabre* as a travesty of Revelation's 'new Jerusalem coming down out of heaven from God, prepared as a bride for her husband'.[56]

Iain Sinclair, the poet and 'psychogeographer', has suggested that the new Apocalypse is to be found in the perpetual observation of urban surveillance cameras, invisibly recording our every move as potential evidence against us.[57] And elsewhere, the profit motive is still at work, turning the millennium into a marketing opportunity with a new computer game entitled *Apocalypse*: 'The end of the world is near. You're Bruce [Willis], starring as Trey Kincaid, nano-physicist and sole defender of the world. It's up to you to defeat the Four Horsemen before it's happy trails to us all...'.[58]

Meanwhile, every time a screen lights up, a fictive world is born; and when it is extinguished, that world dies, if temporarily.[59] Gorky's initial epiphany has proved prophetic: the medium is inescapably an eschatological message.

NOTES

1 On sensation melodrama see Michael Booth, *Victorian Spectacular Theatre 1850–1910*, London 1981, p.62 ff.

2 Morris's *News from Nowhere* was published in 1895. Wells had studied biology at the School of Science in South Kensington, where he was influenced by T.H. Huxley (1825–95), the naturalist and supporter of Darwin. On the fourth dimension, see *inter alia* Robert C. Williams, *Artists in Revolution: Portraits of the Russian Avant-Garde 1905–25*, London 1978, ch. 5.

3 Albert Einstein, *Relativity: the Special and the General Theory* (first pub. 1920), London, 1954, ch. 3 *et seq*.

4 R.W. Paul's preliminary patent application of October 1895 is quoted in Terry Ramsaye, *A Million and One Nights: A History of the Motion Picture Through 1925*, 1926, New York 1986, facsimile edition, pp.155–7.

5 H.G. Wells, *The Time Machine* (1895), in *The Complete Stories of H.G. Wells*, London 1927, p.84.

6 Thomas Edison, Introduction to W.K.L. Dickson and A. Dickson, *History of the Kinetograph, Kinetoscope and Kinetophonograph*, New York 1895, quoted in I. Christie, *The Last Machine: Early Cinema and the Birth of the Modern World*, London 1994, p.96.

7 Reviews in *La Poste* and *Le Radicale*, December 1895, quoted in *The Last Machine*, op. cit. p. 111.

8 Maxim Gorky, 'The Lumière Cinematograph', first pub. Nizhegorodskii Listok, July 1896; trans. in R. Taylor and I. Christie (eds), *The Film Factory: Russian and Soviet Cinema in Documents*, London 1988, pp.25, 28, 31.

9 Andreev was also a pioneer photographer in colour and realized better than most how cinema would develop. His 'First Letter on Theatre' is translated, in part, in *The Film Factory*, op. cit. p.30.

10 Yuri Tsivian, *Early Cinema in Russia and its Cultural Reception*, London 1994, p.151 (also the following quotations in this paragraph). Bely's essay, 'The City', appeared in *Our Monday Paper*, November 1907.

11 *The ? Motorist*, directed by Walter Booth for Paul, 1906; *That Fatal Sneeze*, directed by Lewin Fitzhamon for Hepworth, 1907. Both of these films are included in the British Film Institute's *Early Cinema* video compilation.

12 Ramsaye, op.cit. (n.4), pp.373–6.

13 On Lantern lectures, see Christie, op. cit. (n.6), ch. 4; also Theodore X. Barber, 'The Roots of Travel Cinema', *Film History*, 5/1, March 1993.

14 Richard Alan Nelson, 'Propaganda for God: Pastor Charles Taze Russell and the Multi-Media Photo-Drama of (1914)', in R. Cosandey, A. Gaudreault, T. Gunning (eds), *Une Invention du Diable? Cinéma des premiers temps et religion*, Sainte-Foy, Quebec, 1992, pp.230–55. My thanks are due to David Francis for access to his copy of the accompanying book.

15 *Scenario of the Photo-Drama of Creation*, International Bible Students Association, Brooklyn, New York, 1914, p.92.

16 ibid., p.90.

17 Nelson, op. cit. (n.14), p.255. Robert Christie (my father) recalls seeing it at the Guildhall in Londonderry, some time in 1915–16.

18 Nelson, op. cit. (n.14), p.234.

19 Pathé's *La Vie et la passion de Jésus-Christ* appeared between 1902 and 1905, followed by *La Vie de Jésus* from both Pathé and Gaumont in 1906.

20 Bulwer-Lytton's *The Last Days of Pompeii* was published in 1834. On its subsequent history as opera, stage play and 'pyrodrama', see Maria Wyke, *Projecting the Past: Ancient Rome, Cinema and History*, London 1997, esp. pp.151–7.

21 Griffith was reported as saying to an actress working on *Intolerance* that 'she was working in the universal language that had been predicted in the Bible, which … could end wars and bring about the millennium' (quoted by Miriam Hansen, *Babel and Babylon: Spectatorship in American Silent Cinema*, Cambridge, Mass., 1991, p.77).

22 This play, by Beulah Marie Dix and Evelyn Sutherland, apparently also influenced Griffith, according to Robert S. Birchard, 'Cecil B. DeMille vs the Critics', in Paolo Cherchi Usai and Lorenzo Codelli (eds), *L'Eredità DeMille*, Pordenone 1991, p.288. On McPherson (1860–1944), see Carey McWilliams, 'Aimee Semple McPherson: "Sunlight in my Soul"', in Isabel Leighton (ed.), *The Aspirin Age*, Harmondsworth 1964.

23 John Martin (1789–1854) illustrated *Paradise Lost* and many of the Romantics, and was in turn highly regarded by them. The *Oxford Companion to English Literature* (1985) suggests that 'something of his magnificence lingered on in the lavish productions of Cecil B. deMille [*sic*]', p.623.

24 Gance's claims quoted in Kevin Brownlow, *The Parade's Gone By...*, London 1968, p.621.

25 The novel was published in 1916 and translated into English in 1918. Metro later became part of Metro-Goldwyn-Mayer. Rex Ingram (1892–1950) had already directed two films for Metro before *The Four Horsemen*.

26 When he is shown the Dürer woodcuts, at a World War II field headquarters, the young military scout in *Ivan's Childhood* (1962) responds that he has already seen one of the horsemen, on a motorbike.

27 Reproduced in Liam O'Leary, *Rex Ingram: Master of the Silent Cinema*, Dublin 1980; reprinted London and Pordenone 1993, p.85.

28 Quoted in the programme for the film's revival as a Channel Four Silent in 1993.

29 After 1918 Malevich's Suprematism assumed the dimensions of a cosmic project, with predictions of space travel in 1920 and designs for 'homes for earth dwellers' in 1923–4. See E.F. Kovtun, 'Kasimir Malevich: His Creative Path', in *Malevich 1878–1935*, Amsterdam 1988, p.160.

30 Prologue quoted in Vance Kepley, '*Intolerance* and the Soviets: a historical investigation', in Taylor and Christie (eds), *Inside the Film Factory*, London 1991, p.59.

31 See I. Christie, 'Down to Earth: Relocating *Aelita*', in *Inside the Film Factory*, op. cit. pp.80–102.

32 See, for instance, Adrian Piotrovsky, '*October* Must be Re-Edited!', in Taylor and Christie, op. cit. (n.8), pp.216–17.

33 Yuri Tsivian, 'Eisenstein and Russian Symbolist Culture: An Unknown Script of *October*', in I. Christie and R. Taylor (eds), *Eisenstein Rediscovered*, London 1993, pp.79–109. Also Tsivian's contribution to *Omnibus* on Eisenstein (BBC TV, 1988).

34 R. Taylor (ed.), *Beyond the Stars: The Memoirs of Sergei Eisenstein*, London 1995, pp.629–35.

35 H.G. Wells, *The Shape of Things to Come*, 1933. Wells had already provided scripts for several short comedies in the late Twenties. On his return to Moscow Eisenstein tried to make a comedy about the 'new' Moscow, *MMM*, but failed.

36 See Vita Fortunati, 'From Utopia to Science fiction', in K. Kumar and S. Bann (eds), *Utopias and the Millennium*, London 1993, p.83.

37 On the film's complex history see Christopher Frayling, *Things to Come*, London 1995.

38 Eisenstein wrote enthusiastically about the visionary aspect of *A Guy Named Joe* in 'Judith', in B. Eisenschitz (ed.), *Mémoires 2*, Paris n.d., pp.223–8.

39 See F. Fukuyama, *The End of History and the Last Man*, London 1992, pp.128–30.

40 Miriam Bratu Hansen, '*Schindler's List* is Not *Shoah*', in Y. Loshitzky (ed.), *Spielberg's Holocaust. Critical Perspectives on 'Schindler's List'*, Indianapolis 1997, p.77.

41 Interview quoted in John Brosnan, *The Primal Screen: A History of Science Fiction Film*, London 1991, p.116.

42 Assheton Gorton, production designer of *The Bedsitting Room*, confirmed that he consulted a wide range of apocalyptic sources from the history of painting, in an interview for *Cinema Apocalyptica*, a series of five programmes for BBC Radio 3 by Ian Christie and Mark Burman, April 1999.

43 *On the Beach*, based on Nevil Shute's novel, was produced and directed by Stanley Kramer. *The World, the Flesh and the Devil*, 'suggested by M.P. Shiel's novel *The Purple Cloud*', was written and directed by Ranald MacDougall, and starred Harry Belafonte and Mel Ferrer. On Minnelli's *Four Horsemen*, see Stephen Harvey, *Directed by Vincente Minnelli*, New York 1990, pp.263–71.

44 On Hollywood and the Cold War, see Peter Biskind, *Seeing is Believing*, London 1984; and Mark Jancovich, *Rational Fears: American Horror in the 1950s*, Manchester 1996.

45 On the Russian eschatological tradition see Nikolai Berdyaev, *The Russian Idea*, trans. R.M. French, London 1947.

46 Rev. 8: 10.

47 Tarkovsky spoke about the Apocalypse at St James's Church, Piccadilly, London, 18 July 1984 (where William Blake had been christened, and Tarkovsky's own memorial service would be held in 1986).

48 Nikolai Berdyaev, *The Meaning of History*, London 1936, p.184.

49 Nikolai Berdyaev, *The Beginning and the End* (1947), London 1952, p.251.

50 On quiet or silent Apocalypse see Marina Benjamin, *Living at the End of the World*, London 1998, pp.212ff; on the 'cool Apocalypse' see John Orr, *Cinema and Modernity*, Cambridge 1993, 'Tragicomedy and the Cool Apocalypse', pp.14–34.

51 On Pasolini's use of 'oniricità' (dreamlikeness), see Oswald Stack (ed.), *Pasolini on Pasolini*, London 1969, pp.149–50.

52 D.H. Lawrence, *Apocalypse and the Writings on Revelation*, Cambridge 1980, p.62.

53 Frank Kermode, *The Sense of an Ending: Studies in the Theory of Fiction*, Oxford 1967.

54 Kermode, op. cit. p.24.

55 Susan Sontag, 'Syberberg's *Hitler*', reprinted in Heather Stewart (ed.), *Syberberg: A Filmmaker from Germany*, London and Edinburgh 1992, p.13.

56 Rev. 21: 1–3. I am grateful to Anthony Kinik for the opportunity to consult his MA thesis, '*That Unbearable Recurring Apocalyptic Nightmare*': Crisis and Apocalyptic Visions in British Film, *1987–1994*, University of British Columbia 1997, especially pp.88–9.

57 Iain Sinclair interviewed for *Cinema Apocalyptica*; see also his *Lights Out for the Territory*, London 1997, p.105.

58 Cover publicity, *Apocalypse*, Activision 1998.

59 See Kermode's example of 'tick-tock' as 'a model of what we call a plot... *Tick* is a humble genesis, *tock* a feeble apocalypse', op. cit. (n.51), p.45.

Particular thanks are due to Stephen Bann, Marina Benjamin, Kevin Brownlow, Mark Burman and Robert Christie for help with references and ideas in preparing this essay.

Books and Periodicals cited in Abbreviation

Biblical quotations conform to the authors' preferred versions of the Bible: the Authorized Version is followed in all but the following cases: Chapter 2: New English Bible; Chapter 3 and catalogue entries: Douay-Rheims (N. T. 1582, O.T. 1609); Chapter 4 essay only: Douay-Rheims.

Full bibliographical references are provided in the endnotes to the essays and in the literature attached to the catalogue entries. The principal works cited in abbreviation in the catalogue entries are as follows:

CHAPTER 3
Burlington Magazine: *The Burlington Magazine*, London 1902–

JWCI: Journal of the Warburg and Courtauld Institutes, London 1937–

Lewis: Suzanne Lewis, *Reading Images. Narrative Discourse and Reception in Thirteenth Century Illuminated Apocalypse*, Cambridge 1995

Morgan: Nigel Morgan, *Early Gothic Manuscripts (1) 1190–1250, (2) 1250–1285* (J.J.G. Alexander (ed.), *A Survey of Manuscripts Illuminated in the British Isles*, vol. 4), London 1982, 1988

Sandler: Lucy F. Sandler, *Gothic Manuscripts 1285–1385* (J.J.G. Alexander (ed.), *A Survey of Manuscripts Illuminated in the British Isles*, vol.5), London 1986

Williams: John Williams, *The Illustrated Beatus: A Corpus of Illustrations of the Commentary on the Apocalypse*, vols 1–3, London 1994–8

CHAPTER 4
Bartsch: Adam von Bartsch, *Le Peintre-graveur*, 21 vols, Vienna 1803–21

Briquet: C.M. Briquet, *Les Filigranes: Dictionnaire historique des marques du papier dès leur apparition vers 1282 jusque'en 1600*. 4 vols, Paris 1907. Supplementary edition by Allan Stevenson, Amsterdam 1968

Burlington Magazine: *The Burlington Magazine*, London 1902–
Campbell Dodgson: Campbell Dodgson, *Catalogue of Early German and Flemish Woodcuts Preserved in the Department of Prints and Drawings in the British Museum,* vol.I, London 1903; vol.II, London 1911

Eisler: Colin Eisler, *The Master of the Unicorn. The Life and Work of Jean Duvet*, New York 1979

German Renaissance Prints: Giulia Bartrum, *German Renaissance Prints 1490–1550*, exhib. cat.,British Museum, London 1995

Hollstein: F.W.H. Hollstein, *German Engravings, Etchings and Woodcuts, c.1400–1700*, Amsterdam 1954– and *Dutch and Flemish Etchings, Engravings and Woodcuts, c.1450–1700*, Amsterdam 1949–

Lugt: Frits Lugt, *Les Marques de collections de dessins et d'estampes*, Amsterdam 1921; *Supplément*, The Hague 1956

Mauquoy-Hendrickx: Marie Mauquoy-Hendrickx, *Les estampes des Wierix conservées au Cabinet des estampes de la Bibliothèque royale Albert Ier*, 4 vols, Brussels 1978–83

Meder: Joseph Meder, *Dürer-Katalog: ein Handbuch über Albrecht Dürers Stiche, Radierungen, Holzschnitte, deren Zustände, Ausgaben und Wasserzeichen*, Vienna 1932

Nagler: G.K. Nagler, *Die Monogrammisten*, 5 vols, Munich 1858–79. Facsimile reprint, Nieuwkoop 1977

Passavant: J.D. Passavant, *Le Peintre-graveur*, 6 vols, Leipzig 1860–4

Piccard: Gerhard Piccard (ed.), *Die Wasserzeichenkartei Piccard im Hauptstaatarchiv Stuttgart*, Stuttgart 1961–

Reinitzer: Heimo Reinitzer, *Biblia deutsch. Luthers Bibelübersetzung und ihre Tradition,* exhib. cat., Herzog August Bibliothek, Wolfenbüttel 1983–4
Stimmer: D. Koepplin, P. Tanner *et al.*, *Tobias Stimmer 1539–1584*, exhib. cat., Kunsthistorisches Museum, Basel 1984

CHAPTER 5
Bindman 1986: David Bindman, 'William Blake and popular religious imagery', *Burlington Magazine* CXXVIII, Oct. 1986, pp.713–14

BM Sat.: *Catalogue of Personal and Political Satires preserved in the Department of Prints and Drawings in the British Museum*, vols I–IV (nos. 1–4838) by Frederic G. Stephens, London 1870–83; vols V–XI (nos. 4839–17391) by Dorothy M. George, London 1935–54

Burlington Magazine: *The Burlington Magazine*, London 1902–

Butlin: Martin Butlin, *The Paintings and Drawings of William Blake*, 2 vols, New Haven and London 1981

CW: M.J. Campbell, *John Martin: Visionary Printmaker*, York 1992 (catalogue by M.J. Campbell and J. Dustin Wees)

von Erffa and Staley: Helmut von Erffa and Allen Staley, *The Paintings of Benjamin West*, New Haven and London 1986

Jerusalem: William Blake, *Jerusalem, The Emanation of the Giant Albion*, Morton D. Paley (ed.), in the series *Blake's Illuminated Books*, William Blake Trust/Tate Gallery, I

Keynes, *Blake*: G.L. Keynes, *Complete Writings of William Blake*, Oxford 1957 and subsequent editions

Paley 1973: Morton D. Paley, 'William Blake, The Prince of the Hebrews, and The Woman Clothed with the Sun', in Morton D. Paley and Michael Phillips (eds), *William Blake: Essays in Honour of Sir Geoffrey Keynes*, Oxford 1973

Paley, *Continuing City*: Morton D. Paley, *The Continuing City: William Blake's Jerusalem*, Oxford 1983

CHAPTER 6
Carey and Griffiths: Frances Carey and Antony Griffiths, *The Print in Germany 1880– 1933*, London 1984 (reprinted 1993)

Hofmaier: James Hofmaier, *Max Beckmann, Catalogue raisonné of his prints*, 2 vols, Bern 1990

Ludwig Meidner: Gerda Wagner and Ines Wagemann (eds), *Ludwig Meidner. Zeichner, Maler, Literat 1884–1966*, 2 vols, Darmstadt 1991

Mellerio: André Mellerio, *Odilon Redon*, Paris 1913

General Select Bibliography
(in order of publication)

Montague R. James, *The Apocalypse in Art. Schweich Lectures of the British Academy 1927*, London 1931

Nikolai Berdyaev, *The Russian Idea*, trans. R.M. French, London 1947

Henri Focillon, *L'an Mil*, Paris 1952 (trans. in Cecilia Davis Weyer, *Early Medieval Art 300–1150*, Sources and Documents in the History of Art Series, ed. H.W. Janson, Englewood Cliffs 1971)

Frank Kermode, *The Sense of an Ending: Studies in the Theory of Fiction*, Oxford 1967 (reprinted with an epilogue, Oxford 1999)

Hellmut Rosenfeld, *Der mittelalterliche Totentanz*, 2nd ed., Cologne 1968

Paul Fussell, *The Great War and Modern Memory*, Oxford and London 1975

J.M. Court, *Myth and History in the Book of Revelation*, London 1979

J.F.C. Harrison, *The Second Coming: Popular Millenarianism, 1780–1850*, London 1979

Richard K. Emmerson, *Antichrist in the Middle Ages. A Study of Medieval Apocalypticism, Art and Literature*, Manchester 1981

Robert W. Scribner, *For the Sake of the Simple Folk. Popular Propaganda for the German Reformation*, Cambridge 1981

Peter Martin, *Martin Luther und die Bilder zur Apokalypse. Die Ikonographie der Illustrationen zur Offenbarung des Johannes in der Lutherbibel 1522–1546*, Hamburg 1983

A. Yarbro Collins, *Crisis and Catharsis. The Power of the Apocalypse*, Philadelphia 1984

C.A. Patrides and Joseph Wittreich (eds), *The Apocalypse in English Renaissance Thought and Literature*, Ithaca, N.Y., and Manchester 1984

Saul Friedländer, Gerald Holton, Leo Marx, Eugene

Skolnikoff (eds), *Visions of Apocalypse. End or Rebirth?*, New York and London 1985

Richard Gassen and Bernhard Holeczek (eds), *Apokalypse. Ein Prinzip Hoffnung?*, exhib. cat. Wilhelm Hack Museum, Ludwigshafen-am-Rhein 1985

Morton D. Paley, *The Apocalyptic Sublime*, New Haven and London 1986

Robin Bruce Barnes, *Prophecy and Gnosis: Apocalypticism in the Wake of the Lutheran Reformation*, Stanford 1988

David Bethea, *The Shape of the Apocalypse in Modern Russian Fiction*, Princeton, N.J., 1989

Christopher Hill, *Antichrist in Seventeenth-Century England*, London 1990 (first published 1971)

L.L. Thompson, *The Book of Revelation: Apocalypse and Empire*, New York and Oxford 1990

Richard K. Emmerson and Bernard McGuinn (eds), *The Apocalypse in the Middle Ages*, Ithaca, N.Y., and London 1992

Jon Mee, *Dangerous Enthusiasm: William Blake and the Culture of Radicalism in the 1790s*, Oxford 1992

Marjorie Reeves (ed.), *Prophetic Rome in the High Renaissance*, Oxford 1992

Renata Ulmer, *Passion und Apokalypse. Studien zur biblischen Thematik in der Kunst des Expressionismus.* Europäische Hochschulschriften, vol.144, Frankfurt 1992

Norman Cohn, *The Pursuit of the Millennium*, London 1993 (first published 1957, revised edition 1970)

Norman Cohn, *Cosmos, Chaos and the World to Come*, New Haven and London 1993

Francis Haskell, 'Art and the Apocalypse', *New York Review of Books*, vol.40 no.13, 15 July 1993, pp.25–9

Franz Link (ed.), *Tanz und Tod in Kunst und Literatur*, Berlin 1993

Sergiusz Michalski, *The Reformation and the Visual Arts: The Protestant Image Question in Western and Eastern Europe*, London and New York 1993

John Orr, *Cinema and Modernity*, Cambridge 1993

Marjorie Reeves, *The Influence of Prophecy in the Later Middle Ages: a study in Joachimism*, London 1993 (first published 1967)

Ian Christie, *The Last Machine: Early Cinema and the Birth of the Modern World*, London 1994

Richard Cork, *A Bitter Truth. Avant-Garde Art and the Great War*, New Haven and London in association with the Barbican Art Gallery, 1994

Nicholas Campion, *The Great Year. Astrology, Millenarianism and History in the Western Tradition*, London 1994

Bernard McGuinn, *Antichrist. Two Thousand Years of the Human Fascination with Evil*, San Francisco 1994

Malcolm Bull (ed.), *Apocalyptic Theory and the Ends of the World*, Oxford 1995

Jay Winter, *Sites of Memory, Sites of Mourning*, Cambridge 1995

Rosemary M. Wright, *Art and Antichrist in Medieval Europe*, Manchester 1995

Hans Hillebrand (ed.), *The Oxford Encyclopedia of the Reformation*, 4 vols, Oxford 1996

Hillel Schwartz, *Century's End. An Orientation Manual towards the Year 2000*, New York and London 1996

Christopher Burdon, *The Apocalypse in England: Revelation Unravelling, 1700–1834*, Basingstoke 1997

F.L. Cross and E.A. Livingstone (eds), *The Oxford Dictionary of the Christian Church*, Oxford 1997

Anson Rabinbach, *In the Shadow of Catastrophe. German Intellectuals between Apocalypse and Enlightenment*, Berkeley, Los Angeles and London 1997

Stephen Jay Gould, *Questioning the Millennium. A Rationalist's Guide to a Precisely Arbitrary Countdown*, London 1997

Marina Benjamin, *Living at the End of the World*, London 1998

Morton D. Paley, *Apocalypse and Millennium in English Romantic Poetry*, Oxford 1999

Eugen Weber, *Apocalypses: Prophecies, Cults and Millennial Beliefs through the Ages*, London 1999

Photographic and Copyright Acknowledgements

Index

References are to page numbers; the index does not include the endnotes to the essays or the bibliographical details of the catalogue entries. All the books of the Bible are indexed, with the exception of Revelation, while other terms commonly used throughout, such as Apocalypse, Bible, Christ, and God, are indexed only when referring to particular works or types of representation.